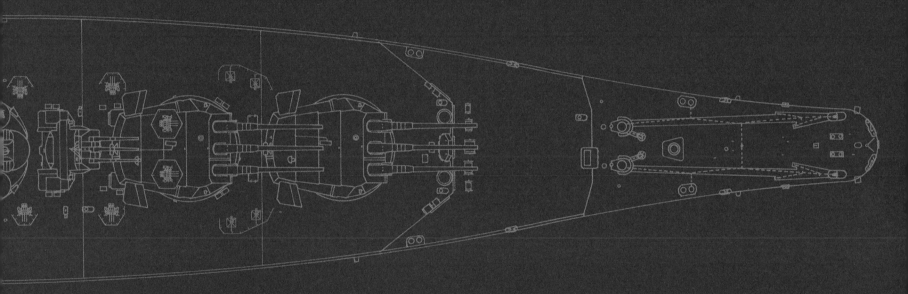

BATTLESHIPS *YAMATO* AND *MUSASHI*

BATTLESHIPS *YAMATO* AND *MUSASHI*

Janusz Skulski
and Stefan Dramiński

C
CONWAY
B L O O M S B U R Y
LONDON · OXFORD · NEW YORK · NEW DELHI · SYDNEY

Conway
An imprint of Bloomsbury Publishing Plc

50 Bedford Square	1385 Broadway
London	New York
WC1B 3DP	NY 10018
UK	USA

www.bloomsbury.com

CONWAY™ is a trademark and imprint of Bloomsbury Publishing Plc

First published 2017
© text, photographs and line artworks, Janusz Skulski, 2017
© illustrations Stefan Dramiński, 2017

Janusz Skulski and Stefan Dramiński have asserted their right under the Copyright, Designs and Patents Act, 1988, to be identified as Authors of this work.

British Library Cataloguing-in-Publication Data
A catalogue record for this book is available from the British Library.

Library of Congress Cataloguing-in-Publication data has been applied for.

ISBN: HB: 978-1-8448-6317-4
ePDF: 978-1-8448-6319-8
ePUB: 978-1-8448-6318-1

2 4 6 8 10 9 7 5 3 1

Design CE Marketing
Printed in China by RR Donnelly Asia Printing Solutions Limited

Bloomsbury Publishing Plc makes every effort to ensure that the papers used in the manufacture of our books are natural, recyclable products made from wood grown in well-managed forests. Our manufacturing processes conform to the environmental regulations of the country of origin.

To find out more about our authors and books visit www.bloomsbury.com.
Here you will find extracts, author interviews, details of forthcoming events and the option to sign up for our newsletters.

CONTENTS

ACKNOWLEDGEMENTS

I would like to express my sincere thanks to those who have helped both directly and indirectly in collecting materials and information for this book.

I would also like to thank the friends who have offered their advice on the work. Their help has made this book possible.

I am especially grateful to Mr Izumi Kozo, Mr Ichimura Masaki, Mr Tsukamoto Hideki, Mr Uchiyama Mutsuo and Mr Kamakura Takumi. Also, special thanks to 'N.Y.' members. Special thanks to Mr Stefan Dramiński author of the splendid 3D illustrations.

Janusz Skulski,
Krakow, May 2016

Port-side view of the Yamato during trials in October 1941. This photo was found by chance three years after the end of the war and was the first portrait of the battleship published – up until then the only known photographs were US aerial pictures taken during the attack on the ship.

INTRODUCTION

In 1988 Conway Maritime Press issued my first book on the Imperial Japanese Navy battleship, *Yamato*, the most powerful and most mysterious warship of the Second World War.

This new book is a significant update, based partly on drawings and partly on my own reconstructions from newly available sources – archival photographs and documentary drawings, all accessed with the invaluable help of my Japanese friends.

In researching the original edition I discovered many details about the ship that it was not possible to reconstruct at the time. But that book led me to new contacts in Japan, including an expert on the ships of the Imperial Japanese Navy. Thanks to him, I gained access to much new material that formed part of the navy yard documentation, including photographs and other documents.

Three expeditions were crucial in finding out more about the ships: the second expedition to the sunken *Yamato* made by the Japanese TV company, Asahi (the first, in 1985, was not fully successful), the expedition by the French ship *Ocean Voyager* in December 1999, and the sensational discovery of the remains of the *Musashi* by the Paul G. Allen expedition in March 2015 after eight years of research.

Since finishing the first book, I have continued my research and study of the *Yamato*, collecting much new material, making new drawings and building study models of the battleship fragments. After this, all done in consultation with Japanese experts, I started to make completely new views of these magnificent ships. It is now possible for the first time to show the beauty and terrible force of these strategic battleships of the Second World War and, as was the case the first time, to make real, not approximate, working plans.

Thanks to my friend Mr Stefan Dramiński, creator of the splendid 3D pictures that accompany the plan drawings, it is now possible to show more clearly the architecture of the ship and equipment.

Of course these splendid battleships will never be able to reveal all their secrets, mainly because a large part of the inner construction and technical achievements will be never be known. Staff of the Imperial Japanese Navy were ordered to destroy all drawings and photographs before the surrender, while the condition of both battleships at the bottom of the sea, as a result of huge explosions at the time of their sinking, is tragic.

And finally, some more interesting, though not official, information. In the years after I finished the first edition I was in contact with still-living members of the *Yamato* crew, from whom I remember two facts. First, during the *Yamato* full-power trials in October 1941 it was announced in an official statement to the crew that the ship had increased its speed to 30 knots. Second, in the middle of her last battle on 7 April 1945, it was announced that the ship had been hit by 16 torpedoes. Please look at the hit scheme on page 43.

YAMATO AND MUSASHI – SUPERBATTLESHIPS

Post-war Allied censorship probably diminished the achievements of the Japanese in the construction of their battleships. The ships, often named superbattleships or strategic battleships, were built mainly to oppose US battleships – with the capability to annihilate them in battle – but the US never in fact fought against them. *Yamato* and her sister ship *Musashi* were sunk by the planes of the US carrier forces. As a result of revolutionary changes in sea warfare tactics, these carrier planes had become the fleet's main force of attack, giving battleships in some measure an auxiliary function. When the Japanese Bureau of Naval Construction began to make plans for the new battleship in 1934, there was no forewarning of the near supremacy of naval air forces and so she more strongly reflected the Tsushima tradition and the sea battles of First World War.

These superbattleships, built by the supreme efforts of their constructors and the naval architects of the Imperial Japanese Navy, were extremely costly and, due to developments in research and new technology, were obsolete almost from the time they were accepted into service – seven years after the first design emerged.

On 16 December 1941, when *Yamato*, the first of four projected ships, entered service, the world's most powerful battleships were:

UK	*King George V* class	227.1 m long 38,000–44,460 tons displacement
USA	*North Carolina* class	222.1 m long 38,000–46,770 tons displacement
France	*Jean Bart*	247.8 m long 42,806–49,850 tons displacement
Italy	*Littorio* class	237.8 m long 41,377–45,963 tons displacement
Germany	*Bismarck* class	(252.0 m long 42,900–52,600 tons displacement).

(*Musashi* was completed on 5 August 1942; *Shinano* was converted into an aircraft carrier and completed on 19 November 1944; the fourth ship, No 111, was cancelled about a third of the way through its construction.)

Yamato exceeded those listed above not only by her 69,100–72,809 tons displacement and the calibre of her guns, but also by the shape and construction of her hull, her armour protection, her gunnery and her optics. By any standards she was a tremendous achievement for the Japanese naval engineers and architects.

Yamato's 46cm (18in) guns, with 42–44km range and superior optical equipment, were the largest and most modern naval guns ever mounted and far exceeded the quality and construction of those of other nations. Her 15.5m rangefinders gave tremendous precision to the main gunfire; her armour protection was a maximum 650mm thick and the side armour plate 410mm thick; and the shape of her hull reduced water resistance to a minimum. All in all, her construction was an extremely difficult and expensive enterprise, significantly outstripping the difficulties encountered building the typical dreadnought.

Yamato and her sister ships *Musashi* and *Shinano* were considered the strategic weapons of the Imperial Japanese Navy; their design and construction were top secret and carefully guarded against recognition.

Unfortunately, just before the Japanese surrender, when the three ships lay on the seabed, orders were given to destroy any documentation about them – including all the drawings and even photographs of the *Yamato*s – which had been deposited in the Japanese Naval Archives.

The special services carried out this task to the letter, so that for many years after the war, the only surviving records of the ships were the aerial photographs taken by US Navy aircraft during their attacks on the giant ships. It was not until 1948 that the first photograph of *Yamato*'s portside, discovered by chance, was published; the most recent was published in 1981. Only fragments of the original documentation have survived, and, became partly available to the public between 1995 and 2015.

It is likely that the explosions on both battleships were ignited partly by 15.5cm, 12.7cm and 25mm rounds, causing the explosion of the powder magazine, and partly by the shells of the 46cm guns when the ships rolled over. With the explosion of *Yamato*'s aft magazines it is possible that the fire that arose after the bomb struck the rear turret of the 15.5cm gun was not extinguished.

DESIGN

The 1922 Washington Treaty, with its prohibitions on the building of new battleships, brought a halt to the 8–8 Project for the development of the Japanese fleet, which comprised the building of eight modern battle cruisers and eight large modern battleships. This was quite a blow for the Japanese, particularly for their designers. Then came a change in the concept of

Starboard view of Yamato *from trials in October 1941*

warship construction. The designers and engineers wanted to increase the quality of the new units. They already considered the US Navy a potential opponent and wanted to ensure that their ships would be stronger and better armed than their US counterparts.

Despite treaty prohibitions, the Bureau of Naval Construction carried on with their studies and research and preparations for building the battleships reached a new phase of development at the beginning of 1930, although work was limited to preliminary studies until 1934. It was in October 1934 that the Bureau of Naval Construction received from the Naval General Staff the order to produce a design study of a new battleship with 46cm guns and a speed of 30 knots (US battleships then had a speed of 24–25 knots and maximum 40.6cm guns).

The first finalised design was completed on 19 March 1935 under the designation A-140. The planned ship was to be bigger than the actual *Yamato*: length 294m, beam 41m, 69,500 tons displacement, 200,000hp turbine engines, speed 31 knots. But this was too large for the Japanese strategists, who reduced the speed requirement to 27 knots.

It was a difficult decision because, until then, they had attached great importance to high speed. The Bureau of Naval Construction's three groups of outstanding naval designers – Fujimoto, Hiraga and Fukada – had drawn

up as many as 23 preliminary designs up to March 1937. After 1 April 1935, when the penultimate design stage had been completed, the naval designers suggested a mixed propulsion system of diesel and turbine engines.

The turbines, with a total of 75,000hp, would drive two propellers; the diesel engines, with a total of 60,000hp, would drive two other propellers. After the second design stage it became the norm in all other versions to install diesel engines as the main machinery.

But, that time the Japanese Navy had a powerful two-cycle, double-acting diesel engine providing more than 10,000hp. These engines had been used successfully as the main propulsion for the submarine tenders *Taigei*, *Takasaki* and *Tsurugizaki* (all these three were converted into aircraft carriers) but at the time the Japanese did not possess any of the 30,000hp diesel engines that were to be used in *Yamato*.

For machinery of the same propulsive power, the diesel had the advantage of appreciably lower fuel consumption than the turbine by about 68 per cent, although the diesel was slightly heavier – about 1.07 per cent.

About two months after the provisional plans had been completed, in July 1936, the designers came across an unexpected difficulty, which caused drastic changes to be made.

Yamato's engine rooms were to be covered with 200mm thick armour-

Quarter view of Yamato *running builder's trials on 30 October 1941. The boat stowage hangar, catapult and lattice antenna mast on the crane platform are clearly visible.*

plating which was an integral element of the hull's armoured box. The plating was not only protective, but an integral part of the ship's structure, so after the diesel engines were installed it would have been impossible to replace them if they happened to cause problems. The designers had to return to their original plan and use 150,000shp turbine engines as the propulsion plant. In March 1937, the final design was drawn up by Dr Hiraga, the leading naval architect of the Imperial Japanese Navy.

On 4 November 1937, the first battleship's construction began and the keel was laid down in the dry dock of the Kure Kaigun Kōshō shipyard. 'Warship No.1' was later given the name *Yamato* – a mystic and especially potent name for the largest and most powerful battleship ever built.

Yamato is Japan's oldest poetic name, the name of the territory on which the first seed of the Japanese state was sown, and it later became the name of the province on the Kii peninsula, in south-western Honshu, whose capital is Nara.

Throughout the Second World War, *Yamato* was not only Japan's most modern new-generation battleship, it was also the pride and symbol of its Imperial Navy. Her loss in the operation 'Ten ichi go', in April 1945, became a symbol of the downfall of the Japanese Empire and was a final confirmation of the eclipse of the world's floating fortresses. Originally built to oppose US battleships – with the capability to annihilate

them in battle – *Yamato* and her sister ship *Musashi* never in fact fought against them.

Both these giant battleships were sunk by the planes of the US carrier forces – as revolutionary changes in sea warfare tactics, these carrier planes became the fleet's main force of attack, giving battleships in some measure an auxiliary function.

When the Bureau of Naval Construction began to make plans for a new battleship in 1934, there was no forewarning of the near supremacy of naval air forces and so she was designed to more strongly reflect the Tsushima tradition and the sea battles of the First World War.

In the Fifth Replenishment Program of 1942 two new warships No.798 and No.799 were projected. They were to have been battleships of a new design, armed with 50.8cm (20 inch)/45cal guns. The last version (Design A-150) featured 50.8cm guns in three twin turrets and many 10.0cm/65 cal HA guns as a secondary battery. The giant gun was constructed in early in 1941 in Kure Navy Yard and tests were made in the same year. The AP shell would have weighed about 2000kg. Battleship No.798 was to have been built at Yokosuka and No. 799 at Kure and laid down in late 1941 or early in 1942, with a total building period of some five years. They were in some ways similar to the *Yamato* class, but the design drawings were destroyed after surrender.

BUILDING HISTORY

Work on the *Yamato* project began with the development and modernisation of four selected shipyards – Kure, Nagasaki, Yokosuka and Sasebo – in which the future ships were to be built, because at that time none of the Japanese shipyards could undertake the building of such gigantic hulls.

Yamato was built in Kure Kaigun Kōshō in Kure naval yard's drydock which was extended by a metre and protected by a special roof on one side to screen her from view from the nearby hill. A gantry crane straddling the dock was used to lift parts weighing more than 100 tons.

A new dock in Yokosuka was built for *Shinano*.

Musashi was built in the Nagasaki naval yard. A sisal rope curtain hid the slipway on which the hull was built from view; the rope was 2710 km long and weighed 408 tons.

Musashi's launch – her hull weight on the slipway was 35,737 tons – was second only to the 37,287 tons of the British passenger liner *Queen Mary*.

The fourth battleship, No.111, which was never completed, was laid down in a new dry dock at Sasebo naval base.

The gigantic 46cm guns and their turrets, manufactured at Kure, were transported by the *Kashino*, a ship built specially for the purpose (displacement 11,000 tons, dimensions 135.0m x 18.8m x 6.7m).

The design works began in October 1934, and in March 1937 the design was finalised.

HULL STRUCTURE

The research and design work was carried out simultaneously with the hull model tests, the main aim of which was to reduce hull resistance and increase propulsive efficiency.

As many as 50 experimental hull models were built and tested in the experimental model basin of the Naval Technical Research Centre in Tokyo. This was then the largest basin of its type in Japan with a length of 245.5m, a width of 12.5m and a depth of 6.5m.

The results of these experiments led to the adoption of a gigantic bulbous bow of such a size and shape that it was unique in the contemporary world. The stern part of the hull was based on the sharp geometric form of the oldest Japanese battleships.

I discovered this sharp form from photographs analysed in about 1995, and the expedition in 1999 confirmed this shape, as did Paul G. Allen's last examination of the *Musashi*.

Principal dimensions of *Yamato* in 1941	
Length overall	263.0m
Length waterline	256.0m
Length between perpendiculars	244.0m
Beam	38.9m max
Beam waterline	36.9m
Draught (trial)	10.4m
Draught (full load)	10.86m
Displacement:	65,000 tons standard
	69,100 tons trial
	72,809 tons full load
Shaft horsepower	153,553 (astern 45,000)
Speed	27.46 kts
Oil fuel capacity	6300 tons
Range in action	7200 nm at 16 knots
Propulsion plant	4 steam turbines
Steam pressure	25kg/cm^2
Temperature	325°C
Armour	75–410mm side belt
	200–230 deck
	190–650 main turrets
	380–560 barbettes
	50mm secondary turrets
Armament	9 x 46cm (18.1in) triple turrets
	12 x 15.5cm (6.1in) triple turrets
	12 x 12.7cm (5in) twin mountings
	24 x 25mm MG triple mounting
	4 x 13mm MG twin mountings
Aircraft	6 (max7) floatplanes
Crew	2500

Thanks to a unique solution, the hull resistance was reduced to 8.2 per cent at a speed of 27 knots, and by improving the fitting of the shaft bracket and the bilge keel, a further reduction was achieved. In terms of effective horsepower, the former alteration resulted in a saving of 1900ehp and the latter in one of 475ehp. Altogether, including the reduction in hull resistance by use of the bulbous bow, sharp stern shape, the saving totalled 7910ehp, or 15,820shp.

In the full-power trial run the 69,100 ton ship, powered by 153,533shp, reached a speed of 27.46 knots (Japanese sources from the late 20th century

Yamato during her full-power trial on 20 October 1941, outside Sakumo Bay. According to information from crewmen, several years after the war, perhaps at that moment the battleship had reached a speed of more than 30 knots.

increased the power of the *Musashi* to 166,520shp and her speed to 28,50 knots).

Yamato's hull was broad and had a relatively shallow draught for a ship with such large displacement (10.86m fully loaded). It meant that the *Yamato* class ships could use the naval bases and dry docks of the Imperial Japanese Navy without extra money being spent dredging or rebuilding.

Another very important feature of *Yamato*'s hull was the method by which the shell plating was joined – namely, the extensive use of lap joints amidships. The butt joint had long been used in shell plating to make the shell surface smooth, reducing its frictional resistance. However, a serious defect had been found in the outer bottom plates of the *Isuzu* class light cruiser and *Fubuki* class destroyers which gave cause for concern over the use of butt-jointed plates in *Yamato*. It was discovered that frictional resistance was greatly affected by the surface of the fore and after parts of a ship where the water pressure was greater than at amidships.

Based on this finding, butt-joint plating was used only in the fore and after parts of *Yamato*, the remaining sections being covered by lap-joint plating. The method proved very effective when the ship was completed.

In the course of constructing *Yamato*'s huge hull, two factors – apparently contradictory – played an important part. The designers wanted to increase its strength and at the same time reduce the hull weight, for which the introduction of new methods was required. Dr. Hiraga applied the method that had earlier been used for the heavy cruiser *Furutaka*, whereby the armour-plating not only served as protection against hits, but was also an integral part of the hull construction. The thickness and rigidity of the armour-plating reinforced the hull strength considerably compared with traditional methods in which the armour merely was added on. This unique method was quite an innovation in international warship-building circles at the time.

Another considerable saving in hull weight was achieved by using electric welding extensively and on a large scale except in such important features as longitudinal members. The technique had not been fully adopted because welded joints on smaller warships built earlier had been found to be weak in comparison with the traditional riveted joints. The Japanese Navy was relatively early in its adoption of electric welding. It was used more widely in the construction of *Yamato*'s upper structure and superstructure than in the hull.

– The largest welded block was 11m high and weighed 80 tons.
– On the hull, the length of the welded joints was 343,422m – and the number of electrodes 5,995,611.
– On fitting and equipment – 120,347m / 1,511,298 electrodes.
– Protection – 15m / 636 electrodes.
– Total length of welded joints was 463,784m / 7,507,536 electrodes.
– Number of rivets used was 6,153,030. For example in building the battleship *Mutsu*, 3,733,753 rivets, were used and in battleship *Hiei* 2,874,622.

Another feature was that the main portion of the longitudinal structure was made with Ducol steel (DS) – the central longitudinal bulkhead was constructed in duplicate – to support the heavy 200–230mm plates plus 9mm DS deck plating. The deck extended to a width of 38.9m – the maximum width of the ship. To ensure the reliability of the electric services, the central ring main electric circuit ran through the watertight compartment inside the central bulkhead.

The weather deck – flush, with an untypical bottle-shape in plan – had its own uniquely characteristic undulating profile. The extremely effective idea of using longitudinal framing – it minimised the structural weight – was another of Dr. Hiraga's innovative methods which had been applied for the first time to the heavy cruiser *Furutaka*.

The characteristic shape of *Yamato's* bow came from the necessity of moving the hawse pipe away from the ship's centre line and as far forward as possible in order to protect the bulbous bow from being damaged by anchors. The lowering of the deck, starting from frame 110 towards the bow, was also connected to the reduction in weight and to the ship's profile.

The boat hangars, which were installed on both sides of the hull aft, were equipped with a single girder crane to lower boats directly to the water and gave the hull a modern and unusual appearance for that time. The middle part of the weather deck was covered with wooden 140mm-wide planking. The planks were made from Japanese 'hinoki' cypress.

The aircraft deck, starting from frame 177 towards the stern, was covered by steel plate partially chequered and reinforced by concrete (under steel plates).

The metal decks – including the anchor deck, part of the superstructure decks and the stern deck were all covered with chequer plating. The chequered plates of the anchor deck were not painted but made of zinc-galvanised steel plates.

The characteristic feature of the decks compared with other battleships was that they were 'empty' – without equipment. This was because of the terrific blast from the 46cm guns.

Ventilators and ventilation openings were constructed and placed in such a way as to avoid or reduce the effect of the blast. The necessary equipment, such as boats, planes and paravane, was kept in completely protected magazines or hangars. The construction and shape of the superstructure sides, the lack of platforms plate supports, and the protection of anti-aircraft batteries and observation and machine-gun control positions by shields were also to reduce blast for its crew. Later on, the open HA and MG stands were manned only when the main 46cm guns were not in action.

Blast pressure (kg/cm²) relative to gun distance				
Calibre	15.5cm		46cm	
Distance	1 barrel	3 barrels	1 barrel	3 barrels
5m	2.1	2.5	10.0	20.0
10m	0.95	1.6	5.8	11.0
15m	0.5	1.15	3.1	7.0

Yamato in 1942; this photo was found about 50 years after the end of the war.

Yamato during a trial run on 26 October 1941.

A blast pressure of 0.28kg/cm² was capable of destroying the boats on board ship and a blast pressure of 1.16 kg/cm² was strong enough to tear the clothing from crew and render them temporarily unconscious. These pressures (1.16 kg/cm³) were felt 30m away from the one-barrel 46cm guns and 50m away from the three-barrel 46cm guns.

Yamato weight breakdown, trial conditions			
	Tons	Tonnes	Percentage
Hull	20,212	20,536	29.2
Armour	21,266	21,807	30.8
Protection	1,629	1,665	2.4
Gun	11,661	11,849	16.9
Machinery	5,300	5,385	7.7
Fittings	1,756	1,784	2.5
Fixed equipment	417	424	0.6
Consumable stores	641	651	0.9
Navigation and optical	95	97	0.1
Electric	1,108	1,125	1.6
Aircraft	111	113	0.2

	Tons	Tonnes	Percentage
Pressurised water in boilers	297	302	0.4
Fuel oil	4,210	4,278	8.1
Reserve feed water	212	215	0.3
Lubricating oil	61	62	0.1
Light oil	48	49	0.1
Total	**69,100**	**70,209**	**100**

SUPERSTRUCTURE

The superstructure was positioned like an island on the huge deck of the battleship.

Its shape differed considerably from the superstructures of the older ships of the Imperial Japanese Navy. The tower – the characteristic 'pagoda mast' – was built as a result of the modernisation and rebuilding of the front tripod mast, which formed the core of their construction.

On the *Yamato* three features rose from the streamlined lower part of the superstructure with sloping sides – the tower bridge under the 15.5m rangefinder, the funnel uptakes and the after tower under the 10m rangefinder. The tower bridge and after tower were constructed around concentric cylinders; the tower bridge from three and rear tower from two.

The inner 1.5m diameter cylinder of both towers was made of 20mm thick DS, inside of which ran the communication lines. On top of these cylinders were Type 98 'Hoiban' low-angle directors in non-rotatable armoured mounting with three 12cm binocular stands and a periscope tower on top. In the space between the cylinders were fitted passages, staff briefing rooms etc. *Yamato*'s tower bridge area was 159m² (front) and 310m² (side) and was smaller than 'pagoda masts' on older Japanese battleships.

The tower bridge posts and rooms had been tested on the battleship *Hiei* – it was especially for that purpose that the the 'pagoda mast' was rebuilt, as a prototype for the *Yamato* class. After the necessary alterations, the tower bridge for the battleship was finally designed.

The main parts of the superstructure and tower bridge were protected by

A view of Musashi *from the anchor deck during trials in May–June 1942.*

20mm armour-plating capable of withstanding the force of projectiles from enemy aircraft.

ARMOUR

The weight of *Yamato*'s armour protection was 22,895 tons – the heaviest armoured ship ever built and a record that has not yet been broken. Her main section was protected by a sort of colossal armoured box. The box sides were protected at the top by 410mm Vickers hardened (VH) armour-plating, which was designed to withstand 46cm armour-piercing (AP) projectiles fired from distance of more than 20,000m. The front and back of the box were protected by 340–300mm VH steel armour. From above the armour deck (on the middle deck of the ship), made of MNC (New Vickers – non-cemented) steel armour-plating 200–230mm thick, formed protection against 46cm AP projectiles fired from a distance of 30,000m and could be penetrated only by a 1000kg AP bomb dropped from a height of 3400m or more.

Another feature was the 9mm DS plating that extended 700mm beneath the armour deck. Its purpose was to protect against possible splinters such as those from armour bolts and rivet heads when the armour deck was hit by a bomb or projectile.

Even part of the fore and after weather deck, in addition to the armoured main section, was protected by 35–50mm CNC (copper alloy – non cemented) steel which was sufficient to repel a 250kg bomb dropped by an enemy dive-bomber. The real achievement of *Yamato*'s design was the fact that the constructors managed to reduce the length of the main box-protected section vitals to 53.5 per cent of the total length. Despite her lower ratio, *Yamato*'s stability in damaged conditions was designed to be better than that of other Japanese capital ships. Heavy armour also protected two steering-engine rooms – for the main and auxiliary rudders – which were situated outside the main armoured section of the ship. They consisted of two armoured boxes: the sides of the main rudder room were protected by 350–360 VC armour, the top part by 200mm MNC and the auxiliary rudder by 250–300mm VC.

Another feature was the fact that the floors of the ammunition magazines were protected by 50–80mm armour-plating which extended from the bottom of the magazines across watertight compartments above the double bottom of the hull shell. The idea was to protect them from explosion from a hostile torpedo or mine beneath the ship.

A new method of armour protection was also adopted for the boiler uptakes. Funnel gases escaped through perforated plates that were adopted after careful tests proved that they reduced the weight of armour compared with conventional grating armour. The 380mm armour-plating was perforated with holes of 180mm diameter (the total area of the holes being less than 55 per cent of the whole plating area). In addition, the inclined surfaces of the funnel were protected by 50mm armour which would detonate bombs before they reached the surface of the perforated plating.

As mentioned previously, *Yamato*'s armour protection was designed to resist the terrific kinetic energy of 46cm projectiles weighing 1460kg and travelling at approximately 500m/sec.

This was the calibre of both *Yamato*'s own, and her sister *Musashi*'s, artillery that was never actually employed on other ships. Such requirements demanded the perfection of new technologies to avoid the increase in thickness of the armour-plating. The builders could not apply the type of steel that had been used before; it took as many as ten years of research and development to solve the problem. An extremely hard surface was a requisite requirement for the armour-plating, but the ordinary method of cementation was expensive and could not achieve the desired plate thickness. A special method was adopted to harden the surface of the thick armour plates, which proved very effective: not only could it harden a portion as far as 140mm into the plate, it also greatly reduced production costs.

The next step was the adoption of armour-plating of larger dimensions, a development connected with the reduction in the number of edges and joints exposed to projectile hits.

The Japanese Navy ignored the expense involved in expanding the necessary facilities to manufacture larger pieces of armour for the *Yamato*-class battleships. According to records, about $10,000,000 (US) were spent on expanding steel-plate manufacturing facilities. As a result, the dimensions of the side armour plates were: thickness 410mm; length 5.9m; width 3.6m = 21.2m²; weight 68.5 tons.

Another problem was the emplacement of the armour, particularly the lower edge of the 410mm side armour, so that it could withstand a hit. Side armour was equipped so as to drive a wedge with an angle of 10° at its lower edge when struck by the shock of a hit, but in the event this method proved insufficient after she was commissioned into service. The underwater protection system was based on a lot of tests carried out on 1:3 scale models by means of well-chosen explosive charges. The last test was carried out in 1939 on a full-scale mock-up of *Yamato* that was attacked with 400kg charges. The holding bulkhead did not remain watertight but was not split open. The principal weakness was at the bottom connection between the holding bulkhead and the shell, and this section was redesigned for *Yamato*.

Prior to construction, however, considerations of underwater projectile trajectories meant that the bulkhead was radically increased in thickness. As installed, it was 200mm thick at the top (the connection with the lower edge of the 410mm main side belt) to 75mm at the bottom connection with the shell – the entire system being designed to withstand an attack by a 400kg charge.

The biggest problem with the change in design was the method for connecting the main armour belt with the newly designed lower torpedo-holding bulkhead. The decision was an unsatisfactory compromise reached over the objection of several officers who felt a delay in completion of the ship was warranted in view of the problems already apparent in the design.

The design of the joint was based primarily on the ability of steelmakers to produce the special shapes required in a reasonable amount of time. That joint was the weak point – and a significant design error – as it was entirely dependent for transfer strength on the shearing strength of tap rivets and three-ply rivets. The joint itself did not give adequate support in the transverse direction.

View from Musashi's tower bridge to the anchor deck, forecastle deck and main gun turrets no.1 and no.2. On the left is part of the 1.5m navigation rangefinder. Small trusses on the left and right barrels and small platforms were fitted temporarily for precise adjustment of the guns.

The aforementioned fears were confirmed by damage to *Yamato* from a single torpedo hit on the starboard quarter, from a torpedo fired from a submarine, on 25 December 1943. A hole about 5m deep, extending downward from the top of the bulge connection (of the armour), and 25m long, between frames 151 and 173, was produced, Water flooded into the No.3 turret upper magazine from a small hole in the longitudinal bulkhead caused by the caving in of the waterline armour.

As a result of the Japanese investigation into this damage, the Fourth Section, Ship Construction, authorised the installation of a 45° sloping plate across the corner of the upper void between the two inboard bulkheads during the January–April refit.

View from Musashi's *tower bridge to the funnel, main mast and aircraft deck in May 1942, during finishing works; the two boats visible were fitted only temporarily.*

Yamato's hull was divided into 1147 watertight compartments (WTC) that comprised 1065 below the armour deck (middle deck) and 82 above. The maximum extension of the WTC increased her buoyancy. Her reserve buoyancy reached as much as 57,450 tons (c.f. 29,292 tons for *Nagato*, 21,300 tons for *Fusō*) – this was 80 per cent (67.6 per cent for *Nagato*, 55.2 per cent for *Fusō*) of her trial displacement. The battleship was also designed to remain fairly stable when in a damaged condition.

In the event of her bow or stern sections, other than the armoured citadel, being flooded, it was believed that she could maintain her stability until she listed to 20°, and that her trim capacity would enable her to function with her freeboard forward reduced to 4.5m – *Yamato*'s fore freeboard was 10.0m, amidships 8.6m, and after 6.4m – even if her fore part was completely destroyed and flooded.

FLOODING AND PUMPING SYSTEM

The flooding and pumping system was designed to fulfil the following requirements:

1. The resultant list and trim from the first torpedo hit should be reduced to under 4° list and 2.3m difference in draught fore and after within five minutes of the damage control system going into action.

2. The resultant list and trim from the second torpedo hit should be controlled within thirty minutes, to the above-mentioned standard.

By flooding the opposite damage control tanks, the battleship could also be heeled by 13.8° maximum, and another 4.5° list could be added by shifting fuel to the opposite fuel tanks. Altogether, it was believed that the system could enable the battleship to return to almost even keel from a list of 18.3°.

MACHINERY

The designers abandoned mixed propulsion (diesel plus turbine) in the last phase of the project.

The battleship was equipped with 150,000hp turbine propulsion machinery using 25kg/cm² and 325°C steam. Twelve boilers, each of 12,500hp, were set up in four rows, three per row, and each located in a separate room. Three boilers in a row propelled each turbine. The Kampon-type boilers were of a standard Japanese Navy design. The banks were nineteen tubes deep with superheaters – which were of the two-pass four-loop type – between inner boiler rows 7 and 8. A peculiarity of Japanese naval boilers was the narrowing of the bank of tubes between the furnace and superheaters. The centre-to-centre length of the first inner rows was 4.25m and rows 4 to 7 were reduced so that the distance between the the superheaters and beyond the passage was only 3.263m. Yamato's boiler rooms had a floor area of 798m² and an engine room floor area of 640m² = 238shp/m². The ship's prismatic coefficient was 0.612 and the block coefficient 0.596.

At maximum speed, when all twelve boilers were in operation, the consumption of fuel oil amounted to 62.700kg/hr = 1233 kg per 1000m of the distance steamed.

Using full power of 153,553shp she reached a maximum speed of 27.46 knots; at a standard (economic) speed 16.47 knots she used 18,596shp with a maximum radius of 7200 nautical miles – all with 4,210 tons of fuel oil on board.

All this data concerning maximum propulsion by steam turbines and maximum speed became available to the public several years after the end of the war. More than 12 years ago new data was published: maximum power 166,520shp with a maximum speed of 28.1 knots for Yamato's sister ship Musashi.

The last preliminary design for the superbattleship A-140-F3 – just before the design of the Yamato class – reached 135,000shp, 65,200 tons trial displacement, dimensions of the hull the same as Yamato – maximum speed 27 knots.

Maybe the previously mentioned speed of over 30 knots during trials in December 1941 is not merely a report and can be assumed to be real.

TURNING ABILITY

The ship's turning ability was also superior compared with other battleships. Yamato's tactical diameter was 640m, the advance diameter 589m, giving a maximum heel of 9° when the ship was turned by the maximum rudder angle of 35° at a speed of 26 knots. The small heeling angle in a turn (necessary from the point of view of evading bombs and torpedoes, and for stability and fire control) was attributed to her metacentric height – GM = 2.88m during trials. Her rolling period was an impressively steady 17.5 seconds.

The battleship had two rudders – main and auxiliary – respectively 46m² and 17m², instead of the twin-rudder system of ordinary large warships. Originally it was planned to install two rudders, one each fore and aft, but the plan was later changed to fit the auxiliary rudder about 15m ahead of the main. In the trial run, however, an unexpected attribute of the auxiliary rudder was discovered, to the disappointment of the designers: so great was the turning momentum of the ship once she had begun to alter course that the auxiliary rudder alone could not reduce the momentum sufficiently to make her resume her course.

ARMAMENT

Main armament – Type 94 46cm/45 calibre guns

The 46cm (18.1in) guns with which Yamato and Musashi were supplied were the only modern guns of this calibre ever mounted in a ship and represented quite an achievement for the Imperial Japanese Navy. Up to that time 40.6cm (16in) guns were the largest in general use, the only exception being the British battlecruiser Furious that was equipped for a short time with two single turrets with 45.7cm Model 1915 guns. Japanese designers had been interested in using very large guns since 1920; the 13–16 class battleships from 8–8 Project's cancelled programme were to be equipped with 46cm guns and at the same time they were testing 48cm (18.9in) guns. In 1934 the building programme for modern 46cm guns was restarted with a view to the new superbattleships. The new guns – being perfected by the engineer C. Hada's team – were ready in 1939 and their production started in 1939–40.

Twenty-seven guns were built, of which 18 – six complete turrets – were mounted in Yamato and Musashi. The maximum weight of a triple turret was 2774 tonnes – about as heavy as a big destroyer. The AP projectile's 1460kg weight was one and a half times the weight of the 40.6cm projectiles.

Building these modern guns was extremely expensive and the designers had to solve a lot of new technical problems. However, the Japanese naval strategists' policy was to make each individual ship so powerful that even the resource-rich industrial United States would scarcely be able to match them.

Shell rooms, hoists and ram mechanisms

The number of projectiles per gun was 130 rounds, of which 60 projectiles were stowed in the turret rotating structure, making 180 projectiles in the turrets (3 x 60). The remainder – 70 projectiles per gun, 210 per turret – were located in the shell rooms. So altogether the ship had 1170 projectiles and the same amount of 330kg powder charges.

It was considered that 60 projectiles per gun was sufficient for battle; while fighting, it was possible to supply the turret rotating structure with projectiles from the shell room, but it was quite a time-consuming process. The projectiles were moved by means of 'push-pull' gear: the projectiles in the turret were moved directly to the hoist (a simple 'pusher type' on a 5° downward-tilting platform for transfer to the hoist proper). The hoist door closed automatically by a spring-loaded crank activated by the weight of the projectile entering the hoist mechanism, and the projectile was seated on the hoist, which was fitted with a set of three lifting and retaining pawls, back and front respectively. When the projectile reached the top of the hoist, it was carried into the tilting bucket (tilted 8° upwards) and held in the bucket by clips. When the projectile was ready, it was moved from the bucket into the waiting tray before its transfer into the shell-loading bogie and rammer. The loading bogie moved forward on rails, at the same time lowering into the gun load angle of 3°. After the gun had been loaded the shell rammer (chain) was taken back and the powder charge loaded.

Magazine and cordite handling room

Each of the three turrets had two cordite magazines. The lower room had one transfer bogie and one hoist servicing the centre gun; the upper room had two bogies and two hoists for the left and right guns. The entire propellant charge weighed 330kg – six charges each of 55kg.

These were stowed in magazines in flash-tight stowage canisters (two charges per canister) from where they were removed and passed through flash-tight scuttles controlled by the cordite roller chute and into the turret rotating structure. A full charge (six 1/6 charges) was then transferred to the cordite hoist cages via the transfer bogie pivot tray. Each end of the hoist had a flash-tight door that was operated by a combination of cams and hand levers.

Opening the upper flash door freed the rammer control. The cordite hoist was a flash-tight 2870 x 950mm trunk equipped to take one cordite cage. The cordite cage was supplied with a flash-tight container for the entire charge (330kg) that was opened at the same time as the charge was loaded into the gun chamber by a cordite rammer (similar in construction to the shell rammer). At low elevation (~20°) a 28-second firing cycle was possible, and 40 seconds for the maximum 45° elevation.

The tower bridge of Musashi *during finishing works in May–June 1942. This photograph was taken from the main deck.*

Train and elevation engine

Each turret was equipped with two sets of training gears, only one being used at a time. Contrary to previous Japanese practice, a worm gear was rejected because of space limitations and a rack and pinion system adopted. Each turret was equipped with two 500hp hydraulic motors for train drive – one for each set of gears.

Each gun was fitted with elevating and shifting cylinders. The rotation rate was 2°/sec, elevation rate 10°/sec, maximum elevation +45°, loading and underway (normal) position +3°, and minimum elevation –5°.

Each turret was equipped with auxiliary hoists with overhead travellers and chain purchase for emergency handling in the gunhouse. Hydraulic winches were used to move the projectiles to the hoists in emergencies; hydraulic valves allowed the magazines to be flooded completely in 20 minutes. Each powder magazine and shell room was equipped with sprinklers.

Gunhouse

Each turret was divided into four compartments, each comprising three guns plus equipment placed in a separate cell. The separate compartment behind the gunhouse was occupied by a 15m turret rangefinder. The armour protection was as follows:

Gunhouse: front 650mm, side 250mm (minimum), back 190mm, roof 270mm.
Barbette: 560mm – 380–440mm after parts.

46cm gun performance		
Elevation	Range (m)	Projectile flight time (sec)
10°	16,843	26.05
20°	27,916	49.21
30°	35,826	70.27
40°	40,700	89.42
45°	42,026	98.60

Power against targets at various ranges		
Range (m)	20,000	30,000
Gun elevation	12° 34'	23° 12'
Striking angle	16° 31'	31° 21'
Striking velocity	522m/sec	475m/sec
Penetration vertical plate	566mm	467mm
Penetration horizontal plate	416mm	230mm

Gun data	
Designation	Type 94 46cm/45cal
Calibre	46cm (18in)
Length in calibres	45
Length overall	21,300mm
Construction type: wire wound radially expanded muzzle	4 layers
Breech	5 layers
Breech type	screw
Rifling No. of grooves Twist uniform Groove depth	 72 1 in 28cal 4.6mm
Bore cross-section	1698cm²
Projectile range	17.59m
Chamber volume	480 litres
Diameter of turret rollers (axle)	12.274mm
Distance from centre of rotation to trunnions in fore and aft line	3520mm
Height from centre line of guns to roller path	4400mm
Distance between centre line of guns	3050mm
Recoil length	1430mm
Ventilation	Three 2.5hp fans for supply and five 5hp exhaust fans
Turret rangefinder	15.5m base, elevation +10° and free train 160 milsec right, 130 milsec left
Local sight	One 10cm telescope per gun
Spreads	Normal spreads in 4- or 5-gun salvoes at maximum range, about 500–600m; somewhat larger in broadside firing

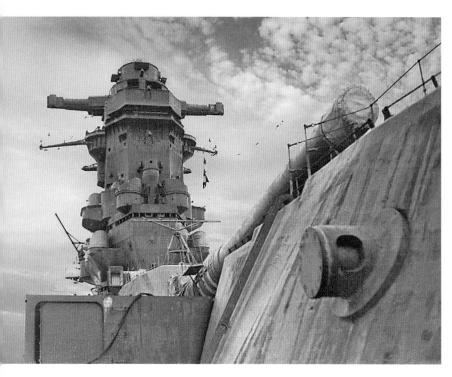

Note the details of the No.1 main gun turret; periscope of the right gun and the 15.5m turret's rangefinder arm with closed opening and a sliding steel screen.

46cm gun mount data (weight in tonnes)	
Rotating turret structure:	
Three guns with breech mechanisms	495
Remainder of elevating parts	228
Turntable minus elevating parts and armour	350
Remainder of training parts below turntable	647
Gunhouse armour	790
Total weight	**2510**
Total weight with ammunition	**2774**

Projectiles

Three basic types of projectile were used in 46cm guns:

1. **Armour piercing (Type 91).** This weighed 1460kg and was designed to enter the water short of the target, maintain its trajectory and penetrate the hull's torpedo defence system. The projectile nose was given a hydrodynamic shape so its trajectory would not alter drastically on entry. The Japanese had been quite impressed by the damage caused by rounds falling short on their partially completed battleship *Tosa* in firing experiments.

2. **46cm type common 'San Shiki' Model 3.** This was originally constructed and designed as AA, acting as an incendiary 'shotgun' projectile. It was fitted with 900 incendiary tubes (rubber thermite) and 600 steel stays. The projectile was supplied with a time fuze set to go off at suitable height when the contents of 1500 incendiary tubes and stays exploded in a cone shape in an angle of about 20° towards any incoming aircraft. In a fraction of a second after firing, the projectile shell was destroyed by a bursting charge, increasing the quantity of shell splinters. The incendiary tubes ignited about half a second later and burned for five seconds at 3000°C, giving a flame about 5m long.

3. **Type HE (high explosive).** This weighed 1360kg and contained 136lb of tri-nitro-anisole (TNA).

46cm projectile data	
Muzzle velocity (AP projectile)	780m/sec
Muzzle velocity ('San Shiki', HE projectile)	805m/sec
Maximum range (AP projectile)	42,050m
Maximum altitude	11,900m
Barrel life (approx)	200–250 service rounds
Bore pressure	32kg/mm^2

Secondary Armament

This consisted of 'Nendo Shiki' (Third Year Type) 15.5cm/60cal guns. Engineer C. Hada designed the 15.5cm guns (as well as the 46cm guns) in 1932 as the main armament for 'B' class cruisers; they were also mounted in the *Mogami* class cruisers. These guns were the finest in use during the Second World War. *Yamato* and *Musashi* originally had four 15.5cm gun turrets. These triple turrets were made available by the conversion of four *Mogami* class cruisers, which were given twin turrets with 20.3cm guns in place. The triple turrets after modernisation were installed in a diamond arrangement, the turrets in superfiring positions over the main battery fore and aft, and the two others were in wing positions, one on each side. The wing turrets were removed to provide space for additional 12.7cm AA guns for *Yamato* in January 1944 and for *Musashi* in April 1944.

The gun mounts and turrets were operated by electro-hydraulic power with mineral oil as the pressure medium (two 100hp motors per turret). Each turret had six hoists – one shell hoist and one powder hoist per gun. The shell handling room and powder hoist equipment were essentially a scaled down version of large-calibre equipment. The hoists were activated by hydraulic motors supplied by the common ring.

15.5cm gun data	
Bore calibre	15.5cm (6.1in)
Length	60cal
Barrel length (overall)	9615mm
Construction	Monoblock radially expanded
Breech mechanism	Normal swinging – hand or hydraulic
Weight with breech	12.7 tonnes
Groove number	40, twist uniform: 1 in 28cal
Chamber length	1129mm
Chamber volume	38 litres
Muzzle velocity	980m/sec
Bore pressure	34kg/mm²
Barrel life	250–300 rounds
Firing rate	7–5 rounds/min
Maximum range (45°) AP	27,400m
Maximum range (common)	26,500m
Maximum altitude	12,600m
Elevation/depression	55°/ – 10°
Projectile weight	55.87kg (all types)
Charge weight	19.5kg
Normal ammunition supply	150 rounds per gun (max 270 per gun)
One 8m rangefinder per turret	

High Angle Guns

As completed, *Yamato* and her sister ship *Musashi* carried twelve Type 89 Model A-1-3 40cal 12.7cm guns in six twin-enclosed mountings. The original shields were enclosed to reduce the effect of the terrific blast from the main 46cm guns. During the ship's refit in January – April 1944 *Yamato* received an extra twin mounting (Type 89 Model A-1 12.7cm/40cal without anti blast protection – it is on open stands) that were installed on existing Model A-1-3 position. The guns with enclosed mountings (towers) were moved to both sides on fitted new superstructure base.

The same modernisation was planned for the *Musashi*, but by the time of the war, difficulties meant that although she had received the additional superstructures on both sides as bases for the 12.7cm and 25mm guns, the six new double 12.7cm guns were not installed, and in its place were fitted six triple 25mm MG on open stands.

The loader's two platforms moved up and down with the elevation of the mounting. The battery was semi-automatic using a spring-operated rammer.

There were fuze setters on the right side of each mount. Simple dredger-type hoists were used to lift the fixed ammunition to the gun platform.

12.7cm gun data	
Designation	Type 89 HA 12.7cm/40cal
Length	40cal
Muzzle velocity	725m/sec
Projectile weight	23.05kg
Charge weight	4.0kg
Maximum range	14,800m
Maximum altitude	9400m
Barrel life	800–1500 service rounds
Rate of fire	14 rounds/min maximum 8 rounds/min sustained
Maximum elevation/depression	90°/–8°
Construction	Monoblock autofrettaged
Rifling	36 grooves, uniform twist – 1 in 28cal
Ammunition supply (normal)	300 fixed rounds per barrel
Ammunition supply (max)	560 fixed rounds per barrel

Light Anti-Aircraft Guns – Type 96 25mm machine guns

Both battleships were armed with a very successful anti-aircraft gun – Type 96, 25mm/60cal triple machine guns of 1941 design, and after 1943 with single 25mm MG of 1943 design. The guns were similar in construction to the French Hotchkiss type and constituted the main AA weapon of the Imperial Japanese Navy. The triple gun mount was manned by a crew of nine, the single (a free-swinging moveable mount) by a crew of three. The usual ammunition supply was 2000 rounds per gun (one barrel) but by some sources the maximum number of rounds per one barrel in 1945 was 10,000. The 15-round magazines were brought up by hoist to the level of the machine gun platforms, and stowed after in ammunition boxes.

25mm machine guns mounted on *Yamato*		
1941	as completed: 8 x III = 8 closed mounts	24 guns
Sept 1943	4 new triple open mounts = 4 x III + old 8 x III	36 guns
Jan–Apr 1944	12 new triple mounts and 26 new single mounts = total 24 x III + 26 x I	98 guns
July 1944	5 new triple mounts = 5 x III = total 29 x III + 26 x I	113 guns
Jan 1945	21 new triple mounts fitted and 24 single mounts removed – total 50 x III – 2 x I	152 guns
April 1945	4 single mounts fitted = total 50 x III + 2 x I + new 4 x I	156 guns

25mm machine guns mounted on *Musashi*		
1942 as completed	8 x III = eight triple enclosed mounts	24 guns
July 1942	4 x III = twenty new triple open	36 guns
April 1944	18 x III plus 25 x I new mounts (30 x III + 25 x I)	115 guns
June 1944	5 x III new mounts (35 x 3 + 25 x I)	130 guns

25mm machine gun data	
Designation	Type 96 'Shiki' 25mm/60cal MG
Length	60cal
Gun length overall	2420mm
Muzzle velocity	900m/sec
Projectile weight	0.25kg
Maximum range	6800m
Maximum altitude	5000m
Rate of fire	220 rounds/min
Maximum elevation/depression	90°/ – 10°

Type 93 13mm machine guns

Two twin 13mm machine-gun mounts were installed on both sides of the tower bridge and were similar in construction to the Hotchkiss type, with a horizontal range of 6000m, vertical range of 4500m, rate of fire 450 rounds per minute and ammunition supply of 2500 rounds per gun. In 1944 *Musashi* carried twin rocket launchers each armed with 28 12cm AA common rockets and four depth charge launchers located on both sides on the stern deck.

Fire control system

Main battery

Both battleships were equipped with the Type 98 low angle fire control system – the ultimate in Japanese low angle fire control installation and specially designed for the *Yamato* class battleships. The principal parts of this installation were as follows:

Four 15.5m rangefinders, one on top of the tower bridge and the remaining three in 46cm gun turrets, and one 10m rangefinder on the top of the after tower. The one on top of the tower bridge was a triple rangefinder with one stereoscopic set. Special attention should be paid here to the high quality of Japanese optics and at the same time to the unusual base length of the 15.5m rangefinders which allowed exceptional range estimation and consequently a high degree of accuracy in shooting, usually bracketing the target with early salvoes.

A rear view of Musashi's *funnel, tower bridge and searchlight platform in September 1942 after fitting Type 21 radar antennas on both arms of the 15.5m rangefinder. Note the white painted 'Hoiban' LA director and antennas – dating from the middle of 1942 to the end of 1943.*

Type 98 low angle 'Hoiban' directors were situated in two completely enclosed towers – one on top of the main 15.5m rangefinder and second on top of the 10m rangefinder. They were manned by a control officer who operated the main telescope searchlight and three others: layer, trainer and cross-leveller. Level and cross-level corrections were handled by a 'match the pointer' system. The director gave train and elevation orders to the guns.

Type 98 'Sokutekiban' was a component of the Japanese fire control system unknown in Western navies. It was a section of the computer and received its information from the directors. It gave target course and target speed information to the computers.

Type 98 'Shagekiban' low angle computer was the latest Japanese fire control table and the first low angle computer with an automatic electrical-mechanical follow-up system.

Type 98 firing device consisted of two components:

1. Trigger time limiting device: limited the time of two or more guns to 0.08–0.2 seconds after the firing circuit was activated.
2. Firing time separator: reduced interference in flight; two guns could not be fired at the same instant.

The battleship's main battery and her fire control system were also adapted for use as anti-aircraft fire.

Secondary guns

15.5cm guns were equipped with an 8m turret rangefinder and a fire control system. This was the same type as used in the main battery system with 4.5m instead of the 15.5m and 10m rangefinders.

12.7cm high angle guns: These were controlled by the Type 94 'Kōsha Sōchi' HA fire control system.

25mm machine-gun batteries: These were controlled by the Type 95 'Shageki Sōchi' short range HA director. It was a simple course and speed system that was not up to Western standards, though all triple 25mm guns had the advantage of remote control.

Sensors

Yamato and *Musashi*, as the most modern and strategically important battleships of the Imperial Japanese Navy, were supplied with the latest radar and electronic equipment.

Type 21

The first radar was installed on *Musashi* in September 1942 and on *Yamato* in July 1943. It was the Type 21 Gō Dentan Kai 3 air and surface search radar. Two Type 7 Gata radar antennas of 'mattress' pattern with combined transmit and receive arrays were installed on both arms of the 15.5 m rangefinder. The Type 21 Kai 3 radar's wave length was 1.5m, power 25–30kW and range 120km (aircraft group), 70km (single aircraft).

Type 22

Surface search/gunnery control radar Type 22 Gō Dentan Kai 4 was installed on *Yamato* in February 1944 and on *Musashi* two months latter in April 1944. The radar antenna comprised two electromagnetic horns – upper for receiving, lower for transmitting. Two Type 22 radars were installed on the sides of the upper part of the tower bridge. The radar was not adapted for fire control. Its characteristics were wave length 10cm, power 2kW, maximum detection range 35 km + – 700m (battleships), 20km (cruisers), 17km (destroyers), bearing error + – 5˚.

The Musashi's *main gun salvo during firing research on the impact of the blast, at Setona-ka in Iyo Nada on 26 July 1942.*

Type 13

The type 13 Gō Dentan air search radar was fitted on *Yamato* and *Musashi* at the same time as the fitting of Type 22 radar. Two ladder-type antennas were located on both sides of the main mast. The characteristics of the radar were a separate set for transmission and receiving, wave length 2.0m, power output 10kW, maximum detection 100km (aircraft group), 50km (single aircraft), range error + – 2–3km, bearing error + – 10˚.

Sonar

Both battleships were equipped with Type '0' sonar arrays that could detect a submarine when the ship was dead in the water or proceeding at low speed.

AIRCRAFT AND CATAPULTS

Yamato and *Musashi* were designed to carry a maximum of seven floatplanes of the Mitsubishi F1M2 Type '0' (allied code 'Pete') and Aichi E13A1 (allied code 'Jake') types. But on both battleships only Mitsubishi F1M2 floatplanes were actually used.

Aircraft were launched into the air by two 19.5m long catapults of Type Kure Shiki 2 G 5 Gata and a 6-ton crane with a 20m long arm was used to lift them out of the water. The floatplanes were stowed in a hangar and before flight were moved across the aircraft deck by a system of trucks and rails to the catapults.

Principal specifications of the Mitsubishi F1M2 two-seat general-purpose floatplane	
Power plant	875hp
Span	11.0m
Length	9.5m
Height	4.0m
Speed (max)	370km/h
Cruising speed	193 km/h
Range max/norm	740km/442km
Weight (max)	2856kg
Ceiling	9440m
Armament	3 x 7.7mm MG + 60kg bombs
Wing area	29.54 m²

BOATS

Yamato and *Musashi* were designed to carry 16 boats but usually carried 14. All the boats were kept in hangars because of the terrific blast from the main battery. They were lowered and raised by an overhead travelling crane (side hangars) or by a 6-ton aircraft crane (boat hangars on the stern deck – UD). The boats consisted of two 17m ceremonial barges with 150hp drive, one 15m ceremonial barge with 150hp drive, one 11m motorboat with 60hp drive, four 12m motor launches with 30hp drive, four 9m cutters unpowered, one 8m and one 6m sampan (unpowered).

SEARCHLIGHTS

After completion, *Yamato* and *Musashi* each carried eight 150cm director controlled searchlights for night fighting. Their number was reduced to six in 1944 and next to four in 1945 on *Yamato*. AA control positions were installed in their place (on *Musashi*, two rocket launchers). Both battleships also carried four 60cm and two 40cm signalling searchlights.

INTERIOR COMMUNICATIONS

These were based on three principal methods: voice tube (146 installed), telephone (491 installed), pneumatic air chute (14). Each ship carried 40 radio receivers and 17 transmitters, with operating frequencies ranging from low frequency (LF) to very high frequency (VHF). Most of the equipment operated at LF, MF and HF.

The Navy Type 2 infrared communications were developed in 1942.

COMPLEMENT

The crews of *Yamato* and *Musashi* as completed were planned as 2500 officers and men, but during service this number was increased by fitting additional armaments and equipment. In April 1945 the number of crew on *Yamato* was increased to 3332 sailors (from this number only 23 officers and 246 men survived on 7 April 1945).

Japanese sources give *Musashi*'s complement on 24 October as 2399 officers and men, and in comparison to *Yamato* the crew looks very understated. Maybe only the number of lost – 1023 officers and men – was correct.

Additionally, on the last cruises of both battleships squads of maritime regiments were transported, but the starting number and number lost were unknown.

WARTIME COLOUR SCHEMES

1. Gold was used for the 120cm diameter chrysanthemum crest on the bow.

2. The hull colour of the Imperial Japanese Navy ships varied in shade, although it was based on regulation colours. The basic grey (medium grey) was made up according to a Paint Mixture Standard Formula and consisted of 15 per cent black, 75 per cent white, 6 per cent brown, 4 per cent blue. This colour was used for the above-water part of the hull, the superstructures, gun turrets, the topside fittings, metal decks and sides of the boats.

3. A reddish-tinged brown was used on the underwater part of the hull, and consisted of 20 per cent red, 65 per cent brown, 10 per cent black and 5 per cent white.

4. White was used for the azimuth scales of the AA rangefinders, the upper part of the tower bridge – above the 15.5m rangefinder (Hoiban, Type 21 radar antenna) – from the middle of 1942 to the end of 1943, the chrysanthemum on both sides of the funnel in April 1945, the stripes of the circular railings of the open triple 25mm gun mounts, the 200mm high numbers on the base of the deck 25mm MG enclosed mounts, the stripes on the edge of the hull – end of 1944–45 – and the inner surfaces of the rangefinder and gun rangefinder openings.

5. Brown (canvas) was used for the blast bags and the gun muzzle covers.

6. Yellowish-brown (like milk chocolate) was used for the non-slip linoleum strips on the aircraft deck (with 20mm brass strips attaching it to the deck surface.

7. Black was used for the upper part of the funnel and mast.

The forecastle of Yamato during construction on 3 June 1940, No.1 main armament gunhouse is nearing completion, and on the barbette of No. 2 main turret are visible rollers with training rack and upper rotating shell stowage and shell and cordite hoists.

8. The chequered steel plates of the anchor deck were zinc coated not painted and were a light grey colour.

9. The wooden deck (main part of FD) was unpainted 'hinoki' cypress wood in a grey tint with a little brown. The planking was made of 140mm wide planks.

10. Aircraft: Upper surface sea green N-1, lower surface gull grey N-2, orange stripes on wing's leading edge (middle part), white-red stripes on floats. White stripes on tailplanes and number codes on fins. The Hinomaru was red with white borders.

11. Wooden decks and probably roof of turret No.1 of main guns were painted black for the night breakthrough in the San Bernardino Strait. This hastily applied camouflage was mainly based on soot from stacks used on both *Yamato* and *Musashi* (18–24 October 1944).

IJN *YAMATO*

The Bureau of Naval Construction's three groups of outstanding naval designers – Fujimoto, Hiraga and Fukada – had drawn up as many as 23 preliminary designs up to March 1937.

March 1937: The final design was drawn up by Dr Hiraga, the leading naval architect of the Imperial Japanese Navy.

4 November: Construction began on 'Battleship No.1' – the keel was laid down in the dry dock of the Kure Kaigun Kōshō shipyard.

September–November 1939: main engines fitted.

May–October: Boilers fitted.

8 August 1940: Launched.

May–July 1941: Main guns fitted.

12 August 1941: Departs Kure for trials.

Admiral Yamamoto (front row, sixth from left) and his staff aboard the Yamato early in 1942. The photo was taken at the after end of the superstructure on the port side. The rear part of the 15.5cm gun turret (turret No.2) is visible in the left background.

5 September 1941: Kure – Battleship No.1 is being fitted out.

8 December: The attack on Pearl Harbor; at the opening of hostilities, Battleship No.1 is still fitting out in Kure.

16 December 1941: Battleship No.1 is completed and registered in the Kure Naval District as *Yamato*. She then joined the First Battleship Division part of the Combined Fleet, which consisted of *Nagato* and *Mutsu,* and began intensive training, next stay at anchor at Hashirajima – Inland Sea.

12 February 1942: *Yamato* became the flagship of Admiral Isoroku Yamamoto, Commander-in-Chief of the Combined Fleet.

20-23 February: The Chief of Staff of the Combined Fleet Rear Admiral Ugaki conducts a series of war games aboard *Yamato* to test plans for the second-stage operations.

9 March 1942: Admiral Yamamoto issues orders to the fleet to prepare for Operation 'C', a raid into the Indian Ocean.

March 1942: Inland Sea – trainings and gunnery practice.

April 1942: Captain Arima, the Chief Equipping Officer of *Yamato*'s sister ship *Musashi,* pays an orientation visit with members of *Musashi*'s fitting-out crew.

April–May 1942: Training and gunnery practice.

Early May 1942: Admiral Yamamoto conducts war games aboard *Yamato* to test plans for the invasion of Midway.

23 May 1942: Returns to Hashirajima.

29 May: Operation 'MI' was begun, at 06.00 *Yamato* departed Hashirajima with the First Fleet, serving as Admiral Yamamoto's flagship as the command centre in the battle. It was intended to use her main artillery at Midway. After the defeat and loss of four aircraft carriers she returned to the Inland Sea. The battle once more confirmed the supremacy of aircraft carriers in war. At that time a decision was made to convert the third battleship *Shinano* (then being built) into a heavy aircraft carrier.

10 June 1942: 1200 miles SE of Tokyo an unidentified submarine fires two torpedoes at *Yamato* and both torpedoes miss.

5 August 1942: *Musashi*, her sister ship, entered service and joined the First Battleship Division.

Kure – 20 September 1941 – Yamato is shown during her final phase of fitting out. The steel mesh supports for the canvas blast bags can be seen above and below the nearest gun barrel, and splinter armoured protection below the gun

barrel elevated to its maximum elevation of 45 degrees. The aircraft carrier to starboard is the Hōshō, and in the background is the stores ship Mamiya.

August 1942: During operations in the Solomon Islands, *Yamato* went to Truk Island to support a series of operations to recapture Guadalcanal Island, but did not take part in the campaign.

28 August 1942: *Yamato* was attacked by the submarine USS *Flying Fish*, and next arrived in Truk where she served there as headquarters and flagship of the Combined Fleet.

9 September 1942: The Combined Fleet main units were transfered to a new anchorage south of Summer Island.

17 October 1942: Truk – oiler *Kenyō Maru* arrived empty, and *Yamato* and *Mutsu* each transferred 4,500 tons of fuel oil to her to refuel IJN warships that were involved in the Guadalcanal operations.

1 November 1942: Aboard *Yamato* was a festive dinner to celebrate the victory at the battle of Santa Cruz.

22 January 1943: *Musashi* arrived at Truk to join *Yamato*.

11 February 1943: *Musashi* became the flagship of Admiral Yamamoto. In the meantime the situation around the Solomon Islands went from bad to worse. The Japanese had to abandon Guadalcanal.

18 April 1943: Admiral Isoroku Yamamoto was killed (his aircraft was shot down over Bougainville Island) and *Musashi* became the new flagship of Admiral Mineichi Koga, successor to Admiral Yamamoto.

8 May 1943: Sailed from Truk to Yokosuka.

13 May 1943: Departs Yokosuka for Kure.

The upper part of Yamato's tower bridge with 15.5m rangefinder, Type 98 LA Director 'Hoiban', with its periscope tower covered by canvas, and signal yards with wind indicators fitted.

Close-up of the top of Musashi's tower bridge and main rangefinder from aft. The lattice structure on the rear wall of the rangefinder may have been strengthening to carry the weight and wind resistance of the radar aerials. On the signal yards are visible platforms for 60cm searchlights, and 2kW daylight signal lanterns.

21–30 May 1943: Drydocked for inspection and repairs.

12 July 1943: *Yamato* drydocked at Kure and was equipped with Type 21 Mod 3 radar. Twelve 25mm MG (4 x 3) were fitted on the forecastle deck before and aft 15.5cm side gun mounts (turret No.3 and 4), and 15.5cm guns were provided with coaming armour and their barbettes with 28mm thick additional armour. *Yamato's* fuel storage was reduced and her main and auxiliary rudder controls were improved.

16 July 1943: Yamato was visited by the German naval attaché to Tokyo Konteradmiral Paul Wenker, (a former Commanding Officer of the pocket battleship *Deutschland/Lützow*). He was not able to see or understand the real calibre of the main turrets during a one-hour visit on *Yamato*. He described the main gun calibre as 40cm. Permission to visit *Yamato* was given in response to a special request made by Adolf Hitler and Admiral Karl Dönitz in reciprocation of Admiral Naokuni Nomura's visit aboard the battleship *Tirpitz* in March 1941.

16 August 1943: *Yamato*, loaded with troops and supplies, departs Kure with *Fusō*, *Nagato* and Destroyer Divisions 16's *Amatsukaze* and *Hatsukaze* next stops at Yashima anchorage.

17 August 1943: *Yamato* departed Yashima via Yokosuka for Truk in task group: *Fusō*, *Nagato*, carrier *Taiyō*, 4' squadron *Atago* and *Takao* and destroyers *Akigumo*, *Yūgomo*, *Ushio*, *Amatsukaze* and *Hatsukaze*.

23 August 1943: The task group arrived at Truk.

17 October 1943: *Yamato*, *Musashi*, *Nagato*, *Fusō*, *Kongō*, *Haruna* with three aircraft carriers, seven heavy cruisers and three light cruisers and destroyers, left Truk to face US forces which were planning a raid on Wake Island.

19–23 October 1943: Japanese forces arrived at Brown Atoll, Eniwetok

26 October 1943: Forces returned to Truk after no contact with enemy forces.

17 December 1943: arrived at Yokosuka.

25 December 1943: *Yamato* was hit by a torpedo fired by the US submarine USS *Skate* near Truk. The torpedo hit her starboard hull near No.3 Main turret (frame 165) with the result that about 3000 tons of water flooded into the upper powder magazine through the small hole in the side armour joint. She arrived in Truk that day for emergency repair.

10 January 1944: Departed Truk for Kure with three destroyers.

16 January 1944: *Yamato* arrived in Japan and was drydocked at Kure for necessary repairs and modifications to the bracket structures of her armour. At the same time her anti-aircraft armament was modernised. In place of two 15.5cm broadside turrets, which were removed, six twin 12.7cm closed turrets were reinstalled. In place of six 12.7cm closed turrets were fitted six new open mounts with 12.7cm guns. Twelve triple and twenty-six single 25mm MG were mounted on her weather deck. Type 22 and Type 13 radar were installed and the construction of the main mast was changed. Two 150cm searchlights were removed and later installed ashore at Kure. Repairs and modernisation lasted until 18 March, when she was undocked.

31 March 1944: Admiral Koga was killed and the new Combined Fleet Commander, Admiral Soemu Toyoda, was appointed.

11 April 1944: *Yamato* departed Kure for trials in the Iyo Nada and returned to Hashirajima that evening.

17 April 1944: Returned to Kure to load supplies.

Details from front of the port-side 15.5m rangefinder arm with the Type 21 (21 Gō) radar mattress type antenna fitted firstly on Musashi *in September 1942 (on* Yamato *eight months later).*

The division between the wooden deck and the steel aircraft deck is clearly visible in this view of Musashi *from July 1942. Note the twin 12.7cm HA gun mount in the foreground and the canvas-covered 150cm searchlight.*

A Mitsubishi F1M2 floatplane aboard Musashi *seen from under the aircraft crane, January 1944. The new type MG control tower can be seen on the left, and in the right foreground the sisal rope curtain that closed off the boat stowage.*

24 June 1943. An Imperial visit to Musashi *anchored in Yokosuka. In the centre sitting is Emperor Hirohito with his brother Prince Takamatsu and Admiral Koga.*

21 April 1944: Departed Kure for Okinoshima, loaded troops.

22 April 1944: Departed Okinoshima with cruiser *Maya* and destroyers *Shimakaze, Yukikaze* and two other destroyers.

28 April 1944: Arrived at Manila, unloated troops and supplies, then departed.

1 May 1944: Arrived at Lingga near Singapore.

3 May 1944: At Lingga she was designated the flagship of Vice Admiral Ugaki.

11 May 1944: Sailed with Vice Admiral Jisaburō Ozawa's Mobile Fleet from Lingga to Tawi Tawi.

14 May 1944: Anchored at Tawi Tawi.

May–June 1944: At Tawi Tawi anchorage – *Yamato* and *Musashi* participated in joint gunnery exercises at ranges of almost 22 miles. At that time the Combined Fleet was reorganised – the main part of the Fleet became a carrier striking force and the battleship group, including *Yamato* and *Musashi,* formed the support force for the aircraft carriers. The Commander-in-Chief of the Combined Fleet hoisted his flag on the light cruiser *Ōyodo.* When the US forces landed on Biak Island, West New Guinea, towards the end of May 1944, the Imperial Japanese Navy decided to use two 46cm gun battleships to attack the enemy invasion force.

7 June 1944: Bongao, Tawi Tawi – *Yamato* received fresh provisions from the supply ship *Kitakami Maru.*

10 June 1944: Operation 'KON' – the relief of Biak. *Yamato* with *Musashi* and *Noshiro* and two destroyers departs Tawi Tawi for Batjan. The operation was not realised and both battleships were recalled on their way because of the imminent US invasion of Saipan Island. After the Mariana sea battle (A Operation, the twin battleships taking part in the battle as part of Admiral Kurita's vanguard group) they arrived on 22 June at Okinawa and 24 June at Hashirajima, going on 29 June to Kure to prepare for the next operation, the defence of the Philippines.

29 June–8 July 1944: Five additional triple 25mm MGs were installed on *Yamato,* making twenty-nine triple and twenty-six single 25mm MG at 113 barrels.

9 July 1944: Both battleships left Japan and, via Okinawa, hurried south to the Lingga anchorage.

16 July: Arrived at Lingga anchorage and underwent training. The surface force remained in the vicinity for three months conducting training and was immediately alerted.

18 October 1944: Black deck camouflage, intended for the night breakthrough in the San Bernardino Strait, is hastily applied to *Yamato* and *Musashi.* The main component was soot from the ships' funnels. On this day the battleships left the Lingga anchorage.

22 October 1944: Arrived at Brunei. After refuelling *Yamato* and *Musashi* left to make a daring dash eastward through the Philippines to launch an attack on the enemy in Leyte Gulf.

23 October 1944: In the early morning, when the surface force was passing northeast along Palawan Island, two heavy cruisers – *Atago,* the flagship of Admiral Takeo Kurita, and *Maya* – were sunk by submarine torpedoes from USS *Darter* and USS *Dace.* Admiral Kurita hoisted his flag on *Yamato.*

24 October 1944: *Musashi's* war career ended on the Sibuyan Sea. As result of air attacks she was hit by a minimum of twenty torpedoes and seventeen bombs and had more than fifteen near misses. And four-and-a-half hours after the last attack the battleship went down with 1039 officers and men.

Yamato was hit by three 1000lb AP bombs during the attack. The first bomb penetrated the anchor deck and demolished the port chain locker and exploded below the waterline. Two other bombs hit turret No.1's 46cm guns and the next penetrated the FD deck to the crew's quarters. These did little damage and she was easily repaired.

25 October 1944: *Yamato* broke through the San Bernardino Strait to the east of the island chain. In the Battle of Samar Gulf *Yamato's* 46cm guns opened fire on the US escort carriers and destroyers. It was the first and the last of her battles with enemy ships. She fired a total of 104 rounds of 46cm projectiles, as a result of which one escort carrier and

Yamato *or probably* Musashi *at Hashirajima in 1943.*

one destroyer were sunk. In the Philippines the Imperial Japanese Navy not only failed to prevent the US forces from capturing the islands, but also suffered irretrievable damage.

After the battle, *Yamato* returned to Brunei Bay in Borneo, but not for a long time because of air raids by the Allied forces. She lost twenty-nine crewmen during these battles.

28 October 1944: Arrived at Brunei and refuelled from oilers.

15 November 1944: Battleship Division was disbanded; *Yamato* was assigned as the flagship of the Second Fleet.

16 November 1944: *Yamato* left Brunei for Kure with *Kongō, Nagato* and escorts.

23 November 1944: *Yamato* arrived at Kure.

25 November 1944: Drydocked at Kure for battle damage repairs and refit. Twenty-four single 25mm MG were removed and twenty-seven triple 25mm MG mounts were fitted – a total of 152 25mm MG barrels.

28 November 1944: *Shinano* left Yokosuka and made her way to Kure, where her fitting-out was to be completed.

29 November 1944: On the way *Shinano* was hit by four torpedoes and sunk; incomplete watertight compartmentation was the cause of her loss.

Admiral Isoroku Yamamoto with staff on Yamato *under main gun turret.*

1 January 1945: *Yamato*, *Haruna* and *Nagato* were assigned to the reactivated Battleship Division 1 of Second Fleet.

3 January 1945: *Yamato* was undocked.

15 January 1945: *Yamato* went from Kure to Hashirajima.

15 March 1945: *Yamato* returned to Kure.

19 March 1945: Under way in the Inland Sea, *Yamato* sustained minor damage by a hit on the bridge by a Helldiver dive-bomber from US aircraft carrier *Intrepid*.

29 March 1945 at Kure *Yamato* received sailing orders. She took aboard a full supply of ammunition – 1170 rounds for her 46cm guns, 1620 rounds for 15.5cm secondary guns, 13,500 rounds for 12.7cm HA guns and 1,500,000 for 25mm MG. She received fuel from the destroyers *Hanazuki* and *Asashimo*, and the light cruiser *Yahagi* from the destroyer *Hatsushimo*. *Yamato* had enough fuel for a one-way trip only.

2 April 1945: *Yamato* left Kure for anchorage at the Mitajiri Bight.

3 April 1945: The Second Fleet received a special order from the Commander-in-Chief of Combined Fleet Admiral Soemu Toyoda alerting it about a sortie to Okinawa.

4 April 1944: Last AA gunnery training.

5 April 1945: Operation 'Ten-Ichi-gō' (Heaven Number One) began. Ships

received the order: 'the surface Special Attack Unit is ordered to proceed via Bungo Strait Channel at dawn on Y-1 day to reach the prescribed holding position for a high speed run-in to the area west of Okinawa at dawn on Y-day. Your mission is to attack the enemy fleet and supply train and destroy them. Y-day is April 8th.' It was a very unusual and grim mission – a suicide mission.

15:00hr: Capitan Ariga informed his assembled crew about the sortie. Sixty-seven naval cadets were sent ashore and the sick and some of the older sailors were disembarked.

Yamato's theoretical task was to destroy the invasion fleet using her artillery or to run the coast of Okinawa and support the Japanese Army. To reach the Okinawa coast or take part in an artillery battle without her own air umbrella and in the face of vast numbers of Allied forces in the air and on the sea was an almost hopeless task. The Commander of the Task Force, Vice Admiral Seichi Ito, was opposed to the operation, the idea for which came from Admiral Toyoda, Commander-in-Chief of the Combined Fleet. But the mission of *Yamato* and the ships accompanying her was to be realised. With her specially selected crew, Samurai traditions, Samurai flag, and the 'Kikusui' Chrysanthemum crest (the crest of Masashige Kusunoki, loyalist hero and 14th century martyr) on her funnel, *Yamato* started out on her final voyage.

6 April 1945: *Yamato* left Mitajiri for the Tokuyama for her last refuelling.

15:20hr: *Yamato* left Tokuyama escorted by Destroyer Division 43 and as far as the Bungo Strait, the Surface Special Attack Force consisted of *Yamato*, light cruiser *Yahagi* and destroyers *Isokaze*, *Hamakaze*, *Yukikaze*, *Kasumi*, *Hatsushimo*, *Asashimo*, *Fuyuzuki* and *Suzutsuki*. The force sailed at a speed of 20 knots.

18.00hr: *Yamato* was in a state of readiness: with one-third of the crew at battle stations, and the remainder sleeping in the vicinity of their stations because of the reported presence of US submarines off the Bungo Strait.

7 April 1945: At night the Special Attack Force, zigzagging at 22 knots on a southerly course, passed the Miyazaki Coast and reached the entrance to Ōsumi Kaikyō Channel and then reduced its speed to 16 knots.

14 Mitsubishi A6M Zeke fighters provided air cover for about three hours from 06:30hr and then returned to base on Kyushu. *Yamato*'s Mitsubishi F1M2 floatplanes were launched (at ~06:00hr) and returned to Kyushu.

07:00hr: there was a ceremonial breakfast, and at 10:00hr radar contact was made with US planes, a state of readiness commanded and the ship closed up for action, with all doors, hatches and ventilators closed; even the escape manholes in the lower portion of the watertight doors were clamped shut. This took about five to seven minutes, after which she was ready for battle in every respect.

Yamato's officers near after part of the superstructure, at right the lower part of the rear tower bridge is visible, on the left, the base of HA 12.7cm guns.

08:40hr: Attack Force sighted several Hellcat fighters but they were not seen by the escorting Zekes.

10:14hr: Attack Force sighted two Martin Mariner flying boats and then turned towards Sasebo.

11:07hr: The operator of Type 13 radar on *Yamato* reported contact with a large aircraft formation at his radio set's maximum range of 63 miles; subsequently all ships increased their speed to 25 knots.

Although the US planes continuously observed the striking forces, an attack did not take place for about two hours. At 11:15hr *Yamato* and *Yahagi* opened fire at a speed of 24 knots and commenced a series of evasive manoeuvres. The Japanese force turned its course towards Okinawa at 11:29hr.

12:32hr: The first attack started and the destroyer *Asashimo* was sunk by aircraft from the US carrier.

12:35hr: *Yamato* stopped zig-zagging, increased her speed to 24 knots and opened fire from her 46cm guns using common 'San Shiki' projectiles and all AA guns.

12:40hr: *Yamato* was hit by two AP bombs in the vicinity of the main mast. Next, two 1000lb AP bombs hit her – the first exploded in the crew's quarters abaft the Type 13 radar shack, the second penetrated the port side of the aft Command Station and exploded between the 15.5cm gun magazine and No.3 upper powder magazine. All detonated above the 200mm

thick deck. The 15.5cm gun turret was completely destroyed – with only one survivor from the gun crew – and the 12.7cm gun turret was destroyed and many 25mm MGs were knocked out.

12:43hr: She was hit by two torpedoes at frames 150 and 125 and probably by a third torpedo at frame 190. After the hits her port list angle of about 5–6° was reduced to 1° by counter-flooding.

13:02hr: The second series of attacks started. *Yamato* was hit by three torpedoes on her port side, on frames 143, 124 and 131, and by one torpedo on starboard frame 124, with a probable hit on frame 148, port side. A port list of about 15–16° was reduced to 5° by counter-flooding, and the bomb hits (one a 1000lb on the fore port superstructure) were negligible.

At that moment all possible starboard compartments had been flooded. The torpedoes striking on the port side caused immediate flooding of No.8 and No.12 boiler rooms, the port outboard engine room and the port hydraulic machinery room. Her speed was not more than 18 knots.

13:45hr: The third series of attacks started. The battleship received more torpedo hits: two hits on frames 135 and 154, and probably frame 164, all on the port side, and one hit on frame 150 starboard. Again the bomb hits were negligible. The initial list was severe: some 16–18° to port and increasing rapidly. The Executive Officer ordered the flooding of the starboard boiler rooms No.3 and No.11 and the hydraulic machinery room. It had some effect and for the time being stopped the ship's list. Her speed slowed to 12 knots.

The hit on the starboard side had caused a leak in the starboard outboard engine room, the two port hits flooding the inboard port boiler room No.10 and the other starting a leak in the port inboard engine room. Soon the list started to increase – the starboard outboard engine room was abandoned and flooded. Only some of the engine room crew managed to leave the compartment. The port list angle was about 22–23°.

Yamato's speed reduced to 10 knots. The effect of the two new starboard torpedo hits, despite the loss of buoyancy, was to make the counter-flooding problem easier to handle and delay *Yamato's* sinking. She was steaming in a large circle and shortly after 14:00hr all power was lost. Temperatures in the aft ammunition magazines were indicated at the danger level, but it was not possible to flood one by the destruction of pumping stations.

14:02hr: The Commanding Officer and Captain Ariga gave an order to prepare to abandon ship.

The Fleet Commander Vice Admiral Ito ordered that the mission was cancelled and directed the remaining ships to pick up as many survivors as possible. The Emperor's portrait was removed.

14:05hr: The light cruiser *Yahagi*, hit by 12 bombs and seven torpedoes sank.

Yamato – officers on aircraft hangar platform.

Yamato's officers near fore starboard part of the superstructure – end of 1944.

Listing heavily to port, Yamato's exposed hull was hit by several more torpedoes. She rolled slowly over her port side on her beam ends. The list was increasing at an alarming rate.

14:23hr: Soon after the abandon order she began to sink with a list of 90°. When she reached an angle of 120° a gigantic explosion in the fore ammunition magazines tore the ship into two parts and some seconds after there was a second underwater explosion of the rear ammunition magazines.

The huge mushroom of smoke reached a celling of 6000m and the fire could be seen by sentries on Kagoshima, more than 200 km away.

Vice Admiral Ito and Yamato's skipper Capitain Ariga and 3055 of 3332 crewmen were lost. Only 277 men were rescued. From the remaining ships of the Attack Force, 1187 crewmen were lost (along with Yahagi and four destroyers).

Yamato sank in the East China Sea at 30–22N, 128–04E in water 350m deep.

31 August 1945: Yamato was removed from the Navy List

IJN BATTLESHIP *MUSASHI*

June 1937: Nagasaki Navy Yard was ordered to build the second gigantic battleship (hull No.800) provisionally designated 'Warship No.2'.

The slipway on which the hull was built was covered by a sisal rope curtain to hide it. The rope was 2710km long and weighed 408 tons.

29 March 1938: Japan's second superbattleship 'Warship No.2' is laid down in Mitsubishi Nagasaki Yard. The first section of the keel structure placed on the slipway No.2 is 21m long.

1 November 1940: Secret launching ceremony. The hull weighed 35,737 tons and was second only to the 37,287 tons of the British passenger liner *Queen Mary*. For security reasons Warship No.2's new freighter *Kasuga Maru* (later escort carrier *Taiyō*) was towed alongside the battleship to block her silhouette from any foreign eyes. A combined force of 1800 policemen, IJ Army Military Police (Kempeitai), and sailors of the Sasebo Sailor Corps patrolled near the shipyard to ensure maximum secrecy during the launch. Following the launch the battleship was moved off Mukojima for fitting out.

On this day the 'Warship No.2' was named *Musashi*.

29 December 1940: Preliminary hull weighing conducted to determine the centre of gravity.

26 May 1941: The fitting of the deck and side armour was completed.

1 July 1941: *Musashi* left Nagasaki Navy Yard for Sasebo under tow by seven tugs.

Yamato (left) and Musashi *(right) at Truk in May 1943.*

2 July 1941: *Musashi* arrived at Sasebo; until 21 July she was drydocked in No.7 dry dock, where the main rudder and propellers were attached and the bottom painted.

1 August 1941: *Musashi* departed Sasebo for Nagasaki towed by fleet oiler *Shiretoko,* and moored the next day at Mukojima wharf.

6 October 1941: IJN special ammunition ship *Kashino* arrived from Kure, carrying the first part of the 46cm guns and one turret. Once aboard, the turret and guns were covered by canvas to maintain secrecy. By 8 December, all nine guns in turrets were installed on *Musashi*.

20 April 1942: After the first bombing of Japan by a 'Doolittle raid', Captain Arima of *Musashi* was ordered to form a skeleton crew to man the AA guns in case of an emergency. All (some hundred sailors) were permanently stationed aboard the ship.

7 May 1942: The permanent crew was transferred to the *Musashi*.

20 May 1942: *Musashi* left Nagasaki for Kure, carrying 1700 crewmen and 1500 engineers and builders from the Mitsubishi yard. The 25mm MG triple mounts were test-fired while the ship was under way.

26 May–9 June 1942: *Musashi* was drydocked in Kure at No.4 dry dock.

18–26 June 1942: The first stage of acceptance and speed trials in Iyo Nada. On 22 June *Musashi* achieved 28.5 knots in an overloaded condition at 70,358 tons displacement on Sata Misaki mile. She returned to Kure after the tests of the counter-flooding system.

27 June–23 July 1942: Kure Navy Yard – twelve unshielded 25mm MG (4 x 3) were added on the forecastle deck (FD) forward and aft of the 15.5cm wing turrets.

24 July 1942: *Musashi* departed Kure for the second stage of trials in Iyo Nada in the calibration, firing and research of the blast of the main turrets, and on 30 July returned to Kure.

5 August 1942: *Musashi* completed and attached to Yokosuka Naval District.

The commissioning ceremony was held at 09:00hr. *Musashi* was assigned to the Combined Fleet's Battleship Division 1 with *Yamato, Nagato* and *Mutsu,* Captain Arima was the Commanding Officer.

10 August 1942: *Musashi* arrived at Hashirajima anchorage and departed on 18 August for Heigun Island in Iyo Nada, conducting additional exercises in the Inland Sea and returning to Hashirajima on 20 August.

3–23 September 1942: At Kure – Type 21 Mod.3 surface fire-control radar was fitted on the 15.5m rangefinder arms of the tower bridge. She returned to Hashirajima on 29 September.

2–22 October 1942: At anchorage at Hashirajima, *Musashi* departed for manoeuvring exercises.

28 October–1 November: *Musashi* participated in gunnery trials in Suō Nada Sea with *Nagato, Ise, Hyūga, Fusō* and *Yamashiro,* departing from Hashirajima for Kure.

In the next few days she undertook a series of radar-controlled gunnery exercises in the Suō Nada Sea, departing from Murozumi Bight on the Inland Sea

3 December 1942: *Musashi* returned to Hashirajima after several short trips between Tokuama Bay, Kure and Hashirajima.

18 January 1943: *Musashi* departed Kure for Truk with aircraft carriers *Zuikaku* and *Zuihō,* light cruiser *Jintsu* and three destroyers, She was carrying over a hundred midshipmen, and arrived at Truk on 22 January.

11 February 1943: At Truk *Musashi* relieved her sister-ship *Yamato* as flagship of Admiral Isoroku Yamamoto's Combined Fleet.

1 April 1943: Operation 'I-gō' for the reinforcement of Rabaul began.

3 April 1943: Admiral Yamamoto and his staff departed from Truk for Rabaul. They were expected to return to *Musashi* on 19 April.

Musashi officers near aft port side part of the superstructure in 1943.

18 April 1943: 18 Army Air Force P-38s fighters over Bougainville shot down Admiral Yamamoto's bomber Mitsubishi GM4 Betty and a second Betty with Vice Admiral Matome Ugaki which survived. This US army operation 'Ultra Codebreaker' was authorized by President Roosevelt.

23 April 1943: A flying boat carrying the ashes of Admiral Yamamoto and six of his staff officers arrived on *Musashi*. The ashes were secretly transferred to the Admiral's sea cabin.

17 May 1943: Admiral Mineichi Koga, the new chief of the Combined Fleet, sortied from Truk for Yokosuka in response to the Attu invasion with Battleship Division 1's *Musashi*, Battleship Division 3's *Kongō* and *Haruna*, heavy cruisers *Tone* and *Chikuma*, aircraft carrier *Hiyō* and five destroyers. *Musashi* also carried Admiral Yamamoto's ashes for a state funeral. *Musashi* dropped anchor at the Kisarazu Bight on the evening of 22 May and a Budist ceremony was held aboard. Yamamoto's ashes were sent ashore the next day aboard destroyer *Yūgumo*.

23 June 1943: *Musashi* returned to Yokosuka for overhaul and over-painting.

24 June 1943: Between 11:03hr and 14:25hr *Musashi* was visited at Yokosuka by the Emperor and other officials. It was a top-secret event; nevertheless, the Imperial flag was hoisted. Admiral Mineichi Koga hosted Emperor Hirohito and his brother Prince Nobuhito Takamatsu, Marquis Kōichi Kido, Admiral Shigetaro Shimada, Admiral Osami Nagano, Admiral Soemu Toyoda, Vice Admiral Toshisuke Sugiyama, Admiral Nishizo Tsukahara, Minister Tsuneo Matsudaira and other officials.

A festive dinner was enjoyed. Later, the Emperor visited the crew's quarters

and an AA defence station on the tower bridge. It seems likely that the Emperor used *Musashi*'s elevator to reach it.

25 June 1943: *Musashi* left Yokosuka for Kure and arrived there on 27 June.

1 July to 8 July: *Musashi* drydocked for some repairs and bottom cleaning.

14 July 1943: *Musashi* departed Kure for trials and returned to Hashirajima and in the next few days to Kure and Yokosuka.

31 July 1943: *Musashi* departed Yokosuka for Truk with Destroyer Division 10 and arrived at Truk on 5 August.

18 September 1943: Flagship *Musashi* remained at Truk with *Fusō*, *Kongō* and *Haruna*.

5–6 October 1943: US Task Force launched a raid on Wake and Marshall Islands.

17 October 1943: Admiral Koga sortied from Truk to intercept the enemy carriers with First Battleship Division; *Yamato* and *Musashi*, Second Battleship Division; *Fusō* and Third Battleship Division; *Kongō* and *Haruna*, three aircraft carriers *Shōkaku*, *Zuikaku* and *Zuihō* and eight heavy cruisers, *Atago*, *Takao*, *Maya*, *Chōkai*, *Suzuya*, *Mogami*, *Chikuma*, *Tone*, light cruisers *Agano*, *Noshiro*, *Ōyodo* and destroyers.

19 October 1943: the fleet arrived at Brown Atoll, Eniwetok.

23 October 1943: The fleet departed Brown Atoll and sortied to a position 25 miles south of Wake. After no contact with enemy forces, the fleet returned to Truk on 26 October.

10 February 1944: *Musashi* departed Truk for Yokosuka escorted by light cruiser *Ōyodo* and four destroyers, with Admiral Mineichi Koga on board.

15 February 1944: *Musashi* arrived at Yokosuka. That evening she commenced embarkation of ammunition, provisions and fuel for the garrison of Palau. No less than 40 Isuzu and Nissan trucks were embarked on the afterdeck. The transfer of cargo continued until 24 February.

22 February 1944: Yokosuka, *Musashi* embarked the 300-strong IJN 87th AA Defence Unit, a 100-strong Army unit and other personnel, including some IJN staff officers destined for re-assignment to Palau. At 10:00hr she departed Yokosuka for Palau escorted by three destroyers. Off Hachijō-jima the group encountered a typhoon and had to reduce speed from 18 to about 6 knots, after some sailors from the destroyer *Shiratsuyu* were washed overboard.

25 February 1944: First Battleship Division's *Yamato* and *Musashi* were reassigned from the First Fleet to the Second Fleet.

29 February 1944: *Musashi* arrived at Koror anchorage on Palau, where her cargo, including 3800 mines, was unloaded.

11 March 1944: At Palau, *Musashi* received fresh provisions from the supply ship *Kitakami Maru*.

29 March 1944: *Musashi* departed from Palau to avoid an anticipated air raid and moved towards the north of the island. She sailed in the company of cruisers *Atago, Takao* and *Chōkai* escorted by eight destroyers and awaited the force at the entrance to the channel. At 17:44hr, *Musashi* cleared the western channel when she was hit in the port bow about 20 feet below the waterline by one of six torpedoes fired by USS *Tunny* (SS-282). The torpedo punched a hole about 10 feet in diameter in her bow. The forward windlass room and the Type '0' hydrophone compartment were flooded. Eighteen crewmen were killed and 7 hydrophone operators. The bow was flooded by about 3000 tons of water, but she continued making 24 knots.

However, Admiral Koga Staff forbade her to return to Palau. As soon as the damaged sections were shored up, *Musashi* departed from Palau that night for Kure escorted by three destroyers.

3 April 1944: *Musashi* arrived at Kure at 09:34hr.

10 April 1944: *Musashi* entered Kure dry dock No.4 where repairs were made to the hull along with the first modernisation of her armament since 22 April.

The two 15.5cm wing turrets were removed and two 150cm searchlights (No.7 and No.8) were removed. With new 25mm MG (16 x 3) and (25 x 1), the number of MG increased to 115 (30 x 3) and (25 x 1). Plans for fitting an additional twenty (6 x 2) 12.7cm HA guns on the new side superstructures were not realised. On the planned 12.7cm stands, 6 x 3 25mm MG were installed. Two Type 22 surface-search radars and two Type 13 air-search radars were fitted. The two searchlights which had been removed, were later installed for use by Sasebo's AA batteries.

27 April 1944: *Musashi* tested radar and AA guns in the Western Inland Sea.

1 May 1944: *Musashi* departed from Kure for Saeki, carrying supplies destined for the garrison of Okinawa, and conducted anti-submarine and AA exercises on route.

11 May 1944: *Musashi* departed Saeki for Okinawa, and joined aircraft carriers *Hiyō, Junyō, Ryuhō, Zuihō, Chiyoda* and *Chitose* plus four destroyers, and sailed to Okinawa.

12 May 1944: *Musashi* arrived at Nakagusuku Bay (Okinawa) and unloaded her cargo, and next sailed for Tawitawi (Sulu Sea), the operating base of the Mobile Fleet. She arrived there on 16 May. The First Battleship Division; *Yamato* and *Musashi* participated in gunnery exercises at a range of almost 22 miles.

10 June 1944: Operation 'KON' for the relief of Biak started. *Musashi* along with *Yamato*, the light cruiser *Noshiro* and three destroyers, made for Batjan on Halmahera Island.

12 June 1944: The US Invasion of the Marianas began and Operation 'KON' was postponed.

The force arrived at Batjan where it was joined by *Haguro* and *Myōkō* and one destroyer. *Musashi* was grazed by the fleet oiler *Genyō Maru* and as a result two port-side 25mm MG triple mounts were wrecked.

13 June 1944: The force departed from Batjan to rendezvous with the Mobile Fleet. The next day, north of Halmahera, after returning from anti-submarine patrol, *Musashi*'s floatplane F1M2 capsized, but its crew was rescued.

19 June 1944: Operation 'A-Gō' began – the Battle of the Philippine Sea.

Yamato and the other ships mistakenly damaged four Zeke fighters but *Musashi* was one of the few ships whose lookout correctly identified the overflying planes in time.

20 June 1944: *Musashi* provided AA support for the retreating aircraft carrier *Zuihō* and next day fired several main guns (common projectiles) at a formation of twenty attacking Helldivers from her aft turret, destroying two dive-bombers. At the same time *Musashi*'s 25mm MG gunners shot down by mistake one A6M5 'Zero' fighter.

24 June 1944: *Musashi* arrived at Nakagusuku Bay, Okinawa, for refuelling, then, escorted by destroyers, departed from Okinawa for Japan the next day.

29 June 1944: *Musashi* departed from Hashirajima for Kure with *Yamato*, arriving at Kure that same day.

2 July 1944: *Musashi* embarked armaments, ammunition and provisions. Five additional 25mm triple MG mounts were installed (the total number of 25mm guns was 130). The Type 22 radar was replaced by Type 22 Mod. 4 with a limited fire-control capability. 2200 infantrymen were embarked.

8 July 1944: After embarking 3522 men and materials of the IJ Army 49th Division's 106th Infantry Regiment on *Yamato* and *Musashi*, both battleships departed from Kure for Okinawa along with Cruiser Division 4's *Atago, Takao, Maya* and *Chōkai*, Cruiser Division 7's *Kumano, Suzuya, Tone* and *Chikuma*, light cruiser *Noshiro* and destroyers as Group 'A', departed Kure. Two hours later Group 'B' consisting of *Kongō, Nagato, Mogami, Yahagi* and destroyers.

10 July 1944: Group 'A' and Group 'B' arrived at Nakagusuku Bay, *Musashi* refueled four destroyers. At evening Group 'A' departed Nakagusuku Bay for Lingga (near Singapore).

16 July 1944: *Musashi* and *Yamato* were detached from Group 'A' and sailed directly to Lingga, escorted by three destroyers. After arriving at Lingga *Musashi* transferred her soldiers and cargo to the 5,289-ton cargo ship *Zuishō Maru*.

19 July 1944: At Lingga the battleships joined the Mobile Fleet.

12 August 1944: Captain Toshihara Inoguchi ordered *Musashi* to be painted a new darker colour.

1, 15, 24 September 1944: While staying on Lingga anchorage *Musashi* received fresh provisions from the supply ship *Kitakami Maru*.

3 October 1944: *Musashi*, *Yamato* and *Nagato* were transfered to Galang – No.3 anchorage north of Lingga. While entering the anchorage *Musashi* grazed an unmarked sandbar and her pit sword became clogged, disabling the pitometer log temporarily. During the next few days *Nagato* ferried the sailors from both superbattleships to Singapore where they enjoyed shore liberty.

6 October 1944: *Musashi* received fresh provisions from *Kitakami Maru*.

15 October 1944: The First Battleship Division's *Musashi* and *Yamato* returned to Lingga anchorage.

18 October 1944: Black deck camouflage intended for the night breakthrough in the San Bernardino Strait was hastily applied to both *Musashi* and *Yamato*. The main component was soot from stacks.

18–20 October: Both superbattleships departed Lingga for Brunei Bay, Borneo.

22 October 1944: Operation 'Shō-Ichi-Gō' (victory) – The Battle of Leyte Gulf – started. The force sortied from Brunei towards the Philippines with Vice Admiral Takeo Kurita's First Mobile Striking Force, Force 'A': First Battleship Division – *Yamato*, *Musashi*, *Nagato*, Cruiser Division 4 and 5 and destroyers.

23 October 1944: During the Battle of the Palawan Passage the Vice Admiral flagship cruiser *Atago* was sunk and the cruiser *Takao* was damaged. Kurita transferred to *Yamato* and resumed command of the First Attack Force. Heavy cruiser *Maya*'s 796 surviving crewmen were picked up by destroyer *Akishimo* and transferred to *Musashi*.

24 October 1944: 'The Battle of the Sibuyan Sea'.

07:43hr: The Centre Force assumed the AA cruising formation, divided into two concentric rings and *Musashi* was stationed on the starboard side of the leading No.1 unit.

08:10hr: Lookouts on *Musashi* reported sighting three Consolidated PBY Catalina patrol bombers.

The air alarm was sounded. A search plane from CV-11 USS *Intrepid* was sighted.

For the next hour, *Musashi* attempted unsuccessfully to jam the plane's radio reports.

10:18hr: Lookouts sighted over 40 enemy carrier planes on bearing 110.

10:25hr: *Musashi* opened AA fire.

10:27hr: *Musashi*, making 24 knots, was attacked by eight Helldivers from *Intrepid*.

Four near misses around the bow caused minor leaks below the waterline. One 600lb bomb hit turret No.1 of 46cm guns but failed to penetrate its roof armour.

10:29hr: Three Avengers from USS *Intrepid* attacked *Musashi* and one torpedo hit starboard frame 130 and quickly flooded the voids in outboard No.9 boiler room causing an initial list of 5.5° which was reduced to about 1° by counter-flooding. Shock damage disabled some instruments in the main turret plotting room. During this attack *Musashi* fired 48 15.5cm and 160 12.7cm rounds at the US aircraft.

11:54hr: *Musashi*'s Type 13 air-search radar detected approaching enemy planes on bearing 290, range 81 kilometres.

11:57hr: Another contact was made with aircraft bearing 210, range 80.

12:03hr: US planes were sighted.

The second attack by eight Helldivers from *Intrepid* caused two bomb hits and five near misses. A hit at frame 15 to port destroyed the crew toilet and washroom and curled up the port bow deck plates. The second bomb penetrated three decks and detonated at frame 138 port and started a fire in the engine room and boiler rooms No.11 and No.12. The damage resulted in the loss of the port inboard shaft. *Musashi*'s speed fell off to 22 knots. Two Helldivers were shot down.

12:06hr: Nine Avengers launched a 'hammer and anvil' attack; one from this group was hit by flak and turned away. The eight remaining Avengers scored three hits on *Musashi* on the port-side at frames 82, 102 and 140. The first torpedo struck near the citadel of No.1 main gun turret, the second flooded the hydraulic machinery compartment No.2 and the third torpedo flooded engine room No.4. Nearby compartments were shored up and the main guns went over to the reserve hydraulic pumps. After immediate counter-flooding, the list was reduced to one degree port, but *Musashi* was down about 2m by the bow. Her three remaining propellers were throttled up for a maximum speed of 22 knots. The bow trim was reduced to 1m.

During this attack, *Musashi* switched over to her second main armament director. She fired nine 46cm type common (San Shiki) shells, seventeen 15.5cm and over two hundred 25mm rounds.

After the first main gun salvo, a bomb fragment (splinter) penetrated the muzzle of the middle 46cm gun barrel of turret No.1 and detonated a common-type shell that had just been loaded.

The resulting explosion disabled the turret's elevating machinery, rendering it inoperable.

After this, the remaining two turrets fired 45 'San Shiki' shells of the 54 that were fired in the battle.

13:12hr: Vice Admiral Kurita ordered the fleet speed reduced to 22 knots so that *Musashi* could keep up.

13:31hr: A third attack took place, this time by 29 aircraft from the US aircraft carriers *Essex* (CV-9) and *Lexington* (CV-16). *Musashi* was strafed by two Hellcats and four Helldivers which scored two near hits starboard amidships and abreast the aft main gun turret No.3 that caused casualties among the nearby AA gun crews.

Six Avengers launched three more 'hammer and anvil' attacks. The first torpedo hit the starboard side at frame 60 and ripped into the ship's shell, forward of the side protection system.

The blast from the explosion penetrated the fuel tanks and watertight compartments, and wrecked the log and sounding rooms. A temporary hospital at the bow filled with carbon monoxide. There were many casualties. Next, three Helldivers scored four bomb hits on the port side near main gun turret No.1.

Another torpedo hit the starboard bow area and flooded store rooms and caused a further list to starboard. The third torpedo hit the port side forward of the main gun turret No.1 and the fourth hit port amidships.

13:50hr: The third attack ended; the heavy list to starboard was reduced by counter-flooding to about one degree (1°). The ship's bow was now down about 4m although all trim tanks were filled. *Musashi*'s speed was reduced to 20 knots. During this attack she fired 35 46cm common shells, 79 15.5cm shells and over 500 25mm rounds.

14:12hr: A fourth series of attacks started, and was directed against *Yamato* and *Nagato* by eight Hellcats and 12 Helldivers from the aircraft carrier *Essex*.

Yamato *during the Battle of Leyte Gulf on October 1944, Photo taken by attacking US aircraft. Note the black camouflage on her wooden deck (and probably main gun turret No.1) intended for the night breakthrough in the San Bernardino Strait.*

14:55hr: A fifth attack by 69 aircraft from USS *Enterprise* (CV-6) and USS *Franklin* (CV-13) began against Vice Admiral Kurita's fleet.

15:15hr: Nine Helldivers from USS *Enterprise* scored four 1000lb AP bombhits and a dozen near misses on *Musashi*. The first three struck in the port bow area and caused damage below decks and this damage was dealt with by the damage control team. The fourth bomb wrecked the Chief Steward's

Upper photo: Musashi *on 22 October 1944 at Brunei.* Lower photo: *The last view of* Musashi *in the late afternoon of 24 October 1944 before her sinking at 19:36hrs*

The Battle of the Sibuyan Sea on 24 October 1944. This photo was taken at the moment Yamato *was hit by two bombs near main gun turret No.1. Her sister-ship* Musashi *was sunk in this battle.*

The last battle of Yamato *on 7 April 1945. In this photo she is turning sharply at high speed. Fire and smoke is visible, caused by the bomb which hit the after 15.5cm gun turret. A bomb detonates in water on her port side.*

room. An attack by eight Avengers resulted in four torpedo hits – two torpedoes to port and starboard near frame 70. The next two torpedoes hit around frame 110 and at frame 138. The hits flooded cooling machinery room No.3 and the hydraulic machinery compartment. She was down about 4m by the bow and making 16 knots on three shafts. After counter-flooding her starboard list was deduced to 1–2°, but her speed fell off to 13 knots.

15:25hr: A sixth attack on the fleet began. Thirty-seven aircraft attacked *Musashi*. Three Helldivers from USS *Franklin* scored two 500lb bomb hits. Next, nine Avengers attacked her and two were shot down.

15:30hr: Seven Helldivers and two Avengers from USS *Intrepid* attacked *Musashi*.

One 500lb bomb penetrated the right wing of the air defence station and detonated on the tower bridge. The bridge and the adjacent operations room were set on fire. Fifty-two crewmen were killed and twenty wounded, including *Musashi*'s captain Rear Admiral Toshihara Inoguchi. After the fire was extinguished, Admiral Inoguchi assumed command from the second aft bridge.

The next three bombs detonated in a row port side on the forecastle deck, abreast the forward main gun turrets and knocked out two single and one triple 25mm MG mounts, the main communications room, telegraph room No.1 and the telephone room. The blast penetrated boiler rooms No.4 and No.8.

The next two bombs exploded on the forecastle deck starboard, abreast the superstructure. They wrecked two single and one triple 25mm MG mounts. The seventh bomb hit the middle AA gun crew shelter, causing extensive damage on the flag deck. The eighth bomb exploded in the port-side crew's space No.5 and demolished the nearby hospital. The ninth bomb struck the main gun turret No.1, and the tenth bomb exploded in the starboard officer's wardroom. Six near-miss bombs caused more damages to the hull's steel plating.

Although the bomb caused numerous casualties and much damage to the superstructure, *Musashi* was finally sunk by an additional 11 torpedo hits:

Three torpedoes struck the port-side frames 40, 60 and 75 causing extensive damage and flooding forward starboard area, including flooding in the No.4 bilge-pump room. The first of these torpedoes hit abreast main gun turret No.1 and flooded its lower powder-handling room. The second torpedo slowly flooded port boiler rooms No.8 and No.12.

The next four torpedoes struck port side on frames 125, 145, 140 x 3, 165, further flooding boiler room No.8 and the aft 25mm ammunition magazine. A 30-foot long section of the ship's side was gouged out. The engine room No.4 was flooded, causing *Musashi* to lose her outer port-side shaft. Her speed fell off to 6 knots.

Next the final torpedoes struck at starboard frames 80 and 105.

Musashi developed a 10° list to port. The crew counter-flooded again and reduced the list to 6°. Her main steering engine was shorted out temporarily and her main rudder jammed at 15° left.

Musashi sustained a total minimum of 20 torpedo hits and a minimum of 17 bomb hits and 18 bomb near misses.

16:21hr: Vice Admiral Kurita's force again approached *Musashi*. She was heading north with a 10° list to port, was down by the bow more than 26 feet, with her forecastle deck was awash. Vice Admiral Kurita dispatched the heavy cruiser *Tone* and destroyers *Shimakaze* and *Kiyoshimo* to escort her.

All free hands and the wounded were assembled topside starboard to counter the list.

The port main anchor was dropped into the sea. Rice and other consumables were loaded on the starboard side. In a last attempt to reduce the list in the crew's spaces starboard aft, some boiler rooms and starboard outboard engine room No.3 were flooded using the Kingston valves. As a result, *Musashi* lost another shaft. Rear Admiral Inoguchi attempted to beach *Musashi*, but her engines stopped before his order could be carried out.

19.15hr: When the list reached 12°, Rear Admiral Inoguchi gave the order to: 'standby to abandon ship'. The Executive Officer Captain Kenkichi Katō assembled the crew on the afterdeck. The battle flag was lowered. The destroyer *Shimakaze* removed 635 live (of 796) survivors of *Maya*, taken aboard *Musashi* a day earlier.

Rear Admiral Inoguchi retired to his cabin and was not seen again.

19:30hr: After her list reached 30° to port, *Musashi* slowly started to turn over. Captain Katō gave the order to abandon ship. He ordered the Emperor's portrait removed.

19:36hr: *Musashi* capsized with a sharp lurch to port and began sinking by the bow.

For some moments her stern was about 40–50m above the sea surface and her two propellers slowly turning were visible as the *Musashi* slid below the water. A short time after she disappeared from the sea surface two giant underwater explosions were heard.

Musashi sank in the Sibuyan Sea at 13–07N, 122–32E in 1300m-deep water.

Destroyers *Kiyoshimo*, *Isokaze* and *Hamakaze* rescued 1376 survivors but 1023 crewmen were lost from her 2399 men. This number of *Musashi*'s crewmen looks somewhat understated in comparison with her sister ship *Yamato*, so perhaps only the number of survivors was correct.

The loss of the *Musashi* was for a long time a top secret in Japan. She was removed from the IJ Navy list on 31 August 1945.

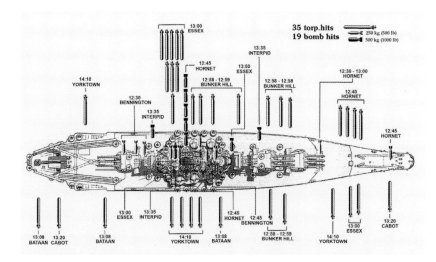

The hits on Yamato in her last battle. (From a new calculation by Gakken)

14:23hrs. Yamato's fore ammunition magazines exploded and some seconds later, the rear magazines also exploded. The huge mushroom of smoke reached a ceiling of 6000m. It was seen by sentries on Kagoshima more than 200km away. The fore magazine would have contained about 250 tons of cordite and 800 rounds for the secondary guns, as well as many tons of HA and MG rounds.

Yamato 1941

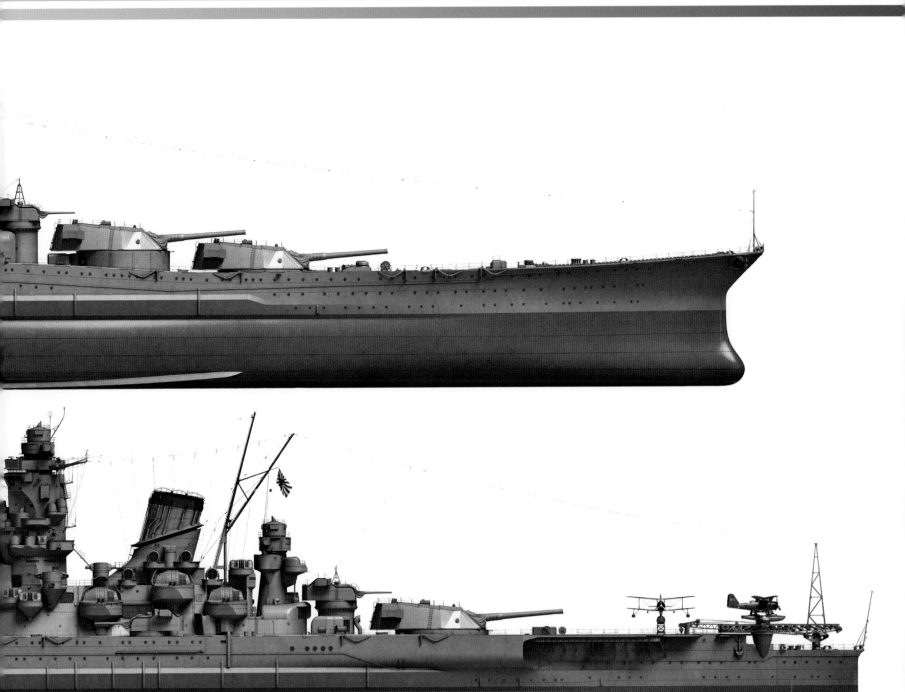

Yamato 1941

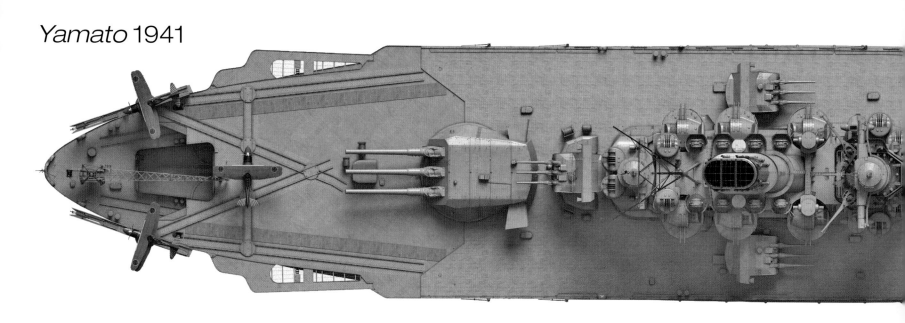

Yamato 1941

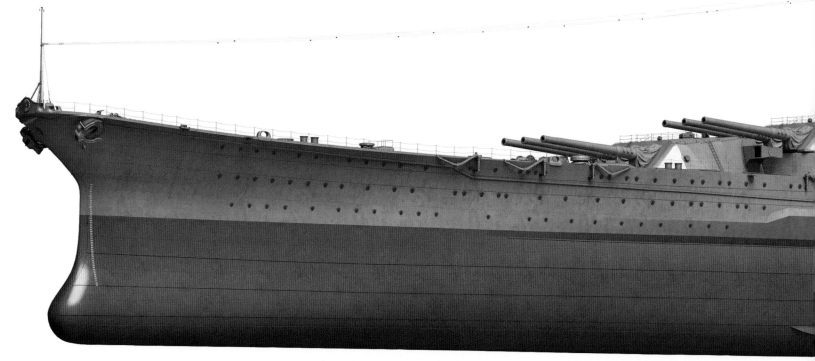

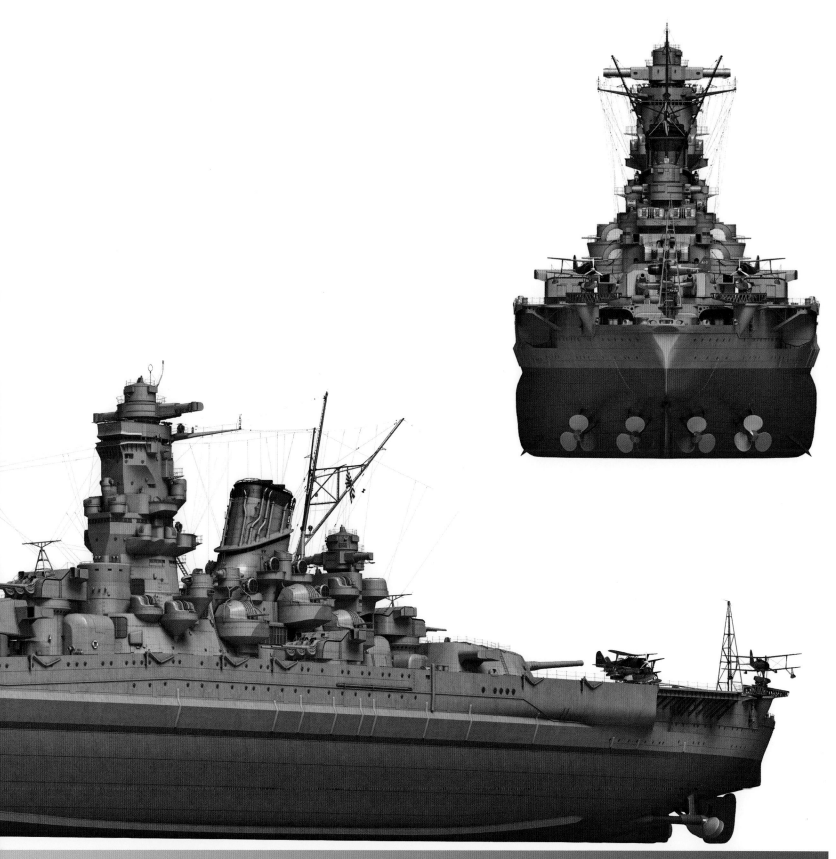

Yamato 1941

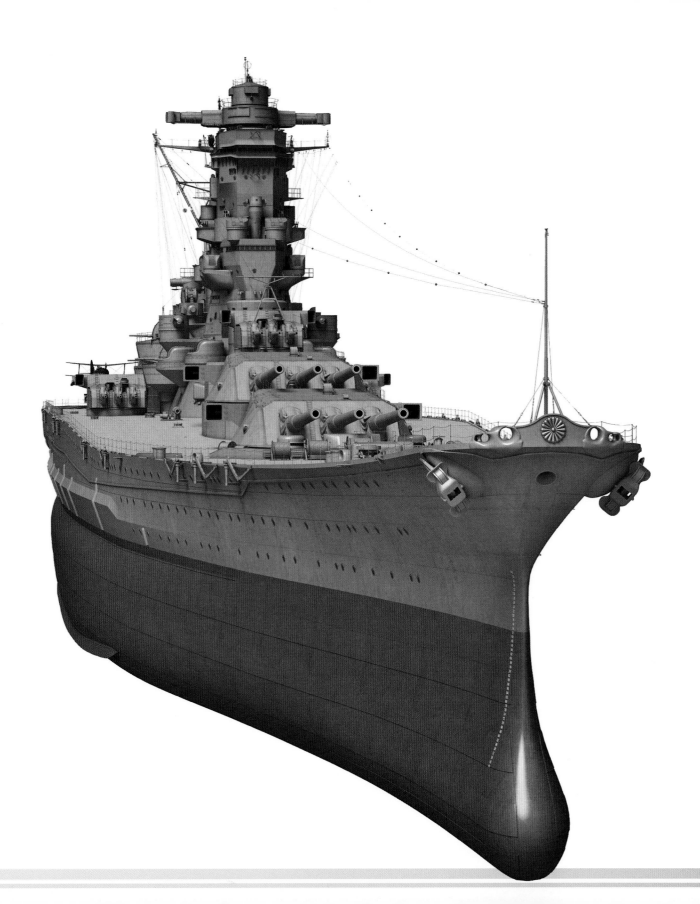

Yamato 1943

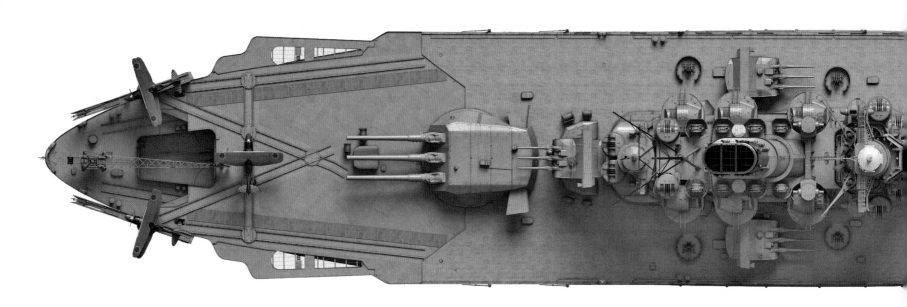

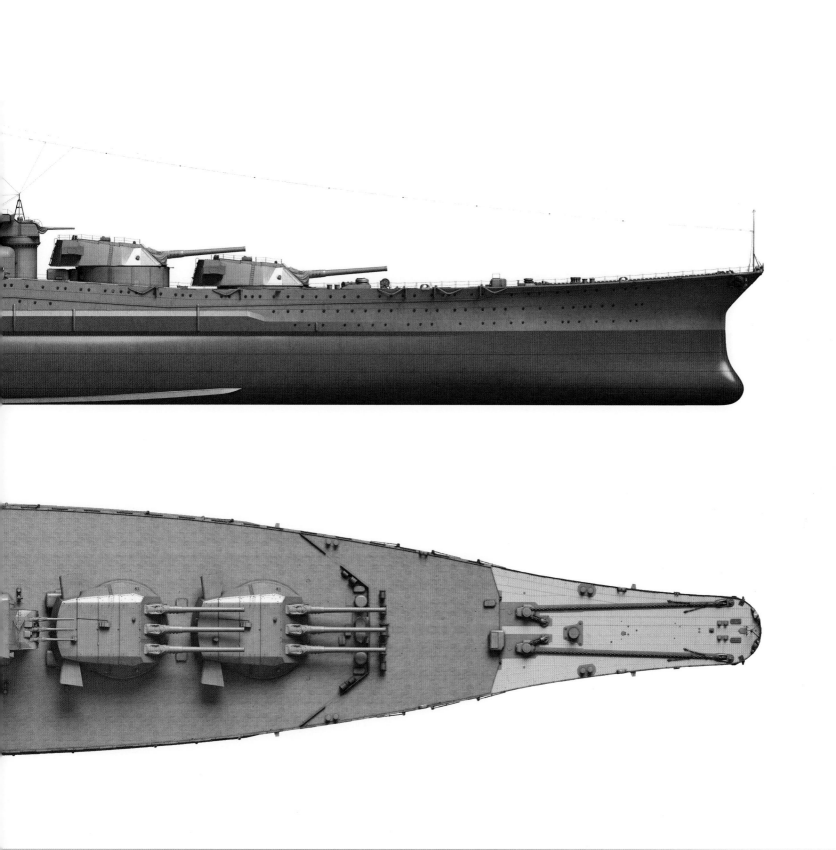

Yamato 1944

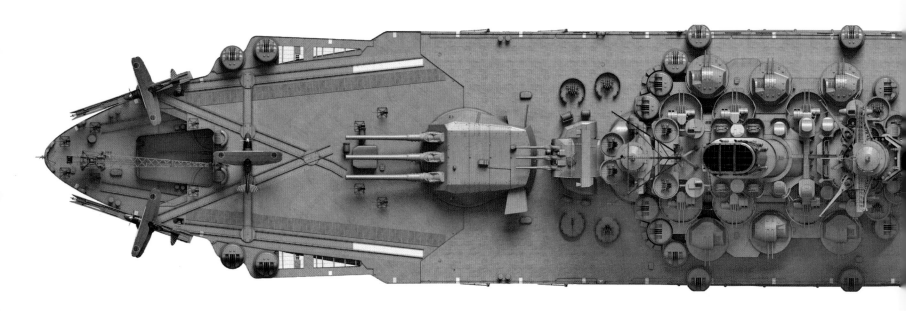

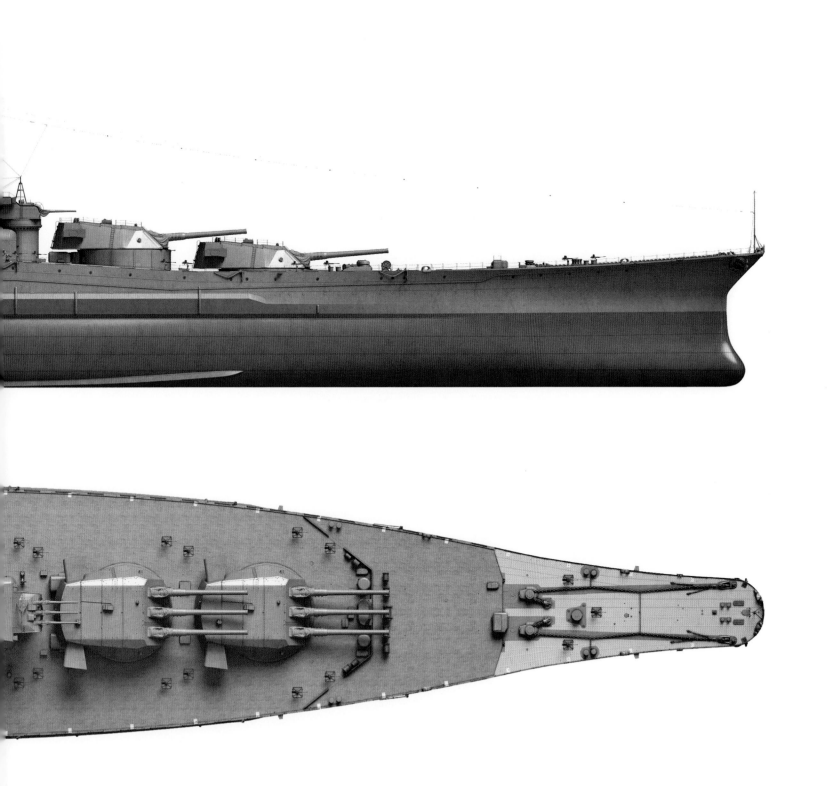

Yamato 1944

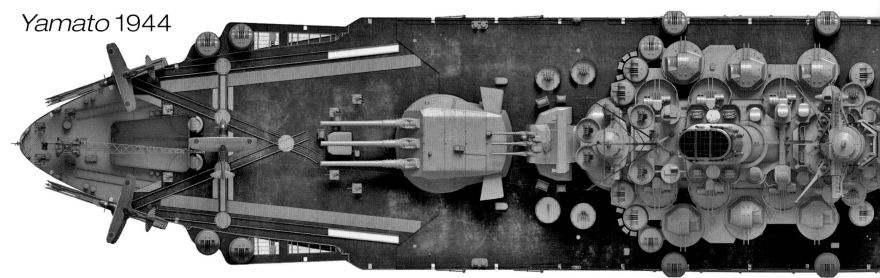

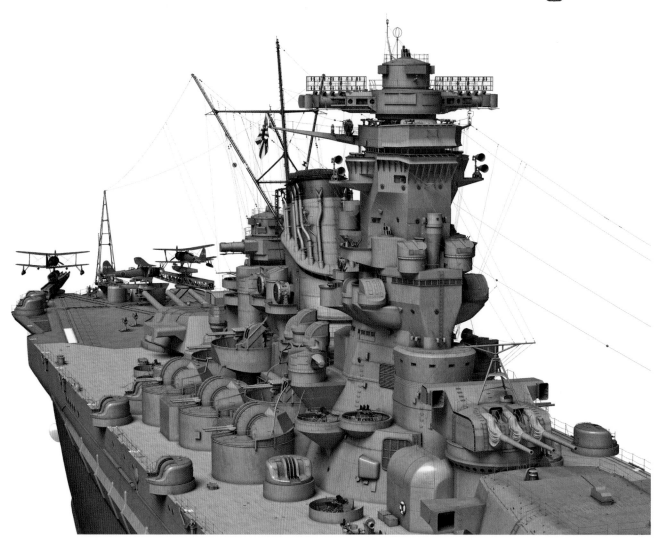

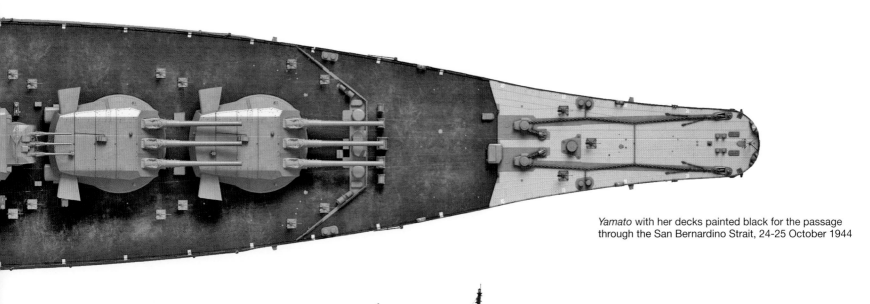

Yamato with her decks painted black for the passage through the San Bernardino Strait, 24-25 October 1944

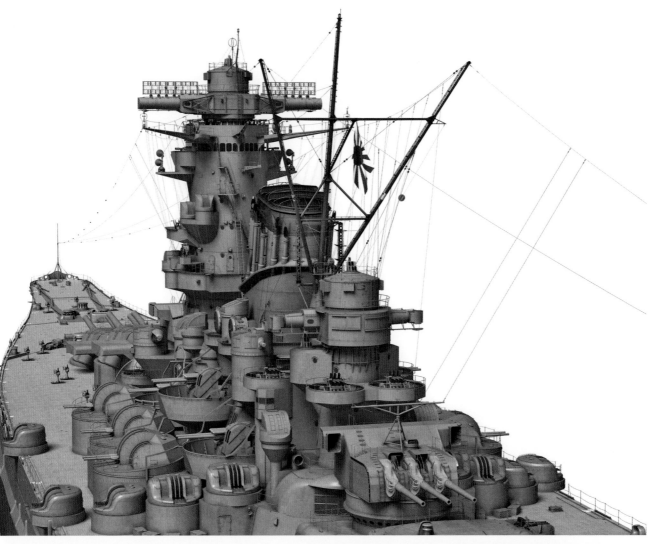

Musashi 1942

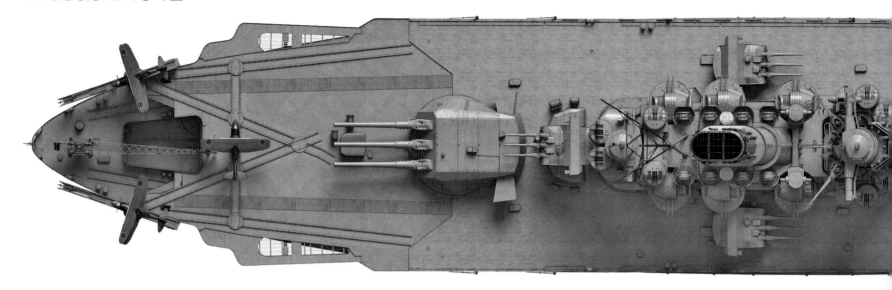

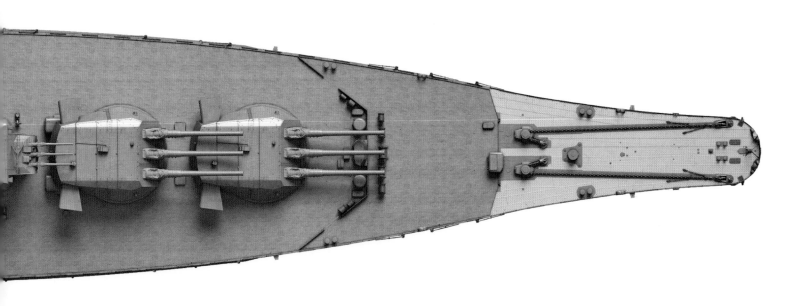

Musashi 1942

Musashi 1944

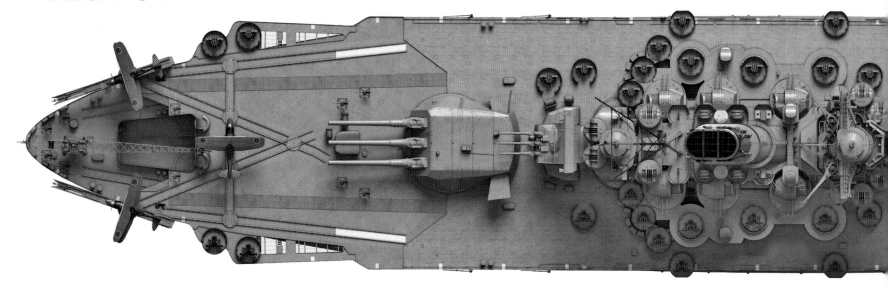

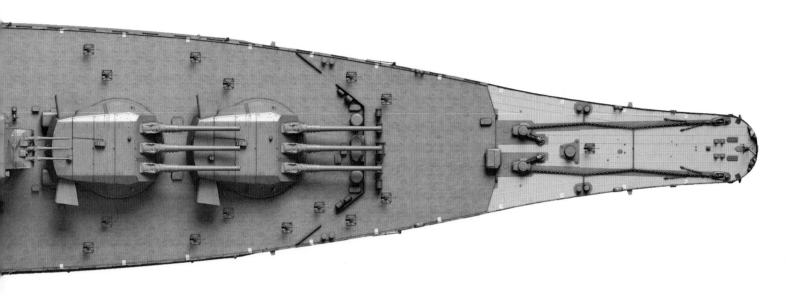

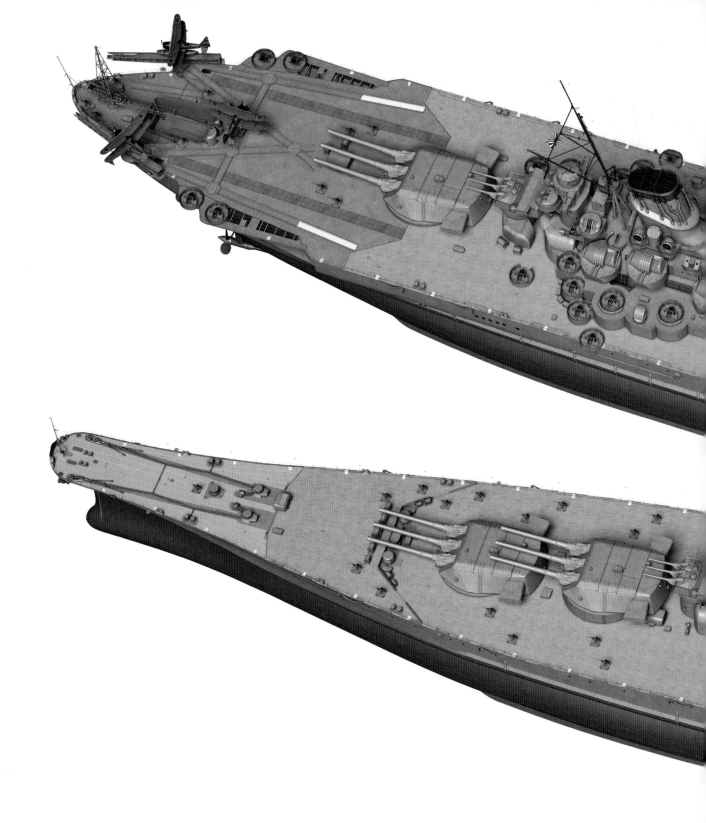

Musashi 1944

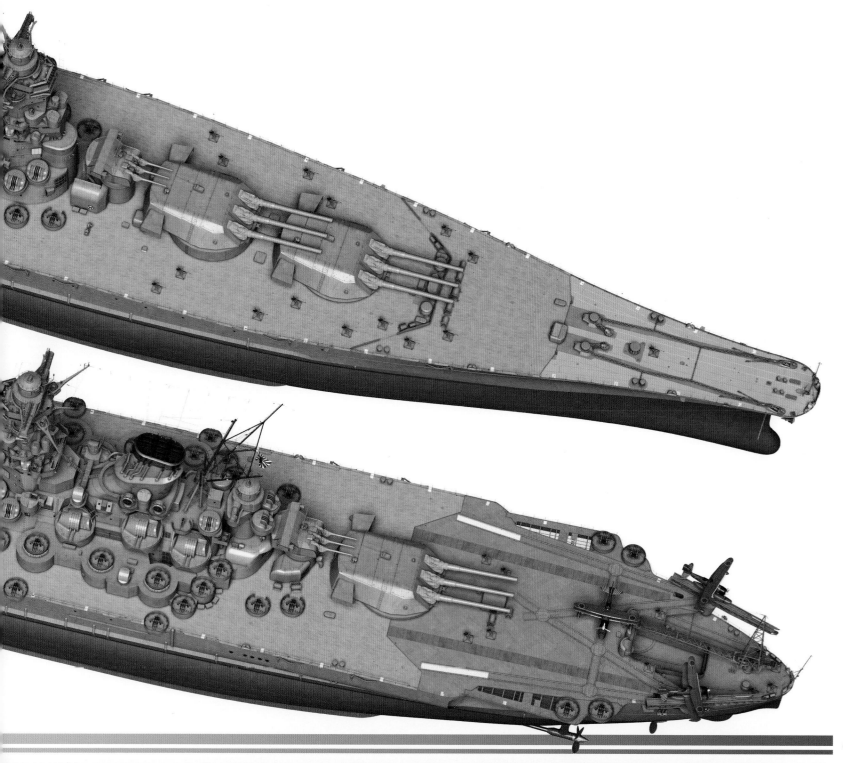

THE DRAWINGS

A General arrangements

A1 *Yamato* 1941 starboard profile (1/600 scale)

A1

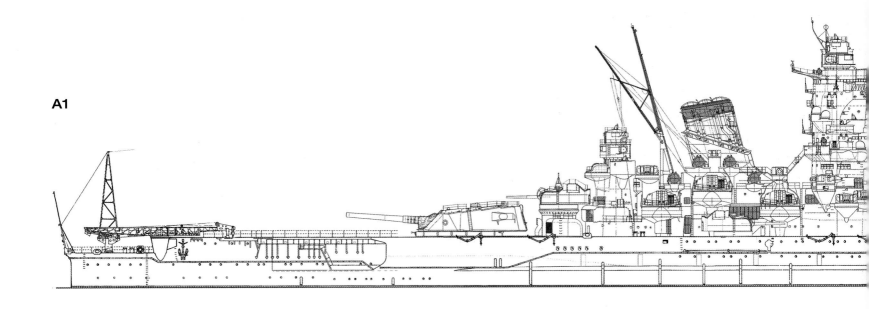

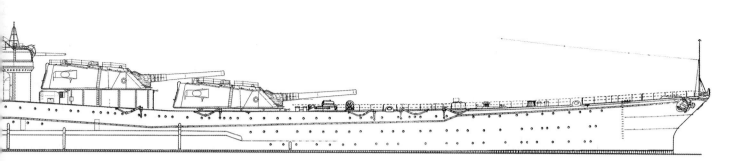

A General arrangements

A2/1 Internal profile (1/600 scale)

1 Store
2 Crew space – living quarters
3 Hangar
4 Hangar shutter door
5 Open hangar deck
6 Crane motor room
7 Flood control section
8 Service machine shop
9 Underwater hydrophone room – Type '0' sonar
10 Bilge pump room
11 Log room
12 Anchor windlass room
13 Anchor cable room
14 Trim tank
15 Oil pump room
16 Sounding room
17 Aviation fuel tank
18 Aviation fuel pump room
20 Cold store
21 Main rudder armoured room
22 Auxiliary rudder armoured room
23 No.1 main gun turret powder upper magazine
24 No.1 main gun turret powder lower magazine
25 No.1 main gun turret shell magazine
26 No.2 main gun turret powder upper magazine
27 No.2 main gun turret powder lower magazine
28 No.2 main gun turret shell magazine
29 No.3 main gun turret powder upper magazine
30 No.3 main gun turret powder lower magazine
31 No.3 main gun turret shell magazine
32 25mm MG ammunition magazine
33 15.5cm gun ammunition magazine
34 12.7cm HA gun ammunition magazine
35 12.7cm HA gun ammunition magazine
36 Hydraulic pump room

A2/1

A2/2

37	Transformer space
38	Wireless room
39	Engine room – turbine
40	Boiler room
41	Gyro room
42	Conning tower
43	Communication tube
44	Bridge No.1
45	Bridge No.2
46	15.5m rangefinder
47	LA director Type 98 – Hoiban
48	10m rangefinder
49	Ventilation and funnel compartment
FD	Forecastle deck
UD	Upper deck

MD	Middle deck
LD	Lower deck
PLD	Platform deck
SHD	Second hold deck
HD	Hold deck (over double bottom deck)

A2/2 Forecastle deck (FD)

1	15.5cm gun base
2	Deck store
3	Ventilation trunk
4	12.7cm gun base
5	Funnel hatch
6	Foundry and welding shop
7	Forge (smithy)
8	Communication tube
9	Tower bridge armoured cable trunking
10	Aft tower armoured cable trunking

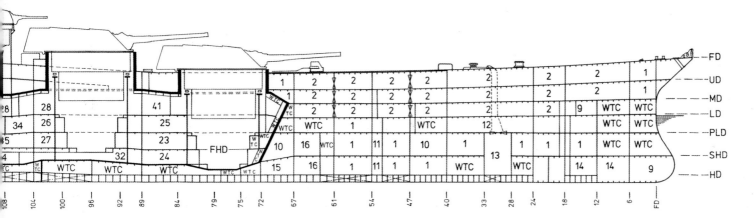

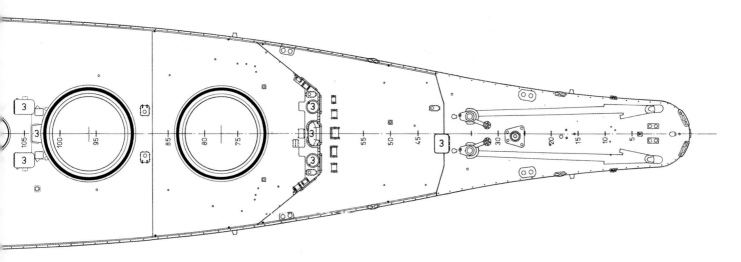

A General arrangements

A2/3 Upper Deck (UD) (1/600 scale)

1 Store
2 Crew space
3 Officer's quarters
4 Passage
5 Wireless room
6 Admiral's day cabin
7 Admiral's cabin
8 Uptake space
9 Machine shop
10 Electrician's shop
11 Carpenter's shop
12 Dynamo room
13 Laundry
14 Galley
15 Wash place
16 Hangar space
17 Boat stowage (starboard two 9m, two 12m, one 8m, one 6m, port side two 9m, one 12m Boat)
18 Raft stowage
19 15.5 cm gun turret base
20 Hall (lobby)
21 Communication hub

A2/4 Middle Deck (MD)

1 Store
2 Crew space
3 Sick-bay (hospital)
4 Boat stowage (starboard one 15m, one 12m, one 11m, port side two 17m boats)
5 Hangar
6 Open hangar deck
7 Warrant officer's quarters
8 Crane motor room
9 Passage
10 Communication tube

A2/3

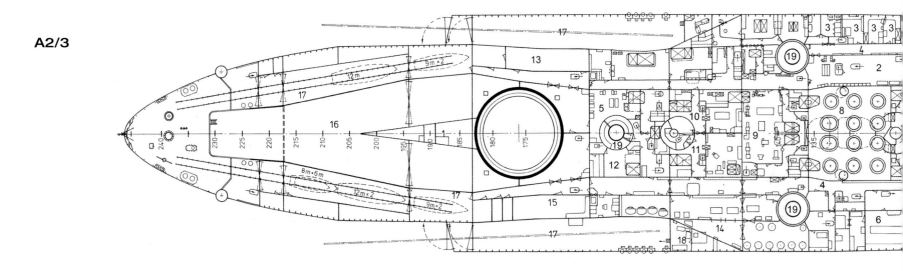

A2/4

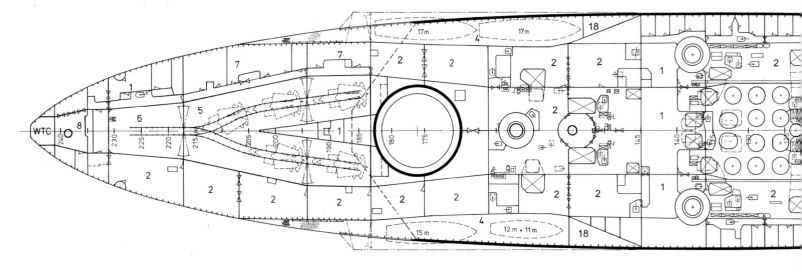

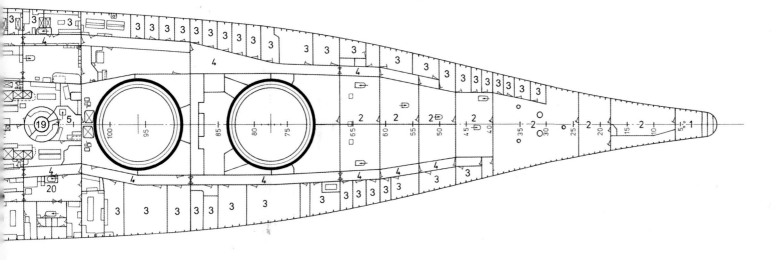

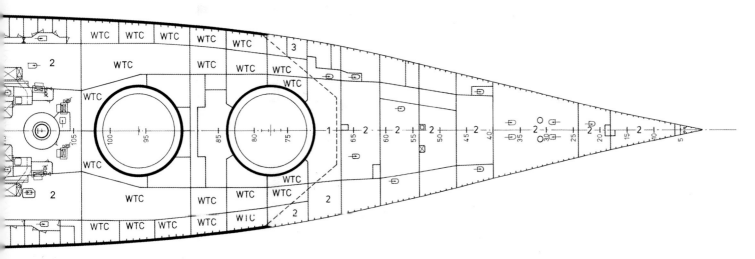

A General arrangements

A2/5 Lower Deck (LD) (1/600 scale)

1 Store
2 Crew space
3 Underwater hydrophone room
4 Isolation ward
5 Crane motor room
6 Main armament transmitting station
7 Wire lead passage
8 Secondary (15.5cm) armament transmitting station
9 HA 12.7cm guns transmitting station
10 Gyro room
11 Telephone exchange
12 Cell room (battery)
13 Fan compartment

14 No.2 main gun turret shell magazine
15 Shell supply room
16 Secondary (15.5cm) armament shell room
17 Dynamo room and ventilation space
18 Dynamo room
19 Cooling machinery room
20 Transformer room
21 Secondary (15.5cm) armament shell magazine
22 Flooding control stand
23 Ventilation and funnel compartment
24 Radio station
25 Wireless room and dynamo room
26 Lower control station
27 Engine room space

A2/6 Platform Deck (PLD)

1 Store
2 Crew space
3 Anchor windlass room
4 Main rudder engine armoured room
5 Black powder store
6 No.1 main gun turret shell magazine
7 Shell supply room
8 No.2 main gun turret upper powder magazine (canister stowage)
9 No.1 main turret magazine cooling machine room
10 Wireless telegraphy room
11 Powder supply room – upper
12 No.3 main gun turret shell magazine

A2/5

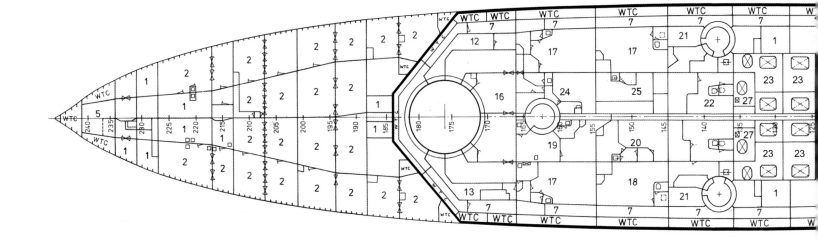

A2/6

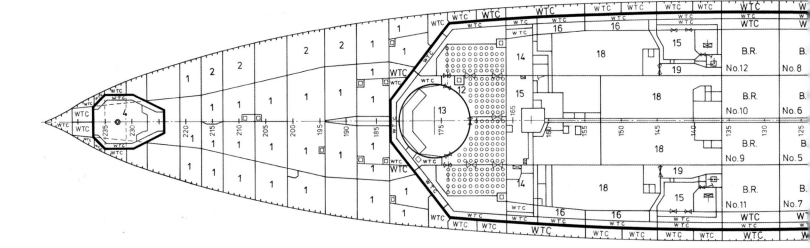

13 Shell supply room
14 Black powder magazine
15 15.5cm gun powder magazine
16 Fresh water tank (hydraulic tank)
17 Dynamo room
18 Main engine – turbine space
19 Boiler steam trunking

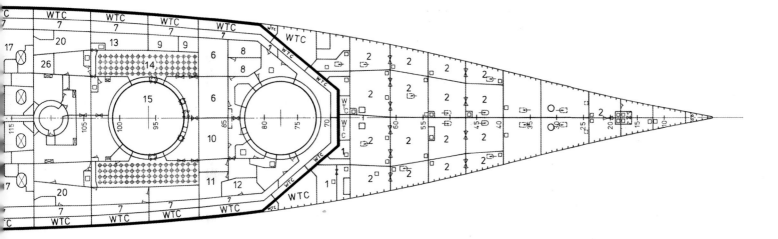

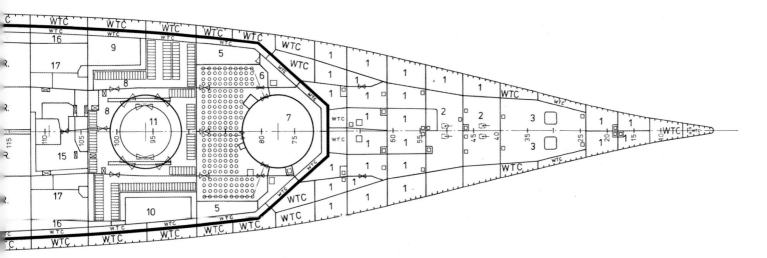

A General arrangements

A2/7 First Hold Deck (FHD) (1/600 scale)

1. No.1 main gun turret upper powder magazine (canister stowage)
2. Powder supply room – upper
3. No.2 main gun turret lower powder magazine (canister stowage)
4. Powder supply room – lower
5. No.2 main gun turret magazine cooling machinery room
6. Small arms magazine
7. 15,5 cm gun powder magazine
8. Passage
9. Pump room
10. Boiler room

A2/8 Section Frame 176

1. Boat stowage
2. Crew space
3. Laundry
4. Cells
5. No.3 main gun turret upper powder magazine
6. No.3 main gun turret lower powder magazine
7. Propeller shaft tunnel

A2/9 Section Frame 141

1. Store
2. Machine service shop
3. Hydraulic pump room
4. Engine (turbine) room
5. 15.5cm gun ammunition magazine

6. Flooding control position
7. Wire trunking passage
8. Steam trunking passage

A2/10 Section Frame 110 (or 107?)

1. Officer's quarters
2. Passage
3. Crew space
4. Transformer room
5. Wire trunking passage
6. Dynamo room
7. Hydraulic pump room
8. Hydraulic measurements compartment

A2/7

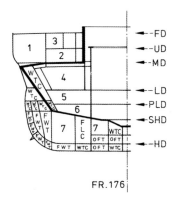

FR.176

A2/8

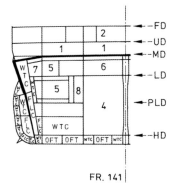

FR. 141

A2/9

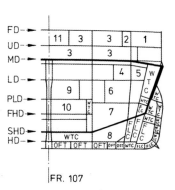

FR. 107

A2/13

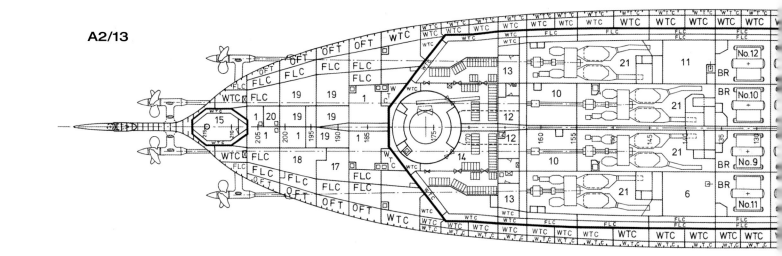

9   15.5 cm gun ammunition magazine
10   12.7cm HA gun ammunition magazine
11   Wireless room

A2/11 Section Frame 96

1   Officer's quarters
2   No.2 main gun turret shell magazine
3   No.2 main gun turret upper powder magazine
4   No.2 main gun turret lower powder magazine
5   25 mm MG ammunition magazine
6   Wireless telegraphy room
7   HA gun transmitting station
8   Passage

A2/12 Section Frame 30

1   Crew space
2   Anchor windlass room
3   Anchor cable room

A2/13 Second Hold Deck (SHD)

1   Store
2   Bilge pump room
3   Anchor cable room
4   Log room
5   Sounding room
6   Cooling machinery room
7   No.1 main gun turret lower powder magazine
8   Flooding pipe room
9   Air (or carbon dioxide) bottle room

10   Hydraulic pipe conduit
11   Hydraulic pump room
12   25mm MG ammunition magazine
13   12.7cm HA gun ammunition magazine
14   No.3 main gun turret lower powder magazine
15   Auxiliary rudder engine armoured room
16   Fresh water pipe room
17   Waste water pipe room
18   Cooling machinery room
19   Cold magazine
20   Aviation fuel control position
21   Engine room

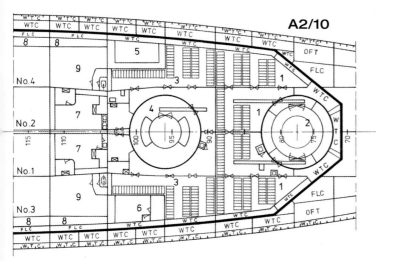

A2/10

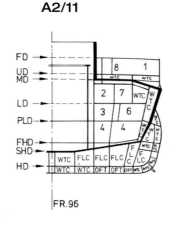

A2/11

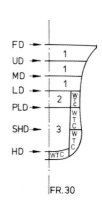

A2/12

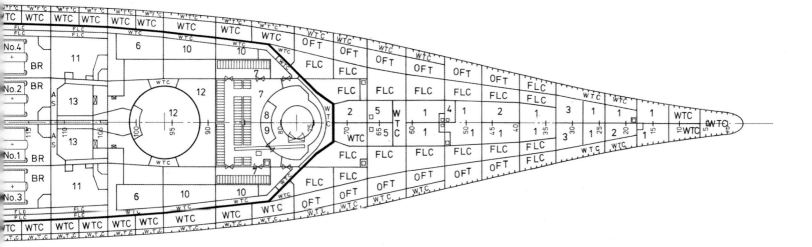

A General arrangements

A2/14 Hatch Deck (HD) (1/600 scale)

1   Store
2   Underwater hydrophone room
3   Trim tank
4   Log room
5   Sounding room
6   Anchor cable room
7   Oil pump room
8   Bilge pump room
9   Hydraulic monitoring compartment
10   Hydraulic pump room
11   Cooling machinery room
12   Engine room – turbine
13   Aviation fuel tank
14   Aviation fuel pump room
15   Propeller shaft tunnel

A2/14

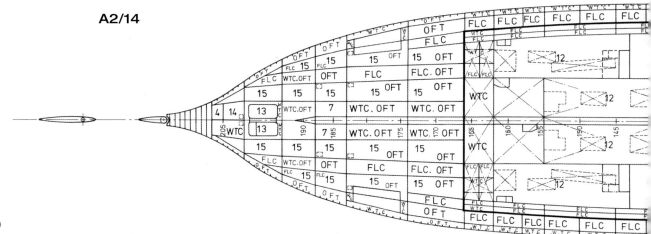

A2/15 Body plan (1/300 scale)
A2/16 Body lines of stern part
A2/17 Body lines of stern part
A2/18 Body lines of stern part

A2/15

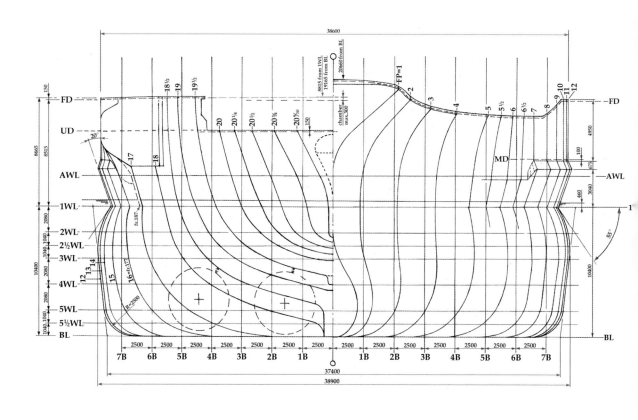

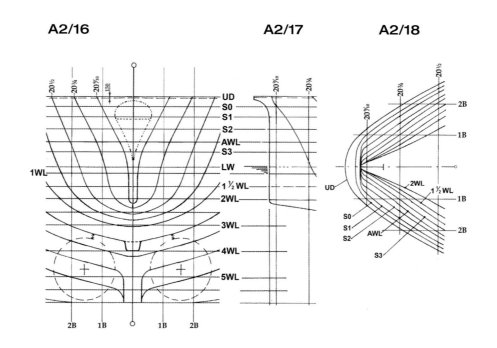

A2/16   A2/17   A2/18

A General arrangements

A2/19 Sheer elevation (1/600 scale)
A2/20 Waterline plan

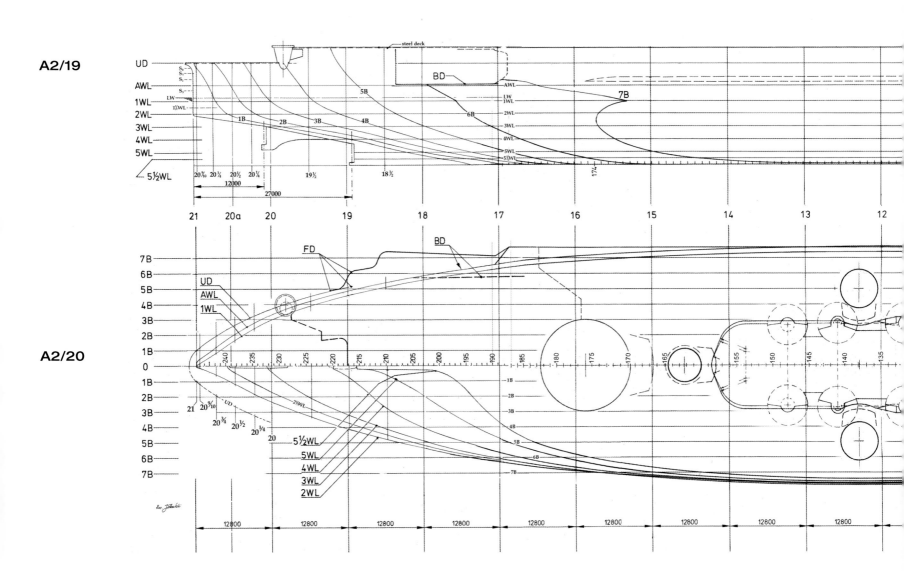

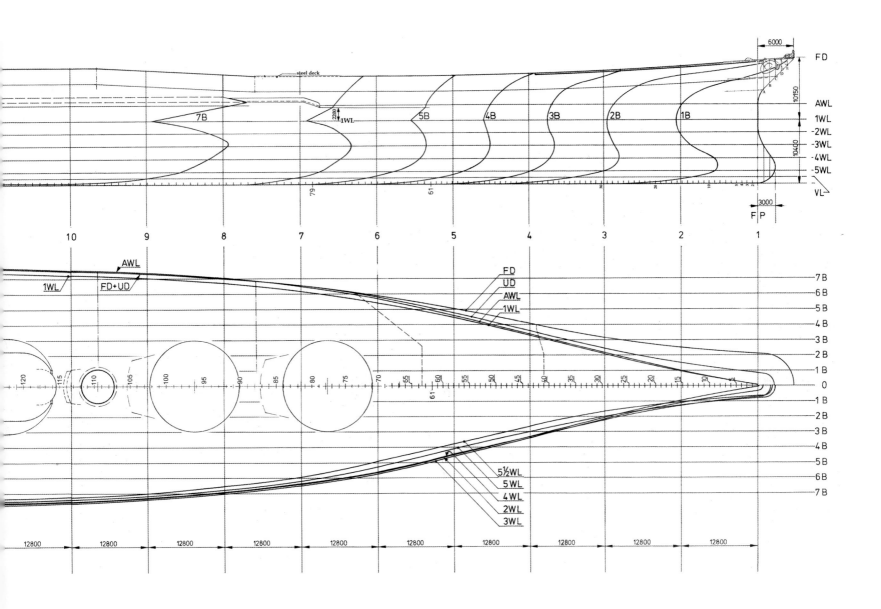

B Hull Structure

B1/1 Midship hull structure (1/300 scale)

B1/2 Armour joints

B1/3 Plan of middle deck armour plates

B1/4 Armour joints (plan)

B1/5 Armour joints (middle deck plate joint)

B1/1

B1/2

B1/3

B1/4

B1/5

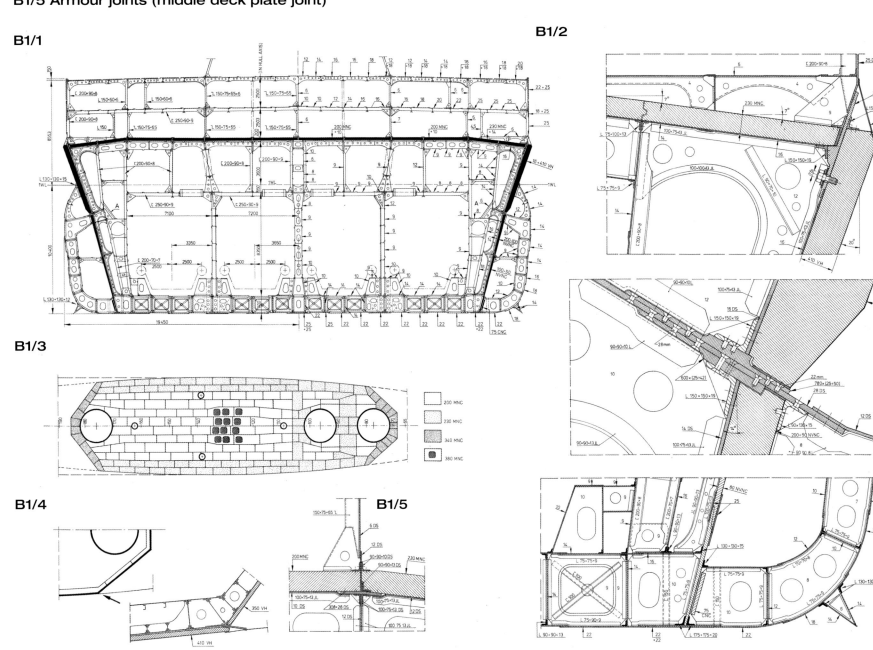

B1/6 Scheme of hull plating
B1/7 Hull plating (thickness in mm)

B1/6

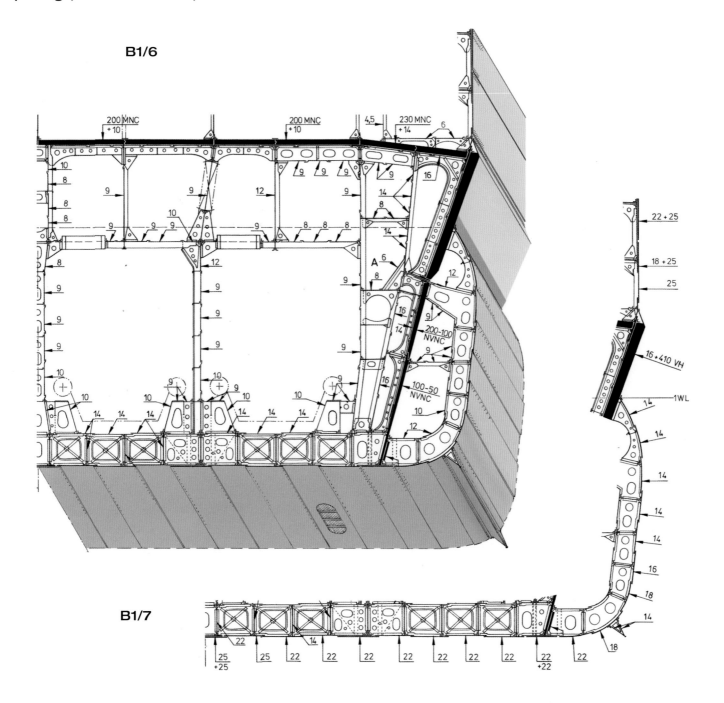

B1/7

B Hull Structure

B1/8 Armour and protective plating – profile (1/600 scale)
Numbers give armour and protective plating thicknesses in mm

B1/9 Forecastle deck and middle deck

B1/10 Second hold deck

B1/11 Section at frame 135

B1/12 Section at frame 77

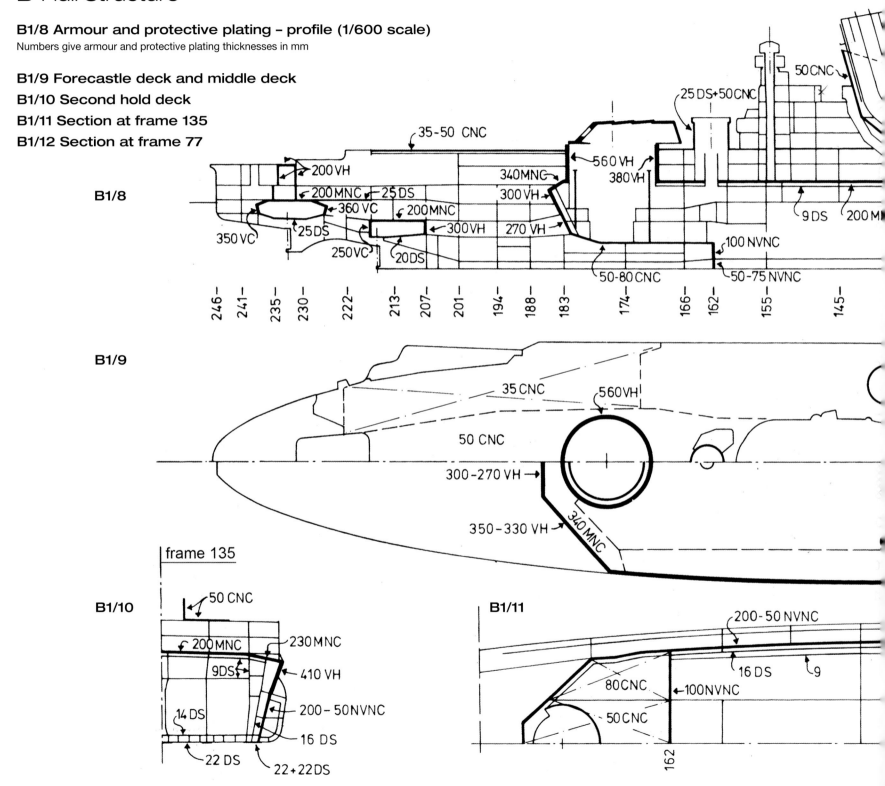

B1/8

35-50 CNC

50 CNC

25 DS+50 CNC

200 VH

200 MNC — 25 DS

360 VC

200 MNC

340 MNC

300 VH

560 VH
380 VH

350 VC

25 DS

250 VC

20 DS

300 VH

270 VH

9 DS

200 M

100 NVNC

50-80 CNC

50-75 NVNC

246 — 241 — 235 — 230 — 222 — 213 — 207 — 201 — 194 — 188 — 183 — 174 — 166 — 162 — 155 — 145

B1/9

35 CNC

560 VH

50 CNC

300-270 VH

350-330 VH

340 MNC

frame 135

B1/10

50 CNC

200 MNC

230 MNC

9 DS

410 VH

14 DS

200-50 NVNC

16 DS

22 DS

22+22 DS

B1/11

200-50 NVNC

80 CNC

100 NVNC

16 DS

9

50 CNC

162

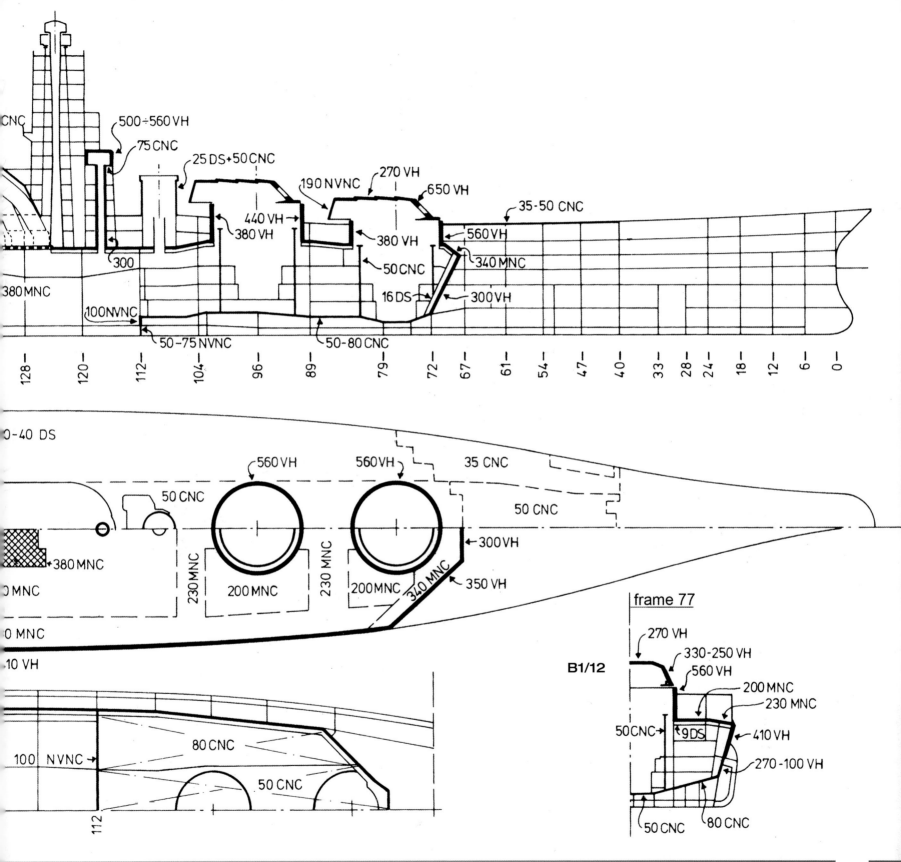

CNC

500÷560 VH

75 CNC

25 DS+50 CNC

190 NVNC

270 VH

650 VH

35-50 CNC

440 VH → 380 VH

380 VH

560 VH

300

50 CNC

340 MNC

380 MNC

100 NVNC

16 DS

300 VH

50-75 NVNC

50-80 CNC

128 120 112 104 96 89 79 72 67 61 54 47 40 33 28 24 18 12 6 0

0-40 DS

560 VH 560 VH 35 CNC

50 CNC

50 CNC

380 MNC 230 MNC 200 MNC 230 MNC 200 MNC 340 MNC 300 VH 350 VH

0 MNC

0 MNC

10 VH

100 NVNC

80 CNC

50 CNC

112

frame 77

270 VH

330-250 VH

560 VH

200 MNC

230 MNC

B1/12

50 CNC 9 DS 410 VH

270-100 VH

50 CNC 80 CNC

B Hull Structure

B1/19

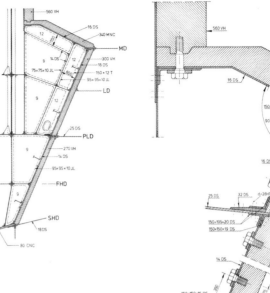
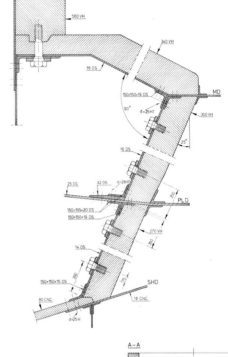

B1/13

B1/14

B1/20

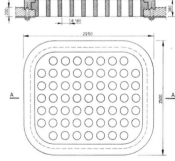

B1/15

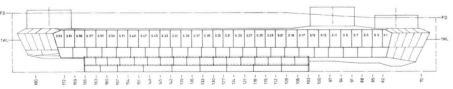

B1/18

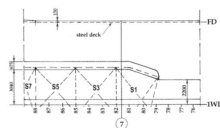

B1/16

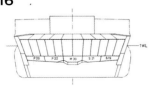

B1/17

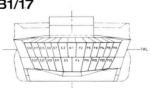

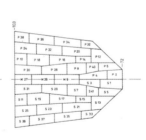

B1/21 Fore and aft side cover of armoured box

B1/22 Vertical joint of fore armour with side plating

B1/23 Typical joints of hull plating

B1/24 Joints of inner armour

B1/21

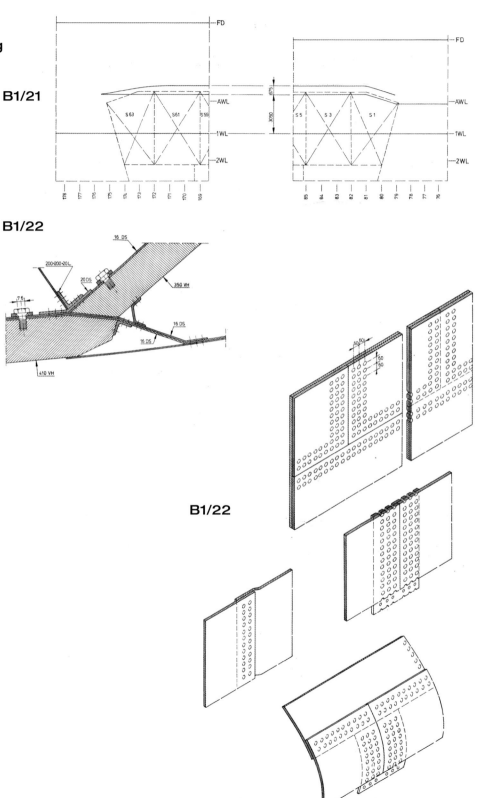

B1/23

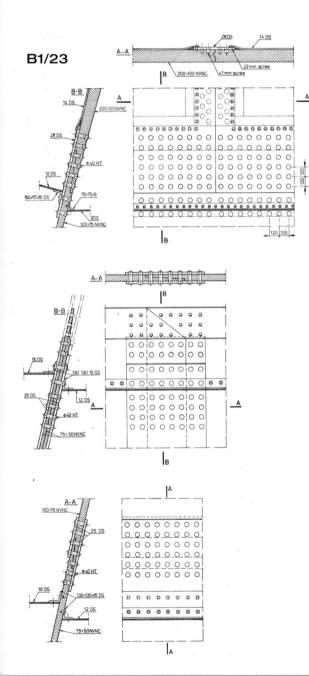

B1/22

B1/22

B Hull Structure – *Yamato 1941 starboard side*

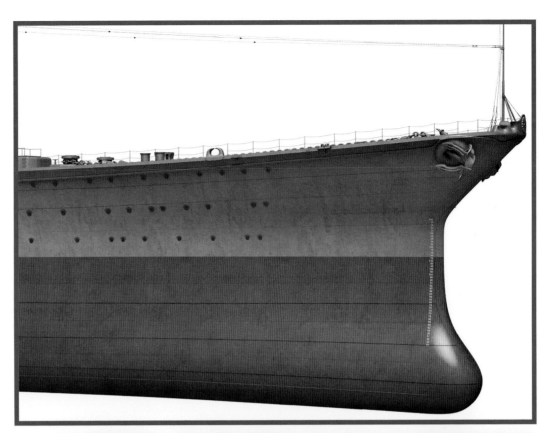
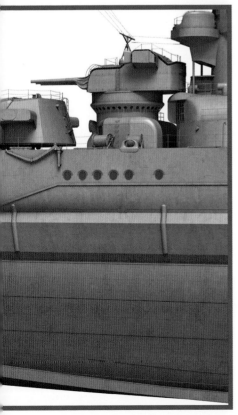

B Hull Structure

B1/25 *Yamato* 1941 – starboard profile (1/600 scale)

B1/26 Side scuttles

B1/27 Degaussing cable socket

B1/28 Support of aircraft deck edges

B1/29 Scupper pipe

B1/25

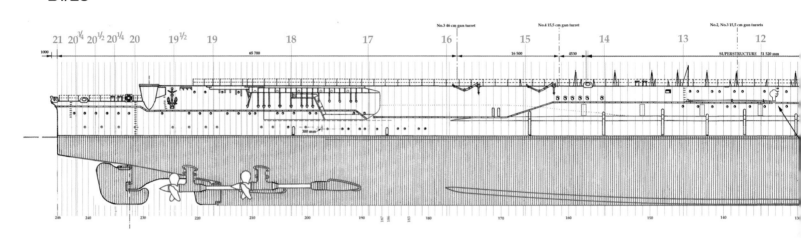

B1/26

Side scuttle fitted only on *Musashi* staff compartments on frame spaces 101–104 and 116–126 on starboard side upper deck

Side scuttle fitted on UD and MD compartments

Side scuttle fitted on LD compartments and on the superstructure

Side scuttle on UD compartments (boats stowage) on frame spaces 156–162

Hull scuttles blanked off by stell rings – 50mm bigger diameter than hole and 25mm thick (after 1944 refit)

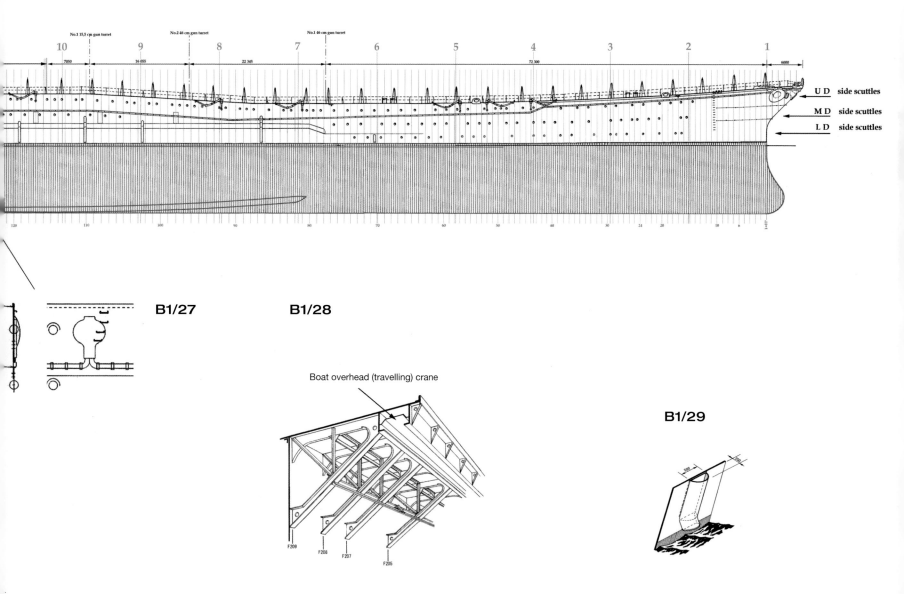

No.1 15,5 cm gun turret   No.2 46 cm gun turret   No.1 46 cm gun turret

| 10 | 9 | 8 | 7 | 6 | 5 | 4 | 3 | 2 | 1 |

7050   16 055   22 345   72 300   6000

U D side scuttles
M D side scuttles
L D side scuttles

120   110   100   90   80   70   60   50   40   30   24   20   10   6

B1/27   **B1/28**

Boat overhead (travelling) crane

F209   F208   F207   F206

B1/29

B Hull Structure

B1/30 *Yamato* 1941 – port side view (1/600 scale)

B1/31 Swinging boom

B1/32 Open hangar doors

B1/33 *Yamato* 1945 starboard profile

B1/34 Degaussing cable

B1/30

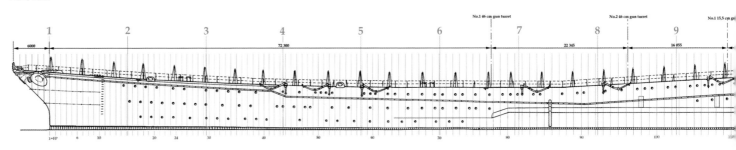

B1/33

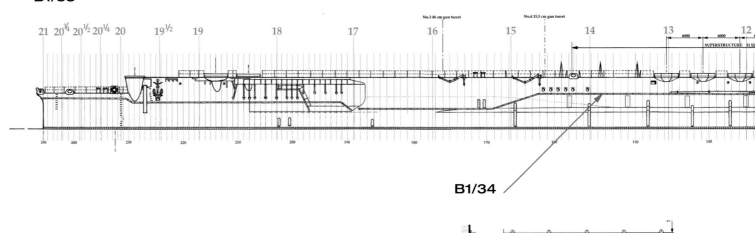

B1/34

Distance between frames		
FP=1 – 61	900mm	60 frame spaces
61 – 62	1000mm	1
62–78	1100mm	16
78–79	1150mm	1
79–90	1200mm	11
90–104	1225mm	14
104–105	1150mm	1
105–111	1200mm	6
111–113	1150mm	2

Distance between frames		
113–119	1200mm	6
119–121	1150mm	2
121–127	1200mm	6
127–129	1150mm	2
129–135	1200mm	6
135–136	1150mm	1
136–140	1225mm	4
140–162	1200mm	12
162–166	1225mm	4

Distance between frames		
166–179	1200mm	13
179–189	1100mm	10
189–190	1000mm	1
190–243	900mm	43
243–246	800mm	3
Distance square stations (1–21) =12 800mm		
Frame FP (fore perpendicular) to frame 246 = 256 000mm		
Length overall = 263 000mm		

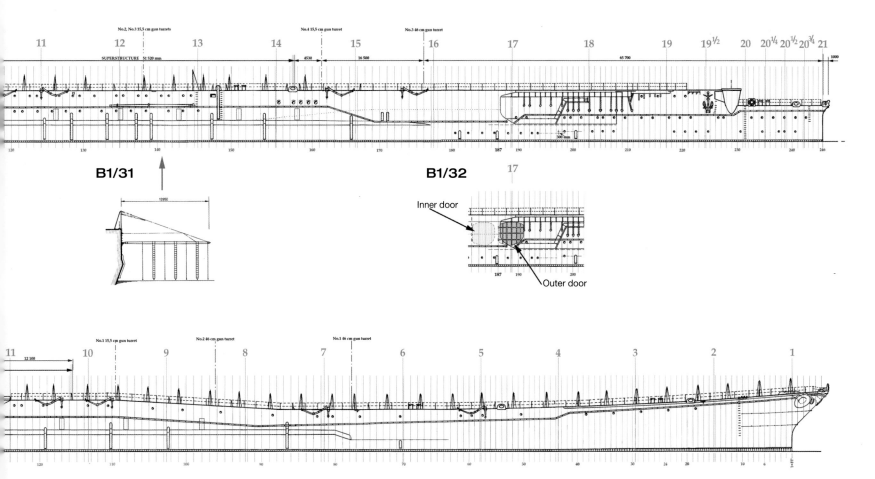

B1/31

B1/32

Inner door

Outer door

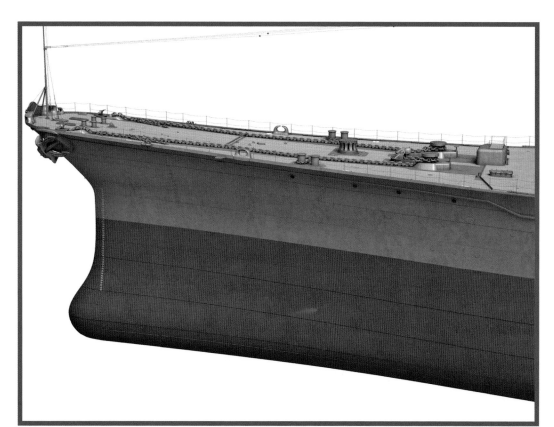

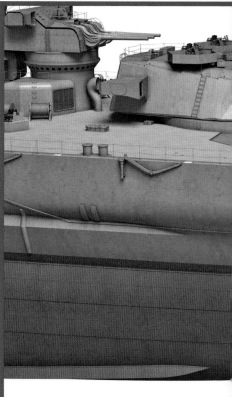

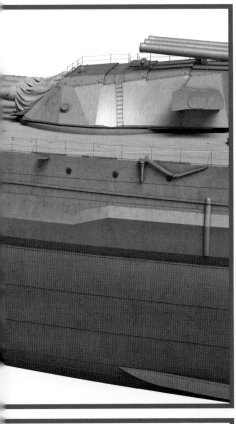

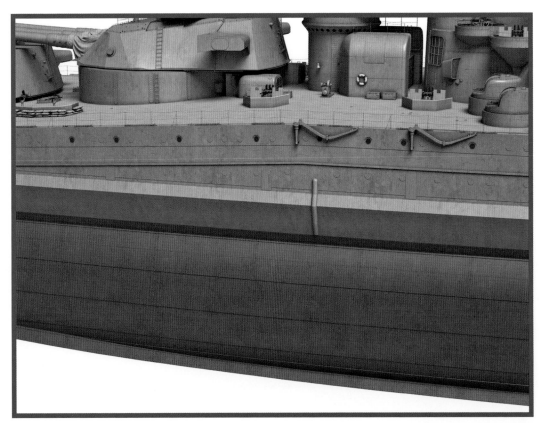

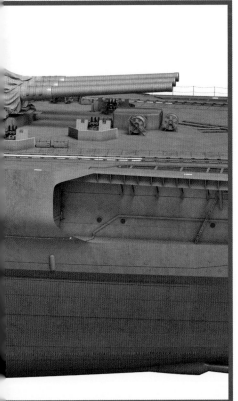

B Hull Structure

B1/35 *Yamato* 1945 port side view (1/600 scale)
B1/36 *Musashi* 1942 starboard profile

B1/35

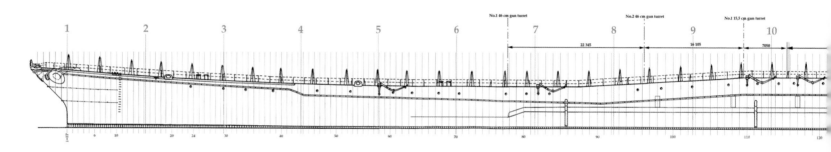

B1/36

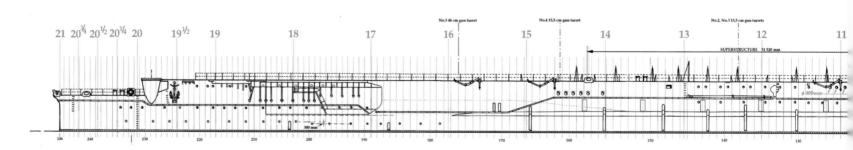

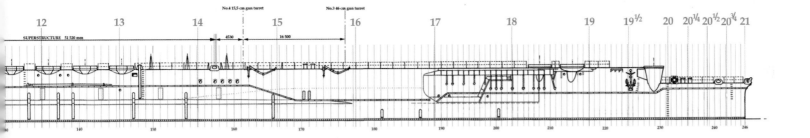

SUPERSTRUCTURE 51 520 mm

No.4 15,5 cm gun turret   No.3 46 cm gun turret

4530   16 500

12   13   14   15   16   17   18   19   19½   20   20¼ 20½ 20¾ 21

140   150   160   170   180   190   200   210   220   230   240   246

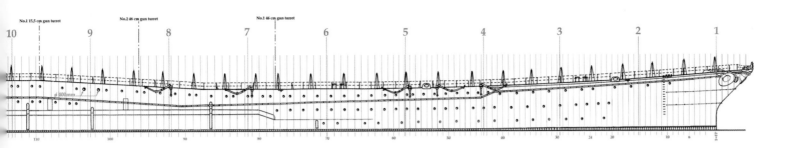

No.1 15,5 cm gun turret   No.2 46 cm gun turret   No.1 46 cm gun turret

10   9   8   7   6   5   4   3   2   1

ø 400mm

110   100   90   80   70   60   50   40   30   24   20   10   6   1 F.P.

B Hull Structure

B1/37 *Musashi* 1942 port side profile

B1/38 Shell plating

B1/39 Bottom openings

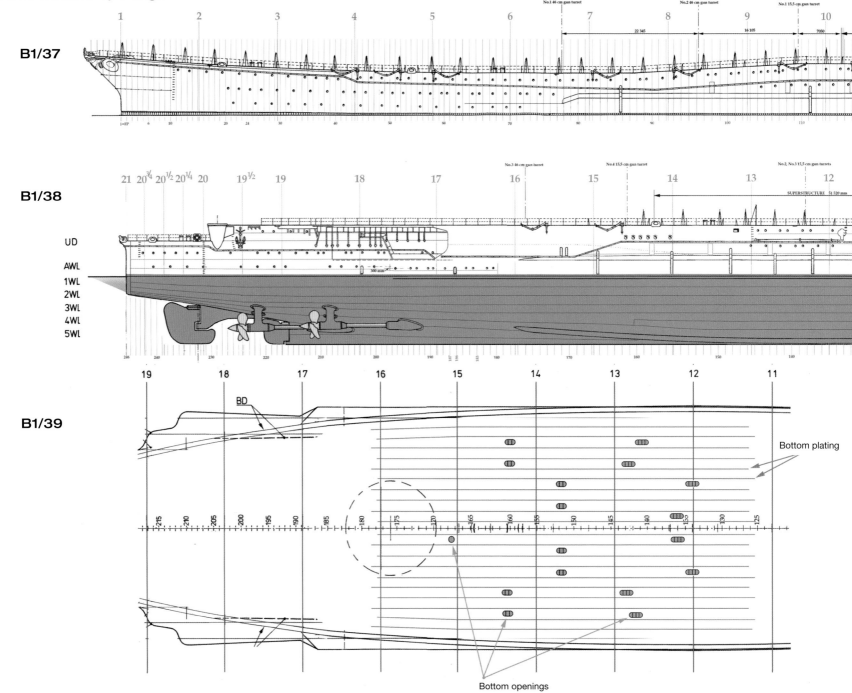

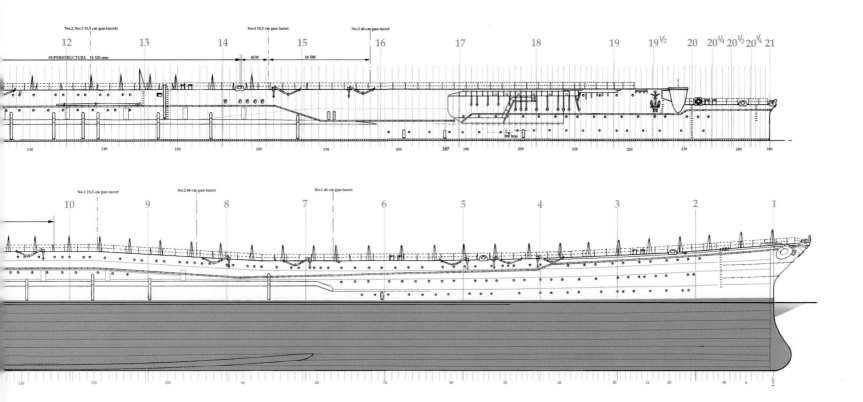

No.2, No.3 15,5 cm gun turrets

No.4 15,5 cm gun turret

No.3 46 cm gun turret

12 13 14 15 16 17 18 19 19½ 20 20¼ 20½ 20¾ 21

SUPERSTRUCTURE 51 520 mm

4530

16 500

300 mm

130 140 150 160 170 180 187 190 200 210 220 230 240 246

No.1 15,5 cm gun turret

No.2 46 cm gun turret

No.1 46 cm gun turret

10 9 8 7 6 5 4 3 2 1

120 110 100 90 80 70 60 50 40 30 24 20 10 6 1

B Hull Structure

B1/40 *Yamato* 1941 forecastle deck plan (1/600 scale)

B1/41 *Yamato* end of 1944 forecastle deck plan

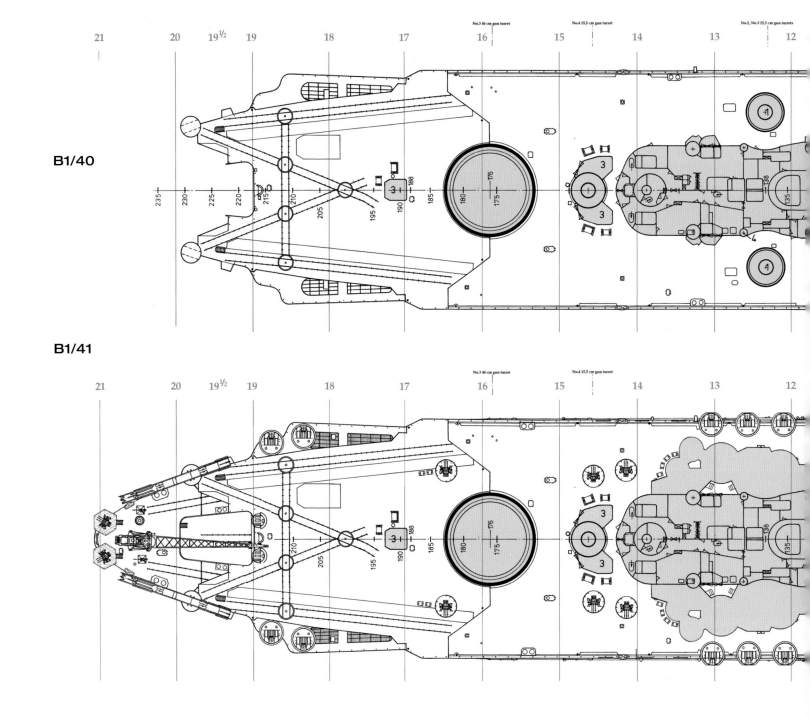

B1/40

B1/41

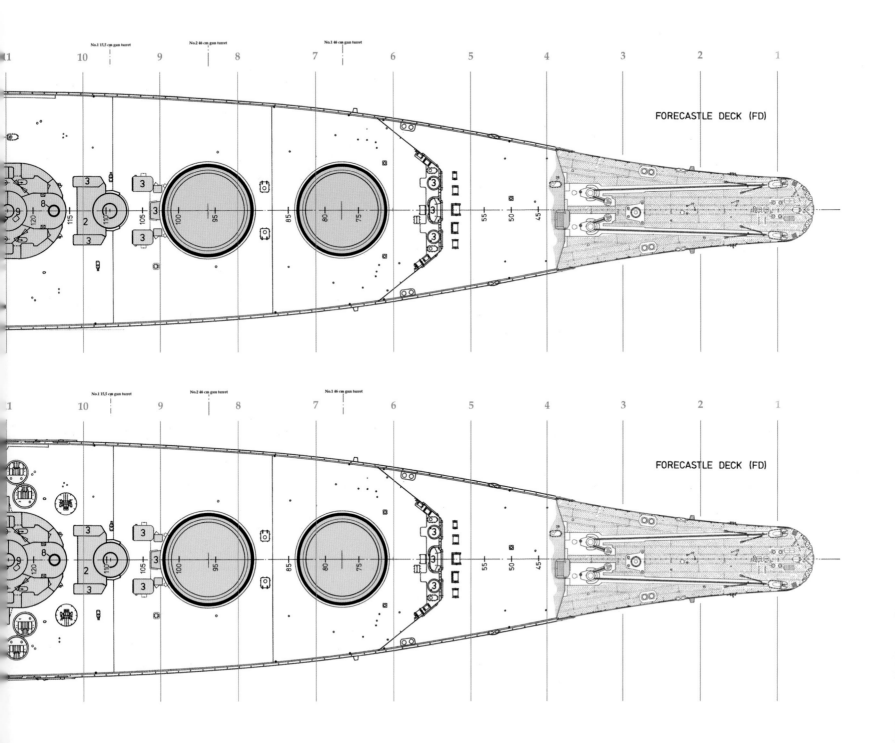

FORECASTLE DECK (FD)

No.1 15,5 cm gun turret   No.2 46 cm gun turret   No.1 46 cm gun turret

FORECASTLE DECK (FD)

No.1 15,5 cm gun turret   No.2 46 cm gun turret   No.1 46 cm gun turret

B Hull Structure

B1/42 *Yamato* – September 1943, *Musashi* – July 1942

Fitting four triple open 25mm MG mountings

B1/43 *Musashi* – October 1944

12 x 12.7cm HA guns, 130 x 25mm MG (35 x III, 25 x I), 4 x 13.2mm MG (2xII), two 12cm rocket launchers

B1/44 *Yamato* – April 1945

24 x 12.7cm HA guns, 156 x 25mm MG (50 x III, 6 x I), 4 x 13.2mm MG (2 x II)

B1/42

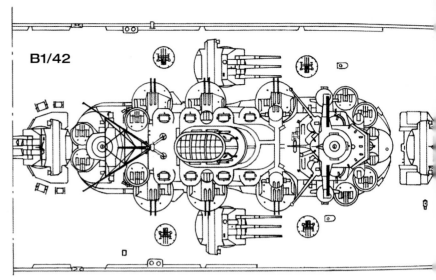

B1/43

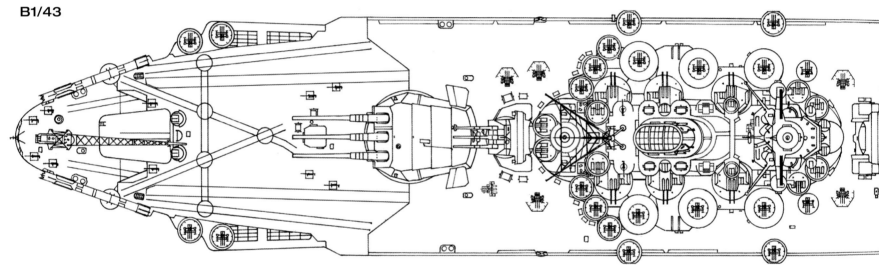

B1/44

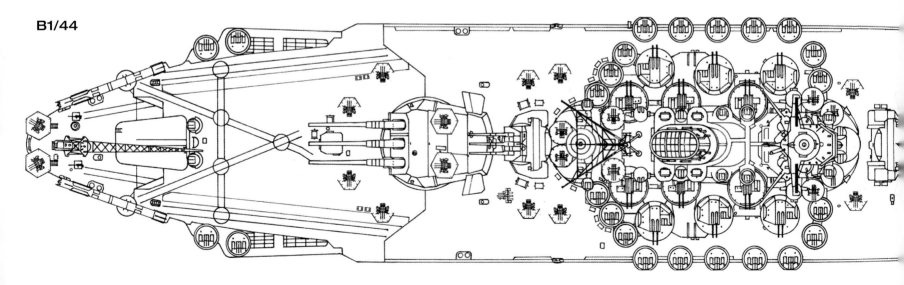

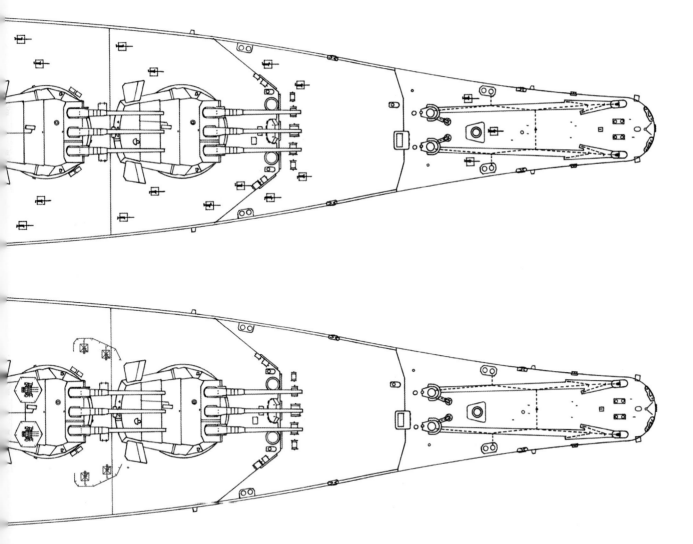

B Hull Structure

B1/45 *Yamato* – April 1945 detail of 25mm MG placement

B1/45

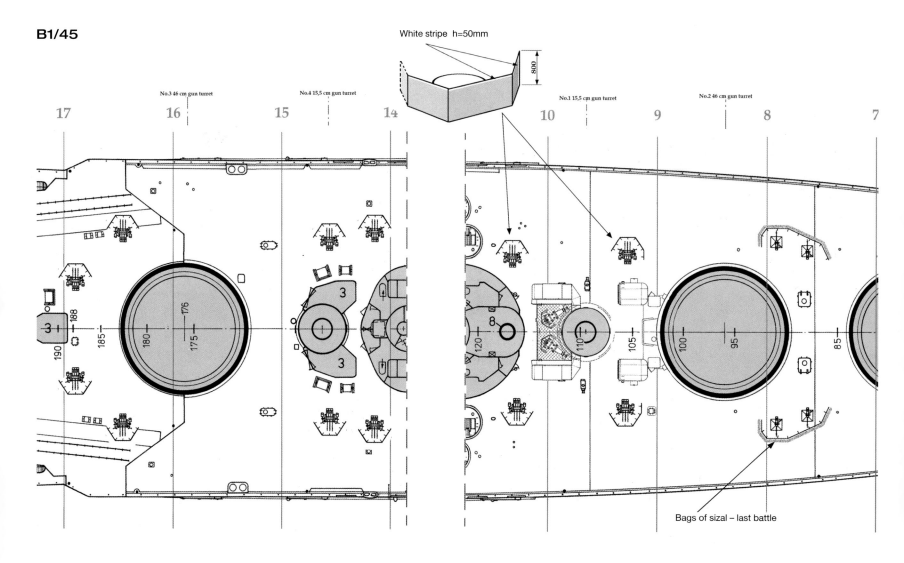

White stripe h=50mm

800

No.3 46 cm gun turret

No.4 15,5 cm gun turret

No.1 15,5 cm gun turret

No.2 46 cm gun turret

17 16 15 14 10 9 8 7

3 176 3 8 3

188 185 180 175 190 120 110 105 100 95 85

Bags of sizal – last battle

B1/46

White painted rectangles on deck edge and white stripes between rails – October 1944 – April 1945 (for crew orientation at night)

B1/46

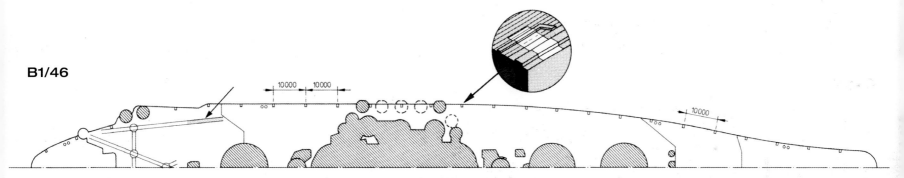

B Hull Structure

B1/47 Forecastle anchor deck plan

B1/48 Chequer plate

B1/49 Chequer plate joints

B1/50 Chrysanthemum crest, towing fairlead, jack staff, hawse pipe

B1/51 *Yamato* – profile

B1/52 Plan

B1/53 *Musashi* – front view

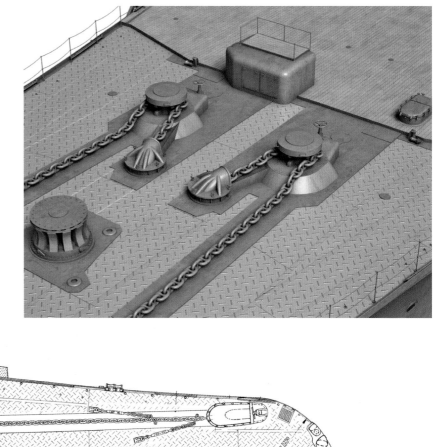

B1/47

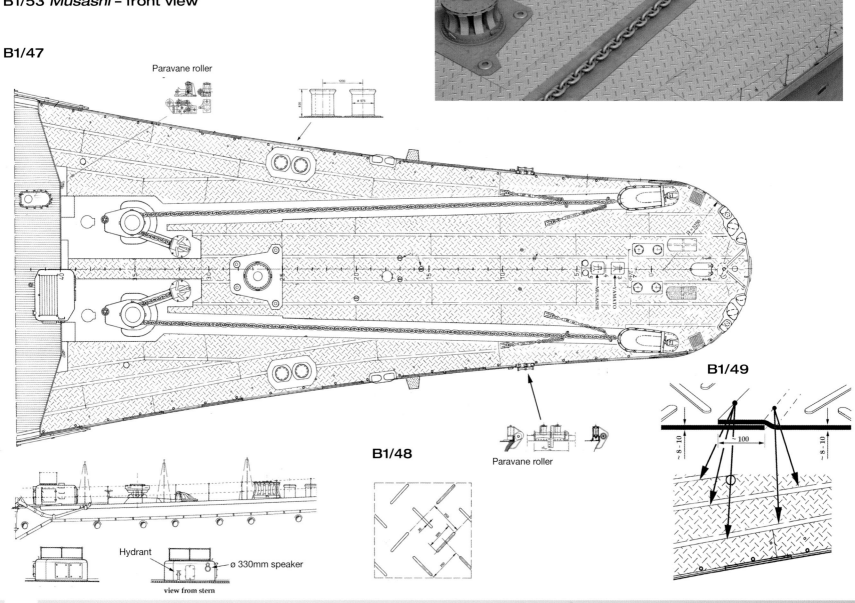

Paravane roller

Paravane roller

B1/48

B1/49

~ 100

8 – 10

8 – 10

Hydrant

ø 330mm speaker

view from stern

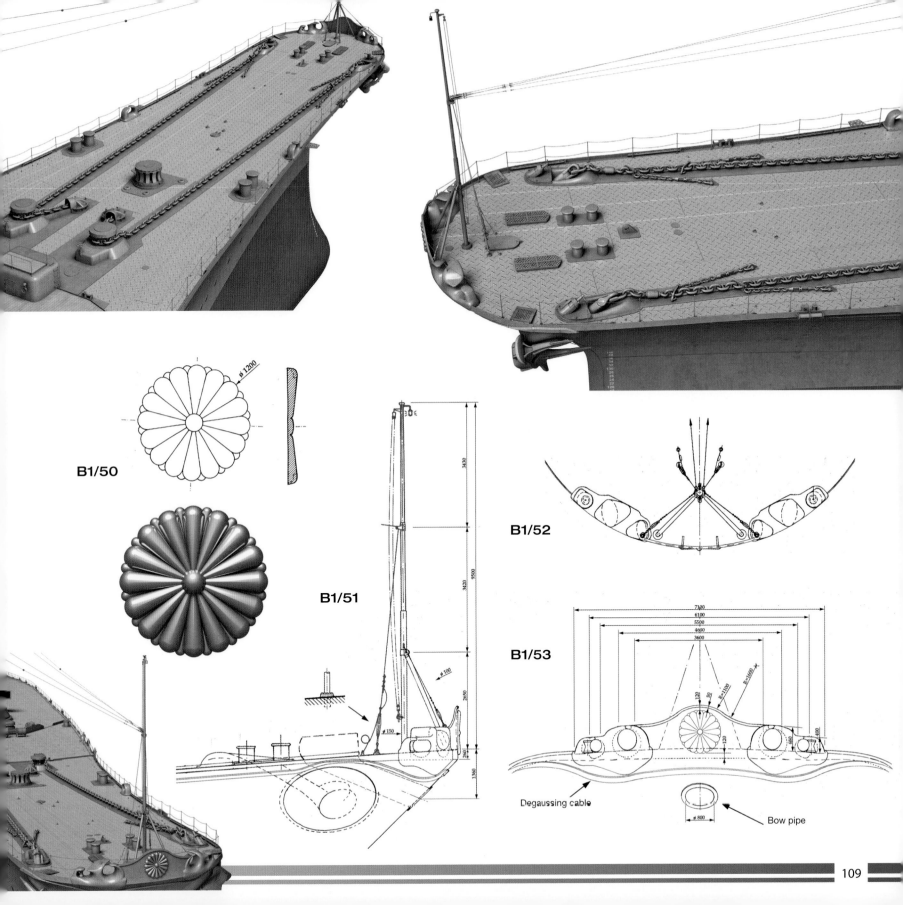

B1/50

B1/51

B1/52

B1/53

Degaussing cable

ø 800

Bow pipe

B Hull Structure

B1/54 Bow view

B1/55 Forecastle deck fittings – frames 40–79

B1/56 Main breakwater

B1/57 Closed deck holes

B1/58 Ventilators on frame 63–64

B1/55

B1/56

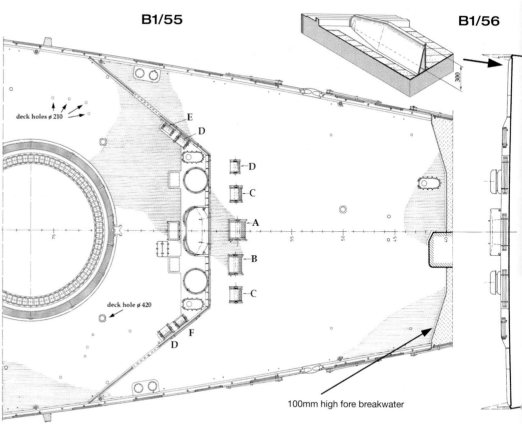

deck holes ø 210

deck hole ø 420

100mm high fore breakwater

B1/54

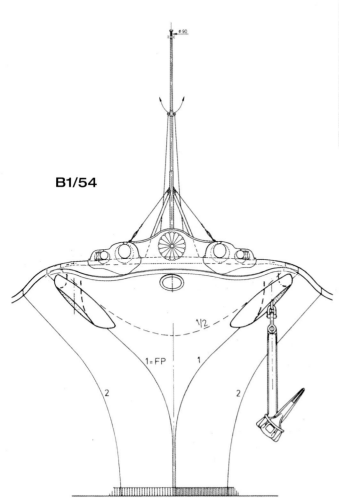

B1/57

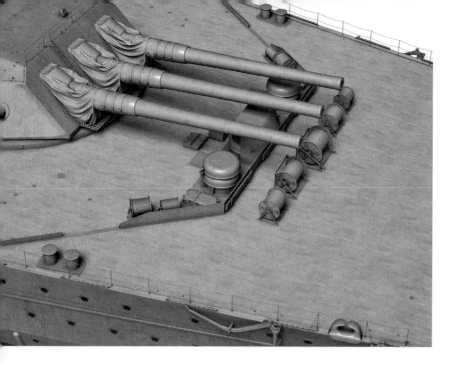

B1/58

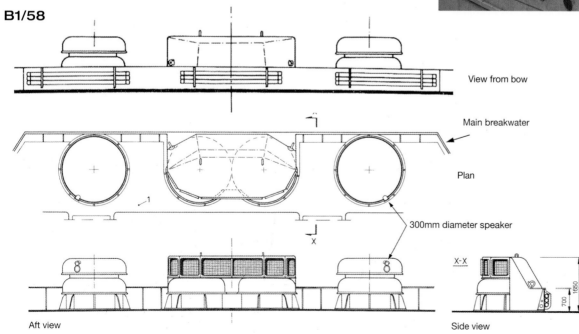

View from bow

Main breakwater

Plan

300mm diameter speaker

X-X

Aft view

Side view

B Hull Structure

B1/59 Midship deck fittings

B1/60 Aircraft deck of *Yamato* 1941
B1/61 Aircraft deck *Yamato* 1944-45
B1/62 Aircraft deck *Musashi* 1942

1 No.3 46cm gun turret barbette
2 Deck rails
3 Rail turntable
4 Ventilator
5 Aircraft hangar platform (middle deck)
6 Ladder
7 Hatch
8 Scupper
9 Anti-blast cover
10 Non-slip linoleum sheets with brass inset strips
11 Bollards
12 Catapult ring
13 After capstan
14 Life buoy
15 After anchor
16 Fairlead
17 After towing fairlead
18 Base of aircraft and boat 6-ton crane
19 Crane capstan
20 Boat overhead travelling crane
21 Platform above travelling crane (chequer plate)
22 100mm high breakwater

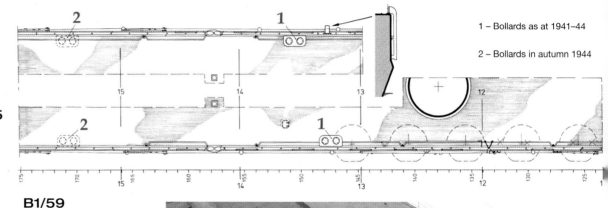

1 – Bollards as at 1941–44

2 – Bollards in autumn 1944

B1/59

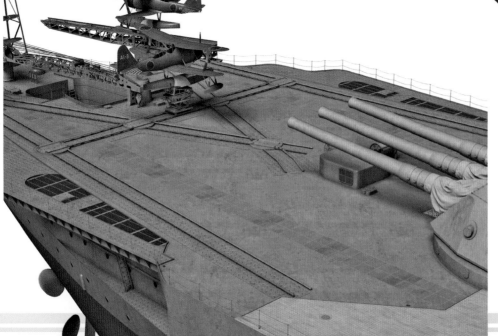

B1/60

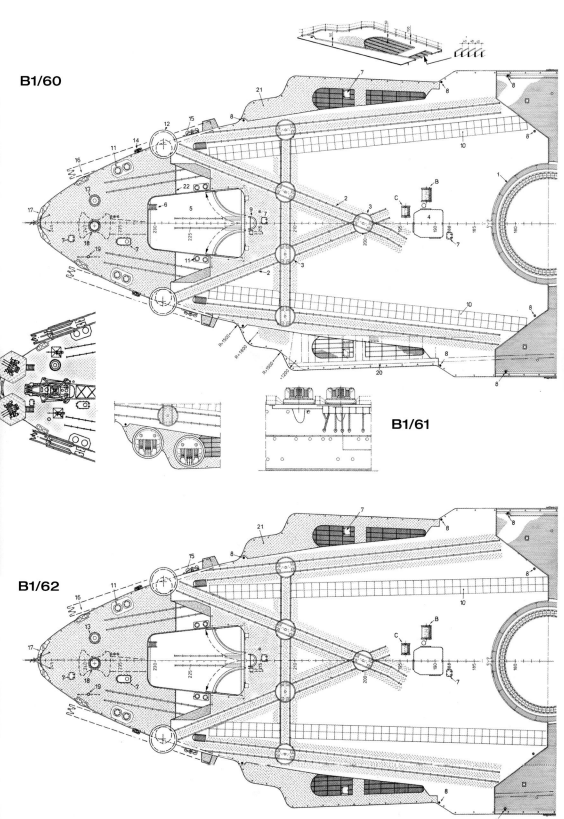

B1/61

B1/62

B Hull Structure

B1/63 Boat hangar doors – plan
B1/64 Side view of boat hangar
B1/65 Sections
B1/66 Bow profile
B1/67 Boat's hangar doors

B1/63

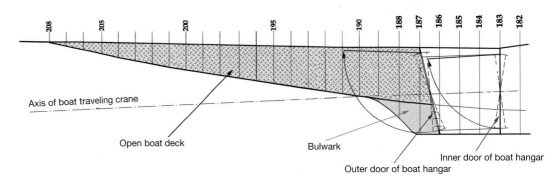

Axis of boat traveling crane

Open boat deck

Bulwark

Outer door of boat hangar

Inner door of boat hangar

B1/64

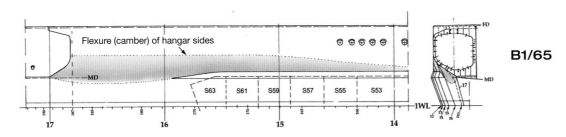

Flexure (camber) of hangar sides

MD

S63 S61 S59 S57 S55 S53

B1/65

B1/66

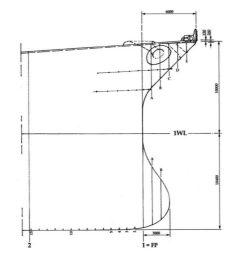

B1/67

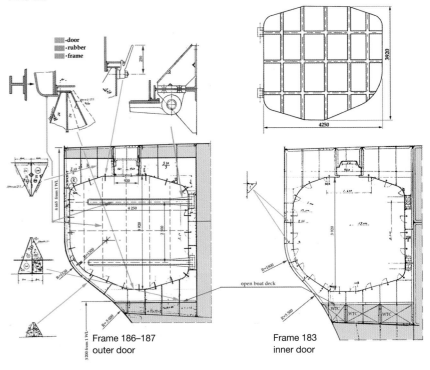

Inner surface of outer door

-door
-rubber
-frame

Frame 186–187
outer door

open boat deck

Frame 183
inner door

114

B Hull Structure – Stern

B2/1 Profile of stern part of hull

B2/1a Ventilator, reels

B2/1a

B2/1

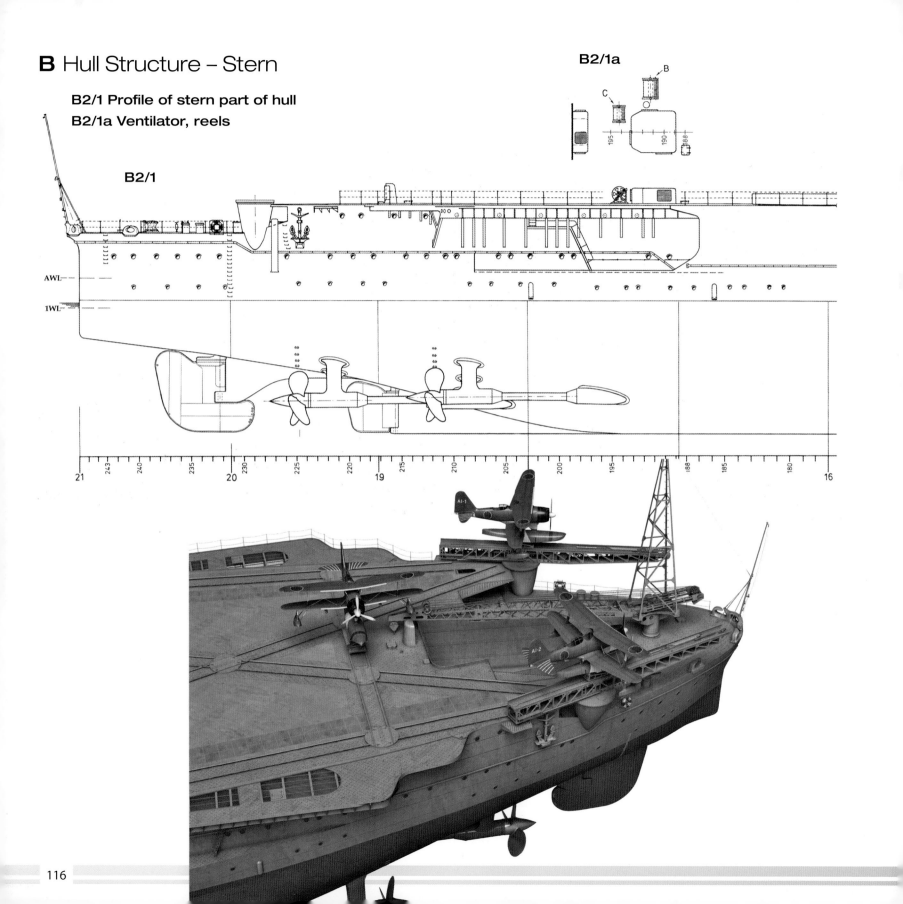

B Hull Structure – Rudders

B2/2 Rudders: fore-auxiliary, rear-main rudder

B2/3 Main rudder side view

B2/4 Main rudder front view

B2/5 Main rudder plan

B2/6 Main rudder bottom view

B2/7 Typical screw – used in rudder assembly

B2/8 Fore auxiliary rudder side view

B2/9 Rear view

B2/10 Plan

B2/5

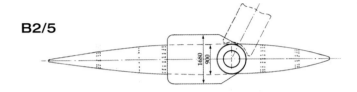

B2/3

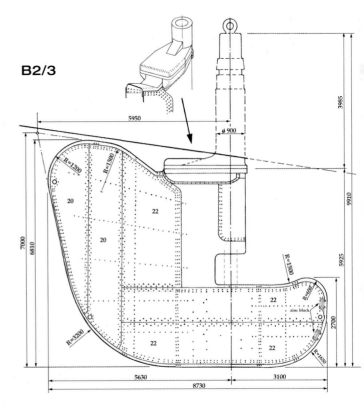

B2/2

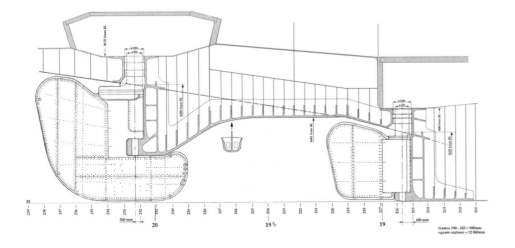

B2/6

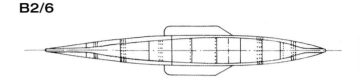

B2/7

B2/10

B2/9

B2/8

B2/4

B Hull Structure – Stern

Open aircraft hangar deck

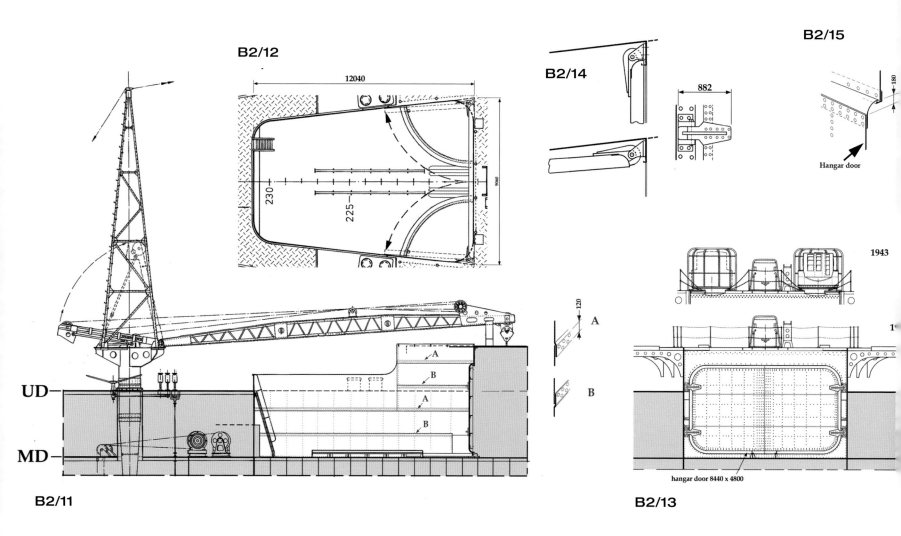

B2/12

12040

230

225

9060

B2/14

B2/15

882

180

Hangar door

1943

120

A

B

A

B

UD

MD

A

A

B

B

hangar door 8440 x 4800

B2/11

B2/13

B Hull Structure – Stern

B2/16 Anti blast covers above hangar doors
B2/17 Starboard pipe near catapult base

B2/16

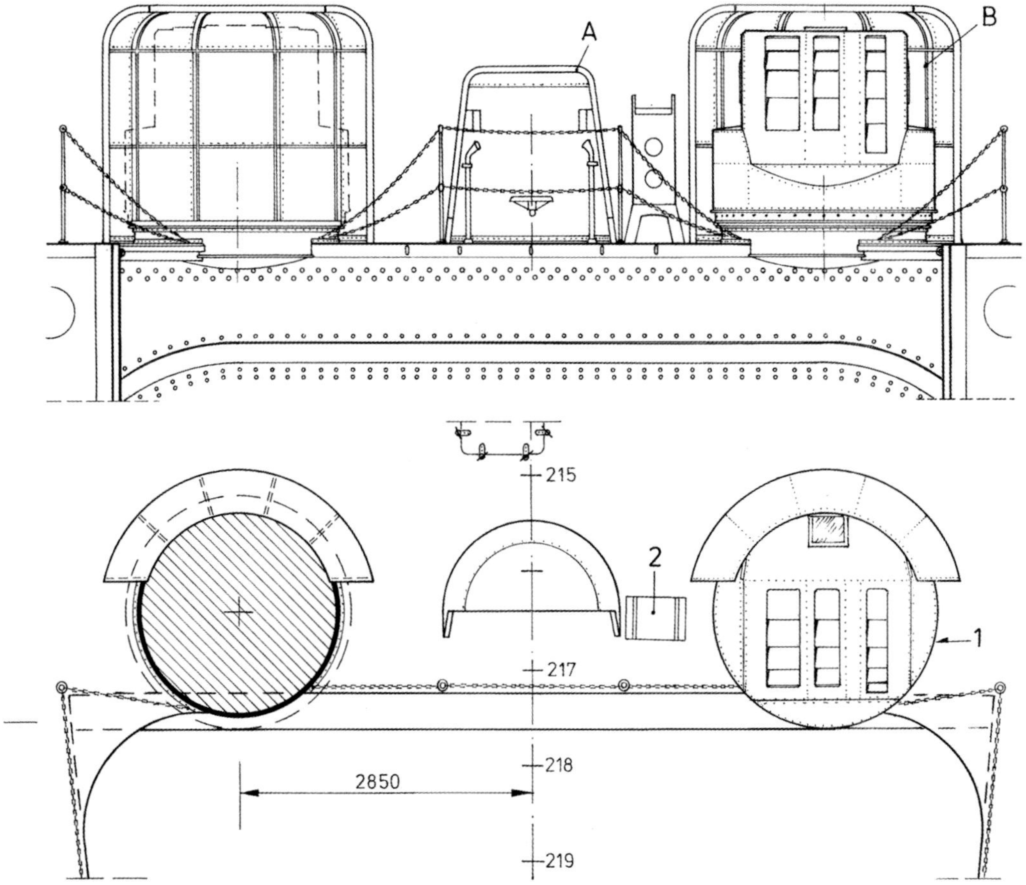

Covers 'B' fitted in 1943

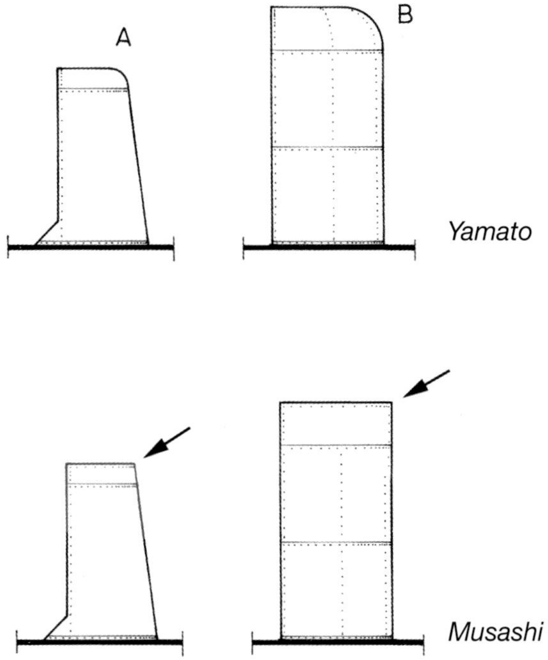

A   B

Yamato

Musashi

215

2

1

217

2850

218

219

B2/17

600

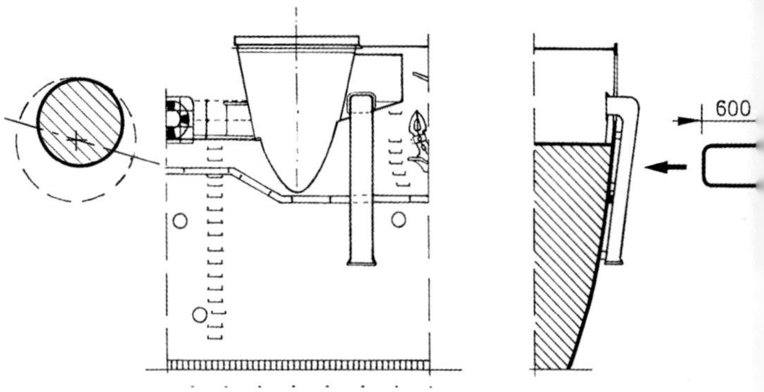

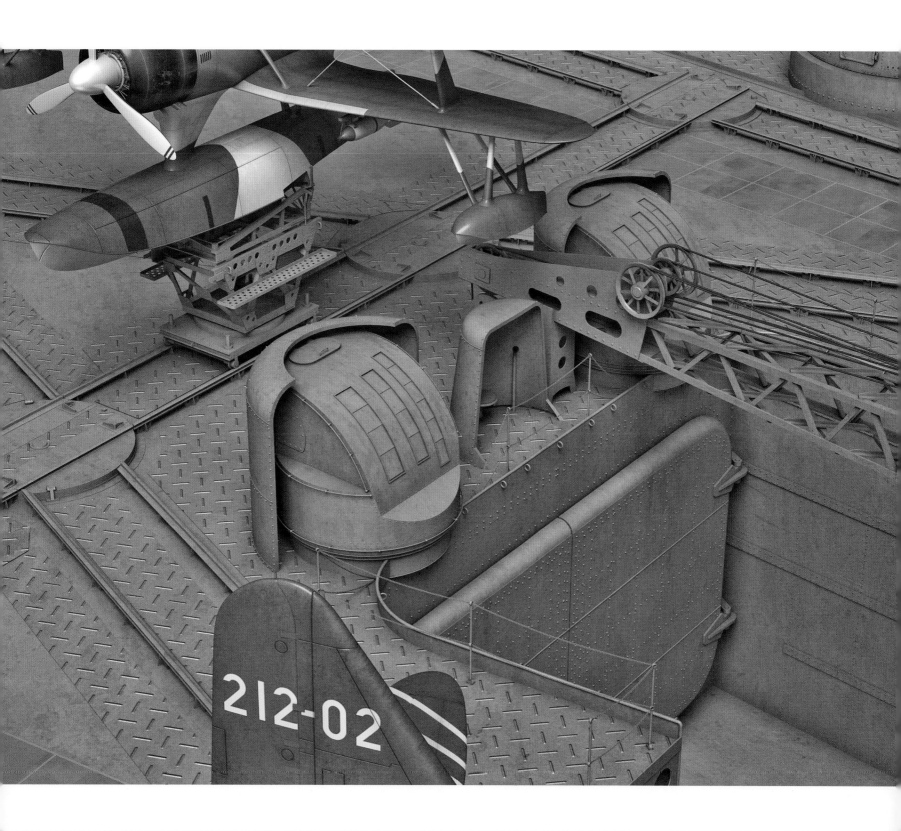

B Hull Structure – Stern and Propellers

B2/18 Stern deck view from astern

B2/19 Stern deck plan and view

B2/18

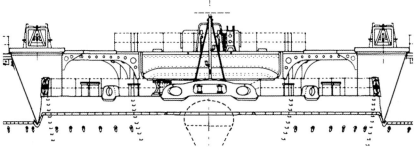

B2/19

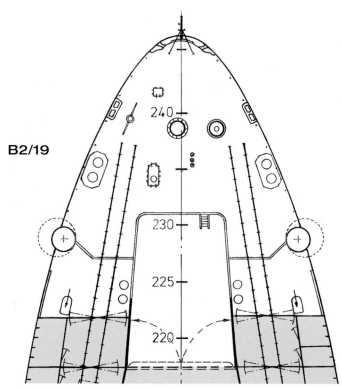

**B2/20 5m diameter propeller (section, view)
(1/100 scale)**

**B2/21 5m diameter propeller (official Japanese
Navy drawings)**

B2/22 Shaft supports (1/150 scale)

B2/23 Anticorrosion zinc plate

B2/21

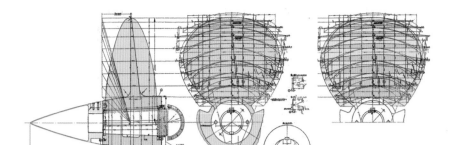

B2/20

B2/23

B2/22

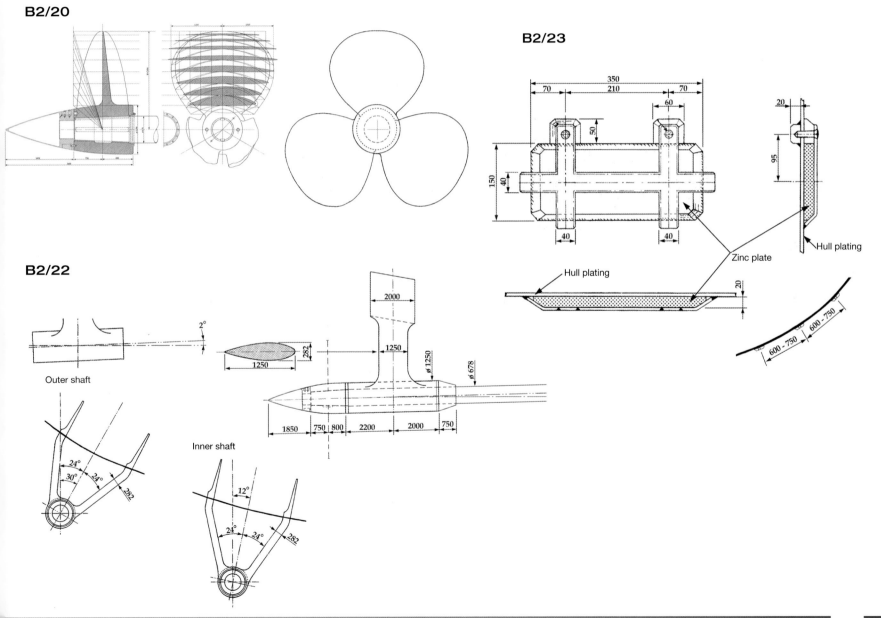

B Hull Structure – Rudder

B2/24 Main rudder (official Japanese Navy drawings)

B2/25 Main rudder (official Japanese Navy drawings)

B2/26 Main rudder vertical sections (official Japanese Navy drawings)

B2/25

B2/24

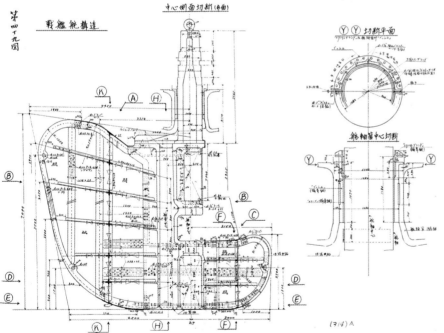

Ⓚ Ⓚ 切断　Ⓗ Ⓗ 切断　舵軸中心切断

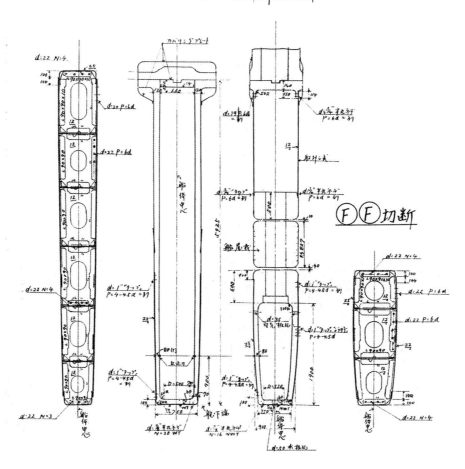

Ⓕ Ⓕ 切断

C Superstructure

C1/1 Superstructure starboard elevation (1/1200 scale)

December 1941 platform levels:	
	Fore tower:
	+31 565
	+28 775
	+26 055
	+23 705
	+21 155
	+18 955
Rear tower:	+16 755
+16 905	+14 355
+14 095	+13 300
+12 635	+12 150
+11 745	+11 050
+10 135	+ 9 950
+ 7 750	+ 7 750
+ 2 450	+ 5 250
+ 0,000	+ 2 900
	+ 2 550
	+ 0,000

Levels	
+- 0.00	Forecastle deck (FD)
+2550/+5250	Lower decks of superstructure
+7750	Upper deck of middle part of superstructure
+9950	Conning tower
+13300	Signal deck (rear part of tower bridge)
+14355	Compass bridge – bridge No.2
+16755	MG control tower (two towers) auxiliary Type 98
	LA directors ('Hoiban')
+18955	Fore part – 1.5m navigation rangefinder, aft – four searchlight control towers
+23705	Combat bridge
+26055	Air defence combat platform and map compatrment
+28775	Axis of 15.5m rangafinder
+31565	Roof of Type 98 LA director 'Hoiban'

C1/1

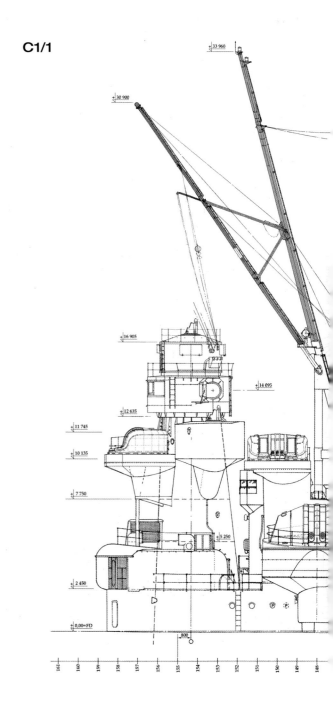

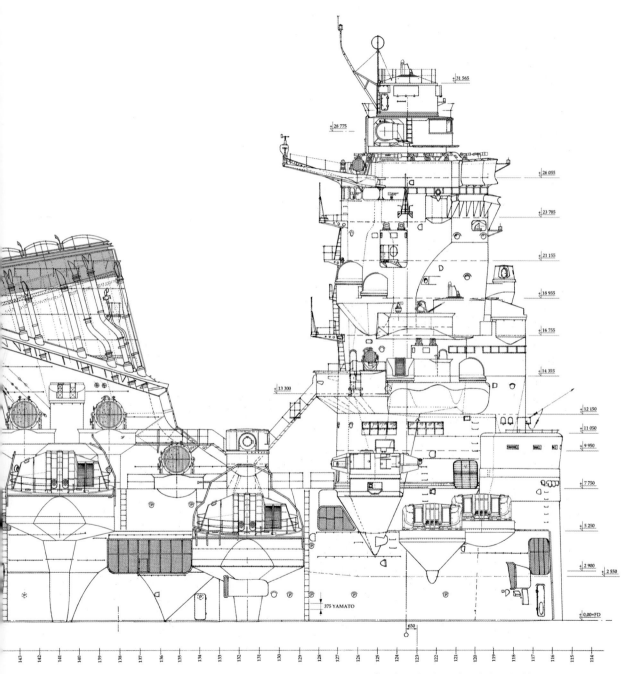

+ 31 565

+ 28 775

+ 26 055

+ 23 705

+ 21 155

+ 18 955

+ 16 755

+ 14 355

+ 13 300

+ 12 150

+ 11 050

+ 9 950

+ 7 750

+ 5 250

+ 2 900   + 2 550

375 YAMATO

+ 0,00=FD

650

143 142 141 140 139 138 137 136 135 134 133 132 131 130 129 128 127 126 125 124 123 122 121 120 119 118 117 116 115 114

Scuttles ○ only starboard ⓟ both sides ⓟ only port side

C Superstructure

C1/2 *Yamato* 1941 level +23 455/+23 705 (1/200 scale)

C1/3 *Yamato* 1941 starboard profile

C1/4 *Yamato* 1941 rear view of tower

C1/2

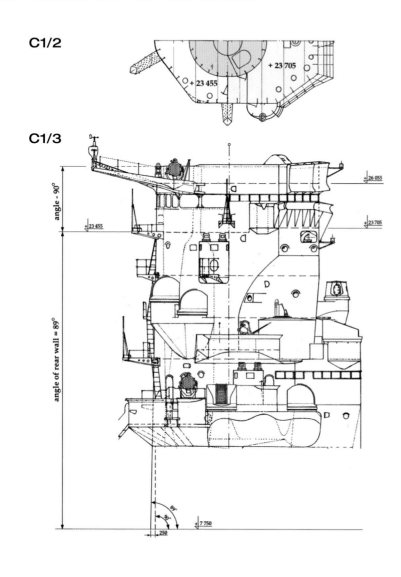

C1/3

C1/4

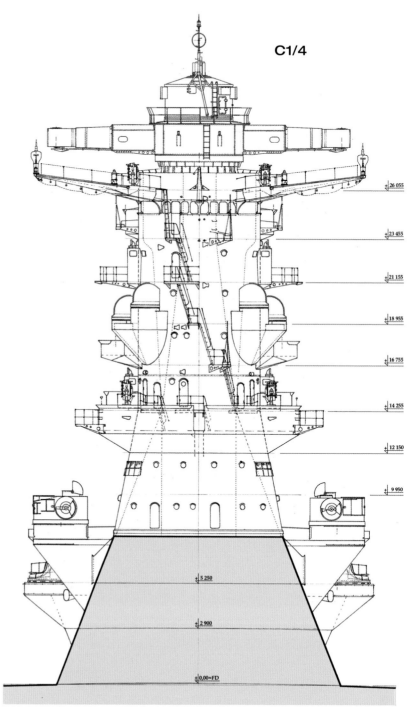

Aft tower of *Yamato* in 1941

C1/5 View from frame 150 from bow

C1/6 View from frame 152 from stern

C1/5

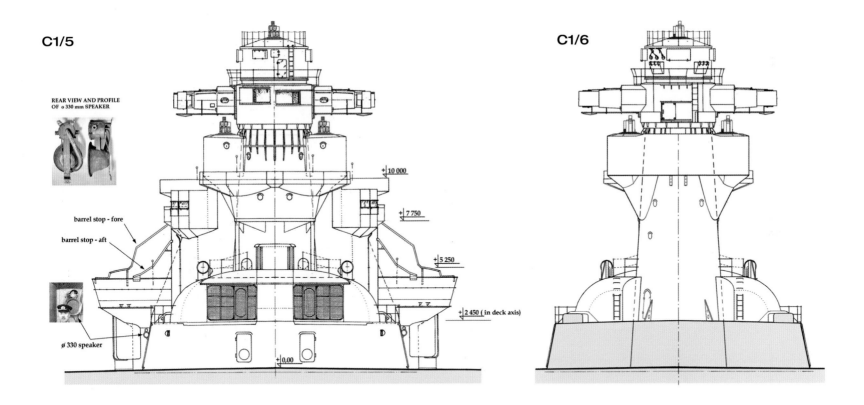

REAR VIEW AND PROFILE
OF ⌀ 330 mm SPEAKER

barrel stop - fore

barrel stop - aft

⌀ 330 speaker

+ 10 000

+ 7 750

+ 5 250

+ 2 450 (in deck axis)

+ 0,00

C1/6

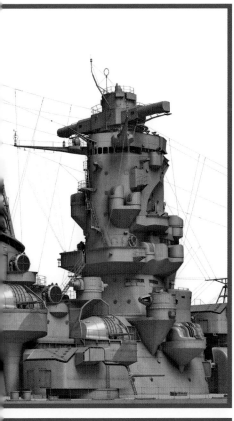

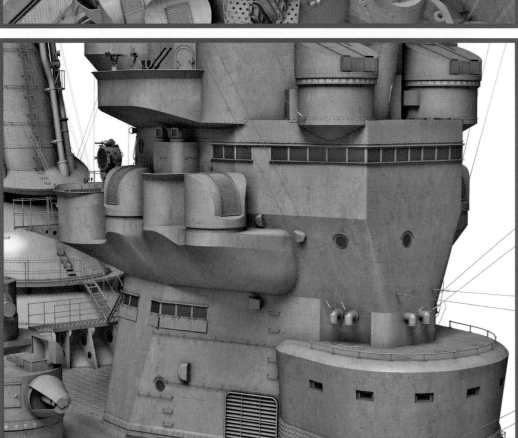

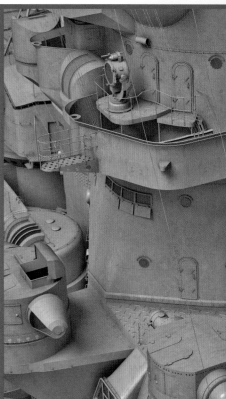

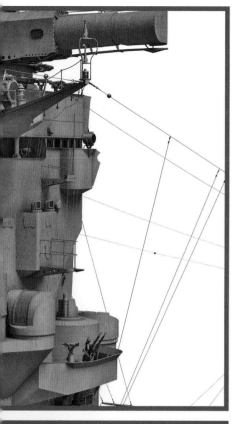

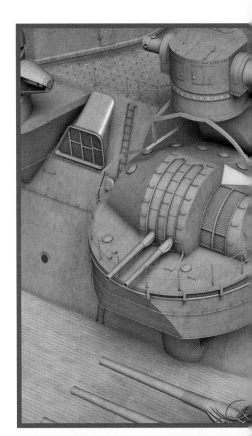

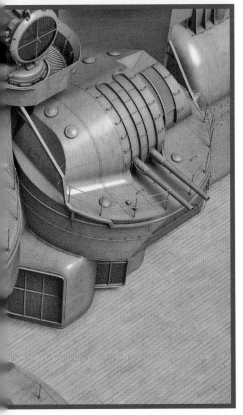

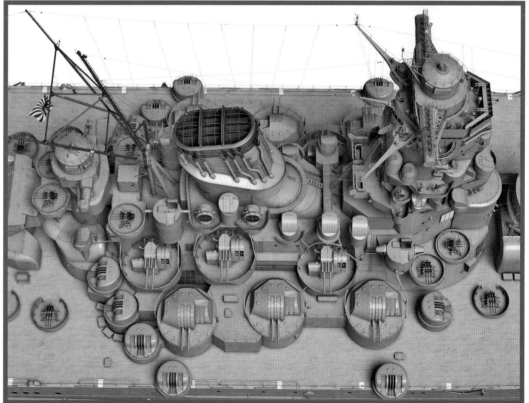

C Superstructure

C1/7 *Yamato* 1945 starboard elevation (1/200 scale)

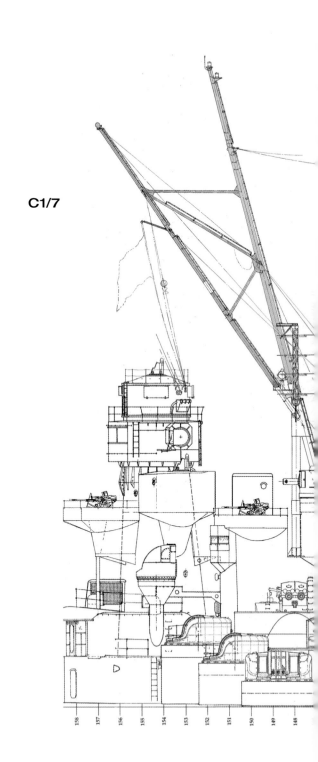

C1/7

158 157 156 155 154 153 152 151 150 149 148

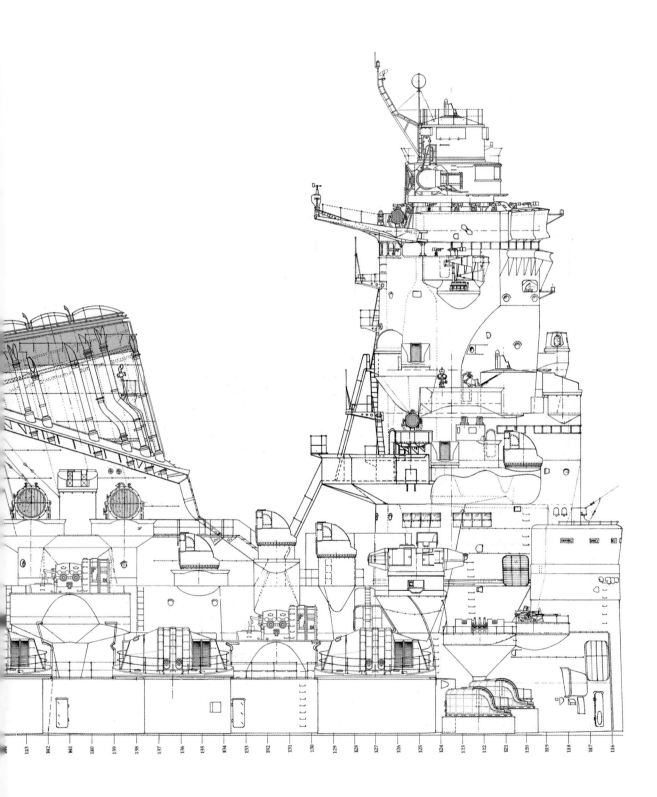

C Superstructure

C1/8 *Yamato* 1945 front view of superstructure (1/200 scale)

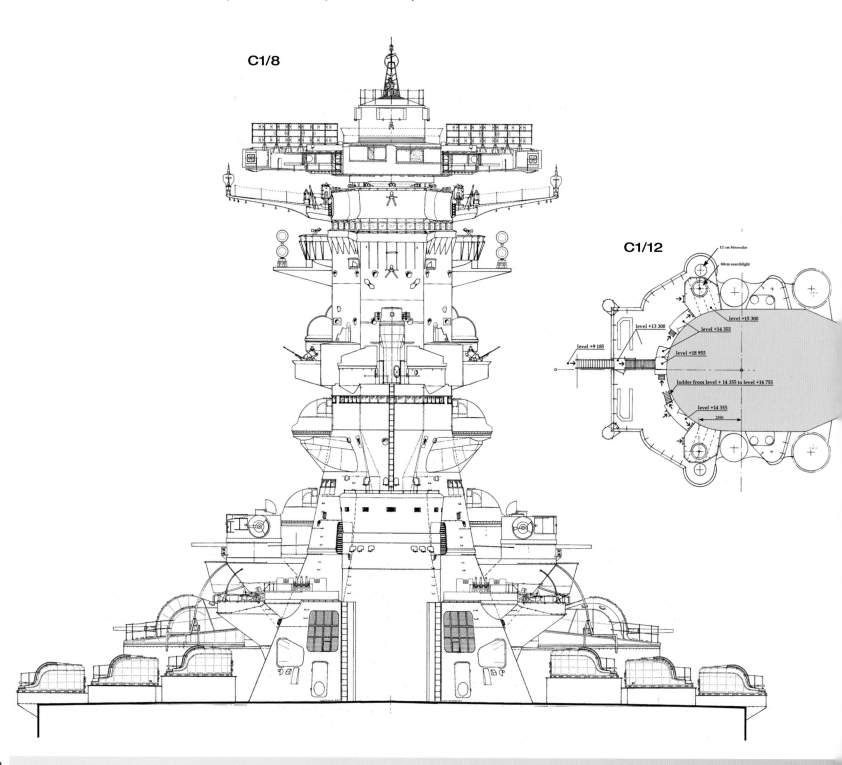

C1/8

C1/12

12 cm binocular

60cm searchlight

level +15 300

level +14 355

level +13 300

level +18 955

level +9 185

ladder from level + 14 355 to level +16 755

level +14 355

2350

C1/9 *Yamato* 1945 rear view of tower bridge

C1/10 *Yamato* 1945 side view of tower bridge

C1/11 Details of tower *Yamato* 1943-45

C1/12 *Yamato* 1945 plan of signal platform

C1/9

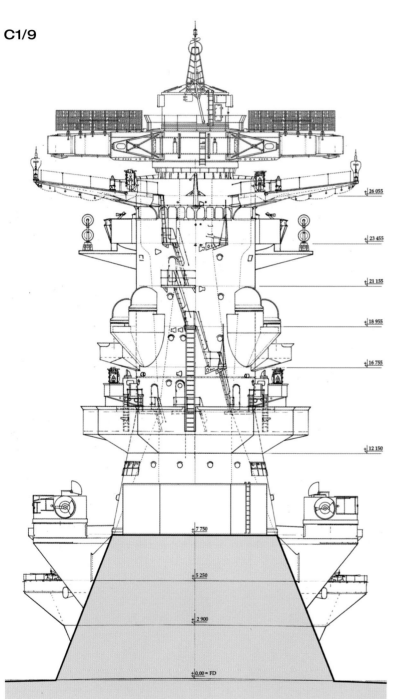

C1/10

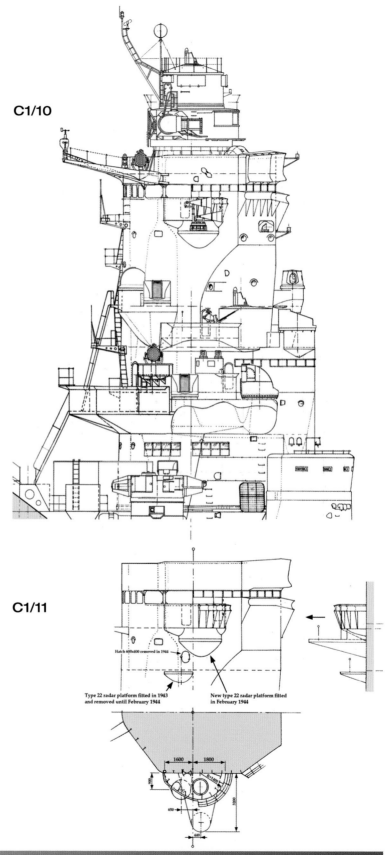

C1/11

Hatch 600x800 removed in 1944

Type 22 radar platform fitted in 1943 and removed until February 1944

New type 22 radar platform fitted in February 1944

C1/13 Rear elevation of aft tower –
***Yamato* 1945 (1/200 scale)**

C1/13

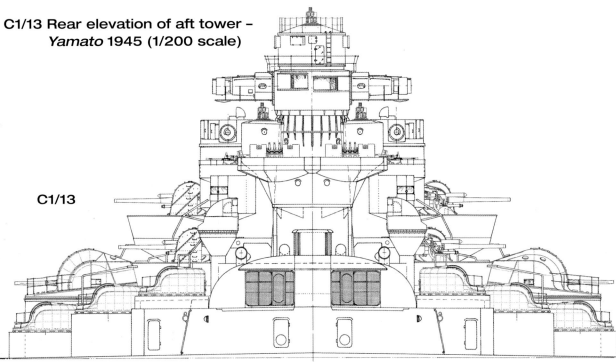

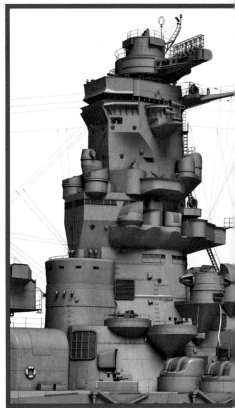

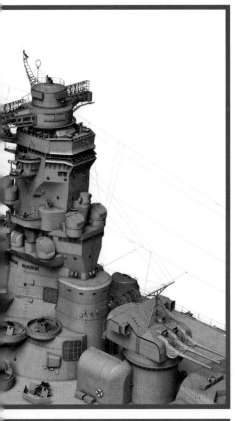

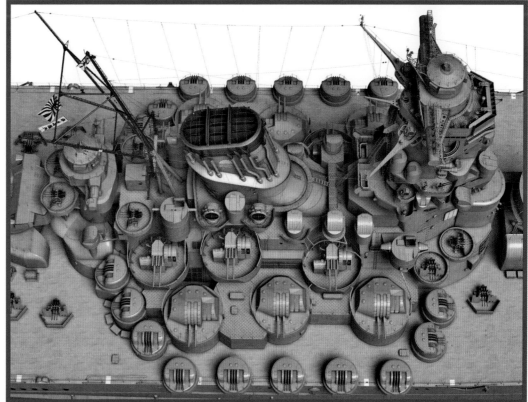

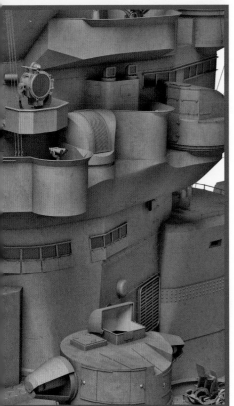

C Superstructure

C1/14 *Musashi* 1942 starboard elevation of
superstructure (levels as on drawing C1/1)
(1/200 scale)

C1/14

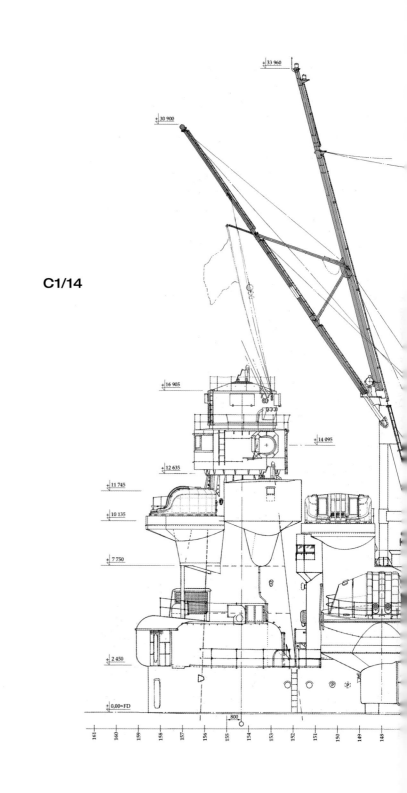

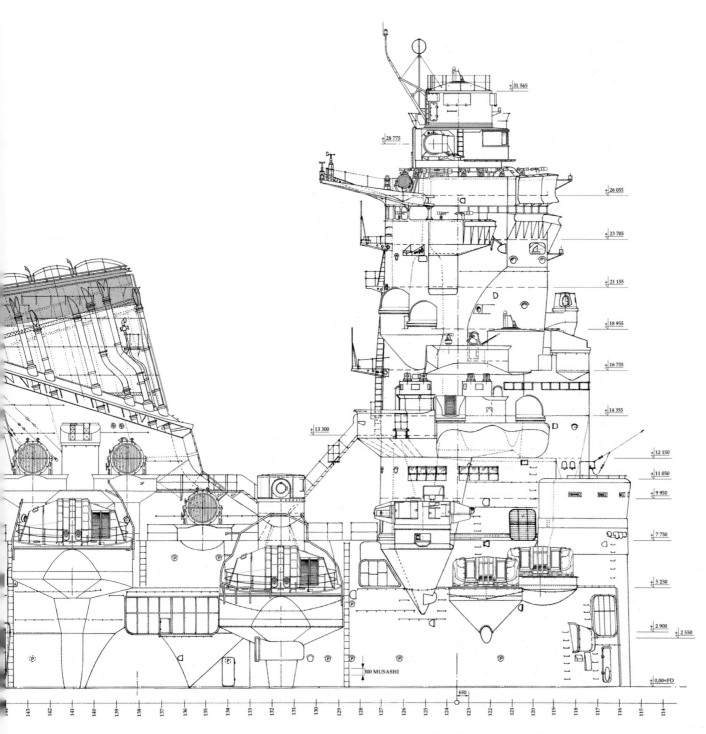

+ 31 565

+ 28 775

+ 26 055

+ 23 705

+ 21 155

+ 18 955

+ 16 755

+ 14 355

13 300

+ 12 150

+ 11 050

9 950

7 750

5 250

2 900

2 550

0,00=FD

300 MUSASHI

650

144 143 142 141 140 139 138 137 136 135 134 133 132 131 130 129 128 127 126 125 124 123 122 121 120 119 118 117 116 115 114

Scuttles ◯ only starboard   ⓟ both sides   ⓟ only port side

C Superstructure

Details of *Musashi* tower bridge in 1942 (1/200 scale)

C1/15 Platform Level +23 455/+23 705

C1/16 Profile

C1/17 Rear view of tower bridge

C1/18 *Musashi* 1942 view of rear tower from frame 159 to bow direction

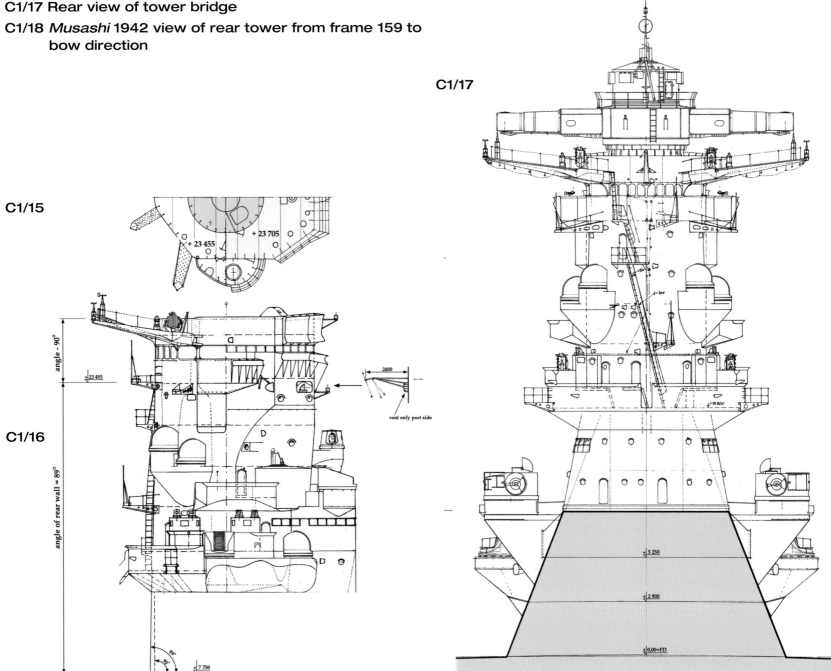

C1/17

C1/15

C1/16

2400

vent only port side

+ 23 455

+ 23 705

angle – 90°

23 455

angle of rear wall = 89°

89°

90°

250

7 750

5 250

2 900

0,00=FD

C1/18

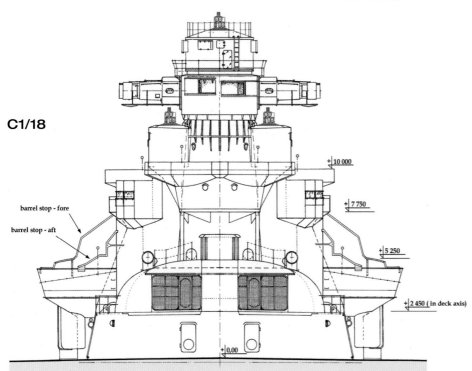

barrel stop - fore

barrel stop - aft

+ 10 000

+ 7 750

+ 5 250

+ 2 450 (in deck axis)

+ 0,00

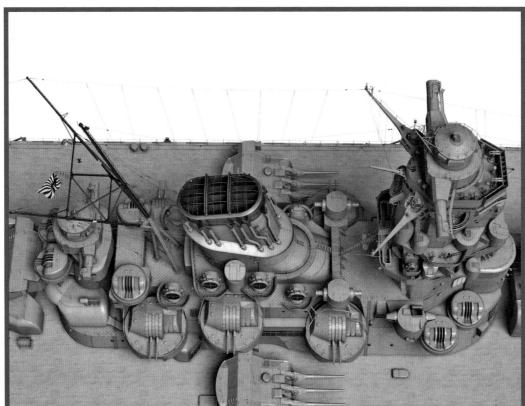

C Superstructure

C1/19 *Musashi* 1944 starboard elevation of
superstructure (1/200 scale)

C1/19

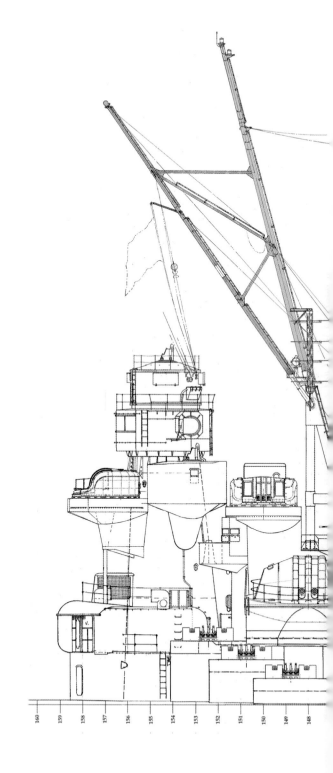

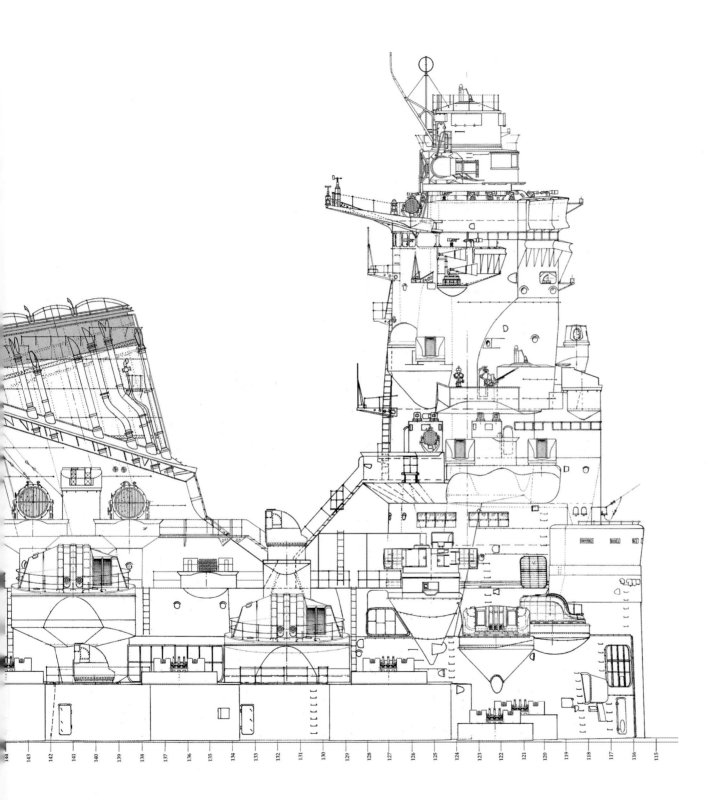

144 143 142 141 140 139 138 137 136 135 134 133 132 131 130 129 128 127 126 125 124 123 122 121 120 119 118 117 116 115

C Superstructure

C1/20 Front elevation of *Musashi* tower bridge in 1944 (1/200 scale)

C1/21 Rear view of tower bridge

C1/22 Side view of tower bridge

C1/23 Signal deck (+13 300 over FD) 1942

C1/24 Signal deck (+ 13 300) 1943-44

C1/25 *Musashi* 1944 rear elevation of aft tower

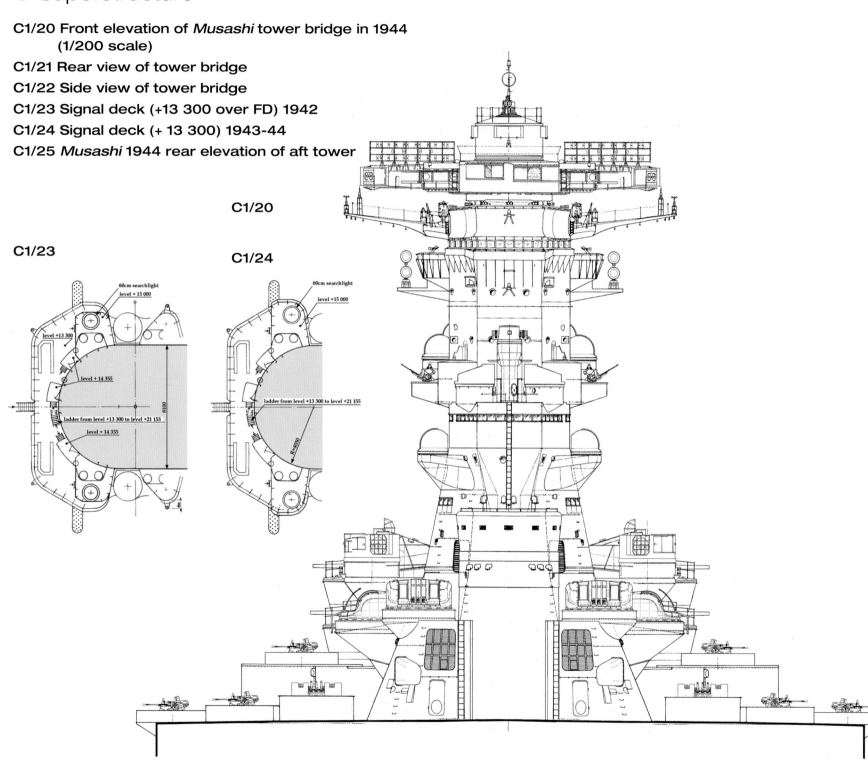

C1/20

C1/23

C1/24

60cm searchlight
level +15 000

level +13 300

level + 14 355

ladder from level +13 300 to level +21 155

level + 14 355

8100

60cm searchlight
level +15 000

ladder from level +13 300 to level +21 155

R=4050

C1/21

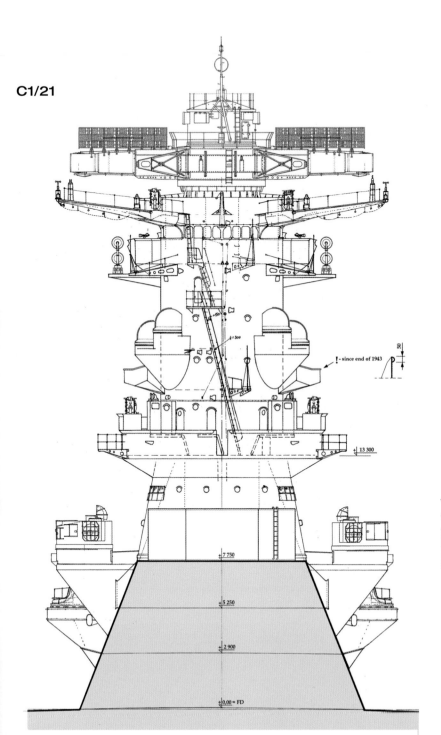

+13 300

50

↓ - since end of 1943

7 750

5 250

2 900

0,00 = FD

C1/22

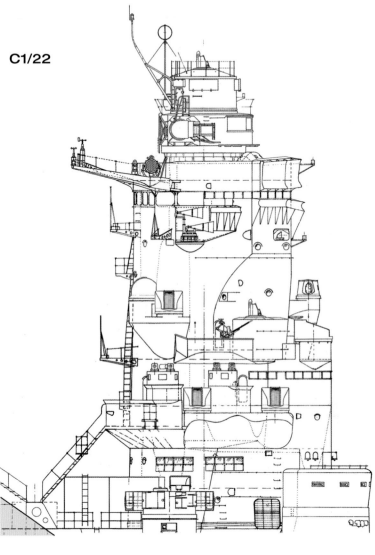

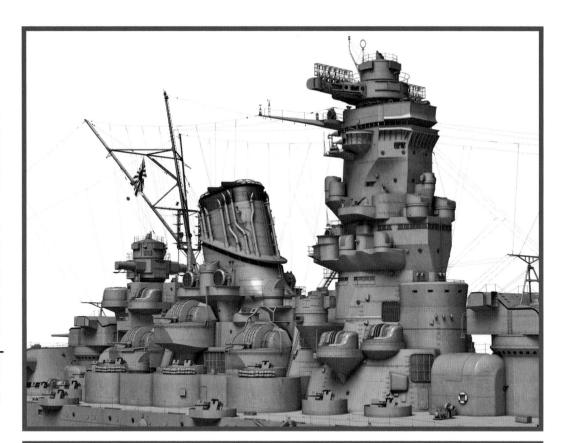

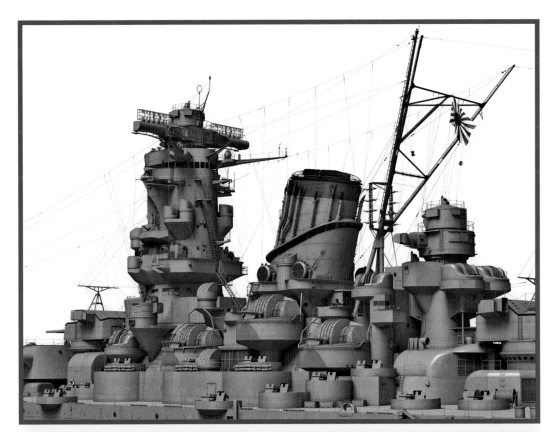

C Superstructure – *Musashi* 1944

C1/25 *Musashi* 1944 rear elevation of aft tower

C1/25

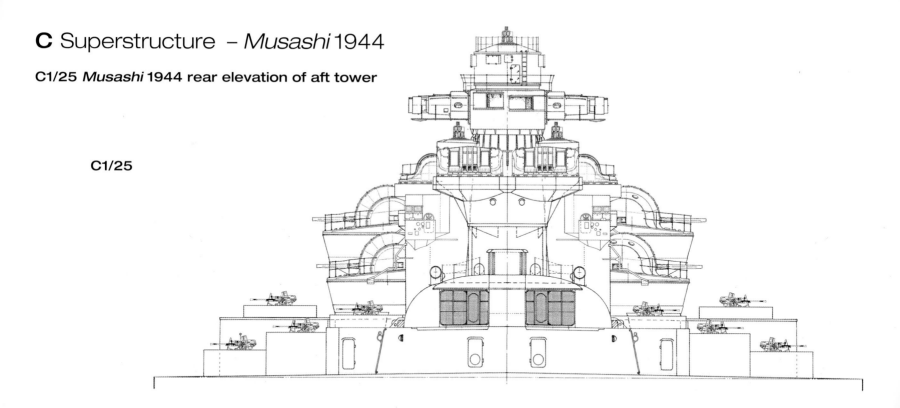

C Superstructure

Rear tower (1/200 scale)
C1/26 Side view – *Yamato*
C1/27 Horizontal body lines of rear tower
C1/28 Detail of *Musashi*

Yamato 1941
C1/29 View from frame 152 to bow direction

Yamato superstructure details after middle of 1943 with fitted radar cabin and passage between superstructure and rear tower:
C1/30 Profile
C1/31 View to stern direction
C1/32 View to bow direction
C1/33 Plan

Musashi 1944
C1/34 Profile
C1/35 View from frame 152 to bow direction
C1/36 Plan

C1/28

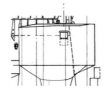

C1/26

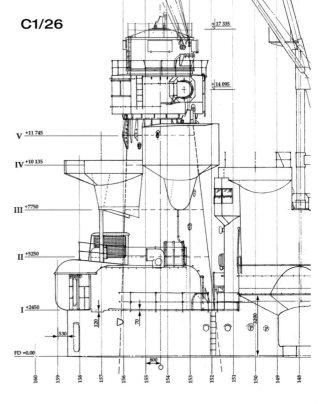

C1/27

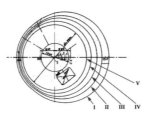

C1/29

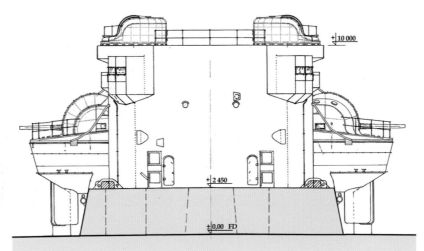

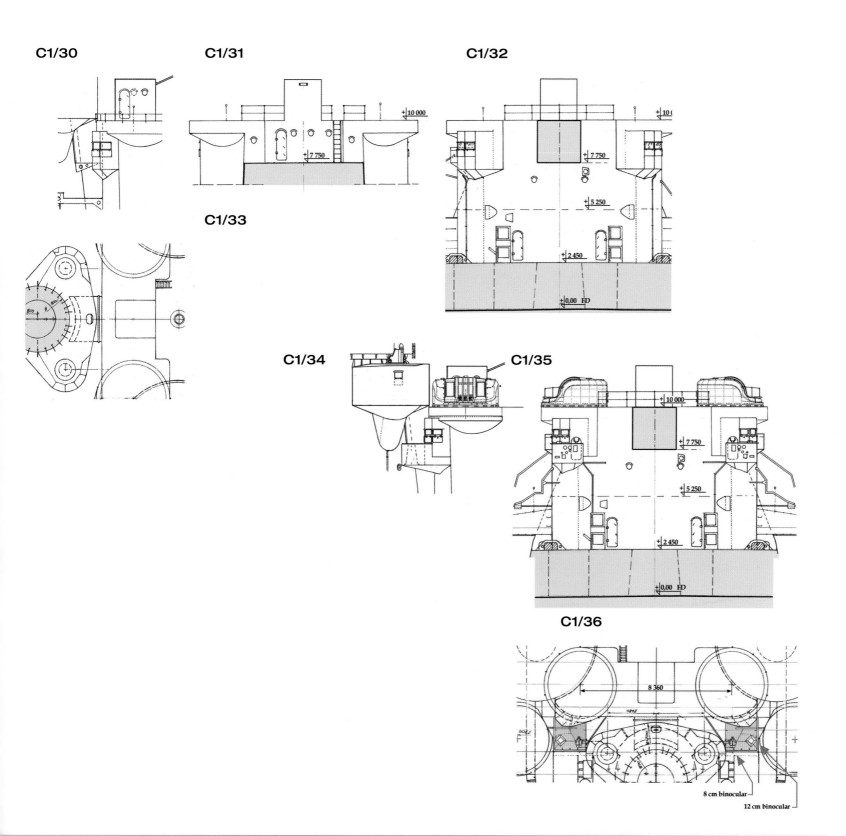

C1/30

C1/31

C1/32

+ 10 000

+ 7 750

+ 5 250

+ 2 450

+ 0,00 FD

C1/33

C1/34

C1/35

+ 10 000

+ 7 750

+ 5 250

+ 2 450

+ 0,00 FD

C1/36

8 360

8 cm binocular

12 cm binocular

C Superstructure

Views from frame 148 to bow direction

C1/37 *Musashi*

C1/38 *Yamato*

C1/39, C1/40 *Musashi* 1942 view from frame 138 to stern
direction

C1/41 *Yamato* 1945 view from frame 138 to stern
direction

C1/37

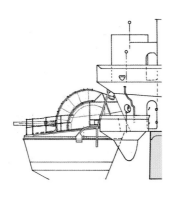

C1/38

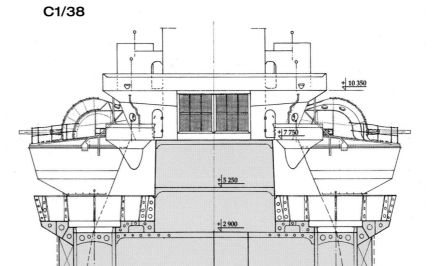

+ 10 350

+ 7 750

+ 5 250

+ 2 900

+ 0,00 FD

C1/39

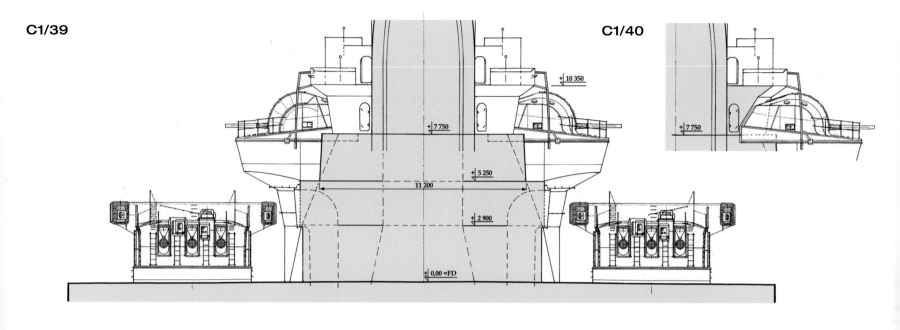

C1/40

+ 10 350

+ 7 750

+ 7 750

+ 5 250

11 200

+ 2 900

+ 0,00 =FD

C1/41

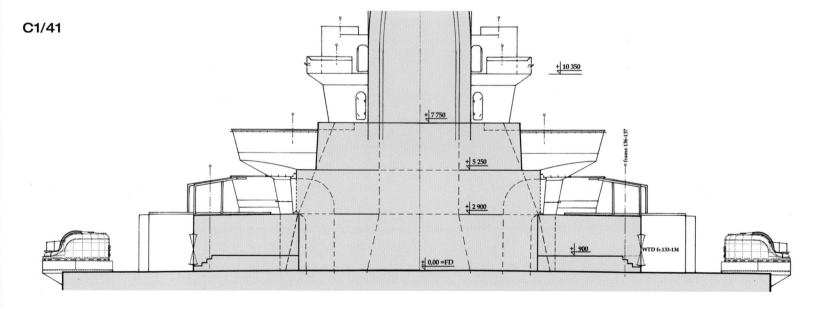

+ 10 350

+ 7 750

+ 5 250

+ 2 900

+ 900

+ 0,00 =FD

WTD fr.133-134

o frame 136-137

C Superstructure

C1/42 *Musashi* 1942 view from frame 138 to stern
direction

C1/43 *Yamato* 1941 view from frame 138 to stern
direction

C1/42

C1/43

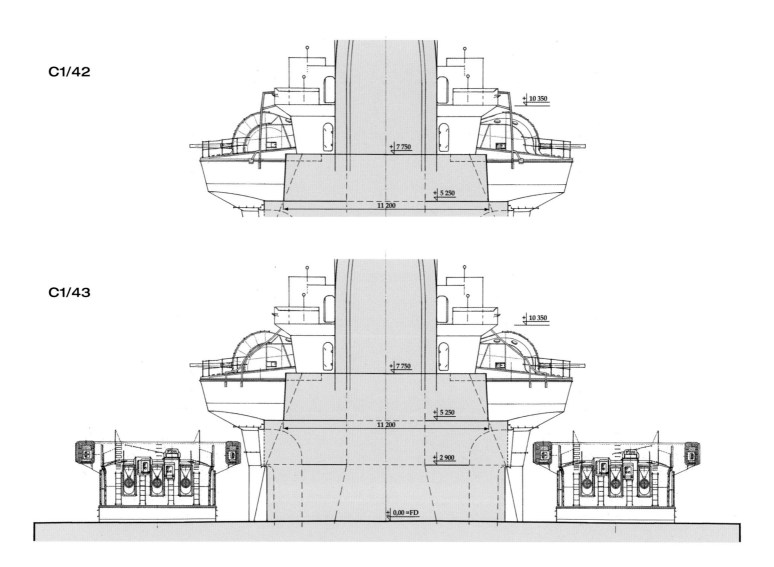

C1/44 *Yamato* 1941 view from frame 138 to bow direction

C1/45, C1/46 *Musashi* 1942 frame 138 to bow (showing differences)

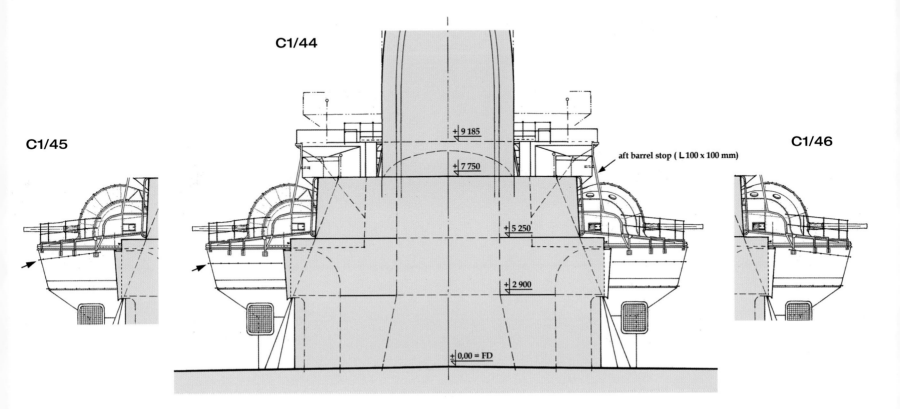

C1/44

C1/45

C1/46

+ 9 185

+ 7 750

aft barrel stop (L 100 x 100 mm)

+ 5 250

+ 2 900

+ 0,00 = FD

C Superstructure

C1/47 *Yamato* 1941 view from frame 128 to stern
direction

C1/48, C1/49 *Musashi* 1942 view from frame 128 to stern
direction (showing differences)

C1/47

C1/48

C1/49

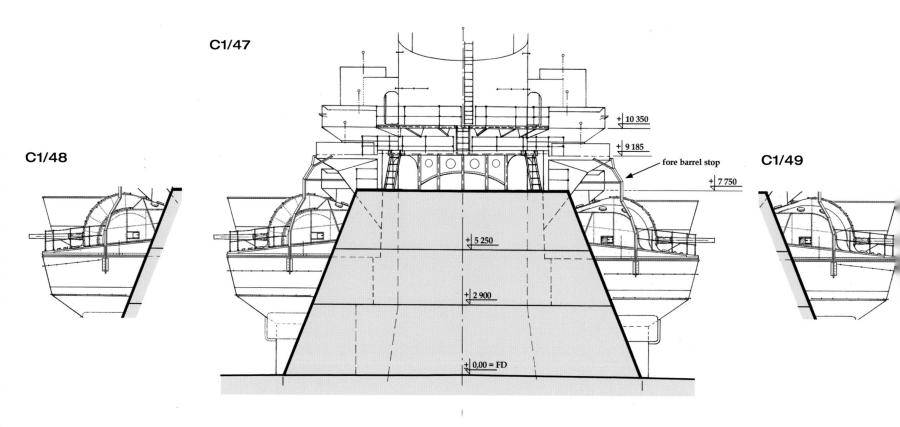

+ 10 350

+ 9 185

fore barrel stop

+ 7 750

+ 5 250

+ 2 900

+ 0,00 = FD

12.7cm HA gun tower bases

C1/50 *Yamato* turrets no.1, no.2, no.5, no.6
C1/51 *Yamato* turrets no.3, no.4
C1/52 *Musashi* turrets no.1, no.2
C1/53 *Musashi* turrets no.5, no.6
C1/54 *Musashi* turrets no.3, no.4
C1/55 *Musashi* turret no.2
C1/56 Handrail details

C1/50

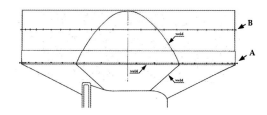

C1/51

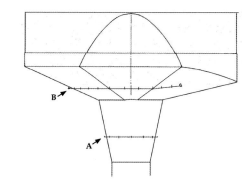

C1/56

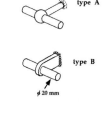

C1/52

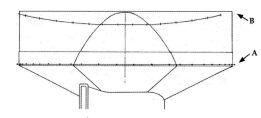

C1/55

C1/54

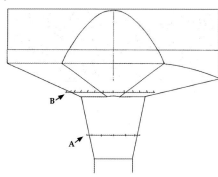

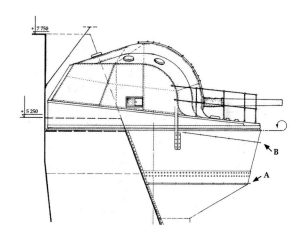

C1/53

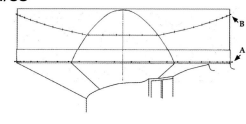

C Superstructure

Rear wall of tower bridge (scheme):

C1/57 Flat surfaces

C1/58 Signal halyards

C1/59 Inclination of superstructure walls

C1/57

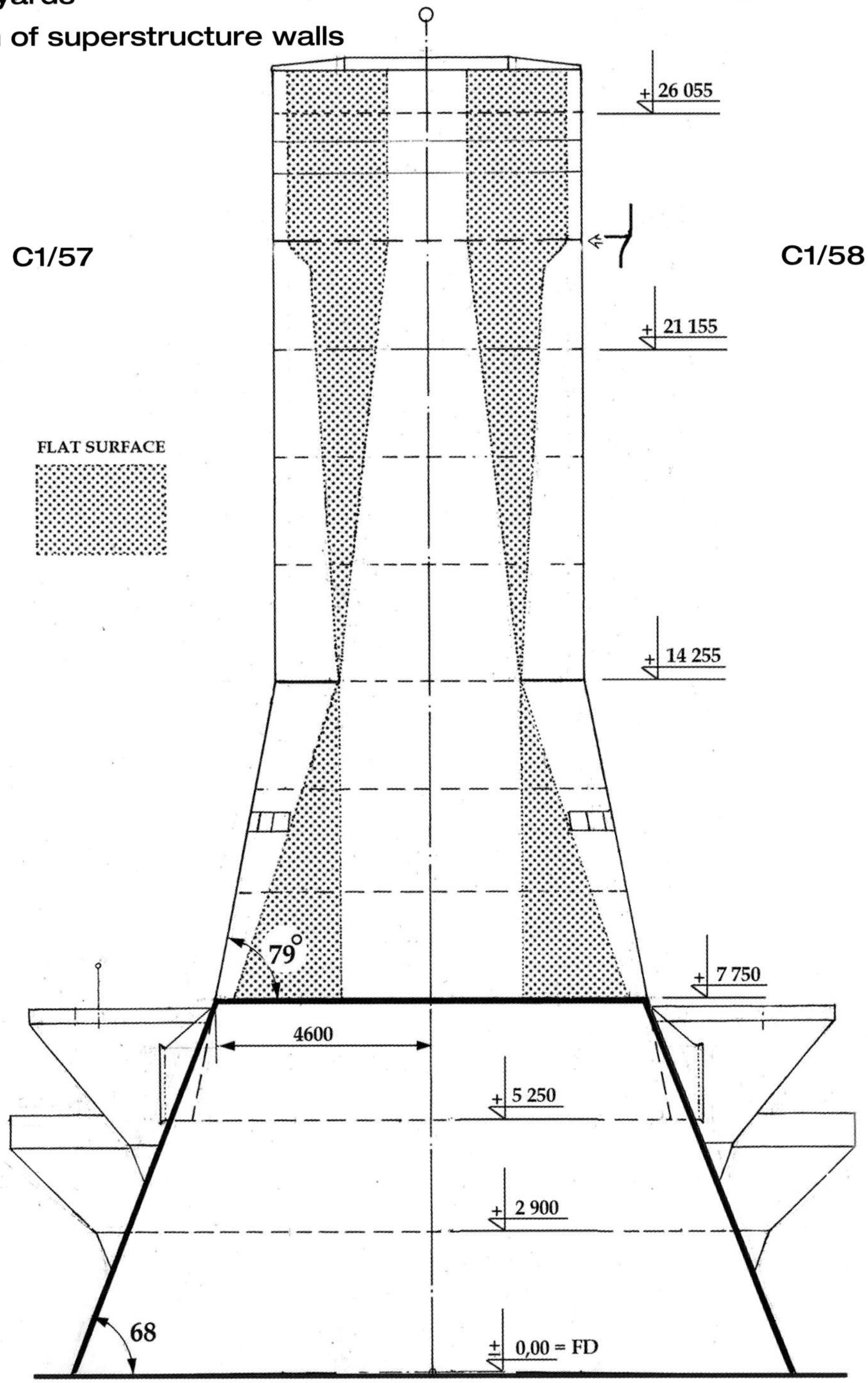

FLAT SURFACE

C1/58

+ 26 055

+ 21 155

+ 14 255

79°

+ 7 750

4600

+ 5 250

+ 2 900

68

± 0,00 = FD

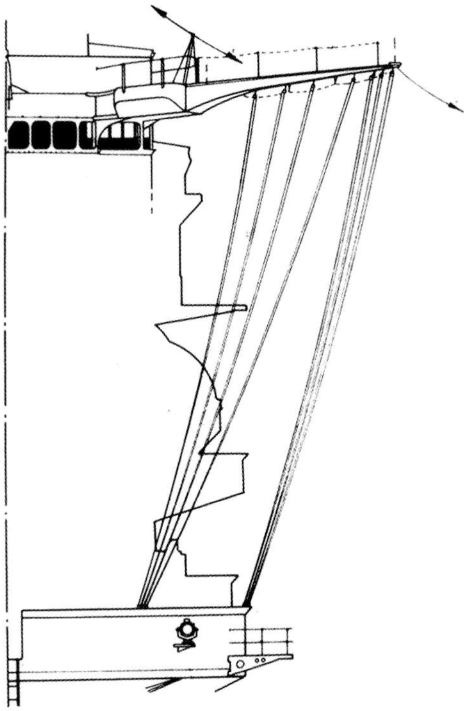

C1/59

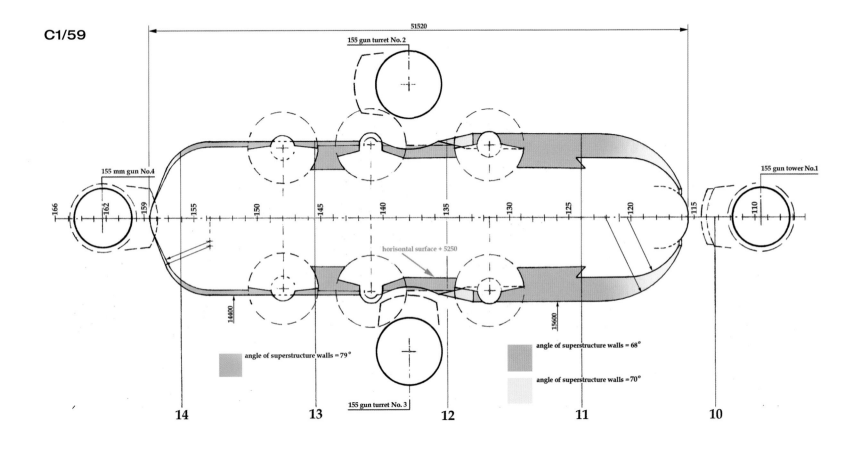

51520

155 gun turret No. 2

155 mm gun No.4

155 gun tower No.1

-166 -162 -159 -155 -150 -145 -140 -135 -130 -125 -120 -115 -110

horisontal surface + 5250

14400

15600

angle of superstructure walls = 79°

angle of superstructure walls = 68°

angle of superstructure walls = 70°

155 gun turret No. 3

14   13   12   11   10

C Superstructure

Inclination of superstructure walls

C1/60 Side view

C1/61 Section

C1/62 Plan

C1/63 Vent intake detail

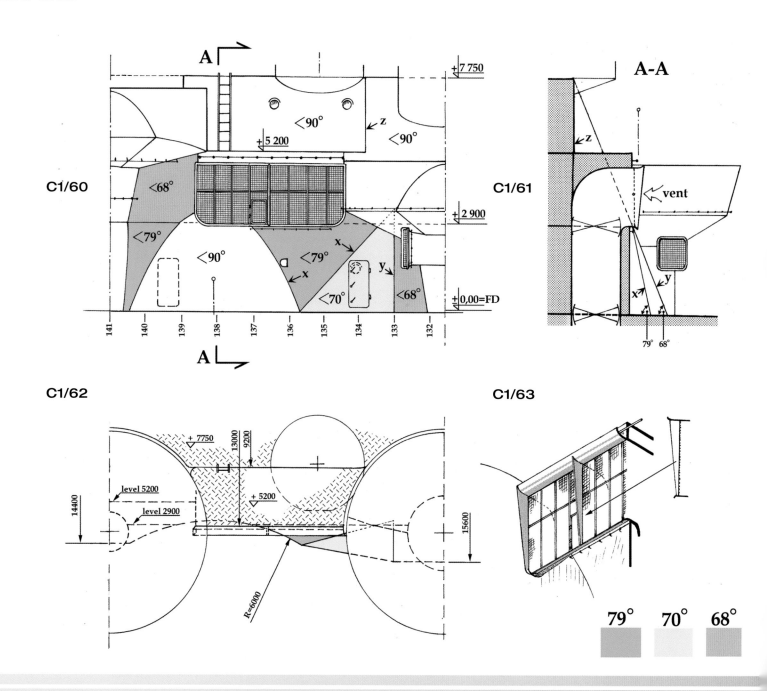

Sponson of searchlight control towers
C1/64 Plan
C1/65 Side view
C1/66 Front view
C1/67 Official Japanese Navy drawing
C1/68 Sections

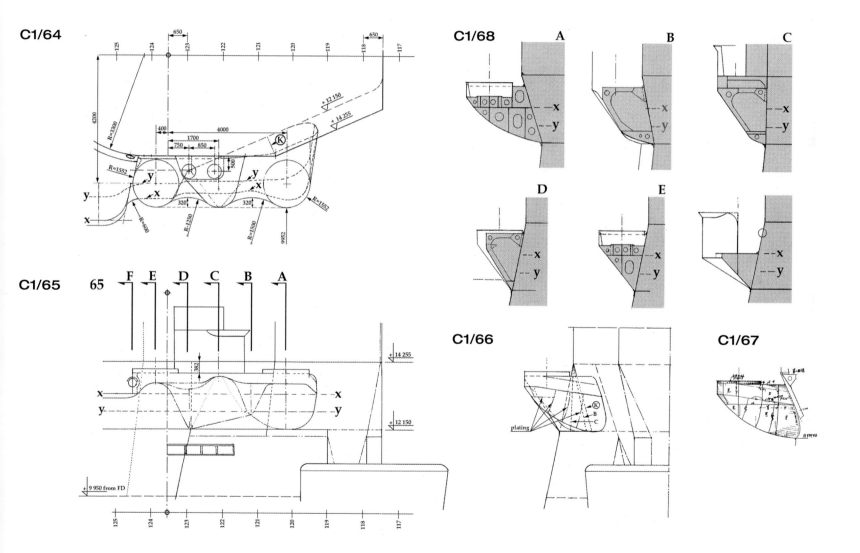

C Superstructure – Tower Bridge

Tower bridge – middle fragment with sponsons of rear searchlights control towers

C1/69 Side view

C1/70 Plan

C1/71 Sponsons

C1/72 Official Japanese Navy Drawing

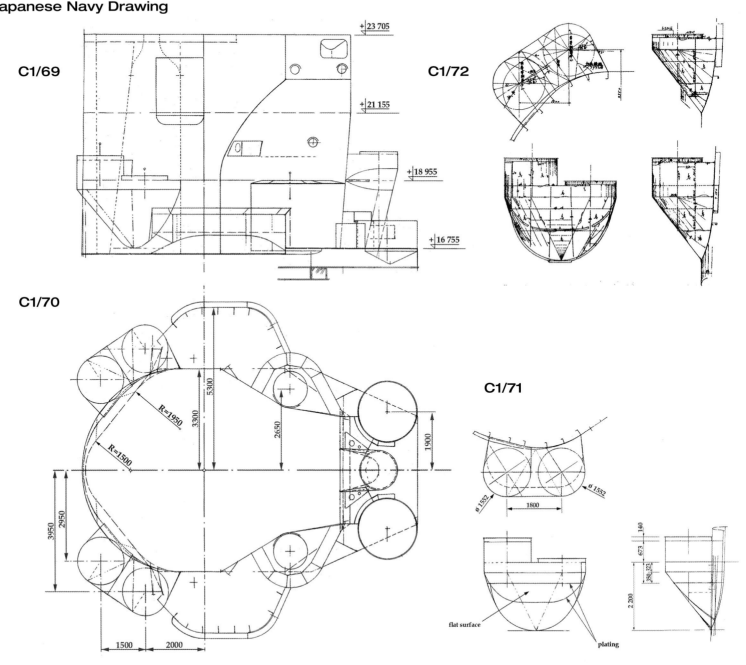

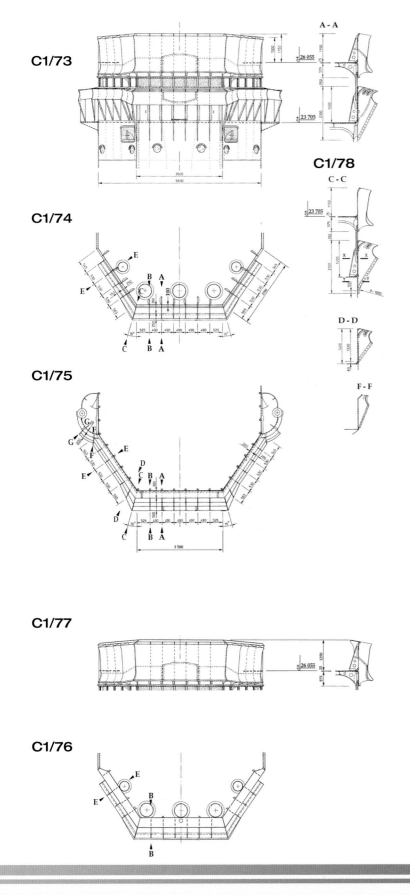

C1/73

C1/74

C1/75

C1/77

C1/76

A - A

C1/78

C - C

D - D

F - F

Wind baffle and periscope on upper part of tower bridge

C1/73 Front elevation

C1/74 Plan of air defence platform +26 055mm from upper deck level

C1/75 Plan of combat bridge compartment +23 705mm

C1/76 Upper fore part after modernisation in 1943

C1/77 Front elevation

C1/78 Sections

C1/79 Periscope window

C1/79

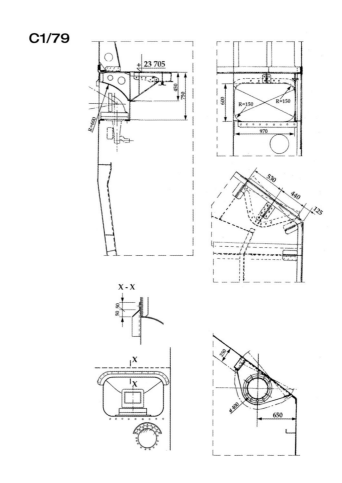

X - X

C Superstructure – Wind baffles

Wind baffle sections:

C1/80 Section of fore wall

C1/81 Section of side wall

C1/82 Detail

C1/83 Fore and side wind baffle with additional angle steel plates (400–300 x 6mm)

C1/84 Section of side small platform (*Yamato* 1941)

Grating from air defence platform level +26 055

C1/85 Section

C1/86 Plan (fragment)

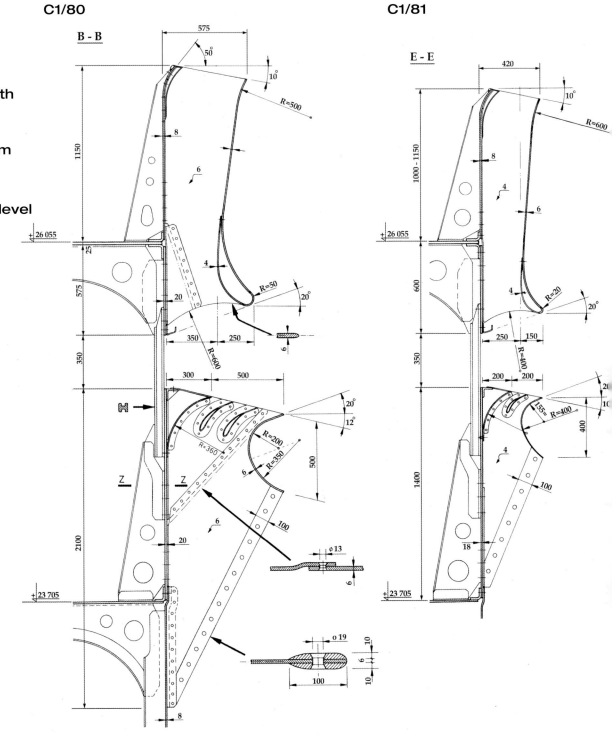

C1/80

C1/81

C1/82

A - A

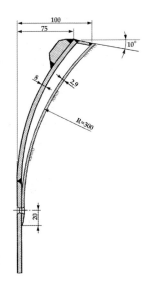

C1/83

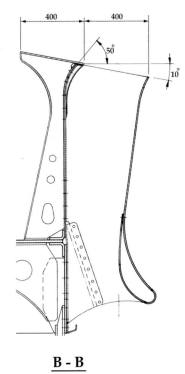

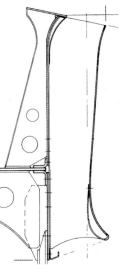

B - B

E - E

C1/84

G - G

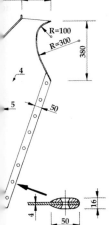

C1/85

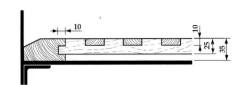

C1/86

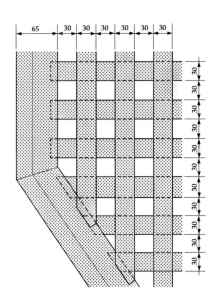

C Superstructure – Platforms

C2/1 Air defence command platform (+26 055)
        (1/150 scale)
C2/2 Fore part of platform in 1943

Construction of signal and antenna yards:
C2/3 Signal yard side sections
C2/4 Plan
C2/5 Antenna yard

C2/1

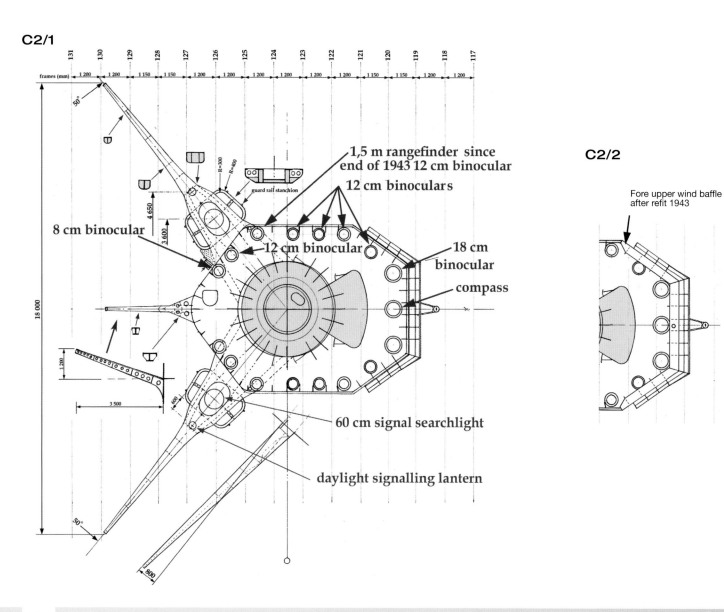

1,5 m rangefinder since
end of 1943 12 cm binocular

12 cm binoculars

8 cm binocular

12 cm binocular

18 cm binocular

compass

60 cm signal searchlight

daylight signalling lantern

guard rail stanchion

C2/2

Fore upper wind baffle
after refit 1943

C2/3

view X

C2/4

view Y

X

scupper

Y

C2/5

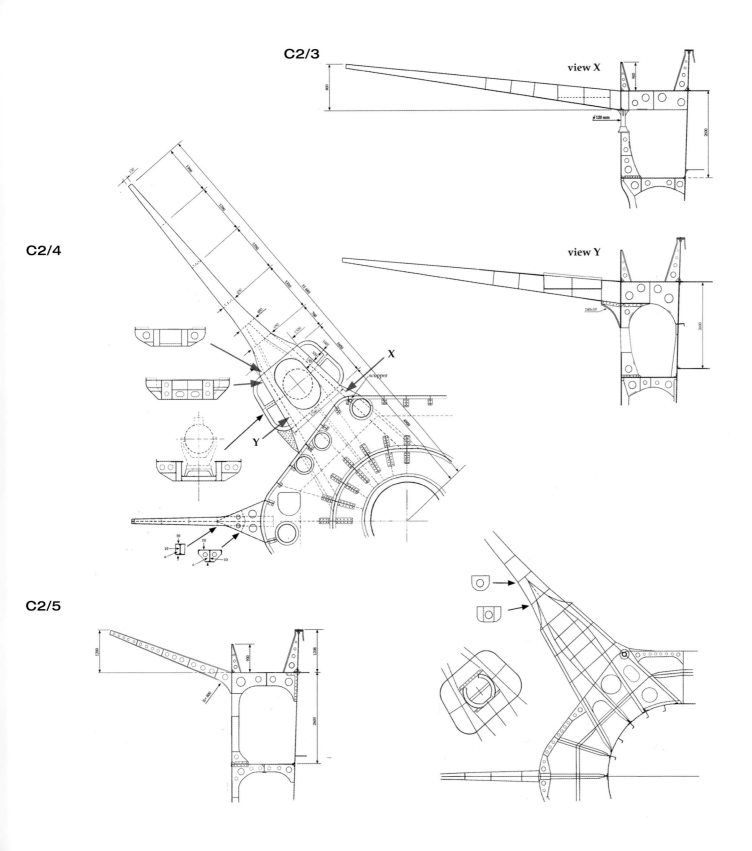

C Superstructure – Platforms

Compact bridge level +23 705 / +23 455 (1/150 scale)

C2/6 *Yamato* **1941**

C2/7 *Musashi* **1942**

C2/8 Platform level +21 155

C2/9 Platform level +18 955

C2/10 Sponsons for searchlight control towers

C2/11 Platform level +16 755

C2/6

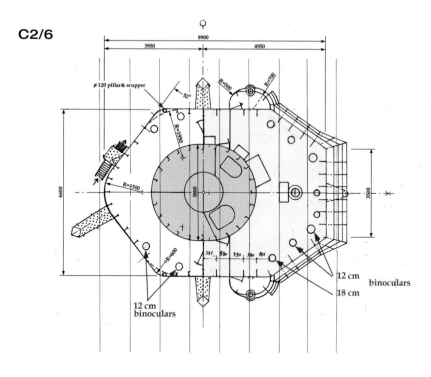

C2/7

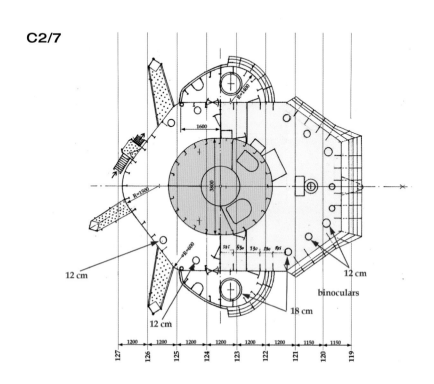

C2/8

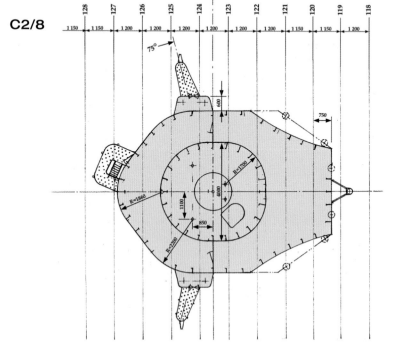

C2/9

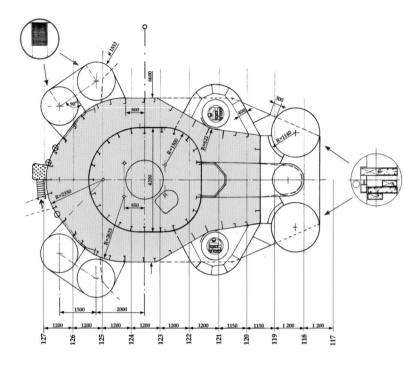

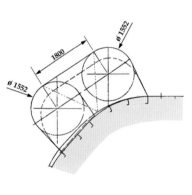

C2/10

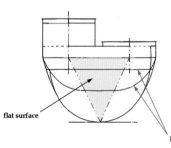

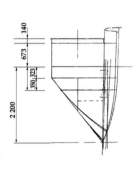

flat surface

plating

C2/11

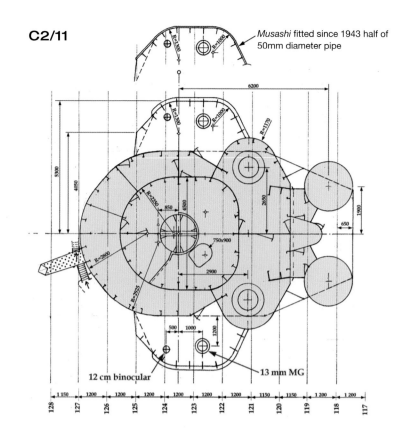

Musashi fitted since 1943 half of 50mm diameter pipe

12 cm binocular

13 mm MG

C Superstructure – Platforms

C2/12 Platform level + 14 355 in 1941 (1/150 scale)

C2/13 Signal platform in 1943

C2/14 Lower platforms of superstructure fore part
  (1/100 scale)

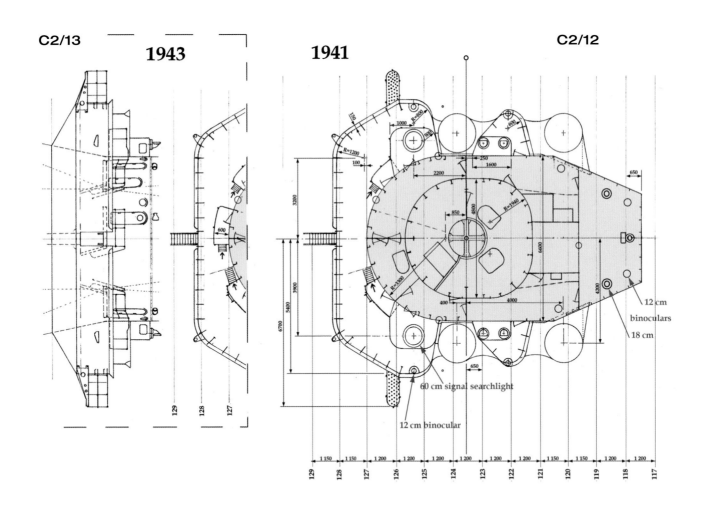

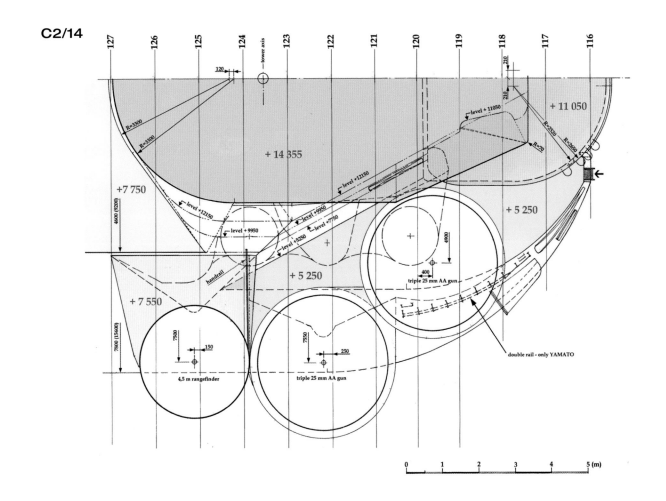

C2/14

127 126 125 124 — tower axis 123 122 121 120 119 118 117 116

120

level +11050

+ 11 050

R=3300
R=3300

+ 14 355

R=3520
R=70
R=2650

level +12150

+7 750

+ 5 250

4600 (9200)

level +12150

level +9950

level +9950

level +7750

handrail

level +5250

+ 5 250

+ 5 250

4900

400
triple 25 mm AA gun

+ 7 550

7500

150

7800 (15600)

7750

250

double rail - only YAMATO

4,5 m rangefinder

triple 25 mm AA gun

0   1   2   3   4   5 (m)

C Superstructure – Platforms

Conning Tower (1/100 scale)
C2/15 Periscope in conning tower – section
C2/16 Conning tower compartment plan

Upper part of rear tower
C2/17 Support plates
C2/18 Plan of support plates

Rear part of superstructure levels
C2/19 Rear elevation
C2/20 Plan
C2/21 Bottom view of 25mm MG sponsons

C2/17

C2/18

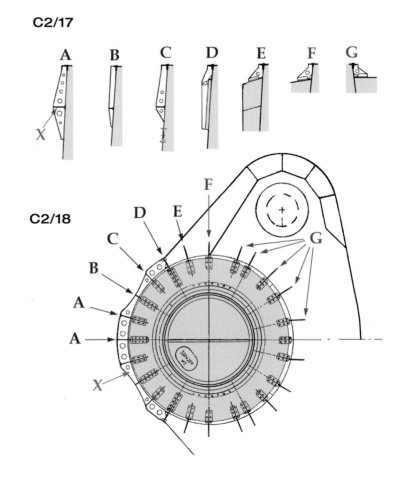

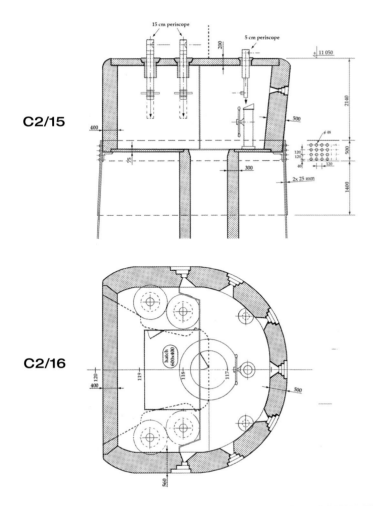

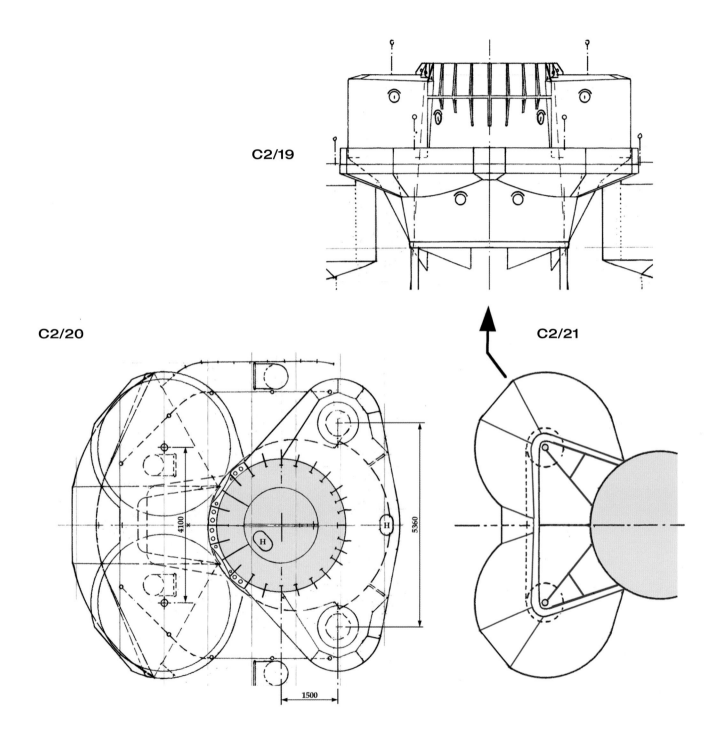

C2/19

C2/20

C2/21

C Superstructure – Platforms

Yamato/Musashi superstructure 1941–1943
(1/200 scale)

C2/22 Plan of lower decks of superstructure

C2/23 Rear view

C2/24 Plan of lower platforms

C2/24 Profile of rear part

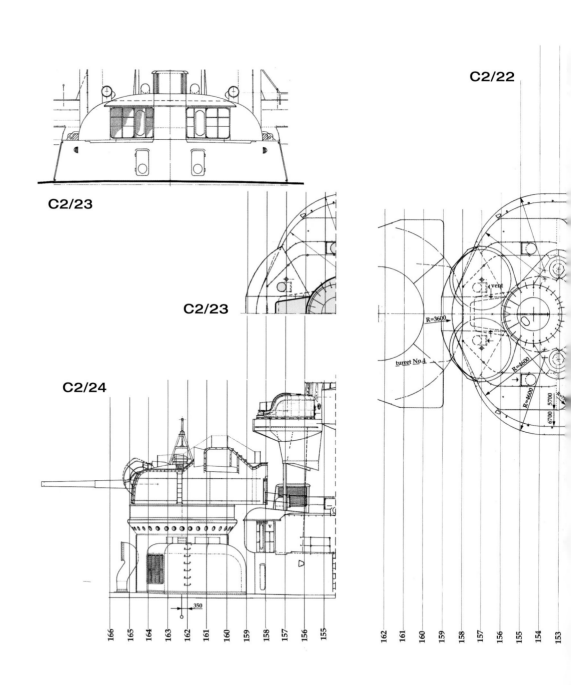

C2/22

C2/23

C2/23

C2/24

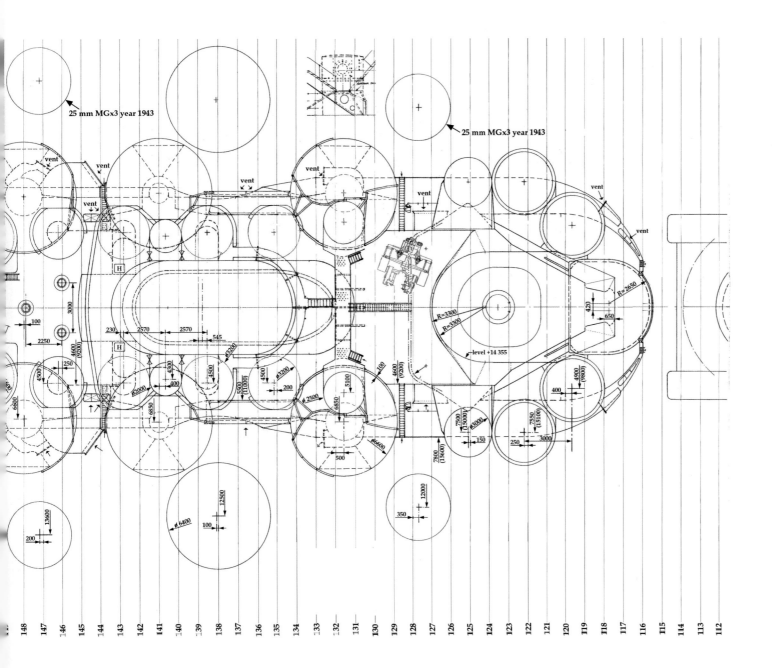

25 mm MGx3 year 1943

25 mm MGx3 year 1943

C Superstructure – Platforms

C2/25 *Yamato* (*Musashi*) 1944-45 plan (1/200 scale)

C2/26 *Musashi* 1944 – differences in comparison to
      Yamato

C2/26

C2/25

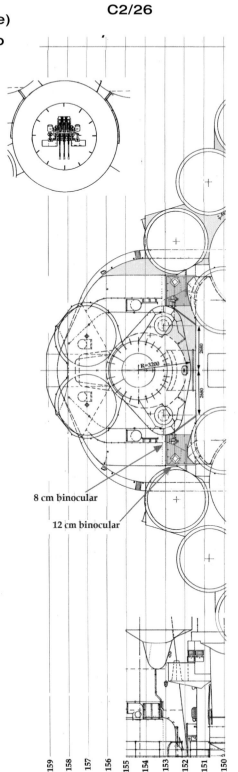

8 cm binocular

12 cm binocular

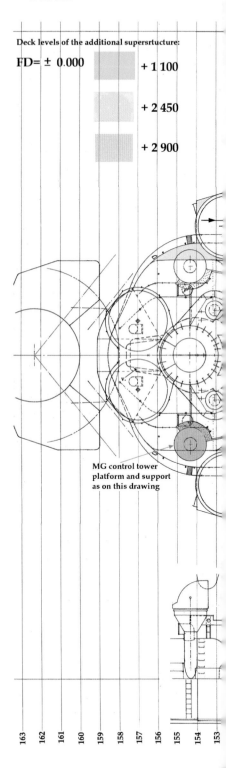

Deck levels of the additional supersrtucture:

FD= ± 0.000   + 1 100

+ 2 450

+ 2 900

MG control tower
platform and support
as on this drawing

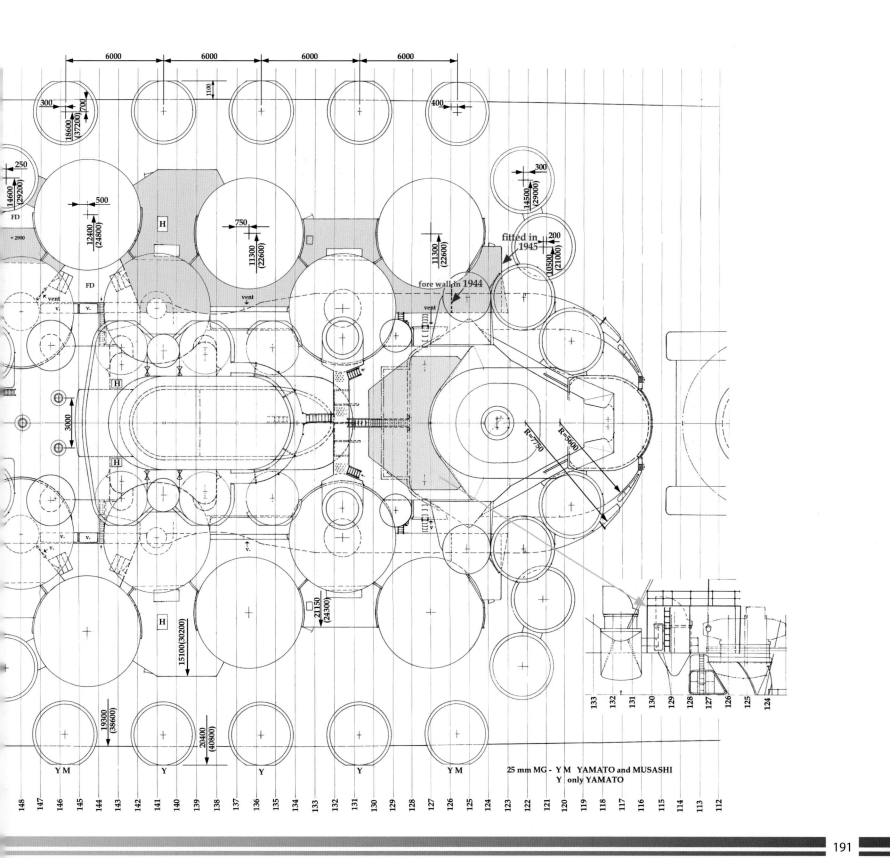

25 mm MG - Y M YAMATO and MUSASHI
Y only YAMATO

C Superstructure – Funnel

C3/1 Starboard profile (1/150 scale)

C3/2 Front elevation of lower part

C3/3 Details of steam pipe

C3/4 Detail of air space rain cover

C3/5 Section X-X

C3/6 Side detail of rain cover

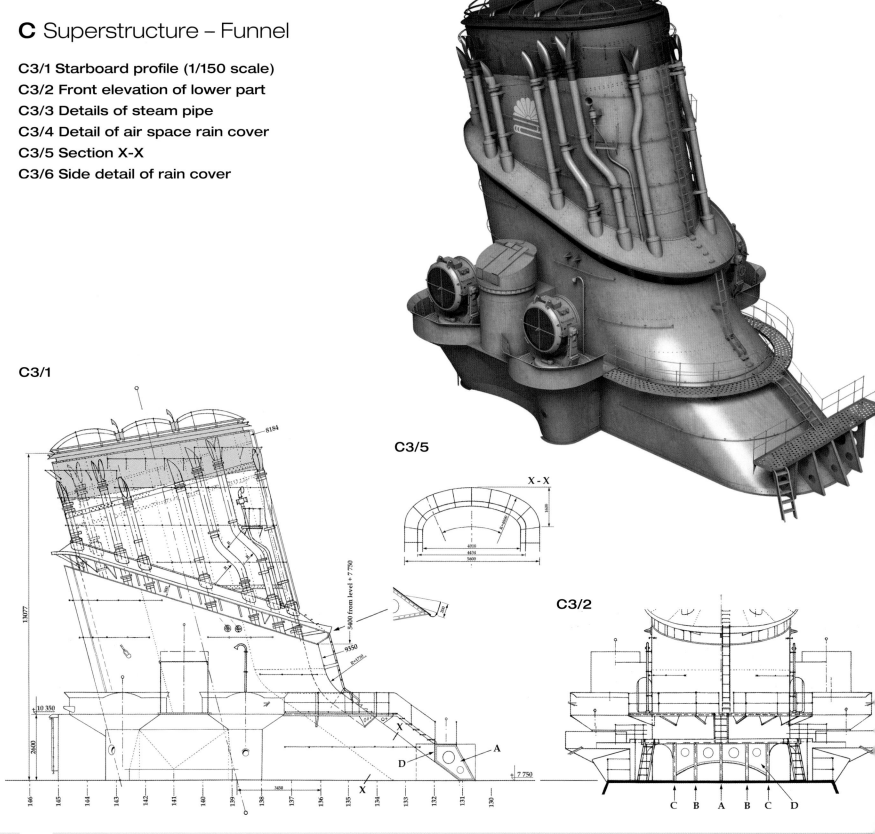

C3/1

C3/5

X - X

C3/2

C3/3

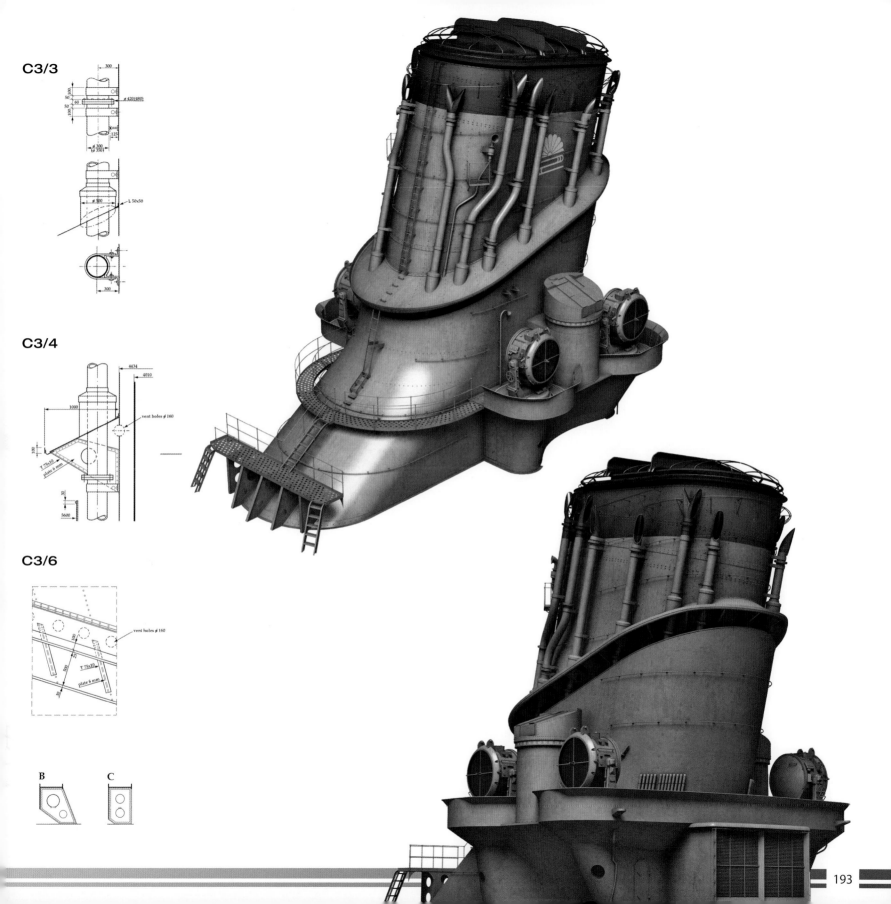

C3/4

C3/6

B   C

C Superstructure – Funnel

C3/7 Front elevation (1/150 scale)

C3/8 Rear elevation

C3/9 Plan of fog horn

C3/10 Detail of riveting

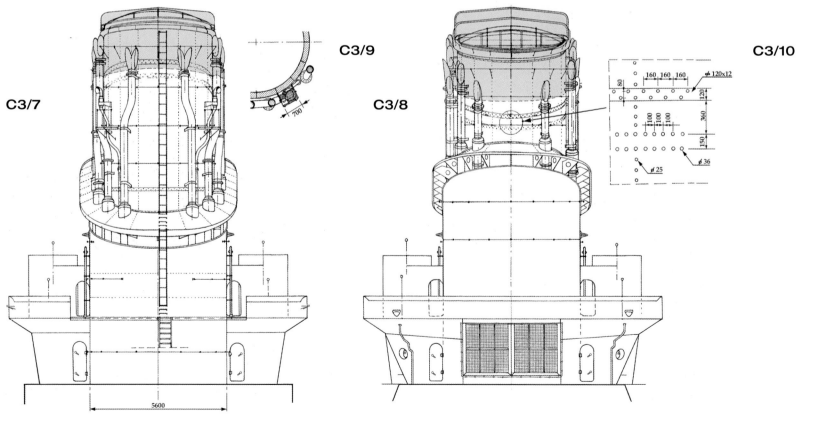

C3/7

C3/9

C3/8

C3/10

C3/11 Plan with 150cm searchlight platform
C3/12 Plan of steam pipes and division plates
C3/13 Upper part of steam pipes

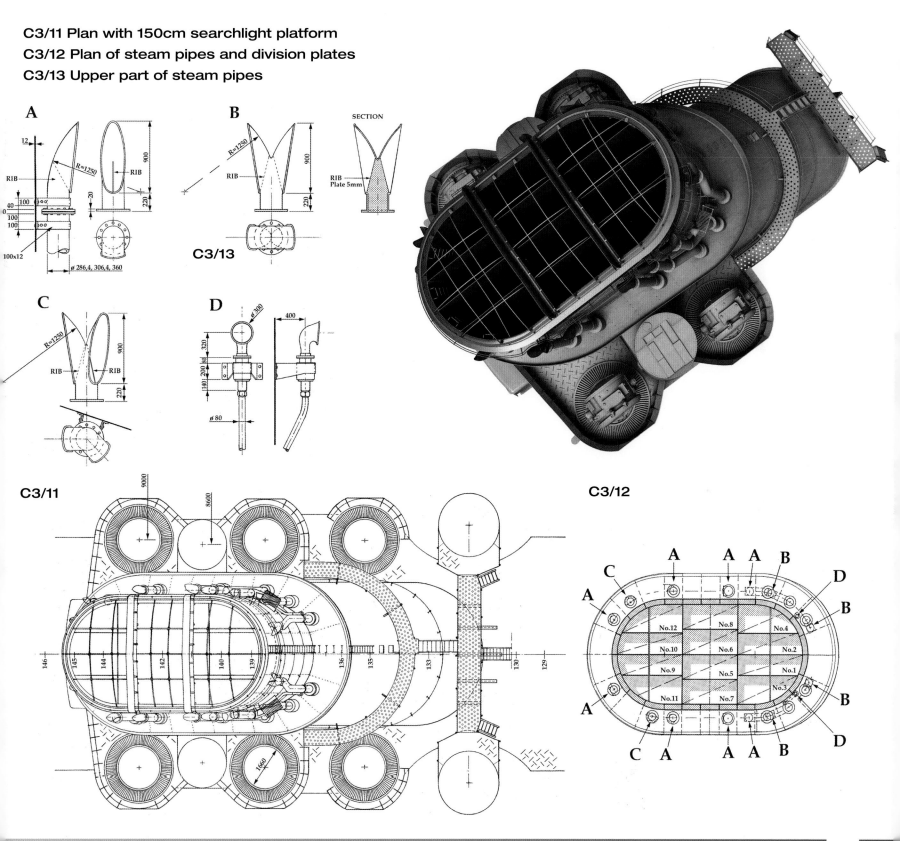

A

12
RIB
R=1250
RIB
900
220
40 100
0
100
100
20
100x12
ø 286,4, 306,4, 360

B

R=1250
RIB
900
220

SECTION
RIB
Plate 5mm

C3/13

C

R=1250
RIB
RIB
900
220

D

ø 300
400
320
200 80
140
ø 80

C3/11

9000
8600
146 145 144 142 140 139 136 135 133 130 129
1660

C3/12

A A A B
C
A
D
A
B
No.12 No.8 No.4
No.10 No.6 No.2
No.9 No.5 No.1
B
No.11 No.7 No.3
A
D
C A A A B

195

C Superstructure – Funnel

C3/14 Funnel dimensions
　　　(1/150 scale)

C3/15 Section (scheme)

C3/16 Geometrical form of
　　　searchlights platform support

C3/17 Section at frame 141

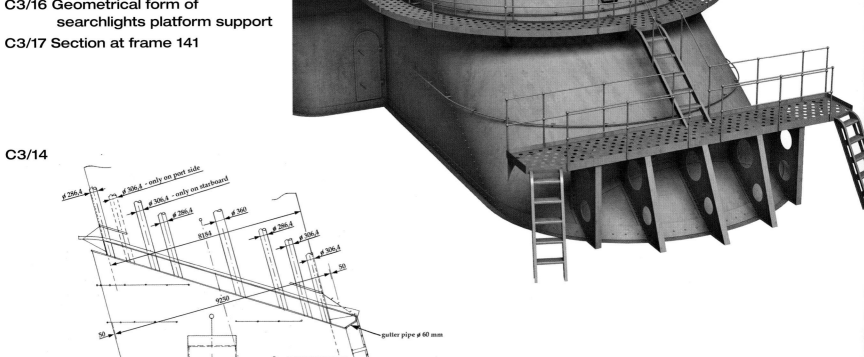

C3/14

ø 286,4
ø 306,4 - only on port side
ø 306,4 - only on starboard
ø 286,4
ø 360
8184
ø 286,4
ø 306,4
ø 306,4
50
9250
50
gutter pipe ø 60 mm

+ 10 350
C-6
C-5
C-4
C-3
C-2
C-1
C-0
WTD 1535x635
+ 7 750

146 145 144 143 142 141 140 139 138 137 136 135 134 133 132 131 130

C3/15

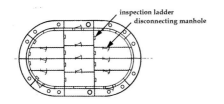

inspection ladder
disconnecting manhole

C3/16

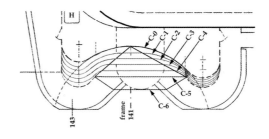

H
C-0 C-1 C-2 C-3 C-4
C-5
C-6
143
frame 141

C3/17

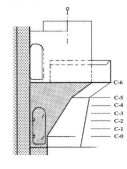

C-6
C-5
C-4
C-3
C-2
C-1
C-0

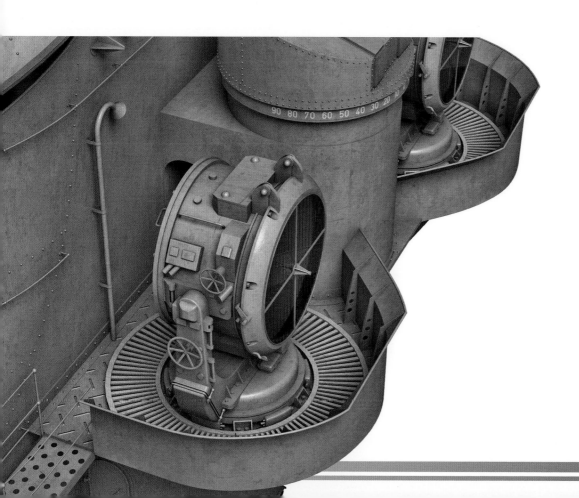

C Superstructure – Funnel

C3/18 Details of hood (no scale)
C3/19 Wind shield and gutter
C3/20 Section
C3/21 Wind shield and gutter
C3/22 Longitudinal section
C3/23 Casting ang uptake

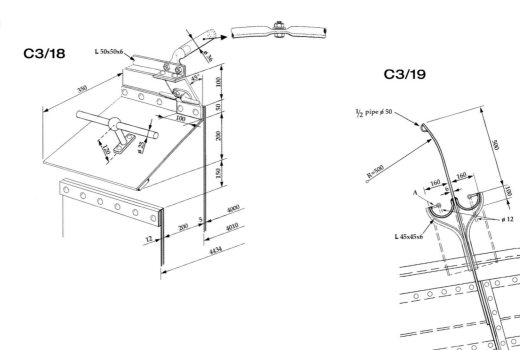

C3/18

C3/19

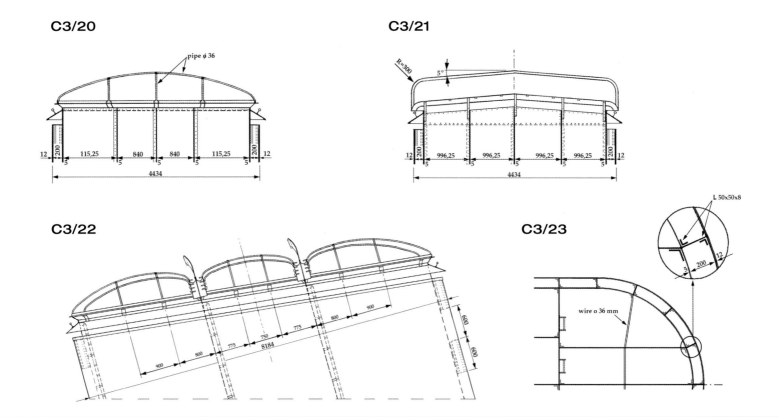

C3/20

C3/21

C3/22

C3/23

C3/24 White-painted chrysanthemum crest at 'Ten Ichi Gō' Operation (April 1945)

C3/25 Imperial Japanese Navy ensign

C3/26 Vice Admiral's flag

C3/27 Jack

C3/28 Main mast flags as flown on 5–7 April 1945 with Samurai banner

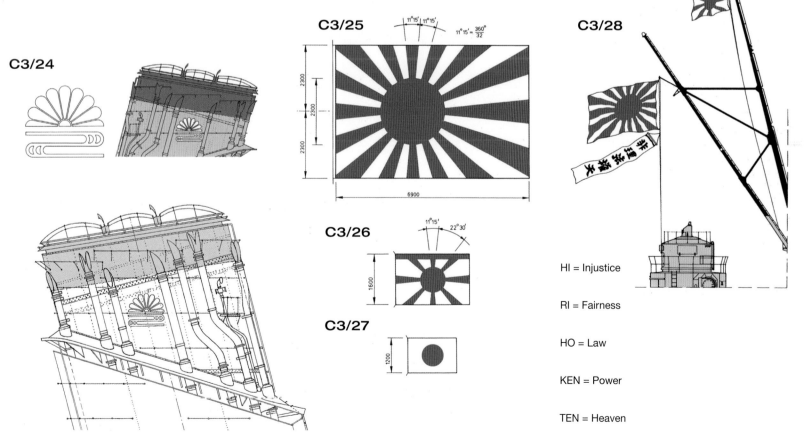

C3/24

C3/25

$11°15' \quad 11°15'$

$11°15' = \frac{360°}{32}$

2300
2300
2300

6900

C3/26

$11°15' \quad 22°30'$

1600

C3/27

1200

C3/28

HI = Injustice

RI = Fairness

HO = Law

KEN = Power

TEN = Heaven

D Rig – Tripod Main Mast

Main mast in the years 1941–43 (1/150 scale)
D1/1 Mast – painting and dimensions
D1/2 Profile

D1/1

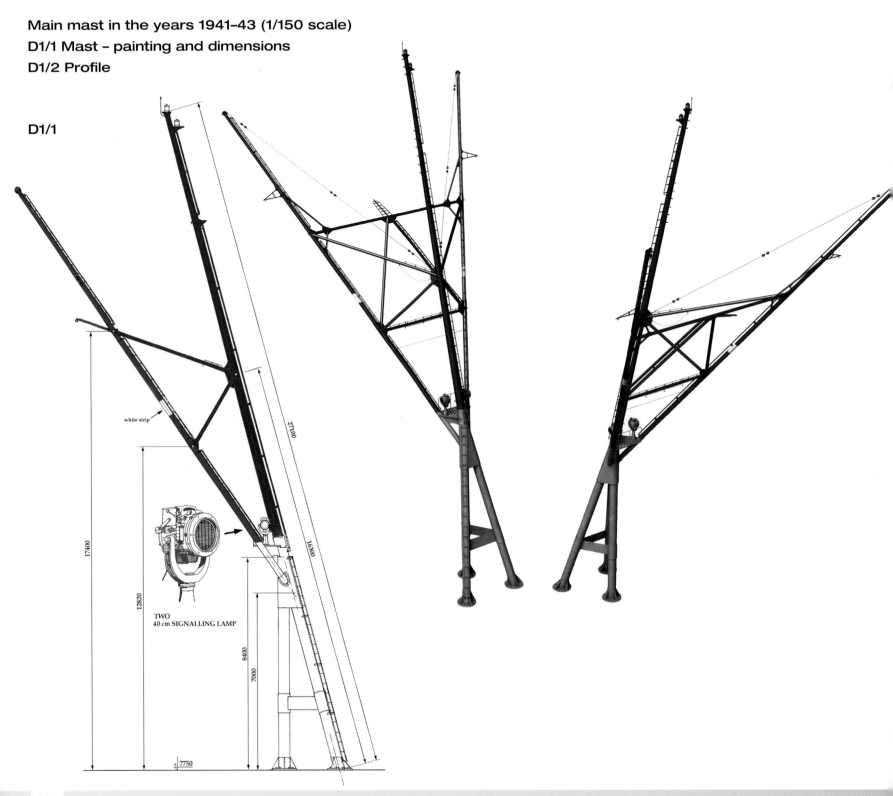

white strip

17400

12820

TWO
40 cm SIGNALLING LAMP

8400

7000

7750

27100

16300

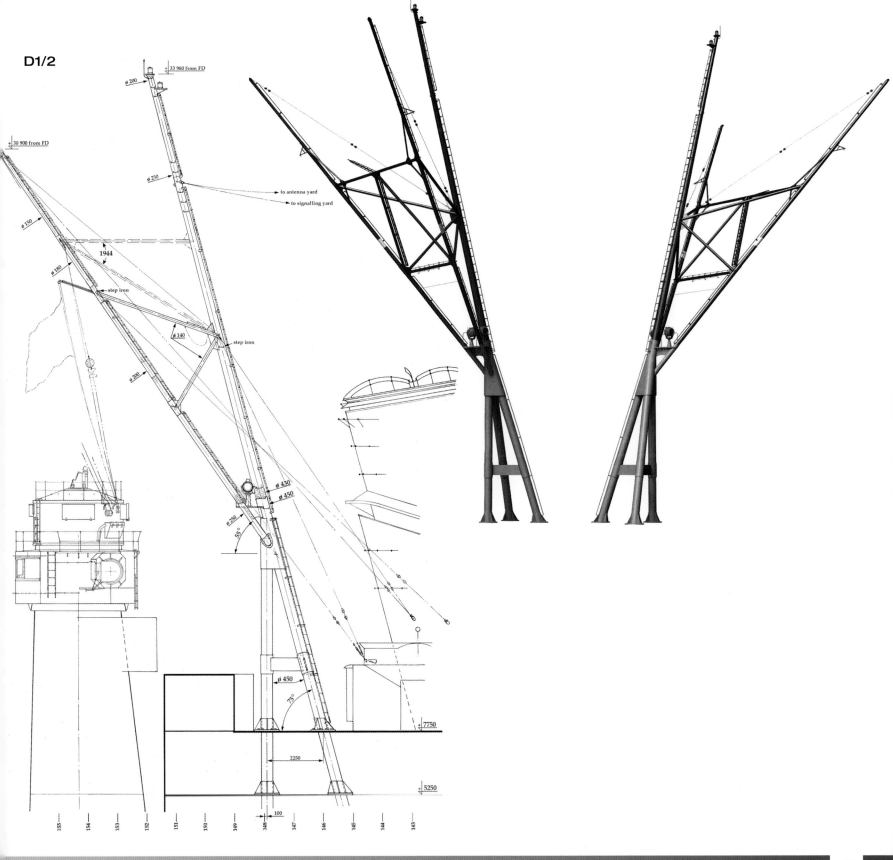

D1/2

+ 33 960 from FD
ø 200
+ 30 900 from FD
ø 250
ø 150
1944
ø 180
step iron
ø 140
step iron
ø 200
to antenna yard
to signalling yard
ø 430
ø 450
ø 250
55°
ø 450
75°
+ 7750
2250
+ 5250
100

155 154 153 152 151 150 149 148 147 146 145 144 143

D Rig – Tripod Main Mast

D1/3 View from bow direction (1/150 scale)
D1/4 Ladder *Musashi* and *Yamato*
D1/5 Scheme of mast 1941-43
D1/6 Scheme of mast 1943-45

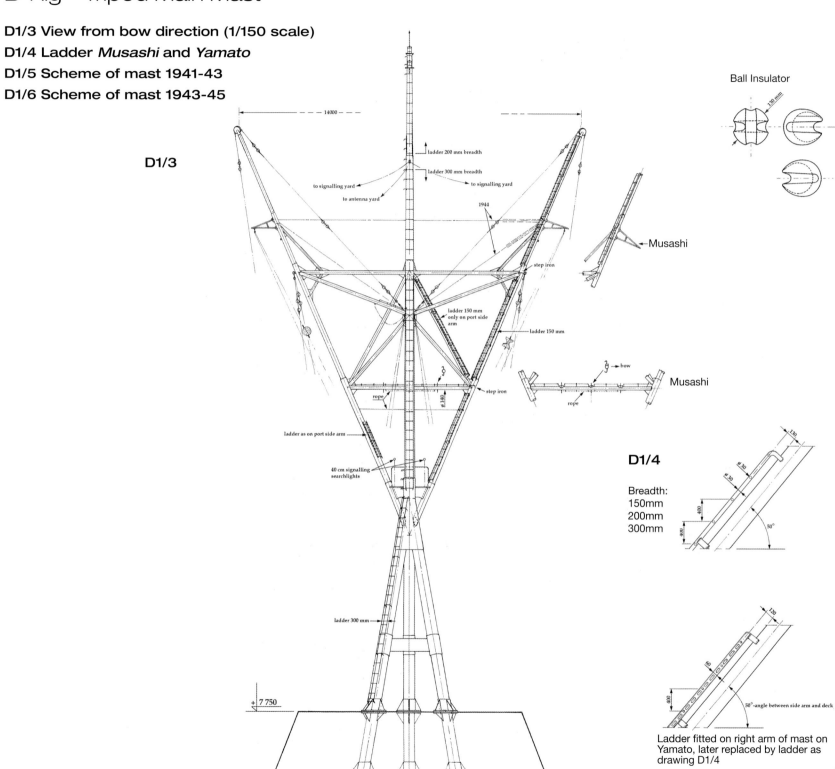

D1/3

14000

ladder 200 mm breadth

ladder 300 mm breadth

to signalling yard

to signalling yard

to antenna yard

1944

step iron

ladder 150 mm
only on port side
arm

ladder 150 mm

Musashi

step iron

rope

ø 140

bow

ladder as on port side arm

Musashi

rope

40 cm signalling
searchlights

ladder 300 mm

+ 7 750

Ball Insulator

130 mm

D1/4

Breadth:
150mm
200mm
300mm

130

ø 30

ø 30

400

400

50°

130

ø 5

400

50°-angle between side arm and deck

Ladder fitted on right arm of mast on
Yamato, later replaced by ladder as
drawing D1/4

202

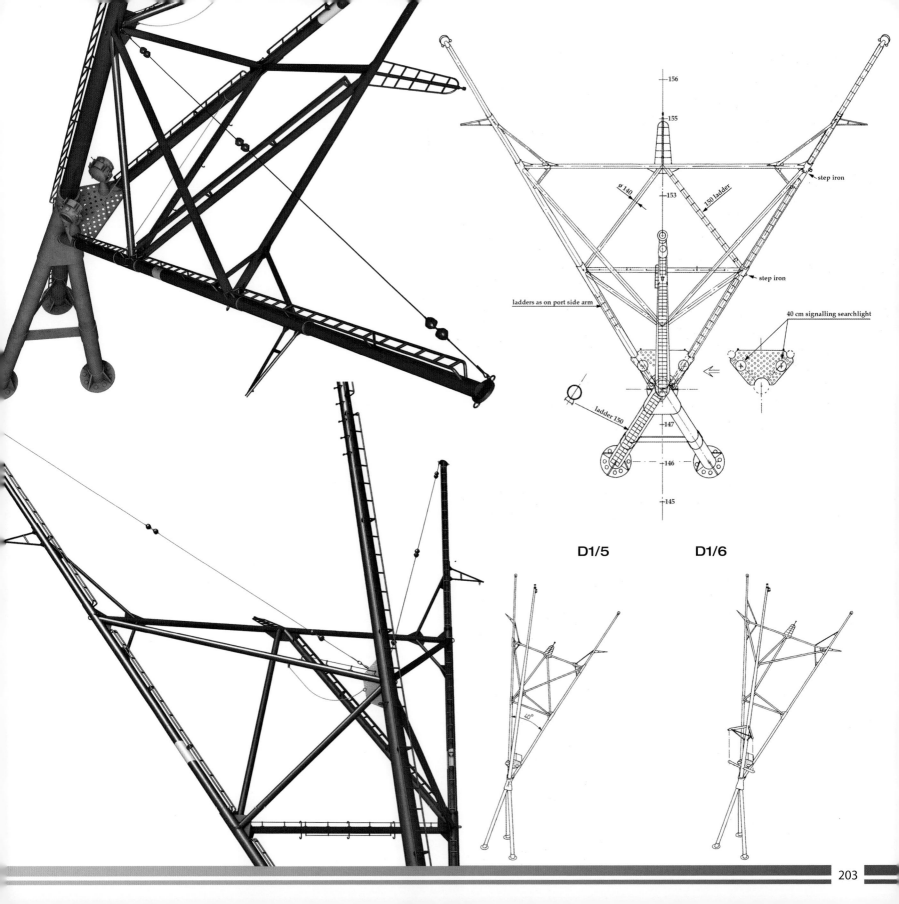

156

155

ø 140

153

150 ladder

step iron

step iron

ladders as on port side arm

40 cm signalling searchlight

ladder 150

147

146

145

D1/5

D1/6

40°

D Rig – Tripod Main Mast

Tripod mast after modernisation (1/150 scale)

D1/7 Profile

D1/8 Front view after April 1944

D1/9 Type 13 ('13 Gō') radar antenna

D1/10 Enlarged antenna arms after December 1944

D1/11 Plan after April 1944

D1/12 Plan after December 1944

D1/8

+ 33 960 from FD

+ 30 900

42 30

+ 15 900 from FD

ladders similiar
to former version

D1/9

14000

ladder 200 mm breadth

ladder 300 mm breadth

to signalling yard

to signalling yard

to antenna yard

rig similiar to
former version

3 100

D1/10

1050

1000

1050

D1/11

5 100

D1/12

upper
support

lower
support

1550   1550

D1/13

upper
support

lower
support

2550   2550

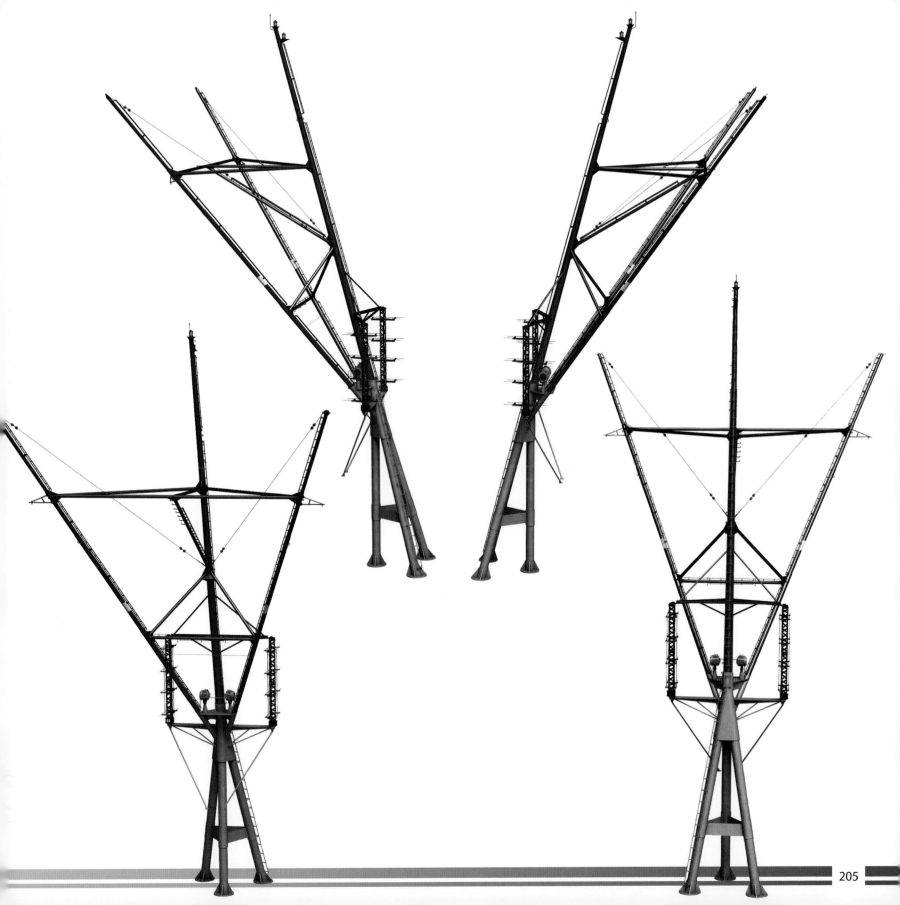

D Rig – Antenna Mast

Antenna mast with crane for aircraft and boats
(1/150 scale)

D1/14 Rear view of mast

D1/15 Profile view

D1/14

D1/15

D1/16 Plan

D1/17 Antenna mast after December 1944

D1/18 Perspective

D1/19 Scheme of crane tackle

D1/17

D1/18

D1/16

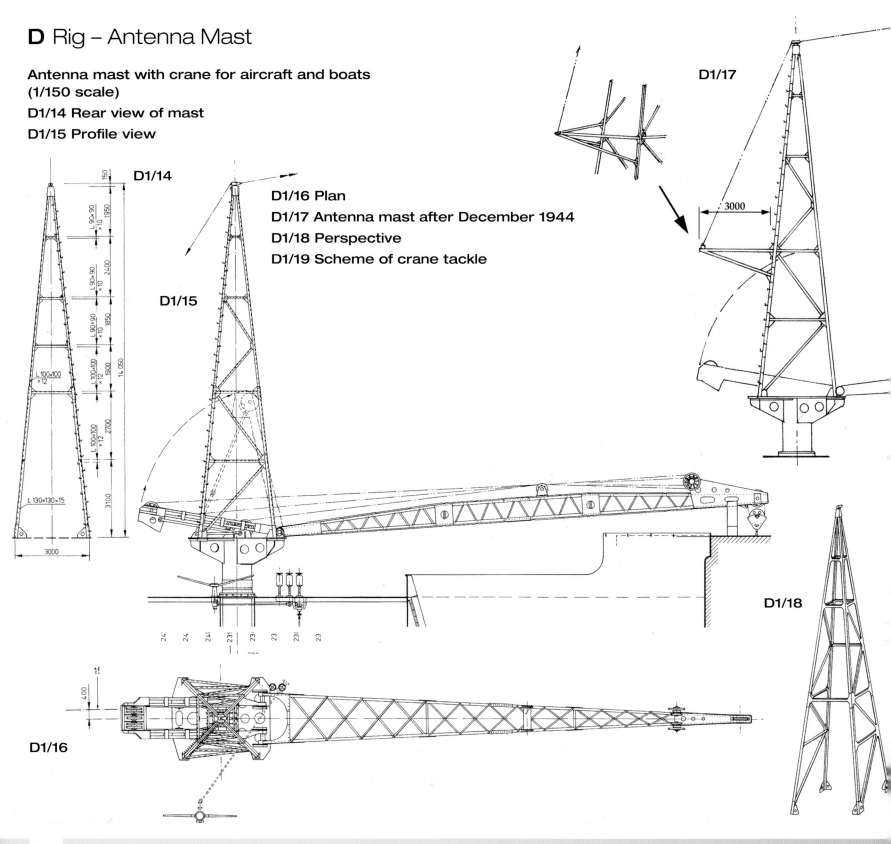

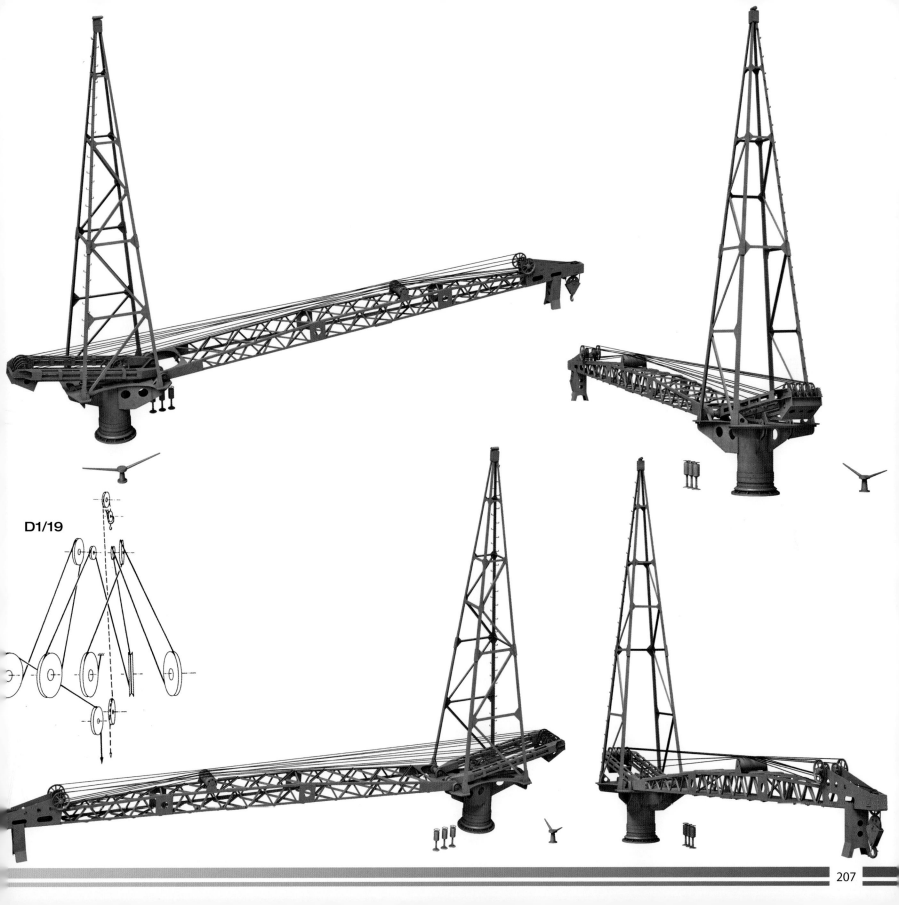

D1/19

D Rig – Crane

Crane Jib (1/100 scale)
D1/20 Profile
D1/21 Plan
D1/22 Bottom view
D1/23 Sections

Crane platform
D1/24 Plan
D1/25 Section A-A
D1/26 Profile
D1/27 Front view
D1/28 Rear view
D1/29 Section B-B

D1/24
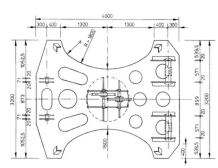

D1/25
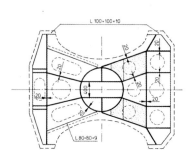

D1/29

D1/26 **D1/27** **D1/28**
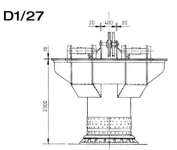

D1/20
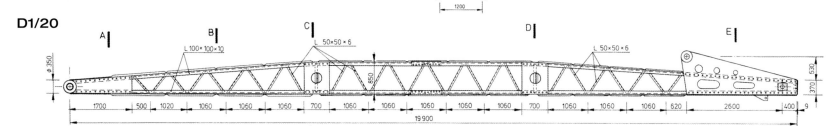

D1/21
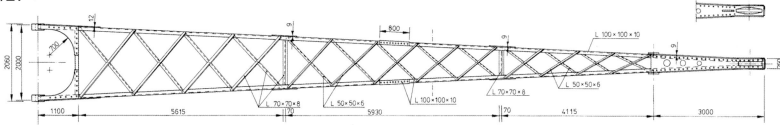

D1/22

D1/23

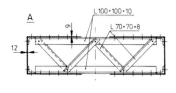
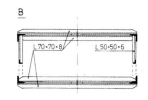
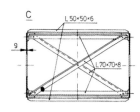
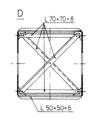
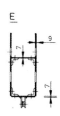

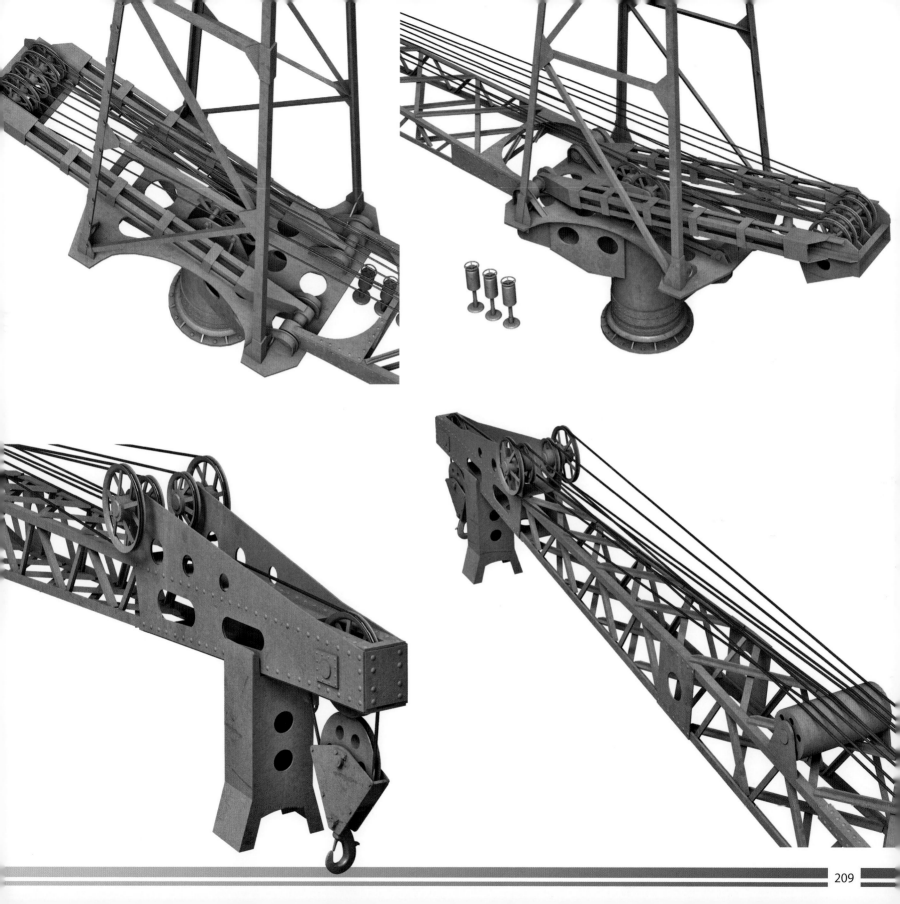

D Rig – Crane

Crane details (no scale)

D1/30 Crane rear frame with luff pulleys – profile

D1/31 Plan

D1/32 Bottom view and sections

D1/33 Folding bracket of rear frame – profile, plan and details

D1/34 Crane hook – front view, section, profile

D1/35 Fore and aft luff pulleys

D1/36 Pulley from platform base

D1/37 Crane electric motor
(this type used as winch for paravane)

D1/38 Deck support of crane arm

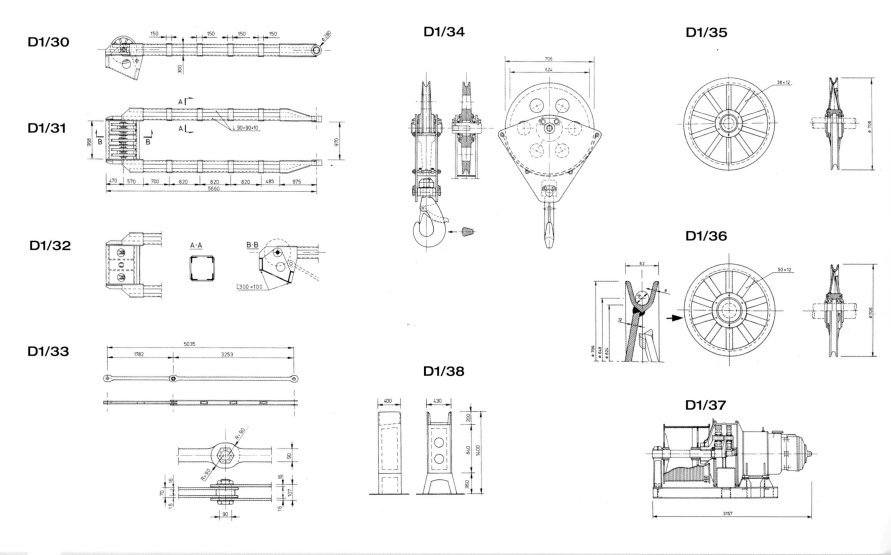

D1/30

D1/31

D1/32

D1/33

D1/34

D1/35

D1/36

D1/37

D1/38

D Rig – Ensign Staff

Ensign staff (1/100 scale)
D2/1 View from astern
D2/2 Side view

D2/1

D2/2

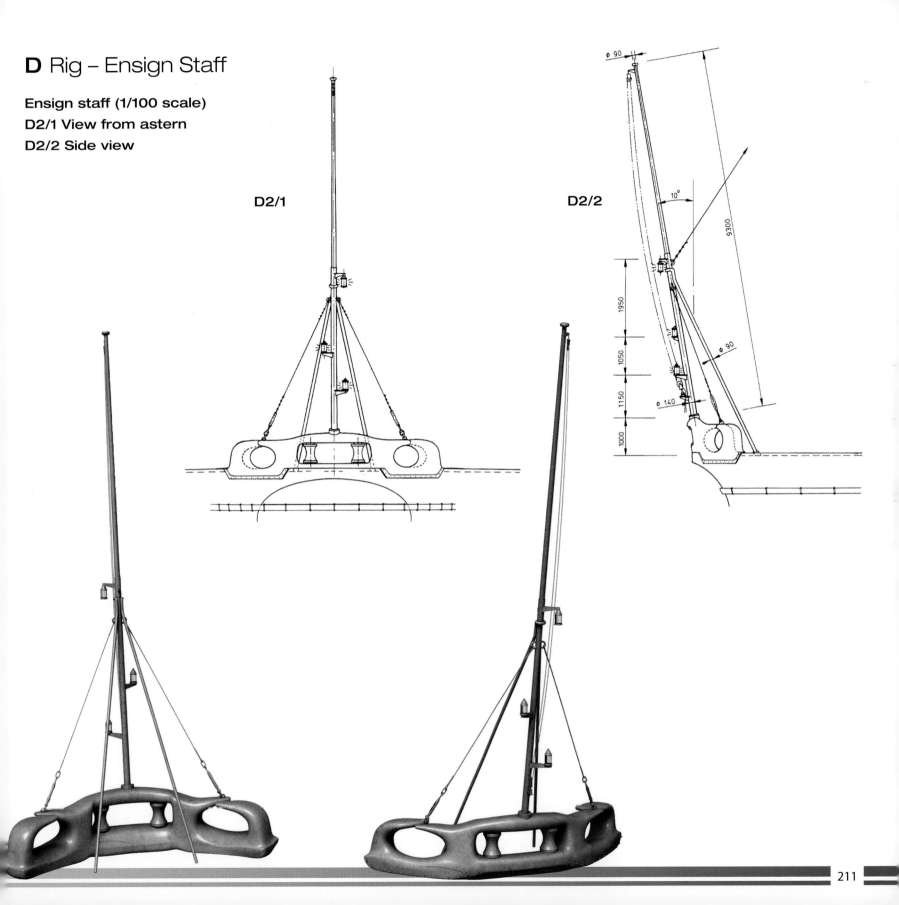

E Armament – 46cm Guns

E1/1 46cm gun turret no.2 – elevation (1/150 scale)
E1/2 Turret no.2 – plan
E1/3 Turret no.3 – plan

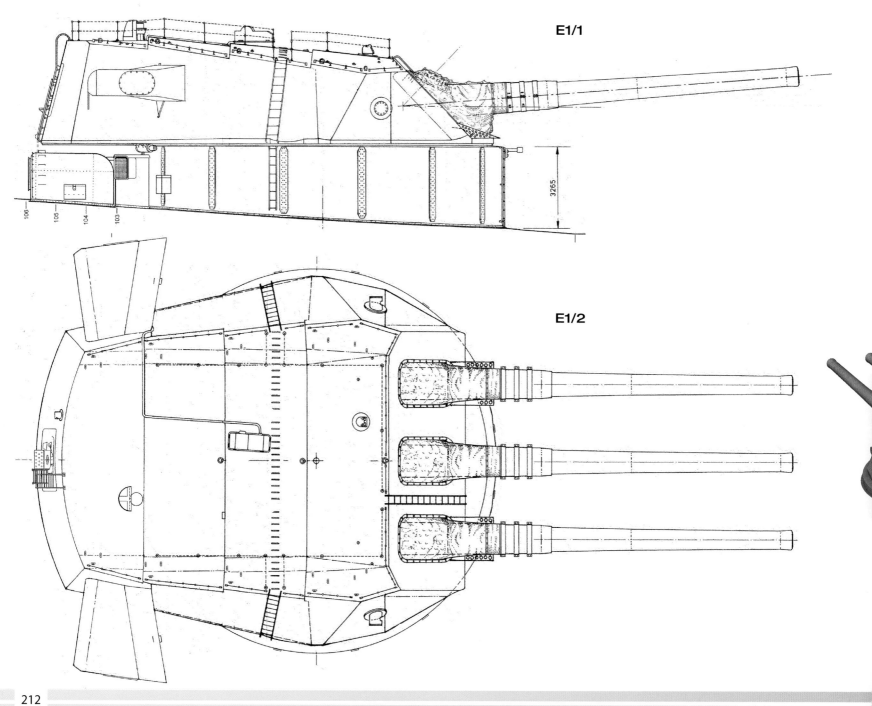

E1/1

E1/2

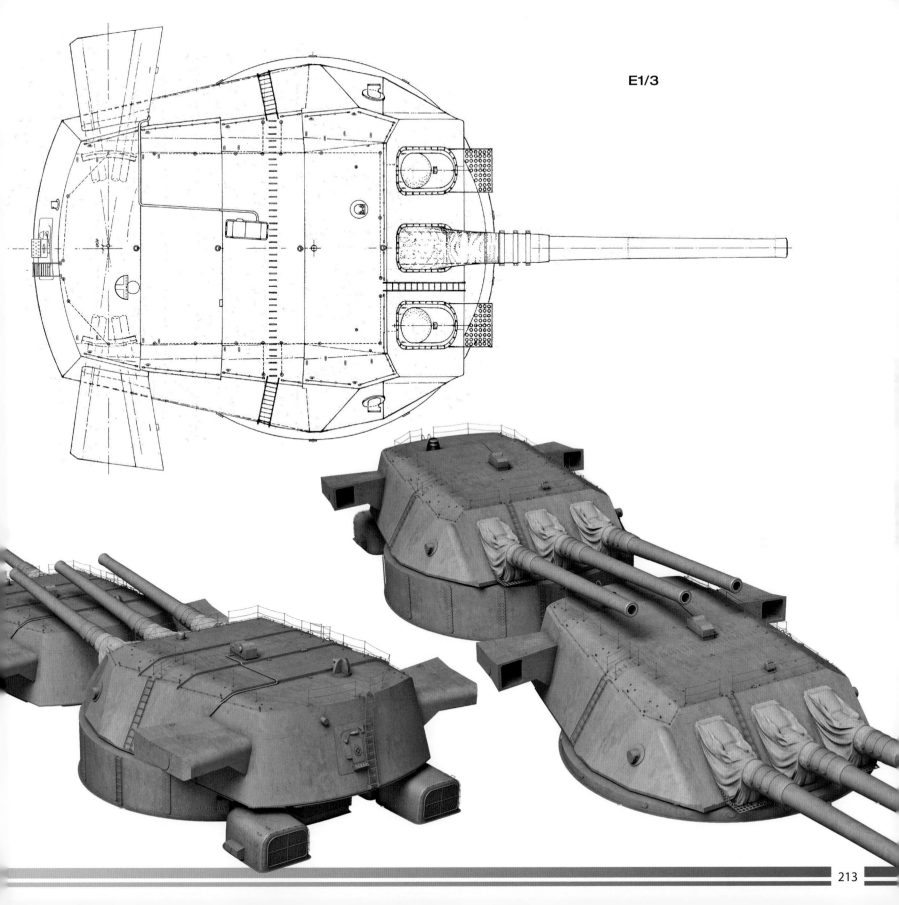

E1/3

E Armament – 46cm Guns

E1/4 Turret no.2 rear view (1/150 scale)

E1/5 Turret no.3 rear view

E1/6 Turret no.1 front view

E1/7 Fragment of front elevation

E1/8 Rear ladder of turret

Barbette of turret no.1 max. Height = 600mm
Barbette of turret no.3 max. Height = 900mm

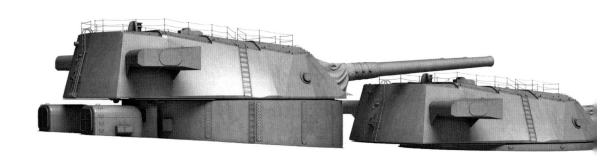

E1/4

E1/5

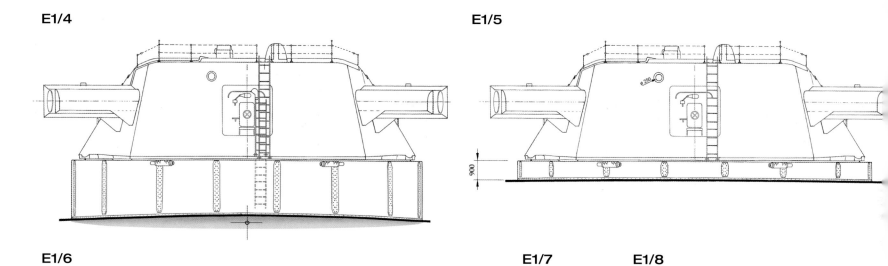

E1/6

E1/7   **E1/8**

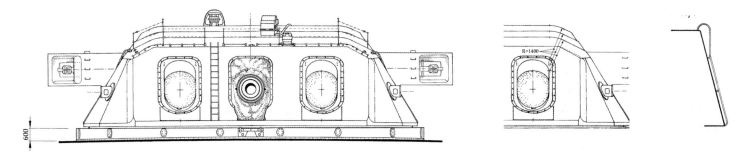

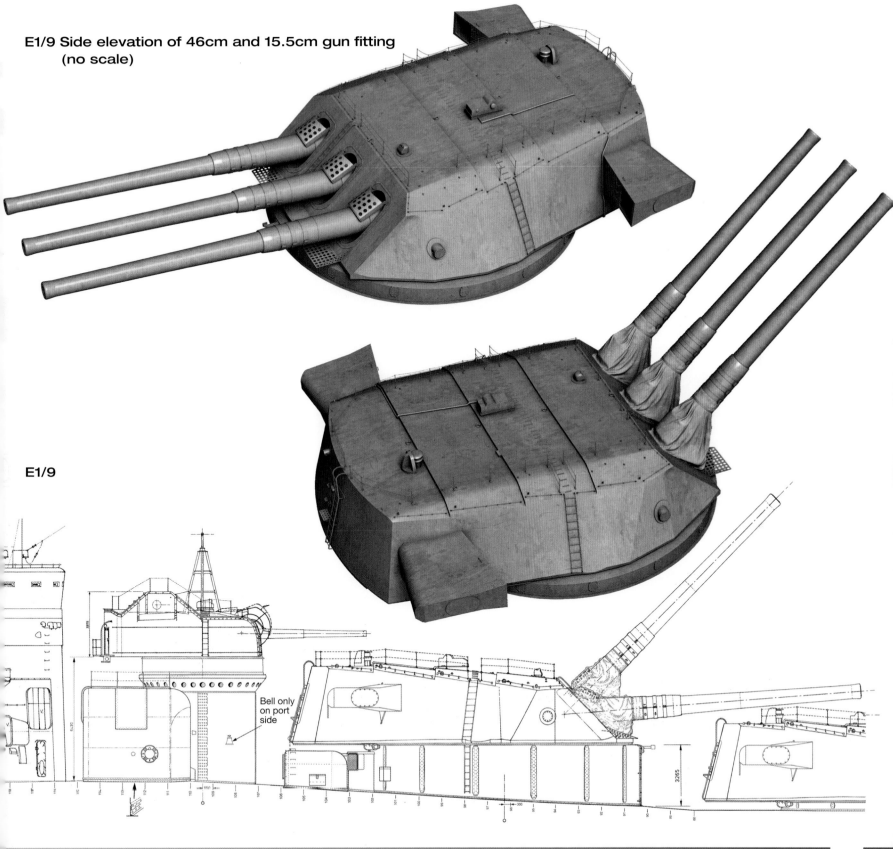

E1/9 Side elevation of 46cm and 15.5cm gun fitting
(no scale)

E1/9

Bell only
on port
side

E Armament – 46cm Guns

E1/10 Rear view of turret no.2 and ventilators
   (1/150 scale)

E1/11 Plan on ventilator intakes

E1/12 Profile view on starboard side ventilator

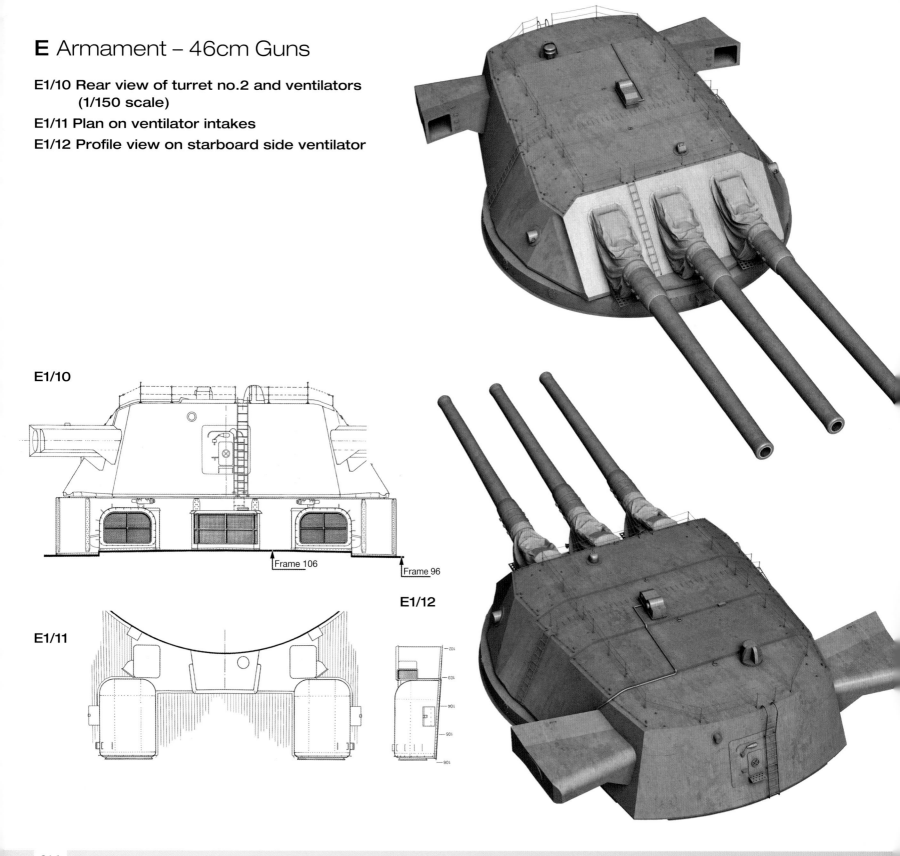

E1/10

Frame 106

Frame 96

E1/11

E1/12

102

103

104

105

106

E1/13 25mm x III MG platforms fitted on *Yamato* turrets
no.2 and no.3 January 1945 (1/150 scale)

E1/14 Side view of triple 25mm MG mount on
turret roof

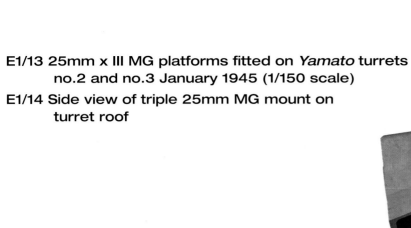

E1/13

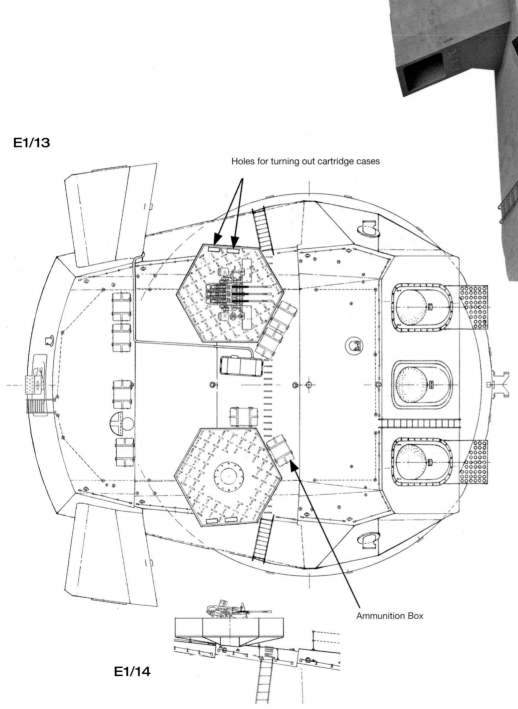

Holes for turning out cartridge cases

Ammunition Box

E1/14

E Armament – 46cm Guns

Geometry of 46cm gun turret

E1/15 Plan of fore 650mm thick armour plate

E1/16 Port side elevation of turret

E1/17 Plan

E1/18 Turret's profiles (body plan)

E1/19 Basket for canvas blast cover

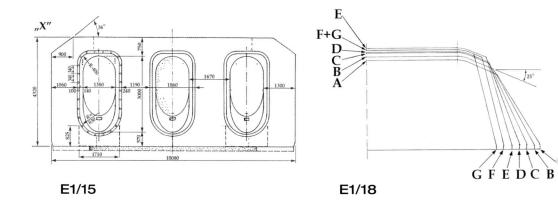

E1/15

E1/18

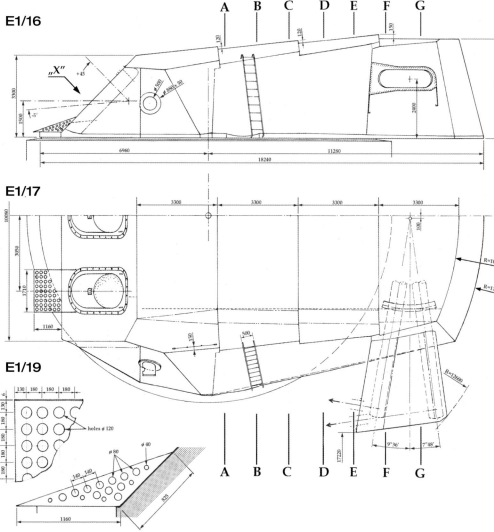

E1/16

E1/17

E1/19

Surfaces of 46cm gun turret

E1/20 Elevation

E1/21 Plan

E1/22 Profiles (sections)

E1/22

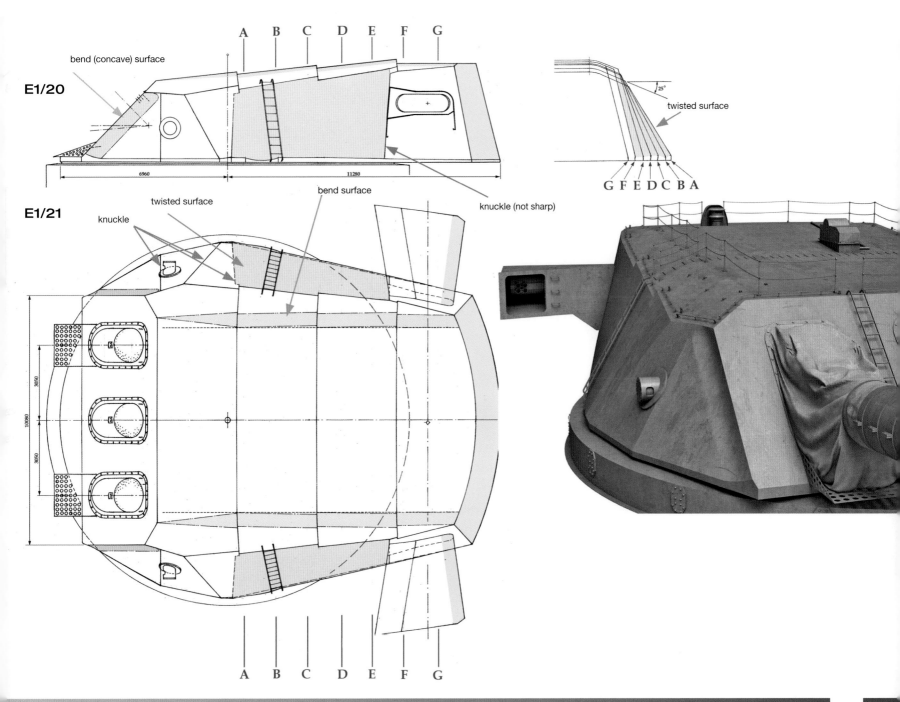

E1/20

bend (concave) surface

A B C D E F G

6960   11280

25°

twisted surface

G F E D C B A

E1/21

twisted surface

bend surface

knuckle

knuckle (not sharp)

3050

10080

3050

A B C D E F G

E Armament – 46cm Guns

Upper support for canvas blast cover (1/75 scale)

E1/23 Profile

E1/24 Plan

E1/25 Front view

E1/26 Fitting the support to fore 650mm
    thick armour plate

Fore 650mm armour plate with canvas blast cover frame (1/75 scale)

E1/27 Section

E1/28 Plan

E1/29 Blast bag mounting

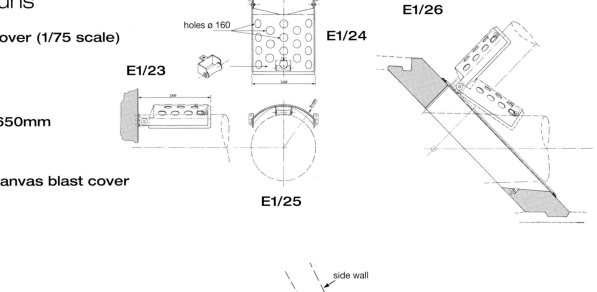

E1/23

E1/24

E1/26

holes ø 160

E1/25

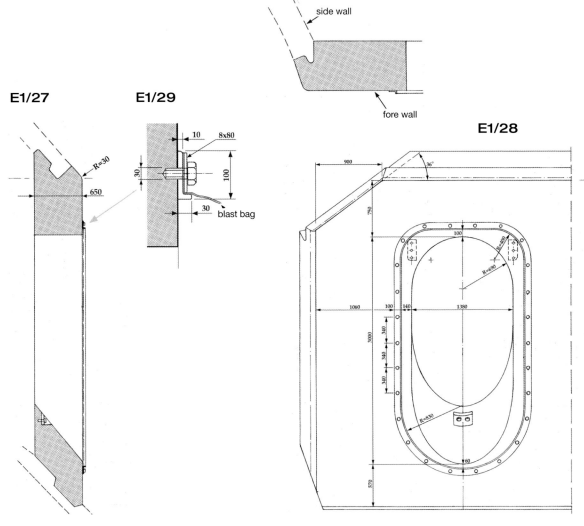

E1/27

E1/29

E1/28

side wall

fore wall

blast bag

R=30

650

10 8x80

30 100

30

900 36°

**15.5m rangefinder arm of 46cm gun turret
(1/75 scale)**

E1/30 Plan

E1/31 Front view – window partially open

E1/32 Open window

E1/33 Side view

E1/34 Type 94 46cm 18.1in / 45 cal gun
barrel (1/150 scale)

E1/35 Muzzle detail

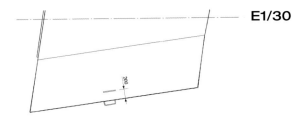

E1/30

E1/31

E1/33

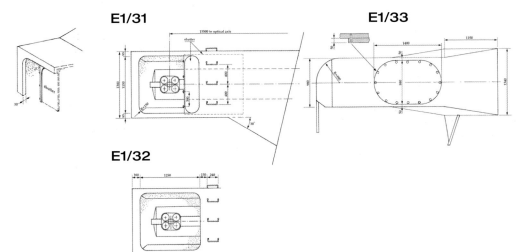

E1/32

E1/34

E1/35

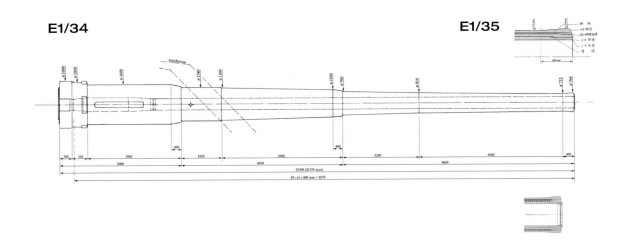

E Armament – 46cm Guns

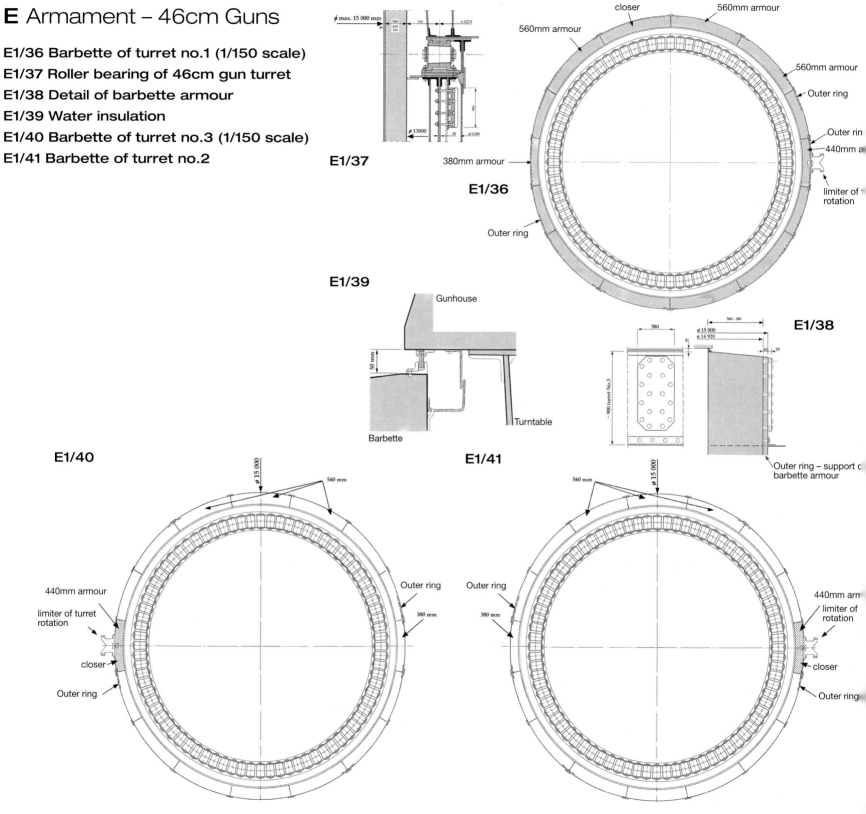

E1/37

E1/36

closer

560mm armour

560mm armour

560mm armour

Outer ring

Outer rin

440mm a

limiter of
rotation

380mm armour

Outer ring

E1/39

Gunhouse

50 mm

Barbette

Turntable

E1/38

380

ø 15 000
ø 14 920

560 – 380

~900 turret No.3

Outer ring – support o
barbette armour

E1/40

ø 15 000

560 mm

440mm armour

limiter of turret
rotation

closer

Outer ring

Outer ring

380 mm

E1/41

560 mm

ø 15 000

Outer ring

380 mm

440mm arm

limiter of
rotation

closer

Outer ring

E1/42 Base of guard rails (no scale)

E1/43 Base of awning stanchions

E1/44 Bases of guard rails and awning stanchions
    (1/150 scale)

E1/44a Turret no.1

E1/44b Turret no.2

E1/44c Turret no.3

E1/45 Guard of turret edge (no scale)

E1/43

E1/42

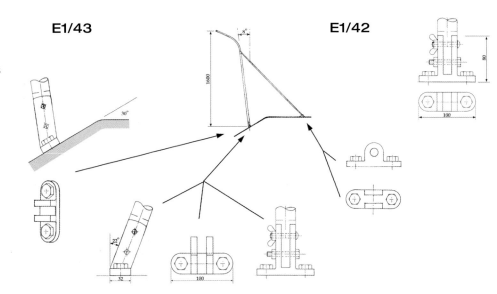

E1/45

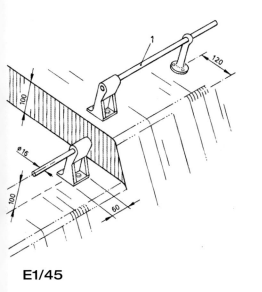

E1/44c

E1/44b

E1/44a

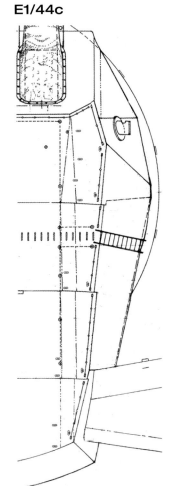

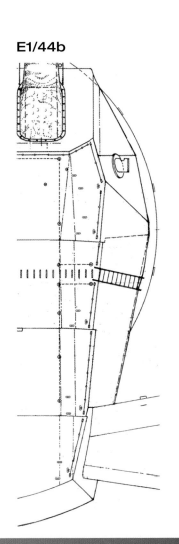

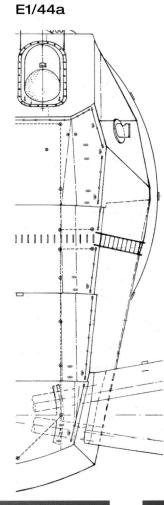

E Armament – 46cm Guns

E1/46

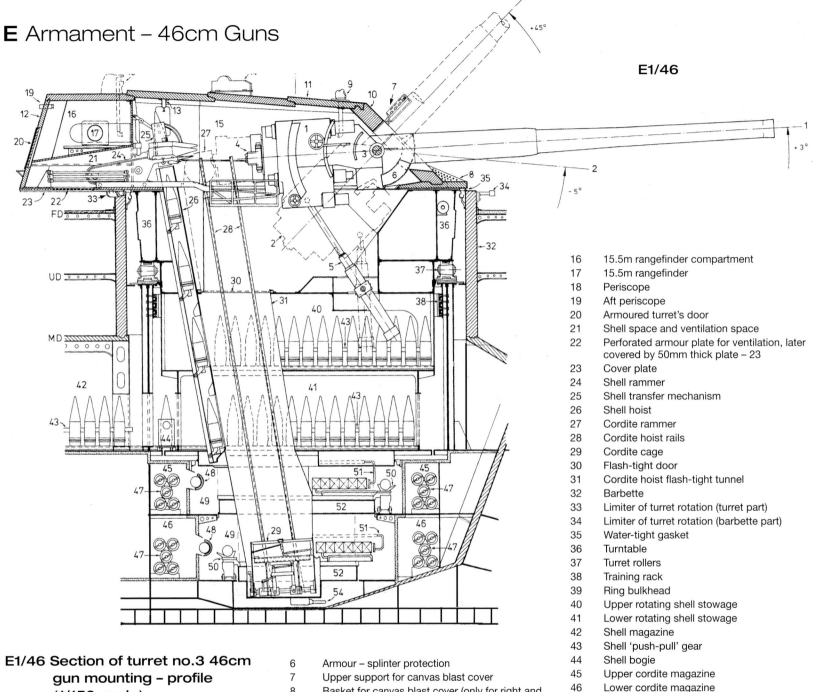

E1/46 Section of turret no.3 46cm gun mounting – profile (1/150 scale)

1 Gun cradle, rest position +3 degrees, max. length of recoil 1430mm
2 Maximum elevation +45 degrees, depression -5 degrees
3 Trunnion bearing
4 Breech mechanism
5 Elevating cylinder
6 Armour – splinter protection
7 Upper support for canvas blast cover
8 Basket for canvas blast cover (only for right and left barrel)
9 Centre gun periscope
10 Fore 650mm armour plate
11 270mm armour plate
12 190mm armour plate
13 Radial service crane and door for crane between gun compartments
14 Exercise aiming device
15 Gunhouse – middle gun compartment

16 15.5m rangefinder compartment
17 15.5m rangefinder
18 Periscope
19 Aft periscope
20 Armoured turret's door
21 Shell space and ventilation space
22 Perforated armour plate for ventilation, later covered by 50mm thick plate – 23
23 Cover plate
24 Shell rammer
25 Shell transfer mechanism
26 Shell hoist
27 Cordite rammer
28 Cordite hoist rails
29 Cordite cage
30 Flash-tight door
31 Cordite hoist flash-tight tunnel
32 Barbette
33 Limiter of turret rotation (turret part)
34 Limiter of turret rotation (barbette part)
35 Water-tight gasket
36 Turntable
37 Turret rollers
38 Training rack
39 Ring bulkhead
40 Upper rotating shell stowage
41 Lower rotating shell stowage
42 Shell magazine
43 Shell 'push-pull' gear
44 Shell bogie
45 Upper cordite magazine
46 Lower cordite magazine
47 Cordite stowage – canisters for two 55kg charges
48 Flash-tight scuttle
49 Powder (cordite) handling room
50 Cordite transfer bogie
51 Cordite swinging rammer – moved 330kg charge into the hoist cage
52 Rotating platform of revolving turret structure
53 50–80mm thick armour
54 Cable lead in

E1/47 Main Gun Turret – Plan (1/150 scale)

1. Right gun – at moment of cordite charge 330kg loading
2. Centre gun – ready to fire
3. Left gun – at moment of shell loading
4. Shell rammer
5. Cordite rammer
6. Shell transfer mechanism and shell hoist
7. Shell waiting tray
8. Hydraulic training engine
9. Training cluth handwheel
10. Auxiliary hoist
11. Breech block
12. Trunnion bearing
13. Side crane arm
14. Hydraulic engine of crane

15. 15.5m rangefinder compartment
16. 15.5m rangefinder
17. Rangefinder rotating rails
18. Hatch
19. Ventilation hole
20. Inner door
21. Rangefinder axis of rotation
22. Left gun periscope
23. Right gun periscope
24. Basket for canvas blast cover
25. 250mm side armour
26. Barbette
27. Flash-tight door for cordite hoist – lower part of turntable
28. Steel bulkheads – separate gunhouse for three gun compartments

E1/47

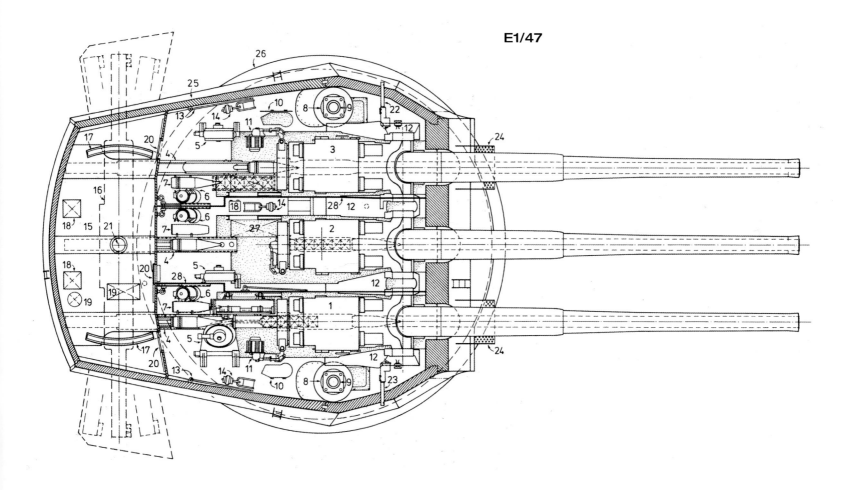

225

E Armament – 46cm Guns

E1/47a Section rear view of central part of turret (1/150 scale)

1   Middle gun periscope
2   Recoil cylinder
3   Run-out cylinder
4   Elevating cylinder
5   Training hydraulic engine
6   Training pinion
7   Training rack
8   Turret rollers
9   Ring bulkhead
10 Turntable
11 Shell hoist
12 Cordite hoist rails
13 Cordite cage
14 Flash-tight door
15 Cordite hoist flash-tight tunnel
16 Barbette
17 Upper rotating shell stowage
18 Lower rotating shell stowage
19 Shell magazine
20 Shell 'push-pull' gear
21 Shell bogie
22 Upper cordite magazine
23 Lower cordite magazine
24 Cordite stowage – canisters for two 55kg charges
25 Flash-tight scuttle
26 Cordite handling room – upper
27 Cordite handling room – lower
28 Cordite transfer bogie
29 Revolving platform – upper
30 Revolving platform – lower
31 Apron
32 Cable lead in
33 50mm-80mm thick armour

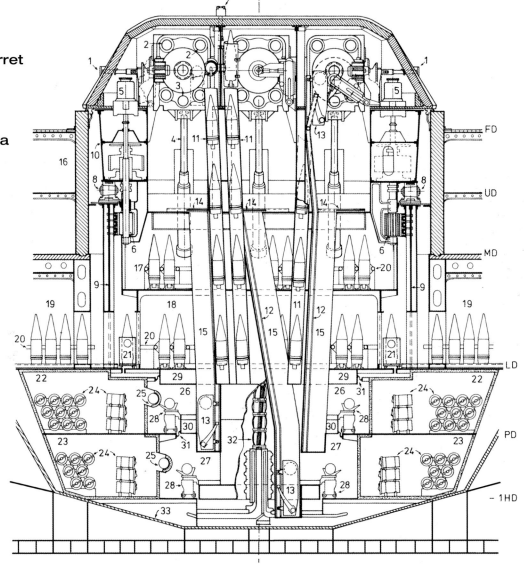

E1/47a

E1/47b Section of 15.5M rangefinder compartment (1/150 scale)

1   15.5m rangefinder
2   Inner door (sliding)
3   Inner deck of compartment
4   Perforated armour plate
5   Shield plate
6   Periscope
7   Limiter of turret rotation
8   Shell rammer
9   Ventilation space
10 Rangefinder cover
11 Rangefinder rotation rails
12 Axis of rotation

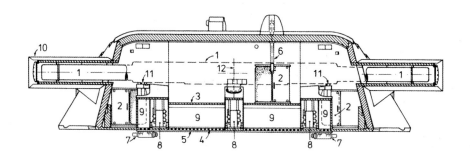

E1/47b

Details of 46cm gun mechanisms

E1/47c Side view of gun cradle (1/75 scale)

E1/48 Rear view and plan of gun cradle and breech
mechanism

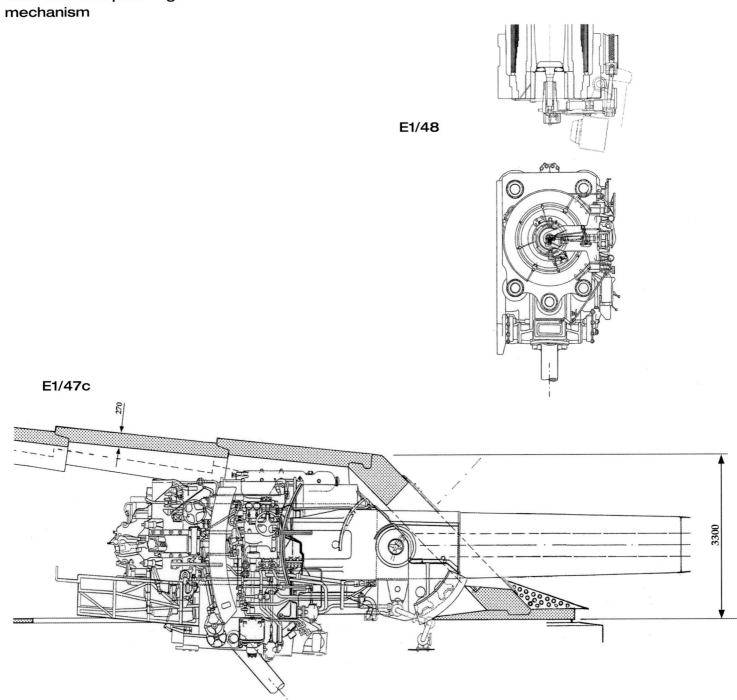

E1/48

E1/47c

270

3300

E Armament – 46cm Guns

E1/48a Turntable of 46cm gun mounting profile and plan (1/150 scale)

1   Left gun axis
2   Centre gun axis
3   Right gun axis
4   Shell hoist
5   Cordite hoist
6   Holes of elevating cylinder
7   Holes of training shaft
8   Hatch
9   Trunnion bearing
10 Roller path seating
11 Hole for training pinion
12 Manhole

E1/48a

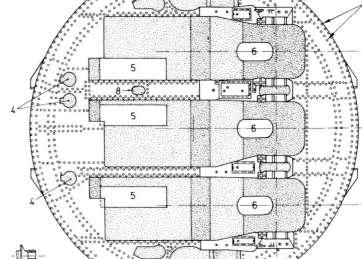

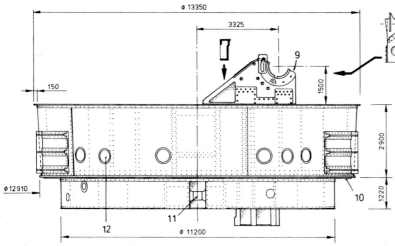

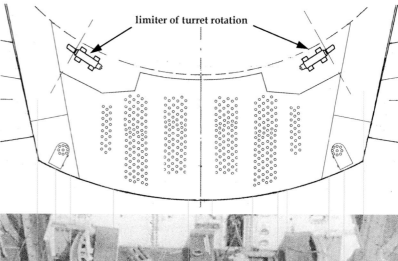

E1/49

E1/49 Perforated armour plate (for ventilation covered later [1944] by steel plates)

46cm gun ammunition (1/20 scale)

E1/50 Type 91, 46cm armour piercing projectiles –
weight 1460kg

E1/51 Cordite charge (weight 330 kg)

E1/52 Copper rotating bands

E1/53 AA common projectile 'san-shiki' weight
1360kg

E1/51

E1/52

E1/50

E1/53

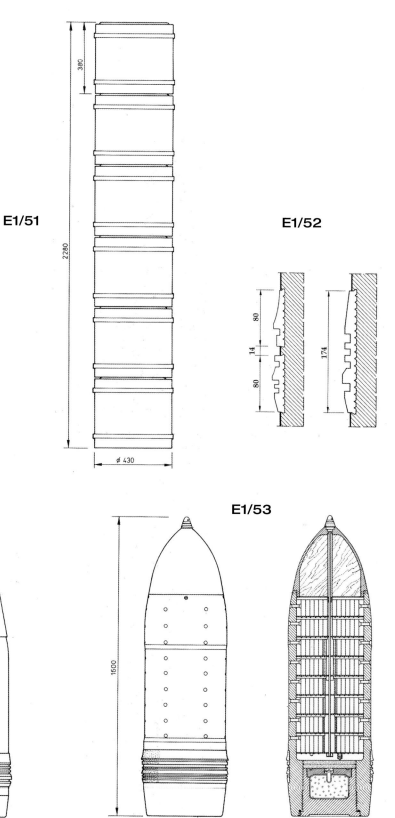
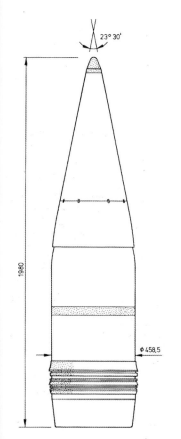
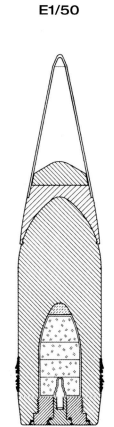
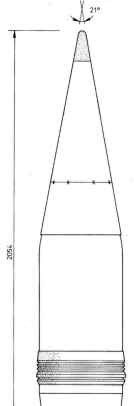

E Armament – 15.5cm Gun turrets

15.5cm/60cal 'Nendo shiki' gun (1/100 scale)

E2/1 Turret no.1 profile view

E2/2 Plan

E2/3 Detail of canvas blast cover support

E2/4 Section 'C'

E2/5 Section 'B'

E2/6 Section 'A'

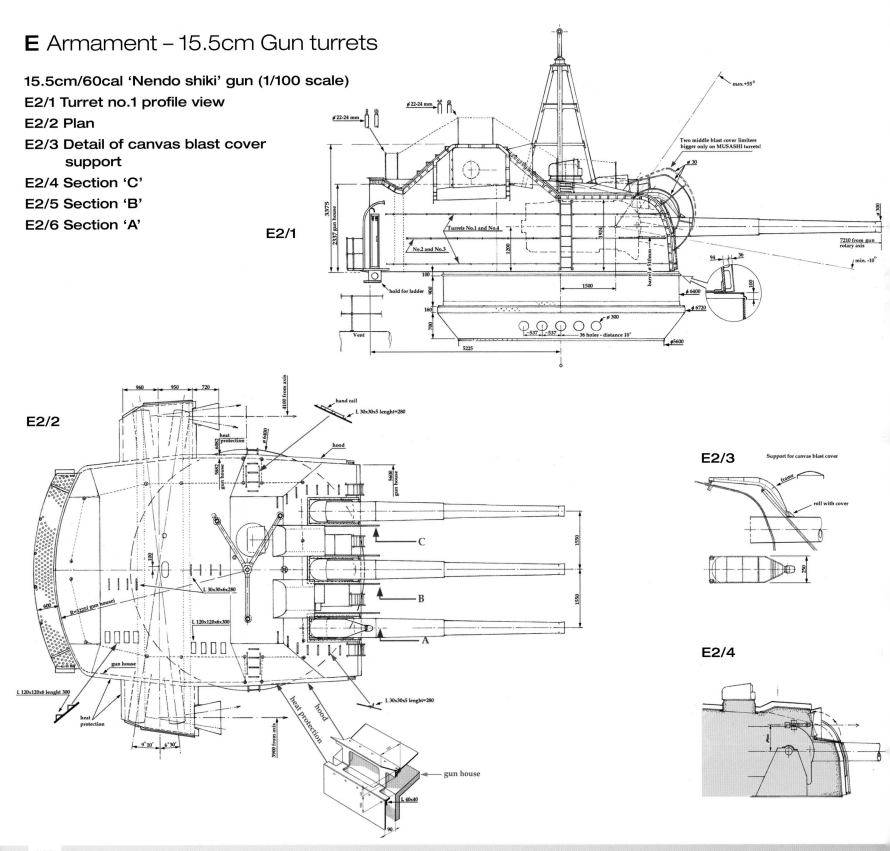

E2/7 15.5cm gun turret no.1 plan (1/150 scale)

E2/8 Turret no.2 plan

E2/9 Turret no.3 plan

E2/10 Turret no.4 plan

E2/11 Scheme of crew positions

E2/7

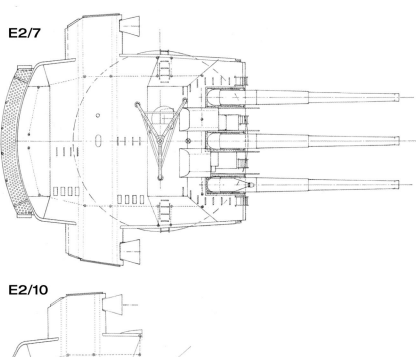

E2/8

E2/9

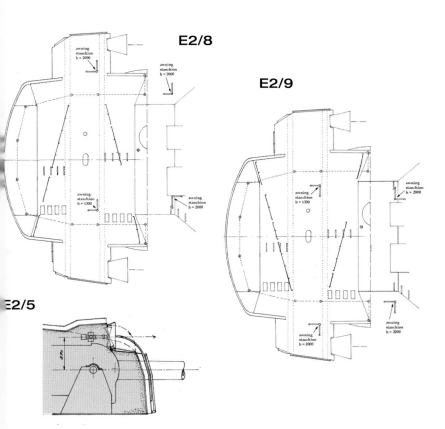

E2/10

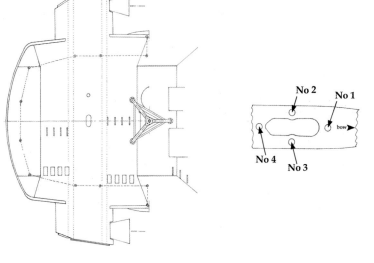

E2/5

E2/6

E2/11

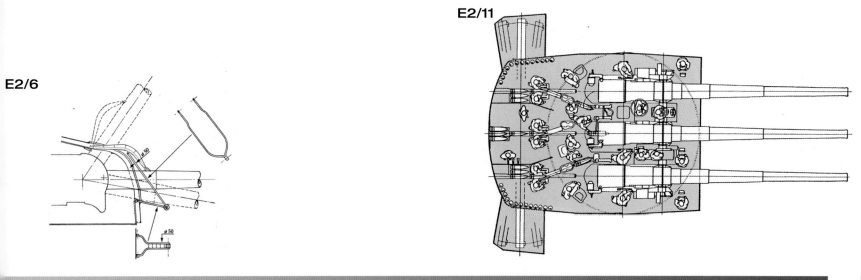

E Armament – 15.5cm Gun turrets

15.5cm gun turret no.1 (1/100 scale)

E2/12 Profile view

E2/13 Front view

E2/14 Rear view

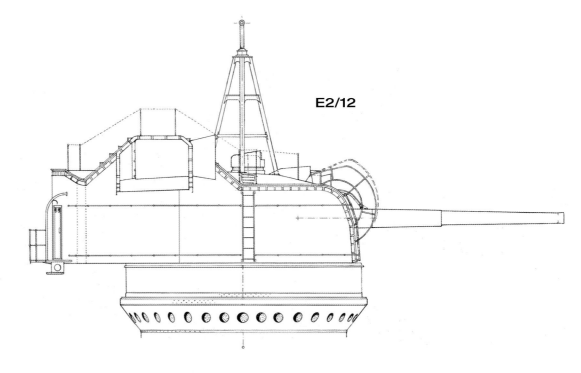

E2/12

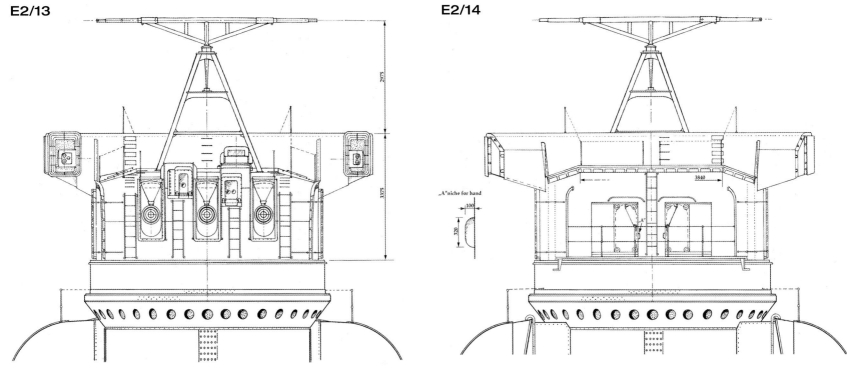

E2/13

E2/14

„A"niche for hand

15.5cm gun turret no.4 (1/100 scale)

E2/15 Profile view

E2/16 Front view

E2/17 Rear view

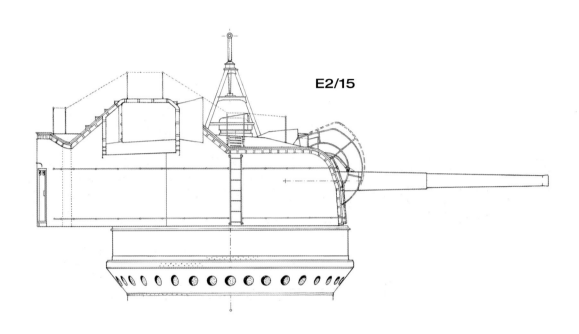

E2/15

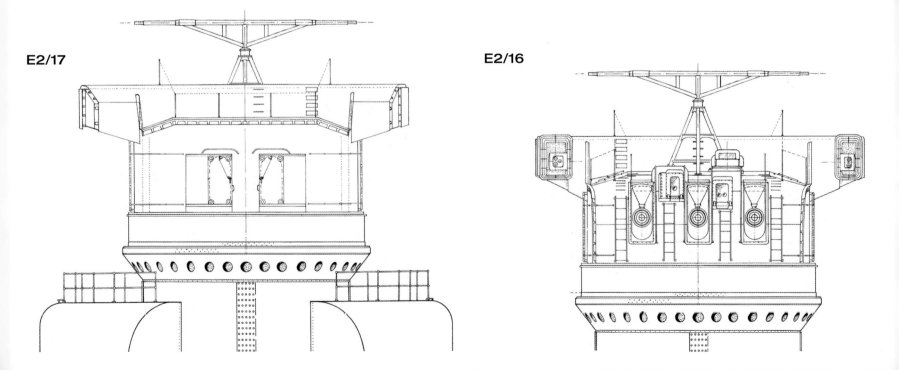

E2/17

E2/16

E Armament – 15.5cm Gun turrets

E2/18 Profile view of turrets no.2 and no.3
(1/100 scale)
E2/19 Turret no.2 front view
E2/20 Turret no.2 rear view
E2/21 Turret no.3 front view
E2/22 Turret no.3 rear view

E2/18

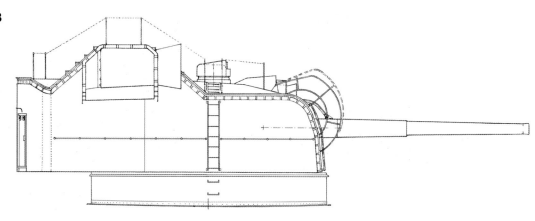

E2/19

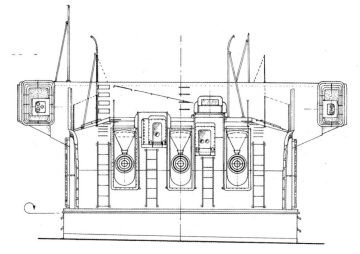

E2/21

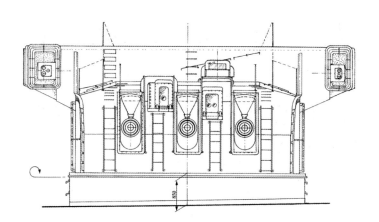

E2/20

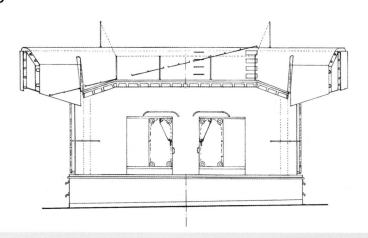

E2/22

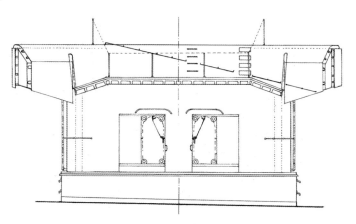

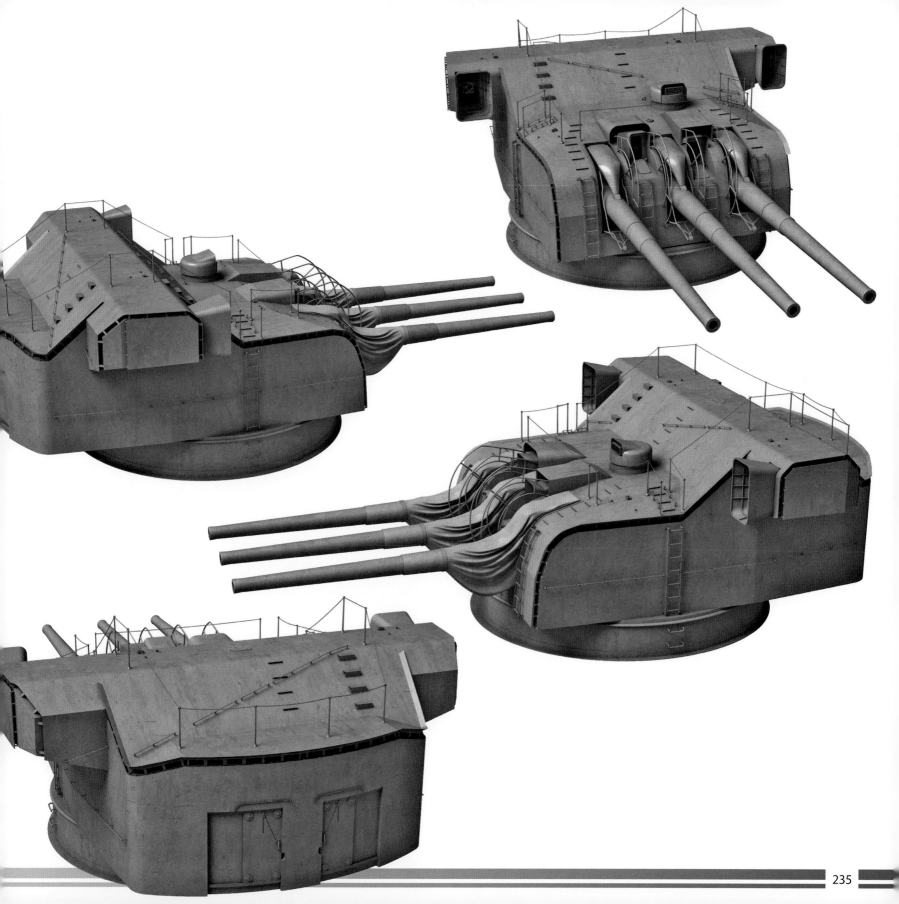

E Armament – 15.5cm Gun turrets

Tripod aerial mast on turret no.1 (1/100 scale)
E2/23 Plan
E2/24 Tripod details
E2/25 Side view
E2/26 Front elevation

Tripod aerial mast on turret no.4
E2/27 Plan
E2/28 Tripod details
E2/29 Side view
E2/30 Front elevation

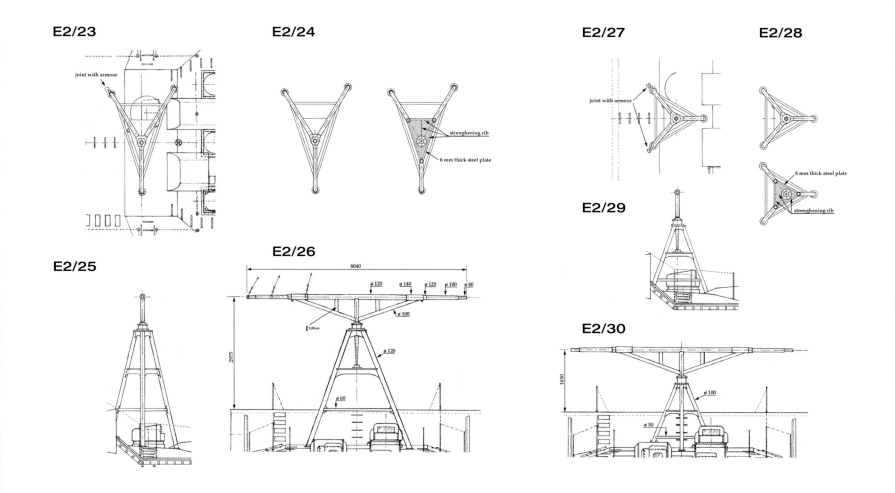

E2/23

E2/24

E2/27

E2/28

E2/25

E2/26

E2/29

E2/30

Details of 8m rangefinder (1/50 scale)

E2/31 Front elevation (*Yamato*)

E2/32 Plan (*Yamato*)

E2/33 Plan (*Musashi*)

**E2/34 Edge rangefinder arms –
front view (*Musashi*)**

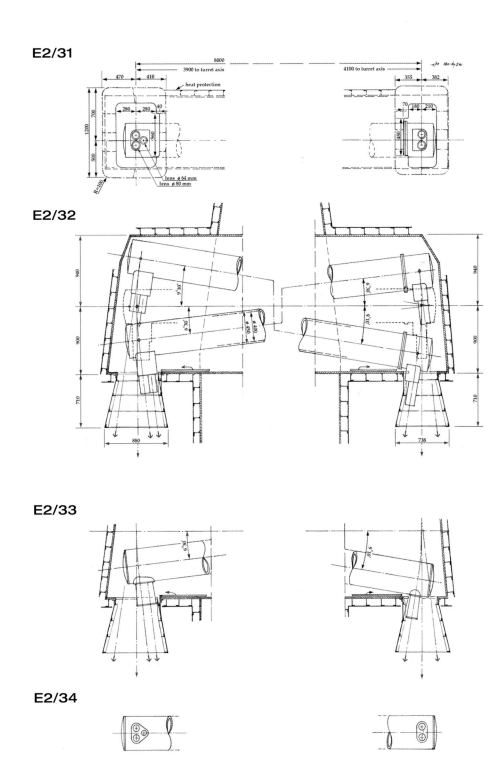

E2/31

E2/32

E2/33

E2/34

E Armament – 15.5cm Gun turrets

Ventilators at barbette no.1 15.5cm gun turret
(1/150 scale)

E2/35 Front elevation

E2/36 Side elevation

E2/37 Rear elevation

E2/38 Plan

E2/39 Section

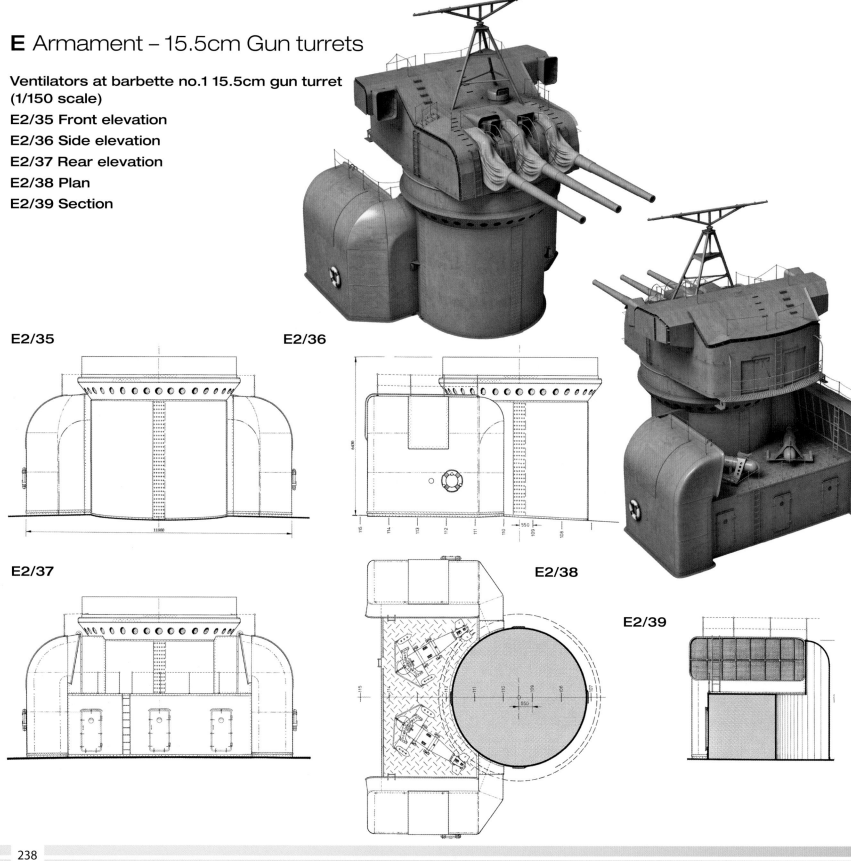

E2/35

E2/36

E2/37

E2/38

E2/39

Ventilators at barbette no.4 15.5cm
gun turret (1/150 scale)

E2/40 Side elevation

E2/41 View from ship's stern

E2/42 Plan

E2/43 View from bow direction

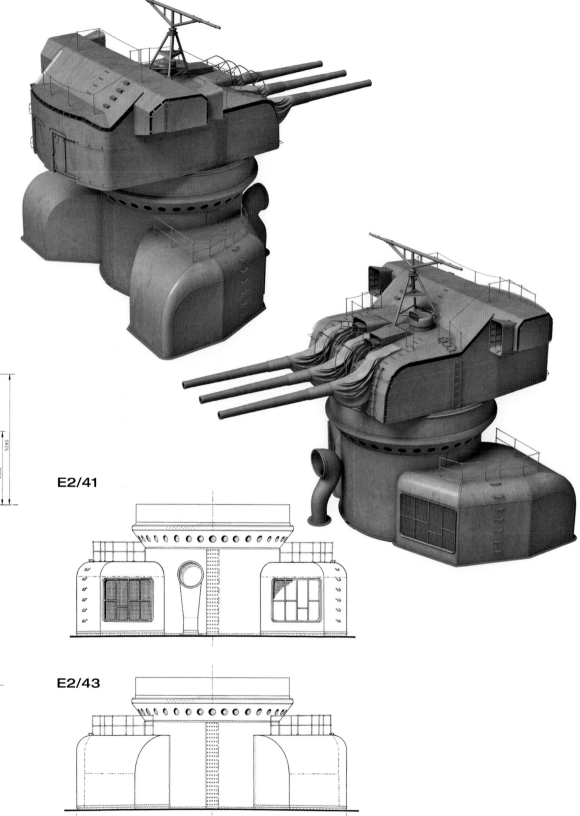

E2/40

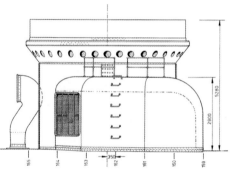

E2/42

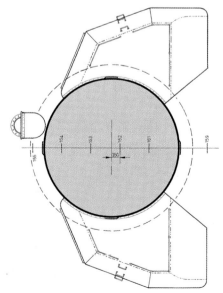

E2/41

E2/43

E Armament – Type 89 12.7cm 40 calibre Anti-aircraft Guns

**Type 89 12.7cm/40 cal AA gun
model A-1-3 turret (1/75 scale)**

E3/1 Plan

E3/2 Left profile

E3/3 Rear elevation

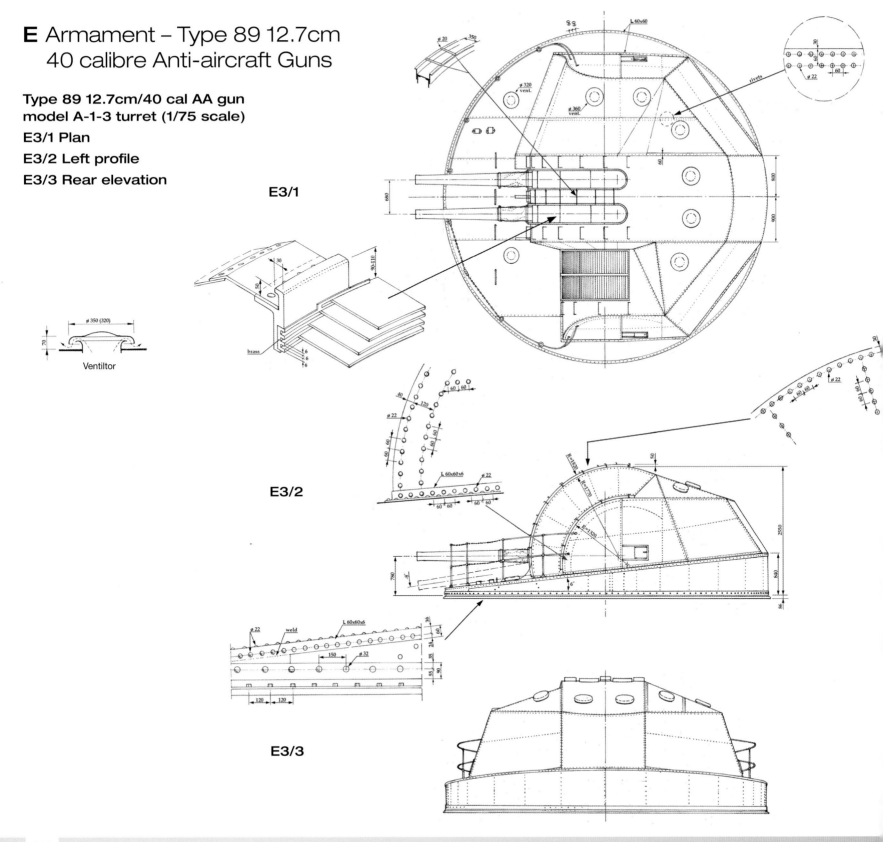

E3/1

Ventiltor

E3/2

E3/3

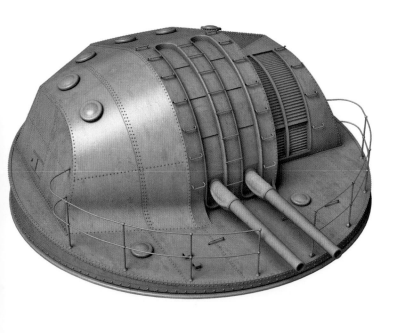
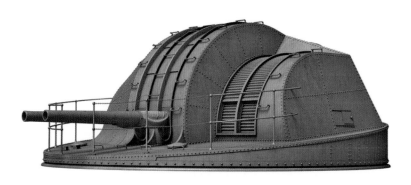
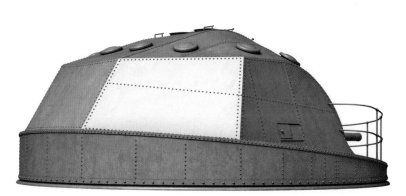
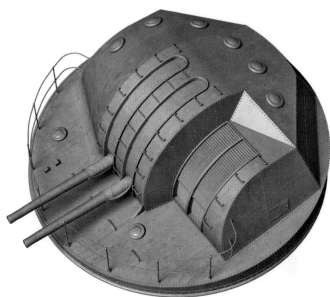
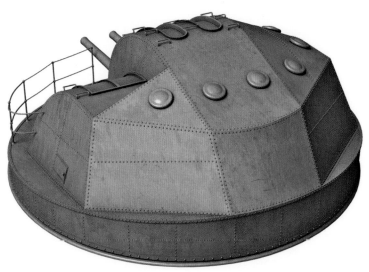

E Armament – Type 89 12.7cm 40 calibre Anti-aircraft Guns

12.7cm gun turret with *Yamato* base
(1/75 scale)
E3/4 Front elevation
E3/5 Right profile

E3/4

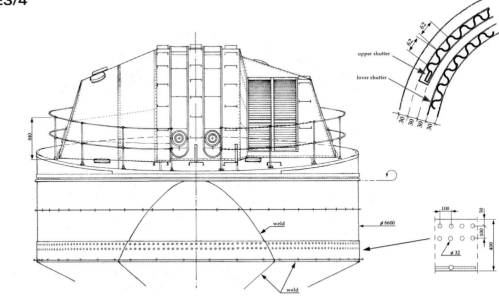

E3/5

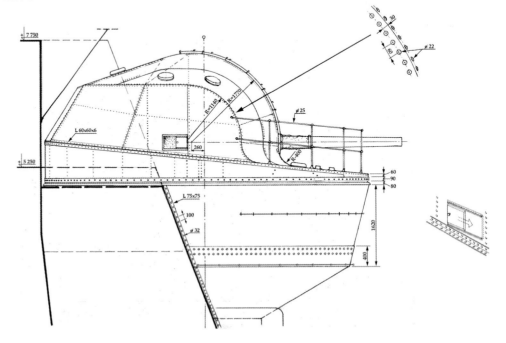

E3/6 Section of turret

E3/7 Roller bearing F turret

E3/8 Typical clamp (from 12.7cm gun turrets
and 25mm MG towers)

E3/6

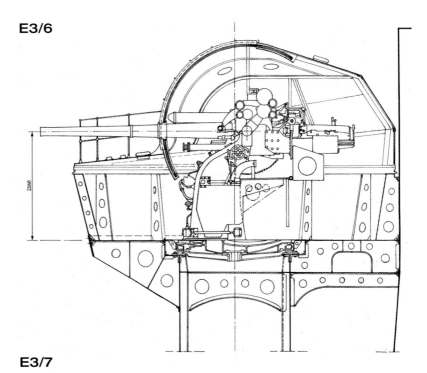

E3/7

E3/8

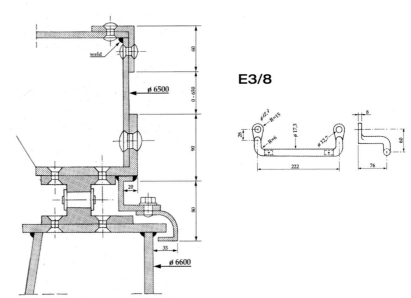

E Armament – Type 89 12.7cm 40 calibre Anti-aircraft Guns

Type 89 12.7cm AA gun model A-1 fitted only on
Yamato in 1944 (1/75 scale)

E3/9 Right profile

E3/10 Front elevation

E3/11 Left profile

E3/12 Plan

E3/13 Rear elevation

E3/14 Details under cover

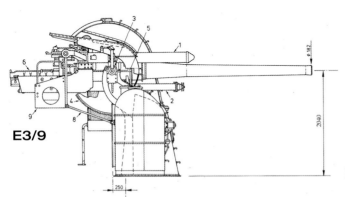

E3/9

E3/11

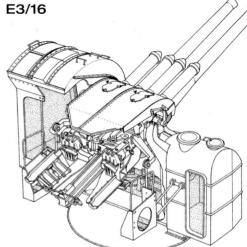

E3/15 Scheme of mounting base ring

E3/16 General view

E3/15

E3/12

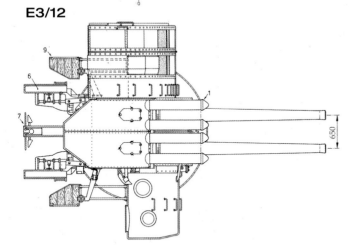

E3/10

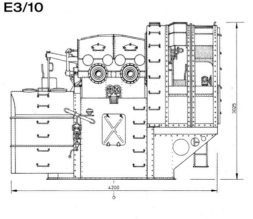

E3/16

E3/13

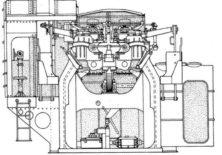

E3/14

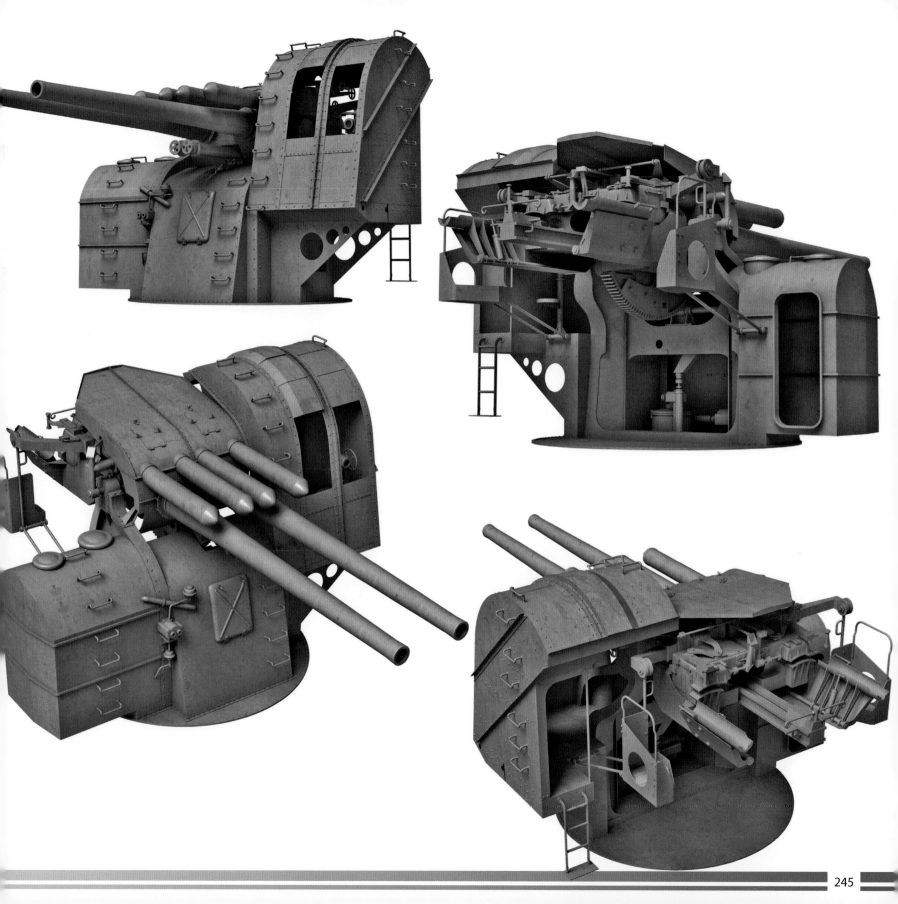

E Armament – Type 89 12.7cm 40 calibre Anti-aircraft Guns

12.7cm Gun crew loading exercise machine – used only in the first months after ship's commissioning and later removed

E3/17 Right elevation

E3/18 Plan

12cm rocket launcher fitted only on *Musashi* in 1944 (1/20 scale)

E3/19 Front elevation

E3/20 Left profile

E3/21 12cm Common AA rocket – profile and section

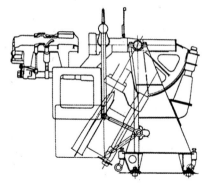

E3/17

E3/18

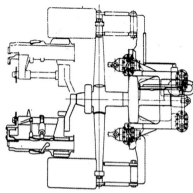

E3/19

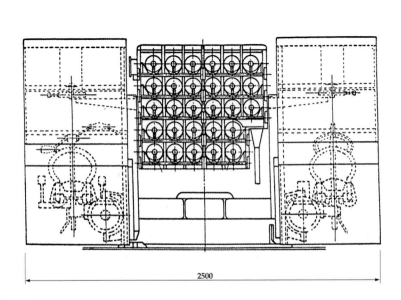

2500

E3/20

70°

8°

E3/21

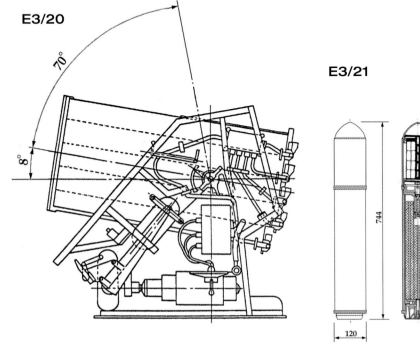

744

120

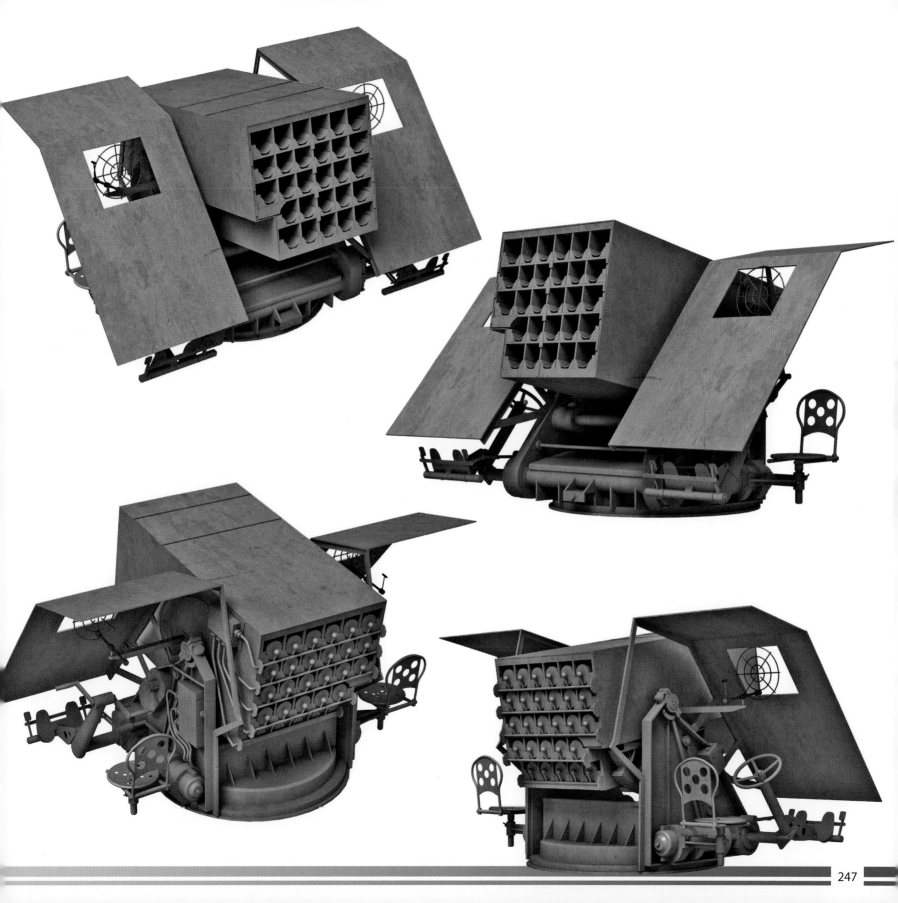

E Armament – 25 and 13.2mm Machine Guns

Type 'A' 25mm MG turret from *Yamato* (1/50 scale)

E4/1 Front elevation

E4/2 Right elevation

E4/3 Plan

E4/4 Section

E4/5 Details of windows (shutter)

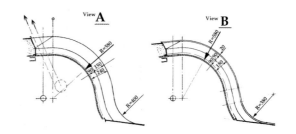

E4/5

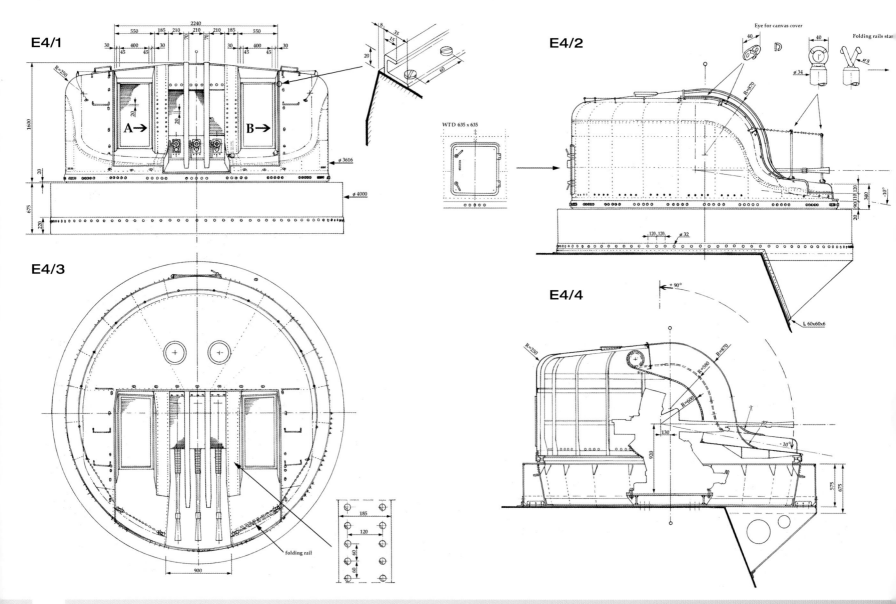

E4/1

E4/2

E4/3

E4/4

E4/6 Detail of roller bearing – side and aft part

E4/7 Detail of roller bearing – fore part of tower

E4/8 Detail of lower part of shield

E4/6

ø 3616

ø 22

40

90

20

ø 4000

Side and aft part

E4/7

ø 3616

ø 4000

Fore part

E4/8

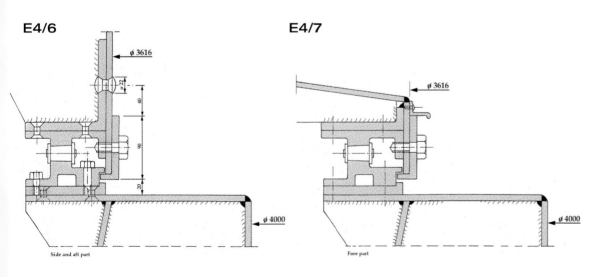

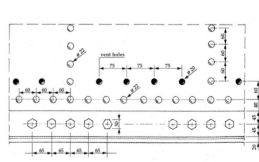

E Armament – 25 and 13.2mm Machine Guns

Type 'B' 25mm MG turret fitted only on _Musashi_ (1/50 scale)

Changes in comparison to _Yamato_ in lower fore part indicated by dimensions

E4/9 Front elevation

E4/10 Profile

E4/11 Arrangement of covered triple 25mm towers on _Yamato_ forecastle deck in 1945

Type 'A' towers – white circles

Type 'B' towers – black circles

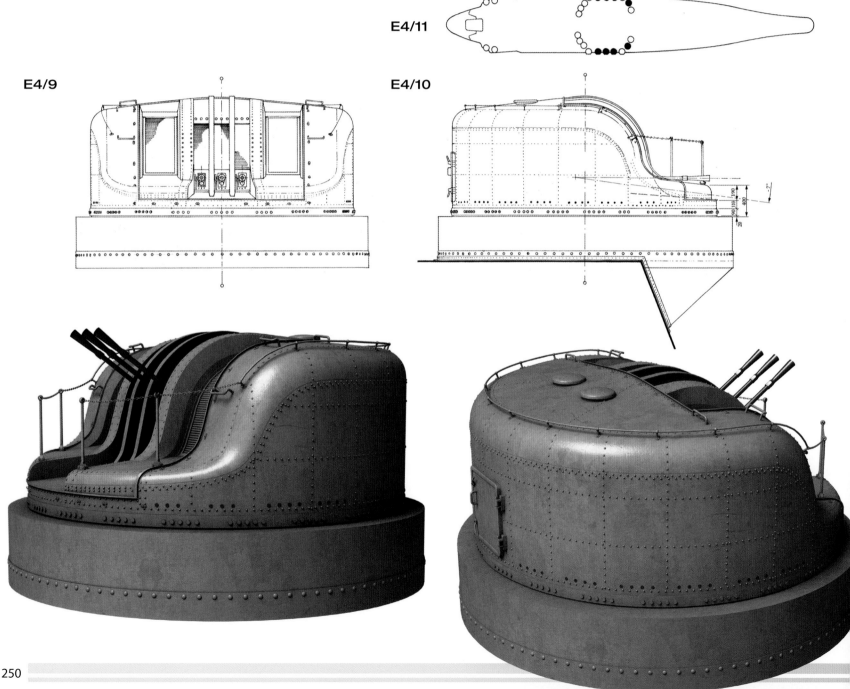

E4/11

E4/9

E4/10

Type 'C' 25mm MG tower fitted only on
Yamato in 1945 (1/50 scale)

E4/12 Front elevation

E4/13 Profile

E4/14 WT door

E4/15 Plan

E4/16 Detail of shutter

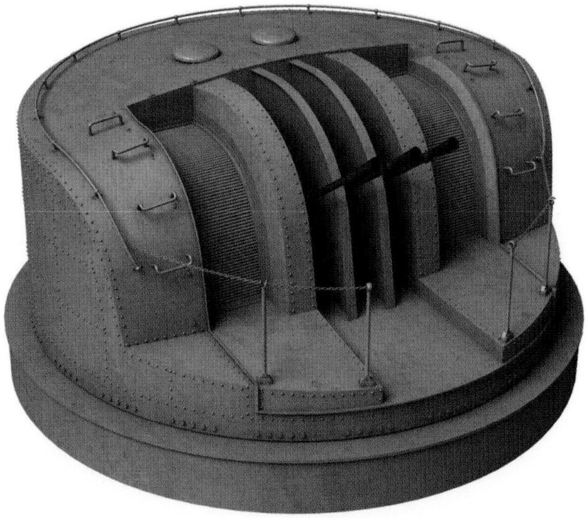

E4/12

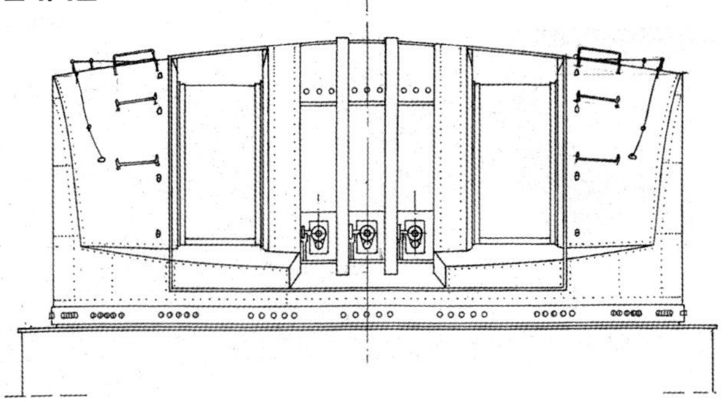

E4/14

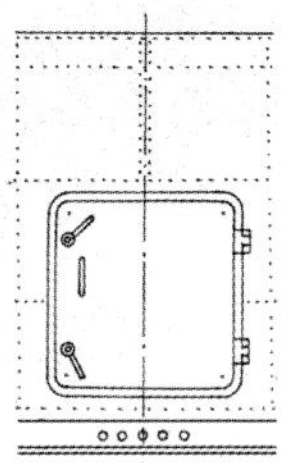

E4/15

E4/13

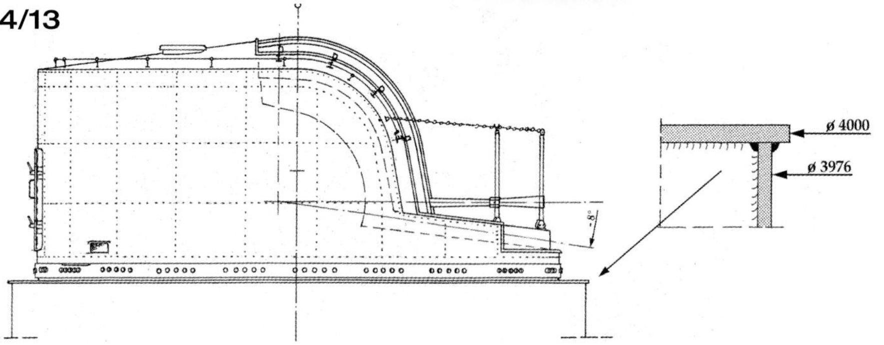

ø 4000

ø 3976

16

20

35

20

E4/16

8

35

20

ø 20

45

120

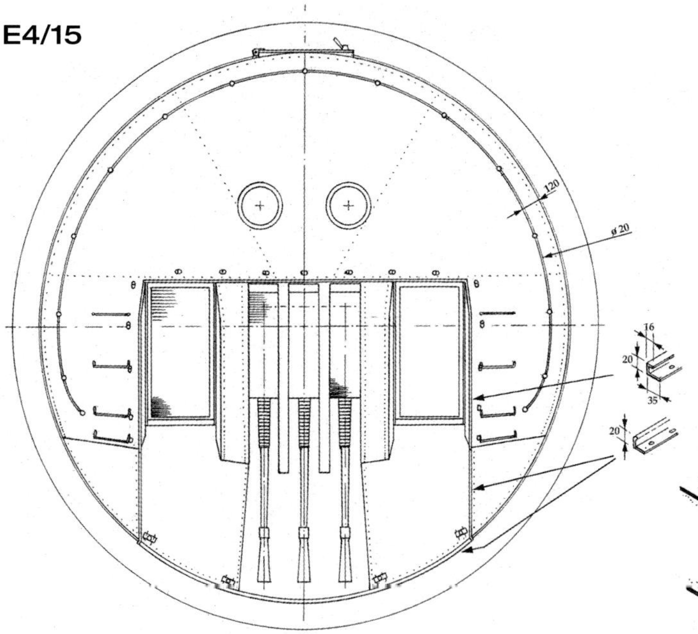

ø 20

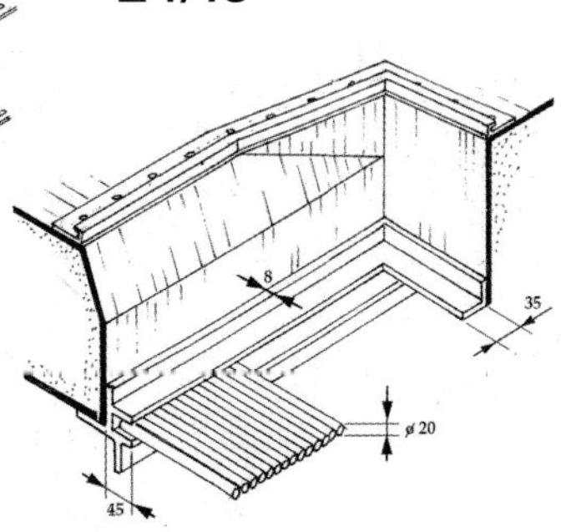

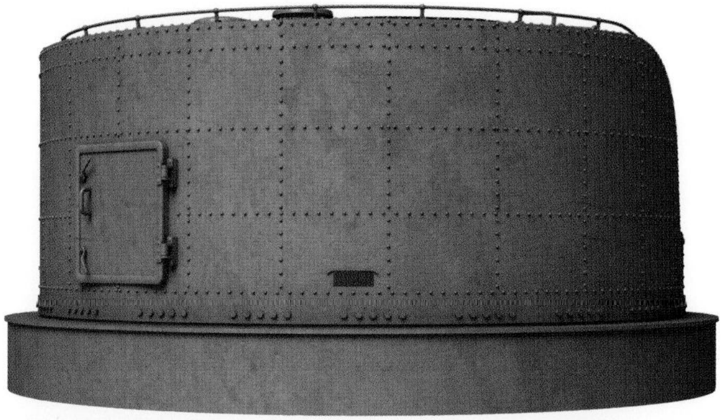

E Armament – 25 and 13.2mm Machine Guns

Ship's side 25mm MG towers fitted on *Yamato*
(1/50 scale)
E4/17 Front elevation
E4/18 Profile
E4/19 Plan

E4/17

E4/18

E4/19

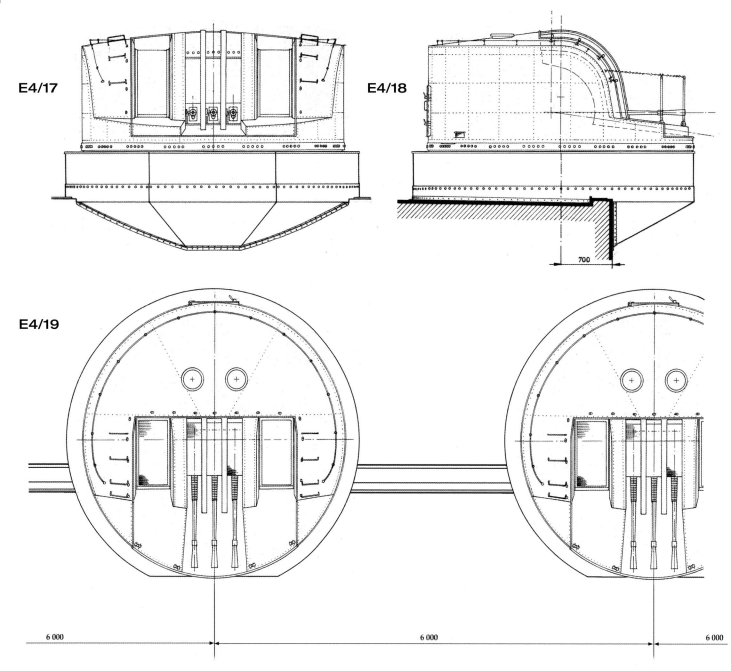

700

6 000   6 000   6 000

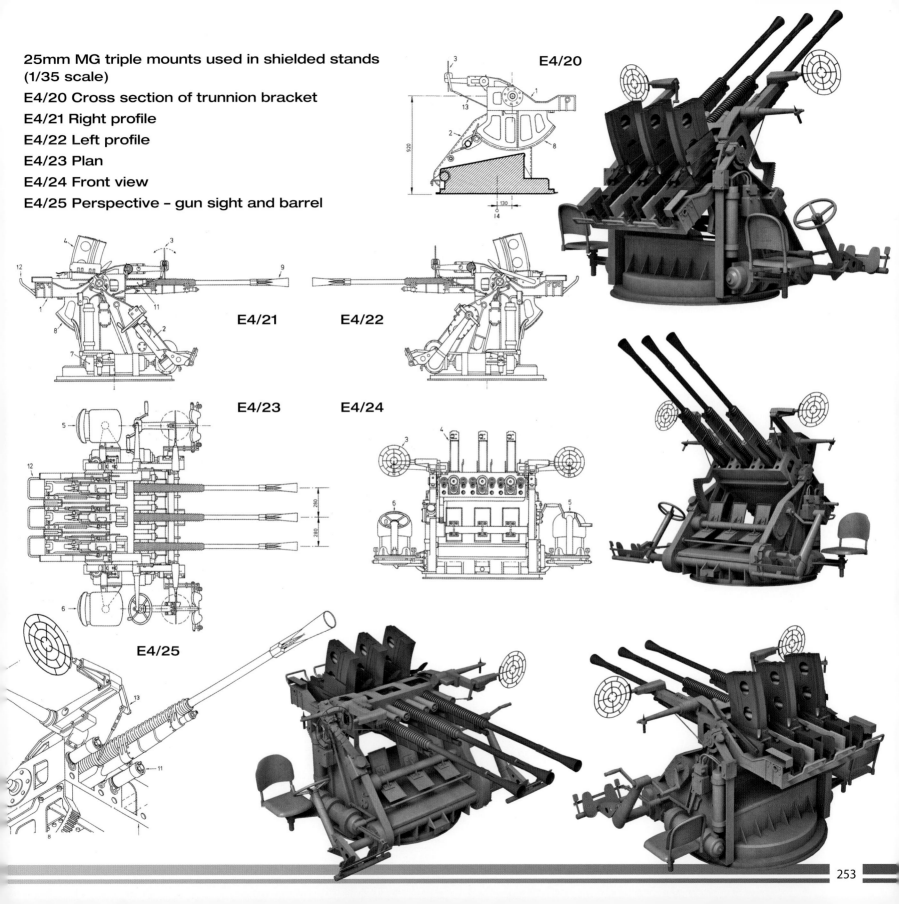

25mm MG triple mounts used in shielded stands
(1/35 scale)

E4/20 Cross section of trunnion bracket

E4/21 Right profile

E4/22 Left profile

E4/23 Plan

E4/24 Front view

E4/25 Perspective – gun sight and barrel

E4/20

E4/21

E4/22

E4/23

E4/24

E4/25

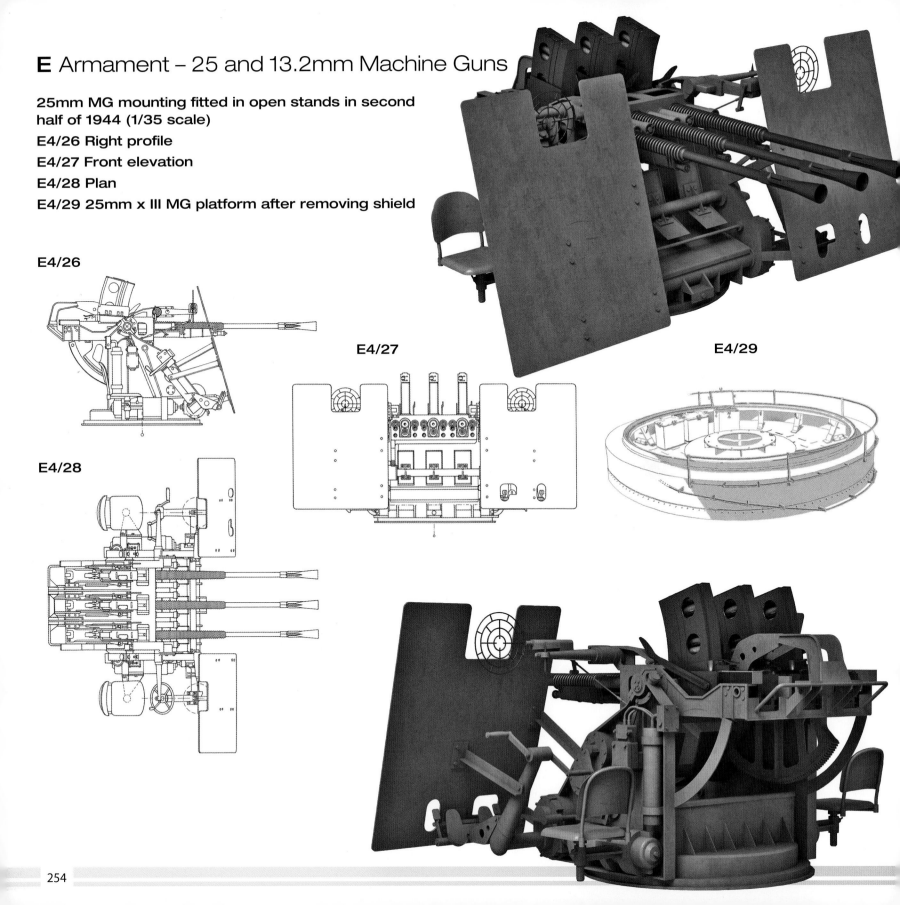

E Armament – 25 and 13.2mm Machine Guns

25mm MG mounting fitted in open stands in second half of 1944 (1/35 scale)

E4/26 Right profile

E4/27 Front elevation

E4/28 Plan

E4/29 25mm x III MG platform after removing shield

E4/26

E4/27

E4/29

E4/28

Type 96 25mm gun barrel (1/20 scale)

E4/30 Profile

E4/31 Plan

E4/32 Sections

E4/30-32 Type 96 25mm MG

1 Muzzle flash eliminator (first model)
2 Radiator
3 Breech block and reloading gas cylinder
4 Pressure regulator for gas cylinder (gas plug)
5 Gas pipe (in shield)
6 Breech block housing
7 Grip – manual operating lever
8 Counter-recoil piston rod lug
9 Slide rail
10 Magazine insert

E4/33 Muzzle flash eliminator used used in guns fitted since April 1944

E4/34 Detail of barrel cooling fins

E4/33-34 Flash eliminator, barrel cooling fins

1 Exhaust ports
2 Barrel
3 Cooling fins
4 Gas pressure regulator (gas plug)
5 Gas pipe for gas cylinder
6 Shield

E4/30

E4/31

E4/32

E4/33

E4/34

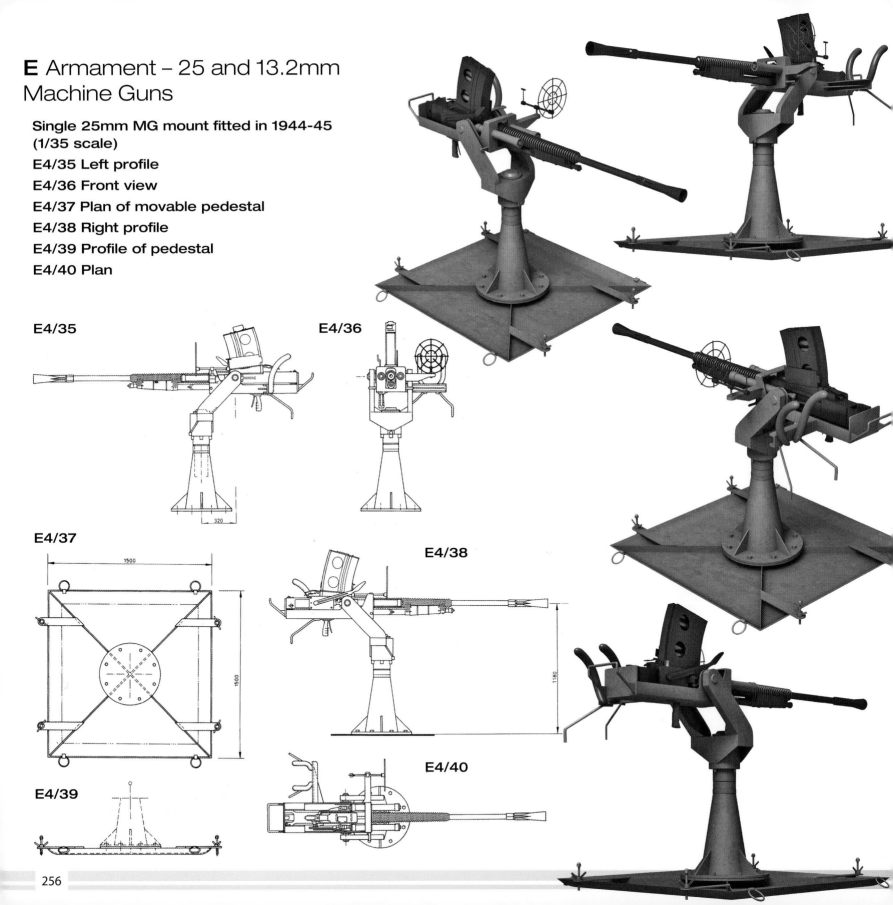

E Armament – 25 and 13.2mm Machine Guns

Single 25mm MG mount fitted in 1944-45 (1/35 scale)

E4/35 Left profile

E4/36 Front view

E4/37 Plan of movable pedestal

E4/38 Right profile

E4/39 Profile of pedestal

E4/40 Plan

E4/35

E4/36

E4/37

E4/38

E4/39

E4/40

E Armament – 25 and 13.2 Machine Guns

Musashi 1944 25mm MG triple mount fitted on base of
not installed 12.7cm HA guns (no scale)

E4/41 Plan

E4/42 Profile

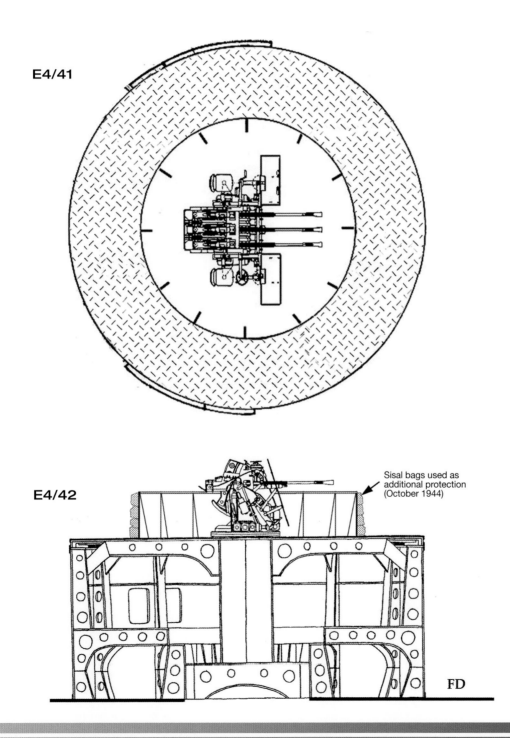

E4/41

E4/42

Sisal bags used as
additional protection
(October 1944)

FD

E Armament – 25 and 13.2mm Machine Guns

13,2mm MG fitted on both sides of tower bridge level
+16 755 (1/20 scale)

E4/43 Right profile

E4/44 Front view

E4/45 Left profile

E4/46 Plan

E4/47 Detail of assembly (no scale)

E4/48 Detail of barrel (no scale)

E4/43-48 13mm Twin mounting

1 Mounting
2 Turnnion bracket
3 Top carriage
4 Sight
5 Pantograph
6 Training wheel
7 Elevation wheel
8 Magazine for 30 rounds

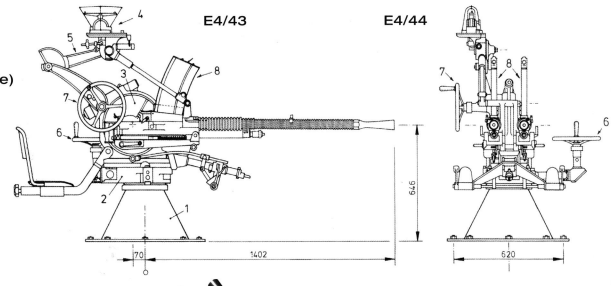

E4/43   E4/44

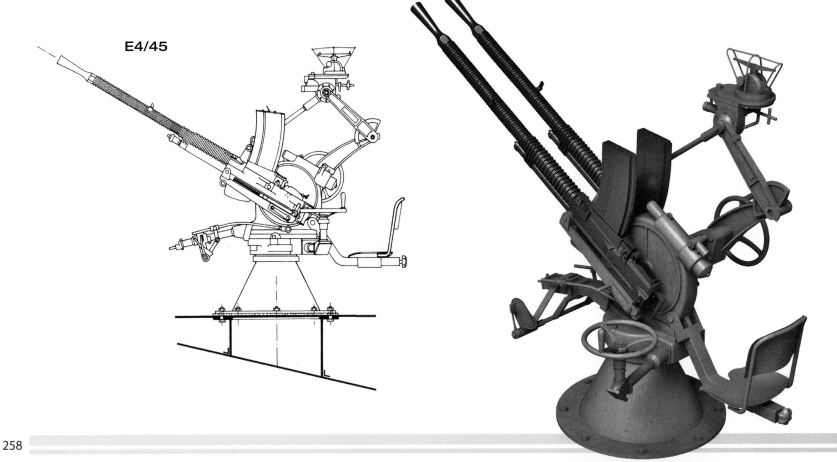

E4/45

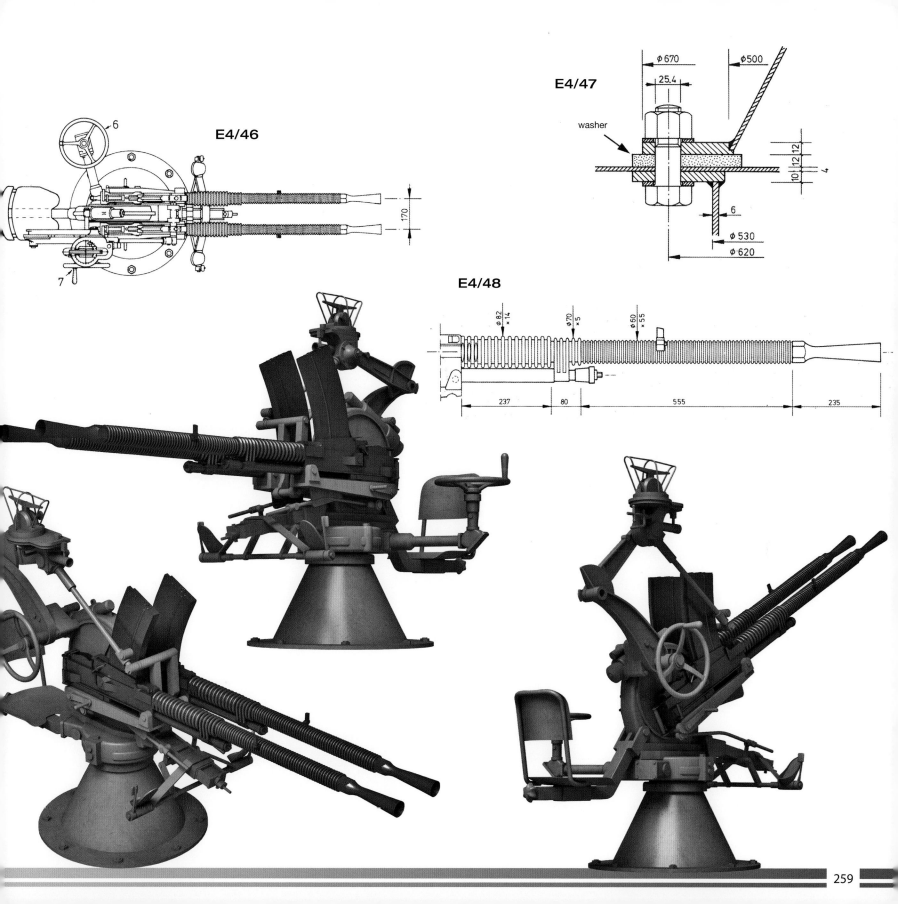

E4/46

6

7

E4/47

washer

φ 670
φ 500
25.4
10 12 12
4
6
φ 530
φ 620

E4/48

φ 82 × 14
φ 70 × 5
φ 60 × 55

237   80   555   235

F Fire Control – 15.5m Rangefinder

Yamato 1941 main low angle director 'Hoiban'
type and 15.5m rangefinder (1/75 scale)

F1/1 Front elevation

F1/2 Plan

F1/3 Right elevation

F1/4 Rear elevation

F1/5 Front view of map cabin

F1/6 LA Director 'Hoiban' – rear view

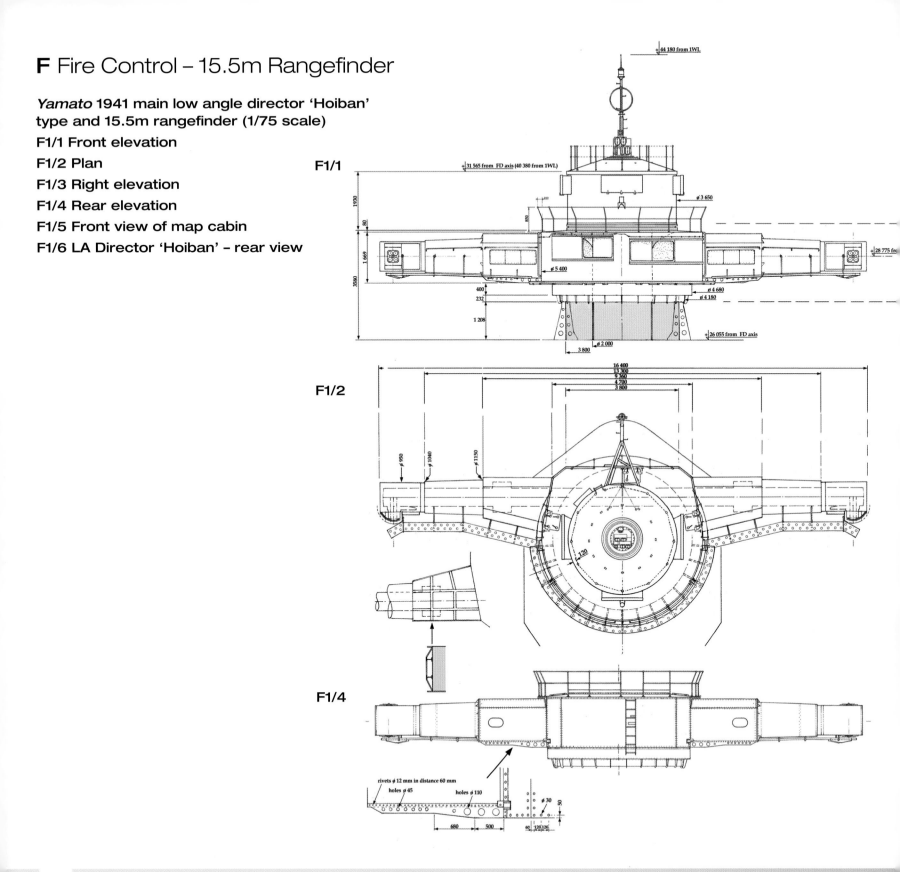

F1/1

F1/2

F1/4

rivets ⌀ 12 mm in distance 60 mm
holes ⌀ 45
holes ⌀ 110

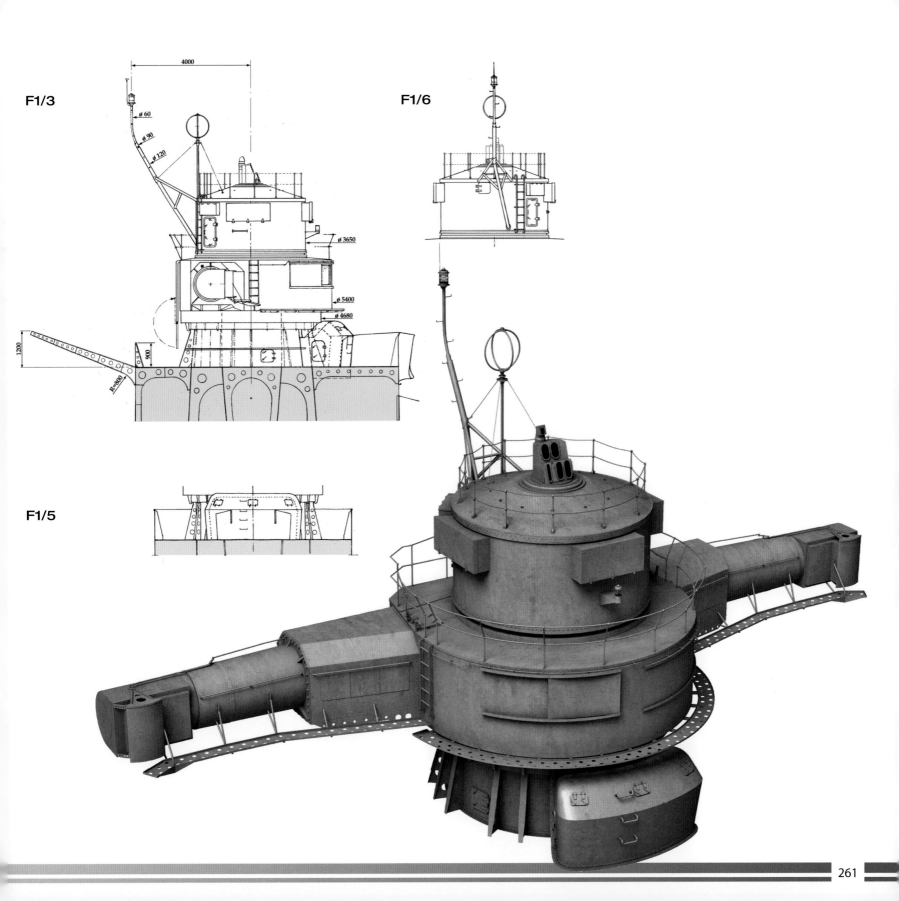

F1/3

4000

ø 60
ø 90
ø 120

ø 3650

ø 5400
ø 4680

1200

900

R=900

F1/6

F1/5

F Fire Control – 15.5m Rangefinder

Rangefinder arm details (no scale)
F1/7 Plan of edge of left arm
F1/8 Plan of open rangefinder window
F1/9 Front view of left arm
F1/10 Platform details
F1/11 Details of movable shield

F1/10

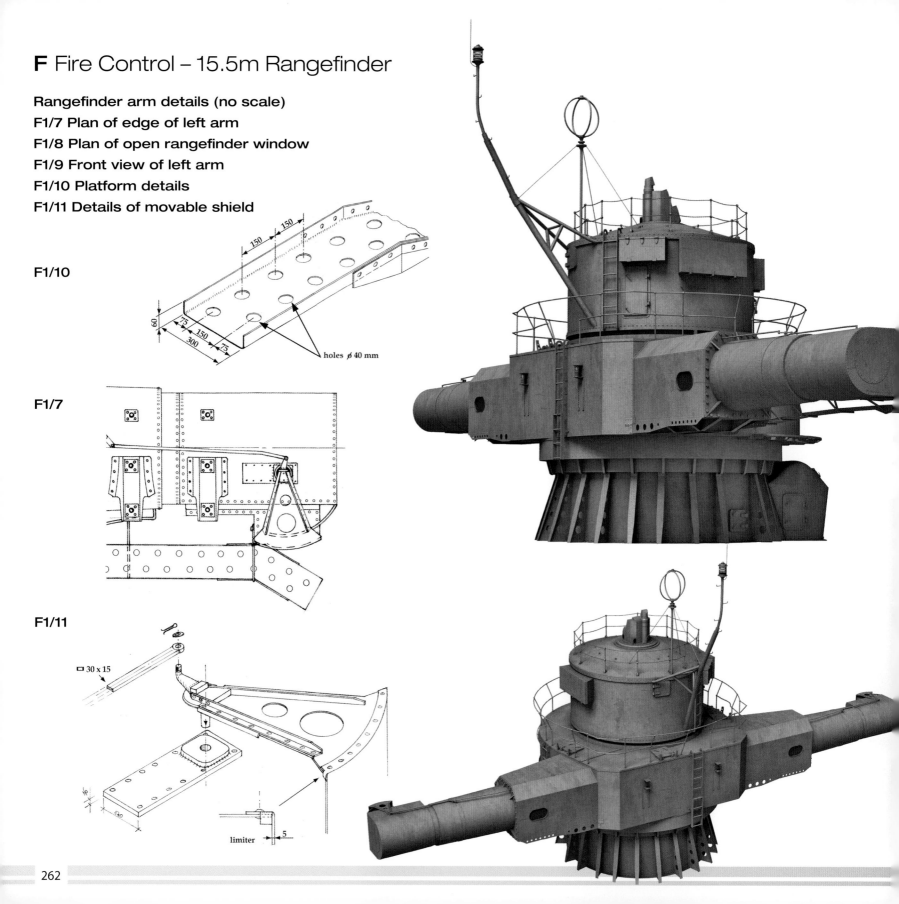

holes ⌀ 40 mm

F1/7

F1/11

□ 30 x 15

limiter 5

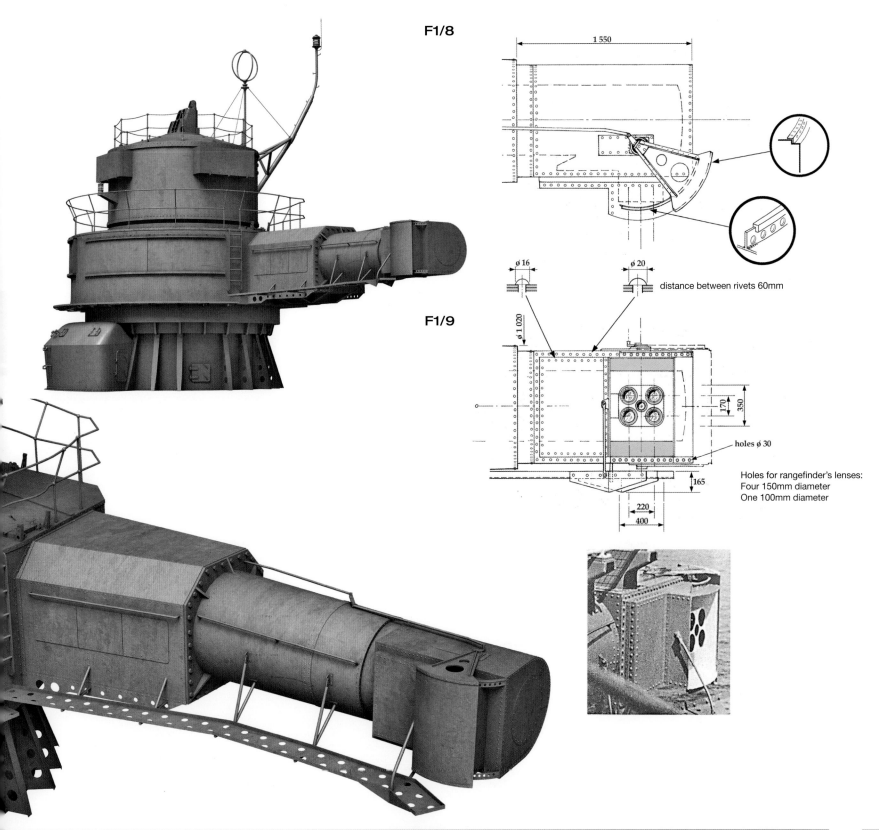

F1/8

1 550

ø 16

ø 20

distance between rivets 60mm

F1/9

ø 1 020

170

350

holes ø 30

165

220

400

Holes for rangefinder's lenses:
Four 150mm diameter
One 100mm diameter

F Fire Control – 15.5m Rangefinder

Yamato 1945 – 15.5m rangefinder
with 'Hoiban' and type 21 radar
antenna (1/75 scale)

F1/12 Front elevation

F1/13 Plan

F1/14 Rear elevation

F1/15 Right profile

F1/16 Rear view of 'hoiban'

F1/17 Section of 'hoiban' base

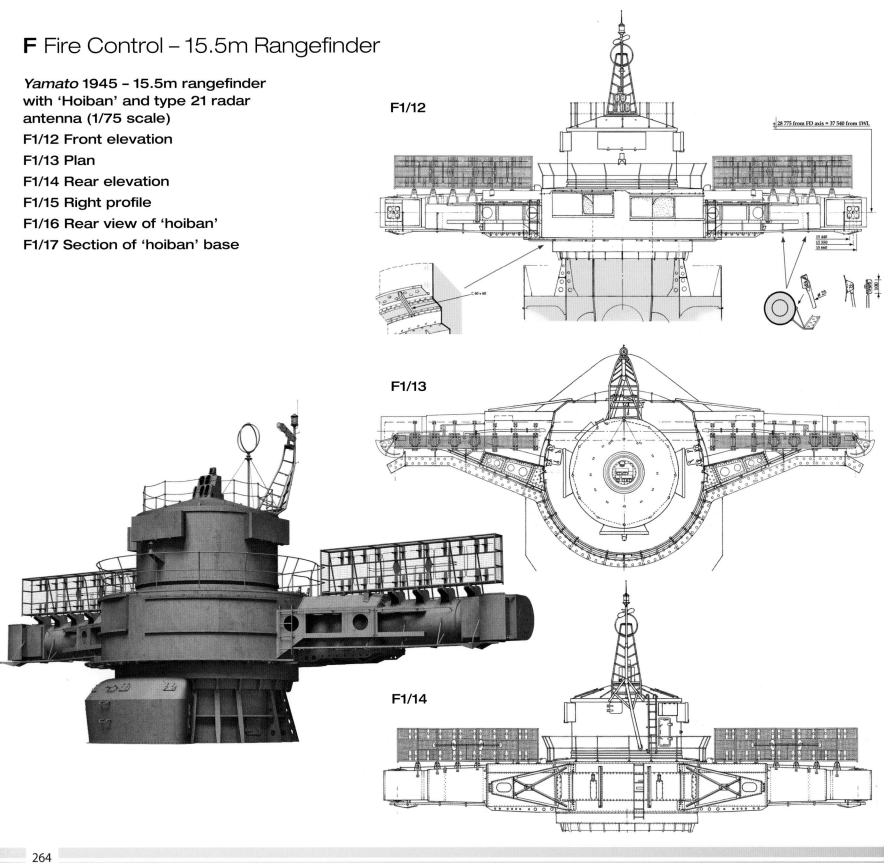

F1/12

+ 28 775 from FD axis = 37 540 from 1WL

15 440
15 550
15 660

F1/13

F1/14

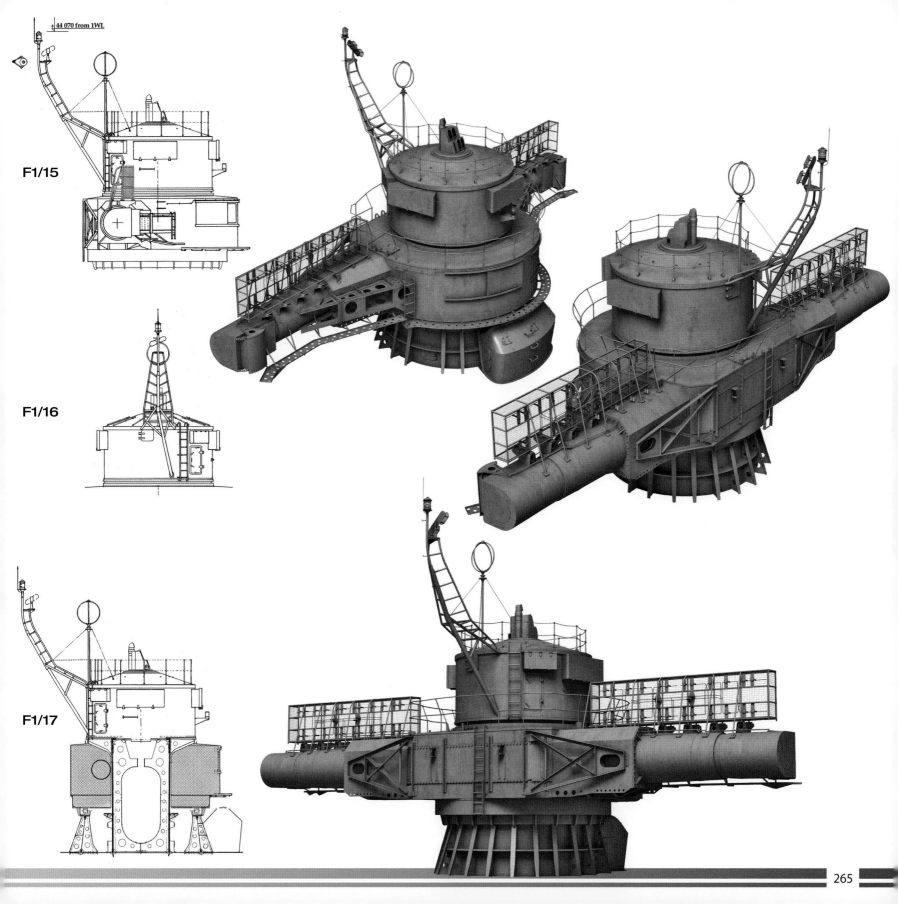

+ 44 070 from 1WL

F1/15

F1/16

F1/17

F Fire Control – 15.5m Rangefinder

Musashi 1944 15.5m rangefinder, 'Hoiban' and type 21
radar antenna (1/75 scale)

F1/18 'Hoiban' right profile

F1/19 Rear elevation

F1/20 Plan (fragment)

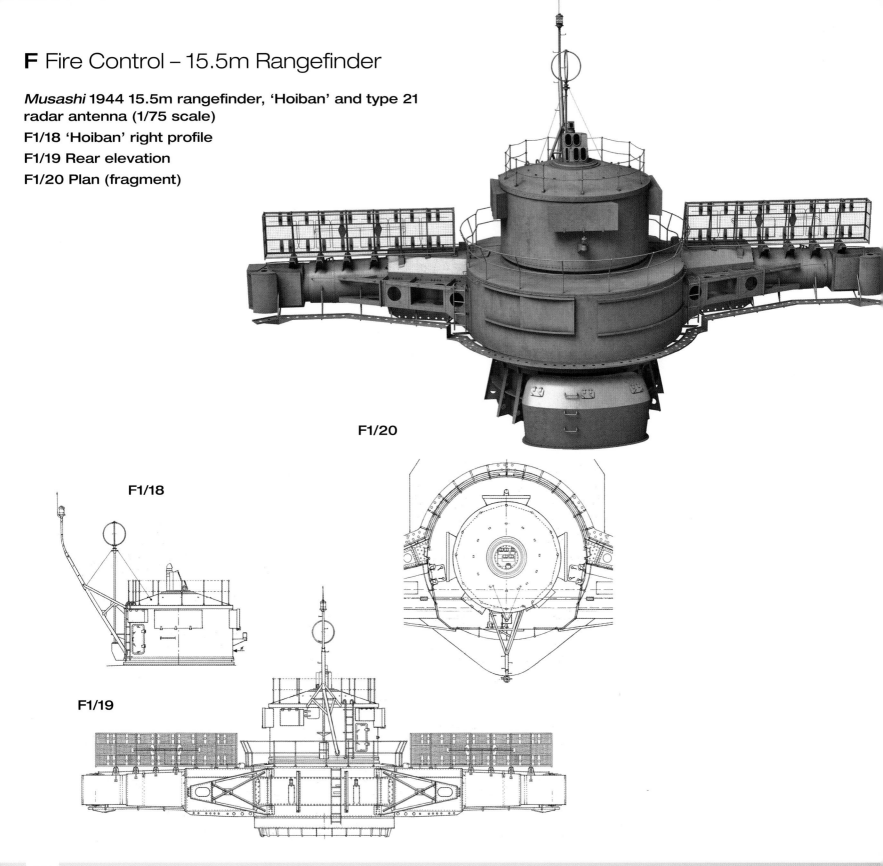

F1/20

F1/18

F1/19

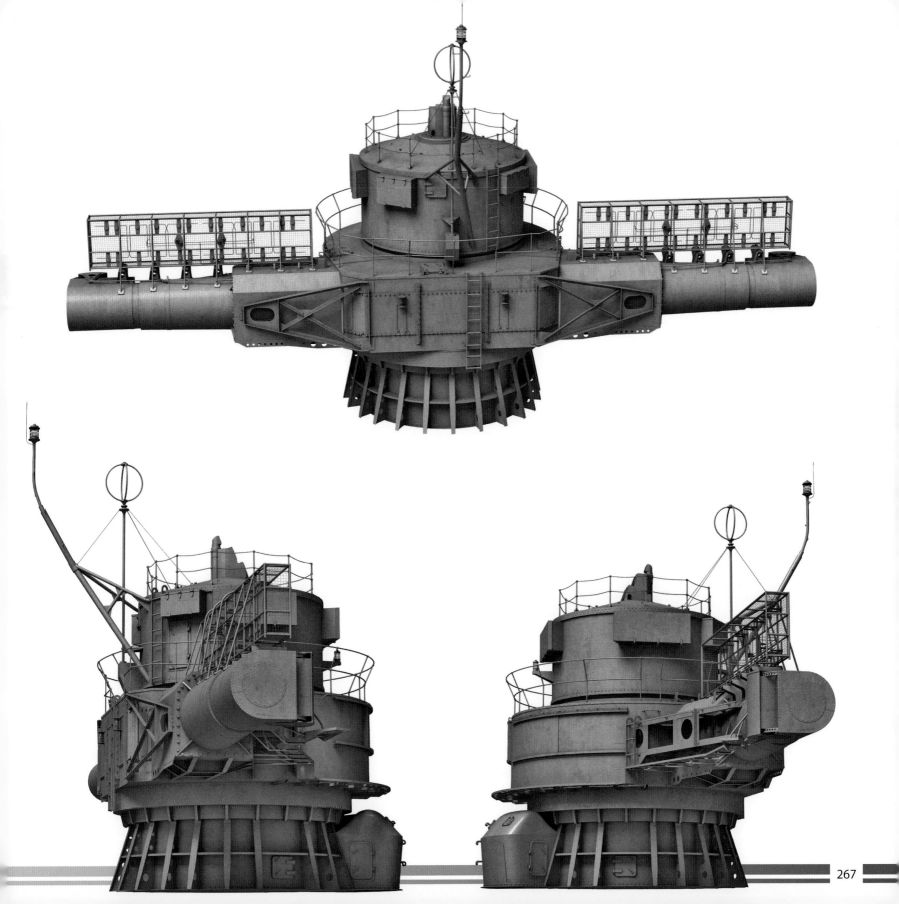

F Fire Control – 15.5m Rangefinder

21 Gō Dentan Kai 3 air search radar mattress type antenna (no scale)

F1/20 View from Hoiban direction

F1/21 Section

F1/22 Assembly detail

F1/23 Wire screen grid

F1/24 Section 'G'

F1/25 Mattress type antenna dimensions (1/50 scale)

F1/26 Front elevation

F1/27 Rear elevation

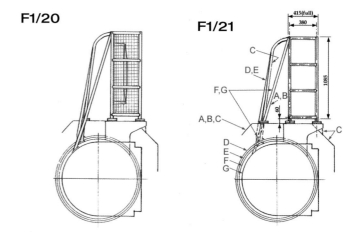

F1/20

F1/21

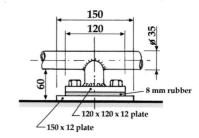

F1/22

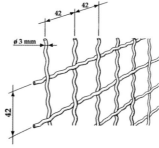

F1/23

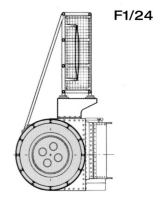

F1/24

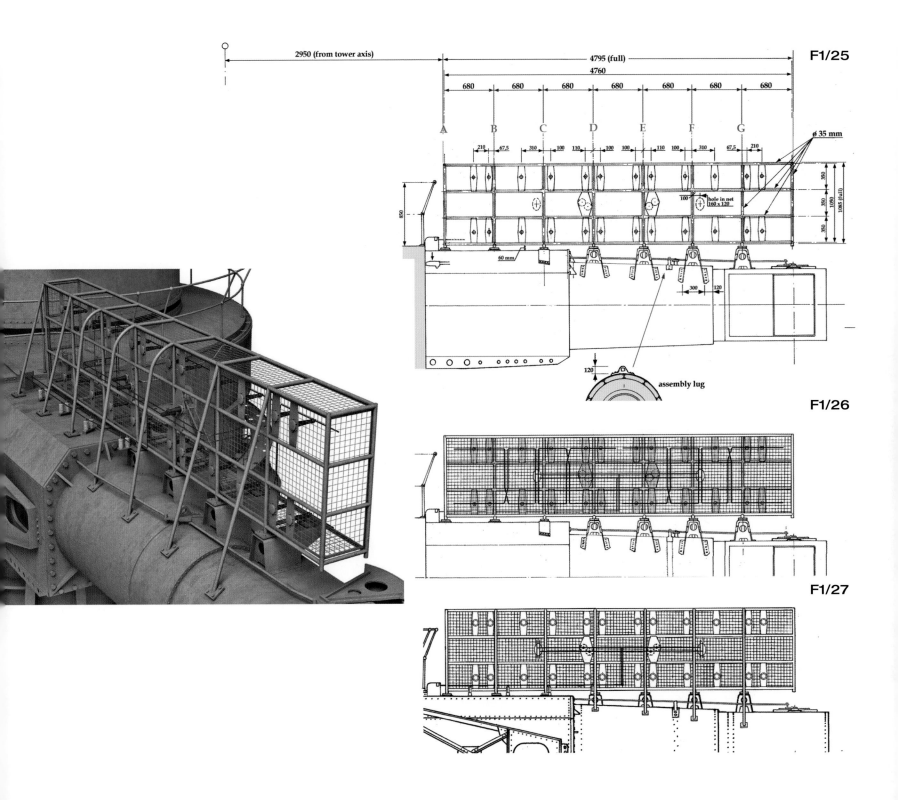

F1/25

F1/26

F1/27

F Fire Control – 15.5m Rangefinder

15.5m Rangefinder arm (no scale)
F1/28 Plan 1941
F1/29 Plan 1943
F1/30 View 'X'
F1/31 View 'Y'

15.5m Rangefinder arm details
F1/32 Section B-B
F1/33 Section A-A
F1/34 Detail of antenna base
F1/35 Rivets
F1/36 Front elevation

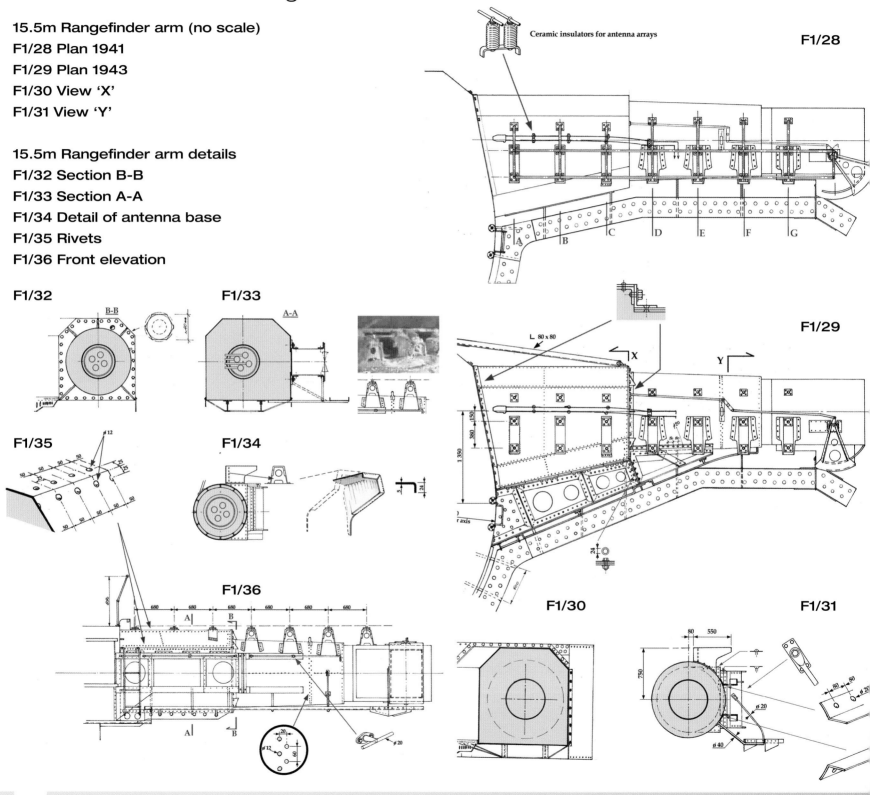

Ceramic insulators for antenna arrays

F1/28

F1/32

F1/33

F1/35

F1/34

F1/29

F1/30

F1/31

F1/36

21 Gō Dentan Kai 3 air search radar mattress type antenna fore insulators and frame (1/5 scale)

F1/37 Section

F1/38 Front view of insulators

F1/39 Rear view of insulator base

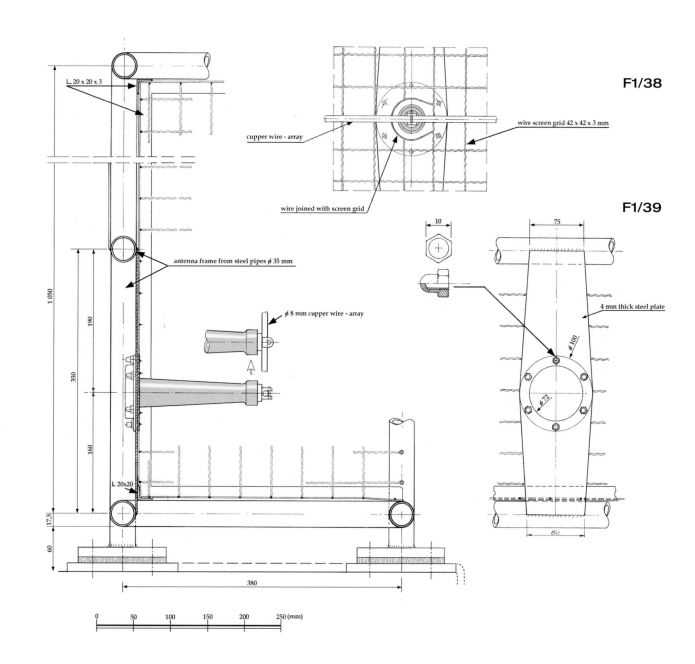

F1/37

F1/38

F1/39

L 20 x 20 x 3

cupper wire - array

wire screen grid 42 x 42 x 3 mm

wire joined with screen grid

antenna frame from steel pipes ∅ 35 mm

∅ 8 mm cupper wire - array

4 mm thick steel plate

∅ 100

∅ 72

10

75

80

1 050

190

350

160

17,5

60

380

0   50   100   150   200   250 (mm)

L 20x20

F Fire Control – 15.5m Rangefinder

F1/40 Rear view of aft insulators

F1/41 Profile of aft insulators (1/5 scale)

Type 21 Gō radar antenna

F1/42 Front view

F1/43 Rear view

F1/42

F1/43

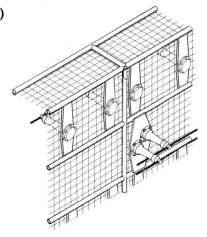

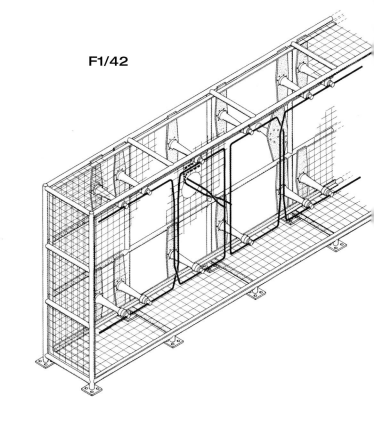

F1/40

F1/41

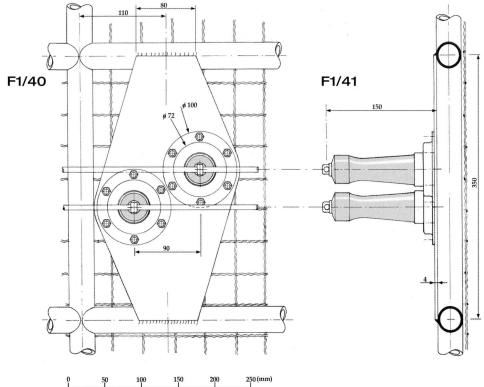

110

80

ø 100

ø 72

90

150

350

4

0   50   100   150   200   250 (mm)

Low angle director 'Hoiban' and 10m rangefinder from rear tower

F1/44 Front elevation – view from stern direction

F1/45 Open arm window

F1/46 Periscope tower

F1/47 Observation angels of periscope tower

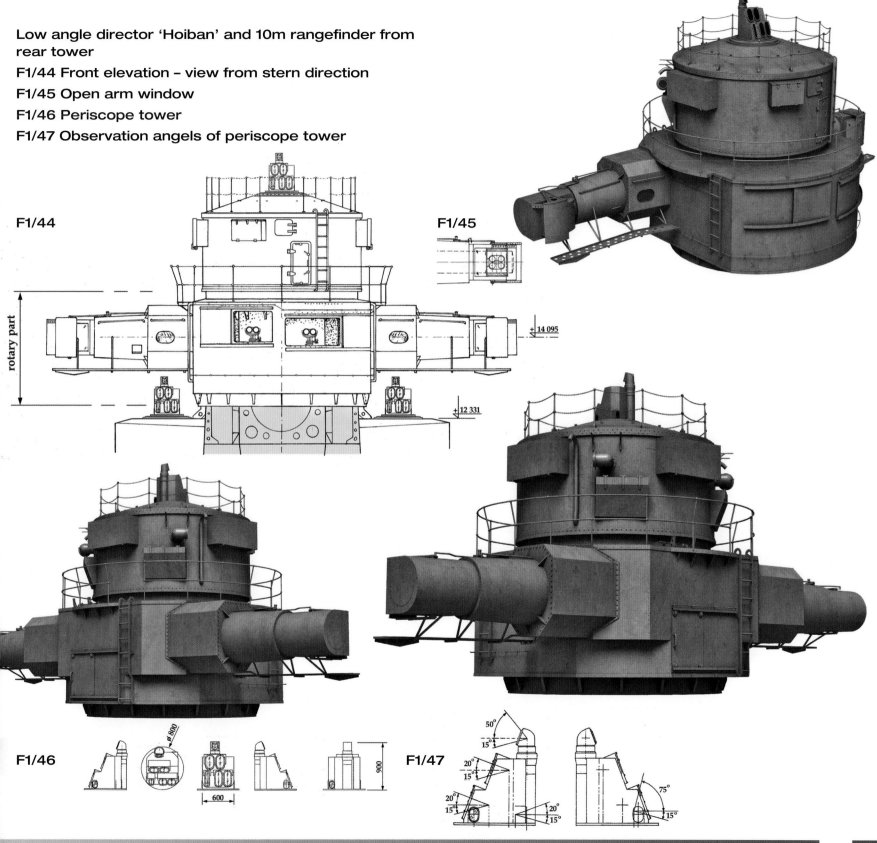

F1/44

rotary part

+ 14 095

+ 12 331

F1/45

F1/46

ø 800

600

900

F1/47

50°

15°

20°

15°

20°

15°

20°

15°

75°

15°

F Fire Control – 'Hoiban' and 10m Rangefinder

'Hoiban' and 10m rangefinder
F1/48 Plan
F1/49 Plan of rangefinder's room – rotatable part
F1/50 Plan of rangefinder arm
F1/51 Front view of open window
F1/52 Rear elevation – view from bow direction
F1/53 Starboard elevation
F1/54 Water-tight seal of rotatable periscope tower

F1/52

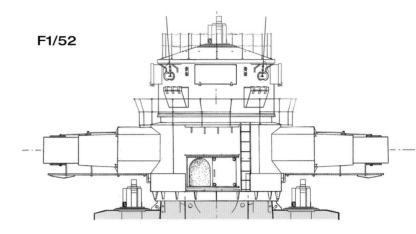

F1/48

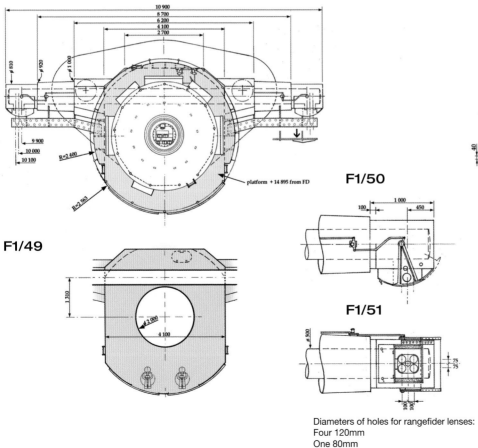

F1/49

F1/53

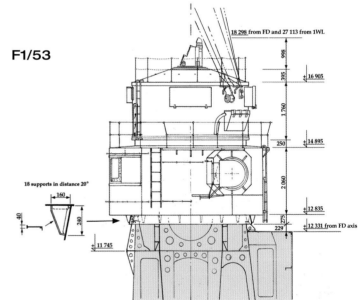

F1/50

F1/51

Diameters of holes for rangefider lenses:
Four 120mm
One 80mm

F1/54

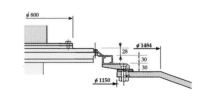

Type 13 Gō air search radar antenna installed on both
sides of main mast (1/50 scale)(1/50 scale)

F1/55 Profile
F1/56 Front view
F1/57 Rear view
F1/58 Plan
F1/59 Section of pillar

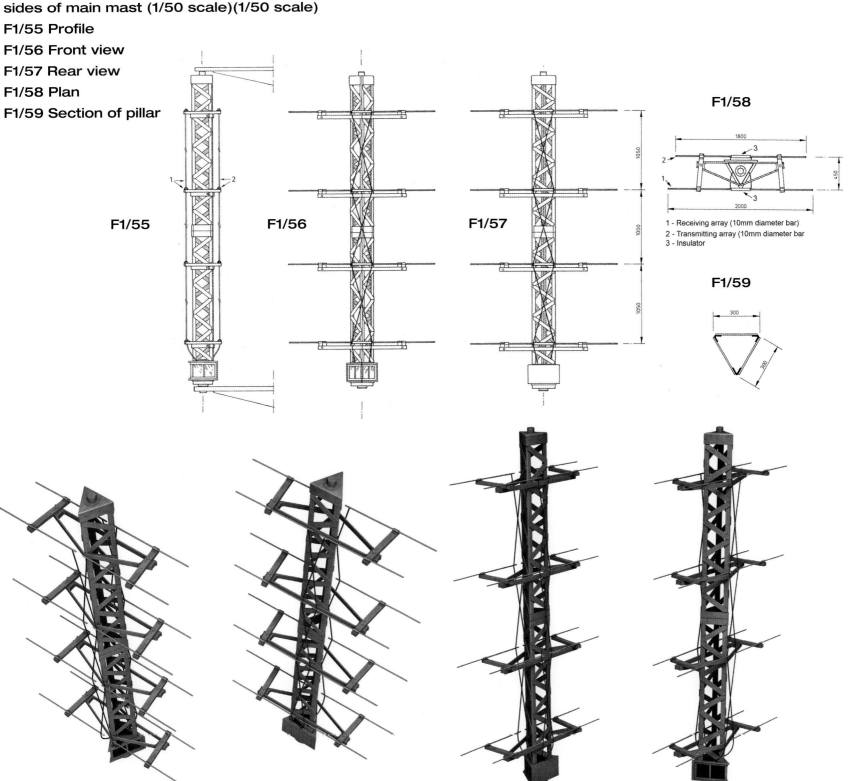

F1/55

F1/56

F1/57

F1/58

1 - Receiving array (10mm diameter bar)
2 - Transmitting array (10mm diameter bar
3 - Insulator

F1/59

F Fire Control – 15.5m Rangefinder

Type 22 Gō Dentan Kai 4 surface search radar horns
Antenna fitted in January – April 1944 (1/20 scale)

Receiving horn – upper
Transmitting horn – lower

F1/60 Side view
F1/61 Plan

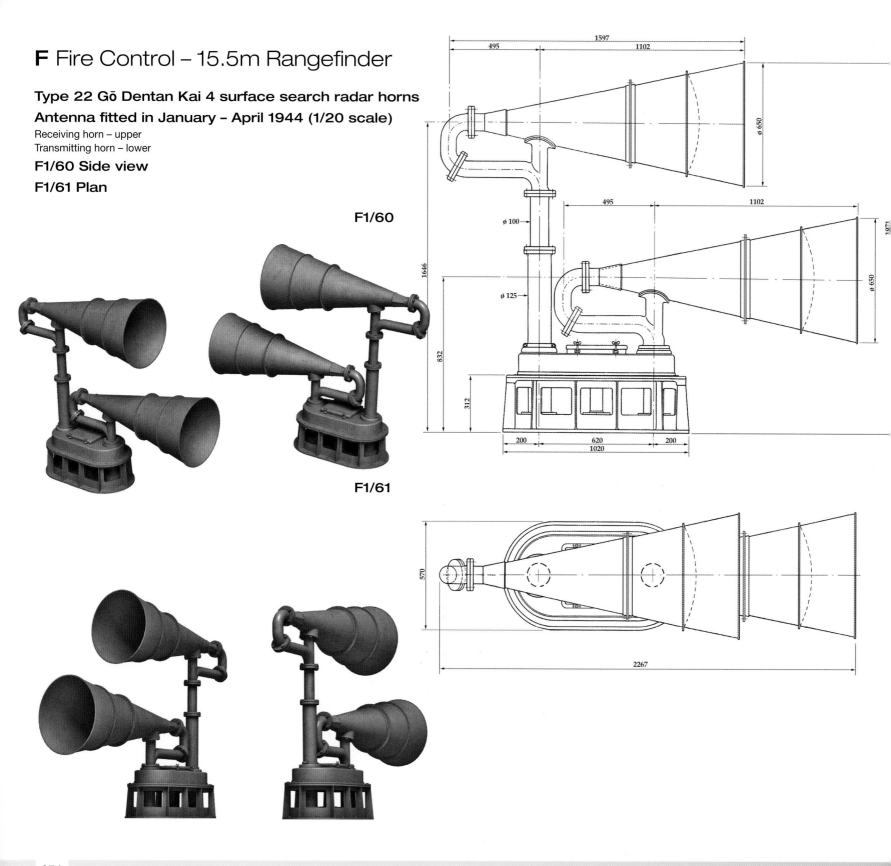

F1/60

F1/61

F Fire Control – 4.5m to 1.5m Rangefinders

4.5m Rangefinder type 94 for high angle fire control fitted on *Yamato* and *Musashi* (*Musashi* version until end of 1942) Fitted at frame 125 (1/100 scale)

F2/1 Left profile (closed windows)

F2/2 Front (port side) elevation

F2/3 Right profile

F2/4 Plan

F2/5 Left profile with open windows and rotating shield of rangefinder arm

F2/6 Right profile with open windows and rotating shield

F2/7 Observation port cover

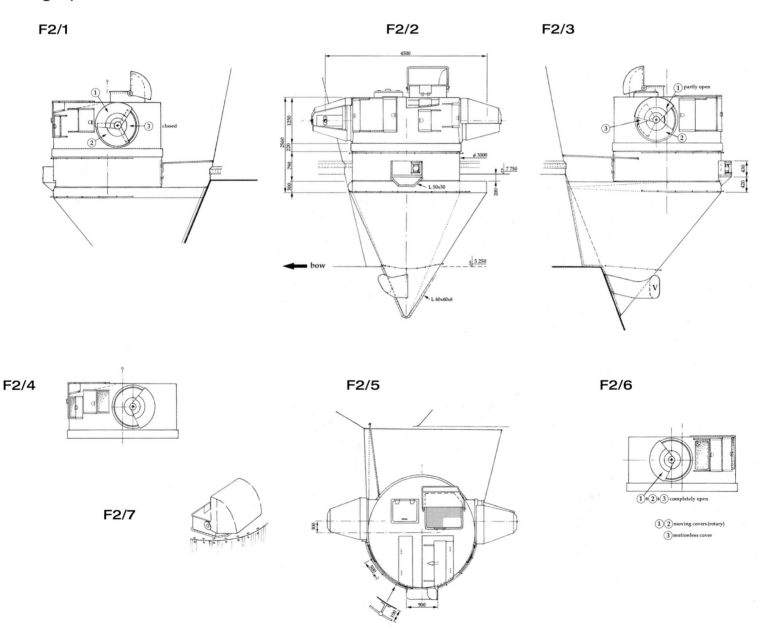

F2/1

F2/2

F2/3

F2/4

F2/5

F2/6

F2/7

F Fire Control – 4.5m to 1.5m Rangefinders

Perspective views of 4.5m Rangefinder type 94 for
high angle fire control fitted on *Yamato* and *Musashi*
(*Musashi* version until end of 1942) Fitted at frame 125

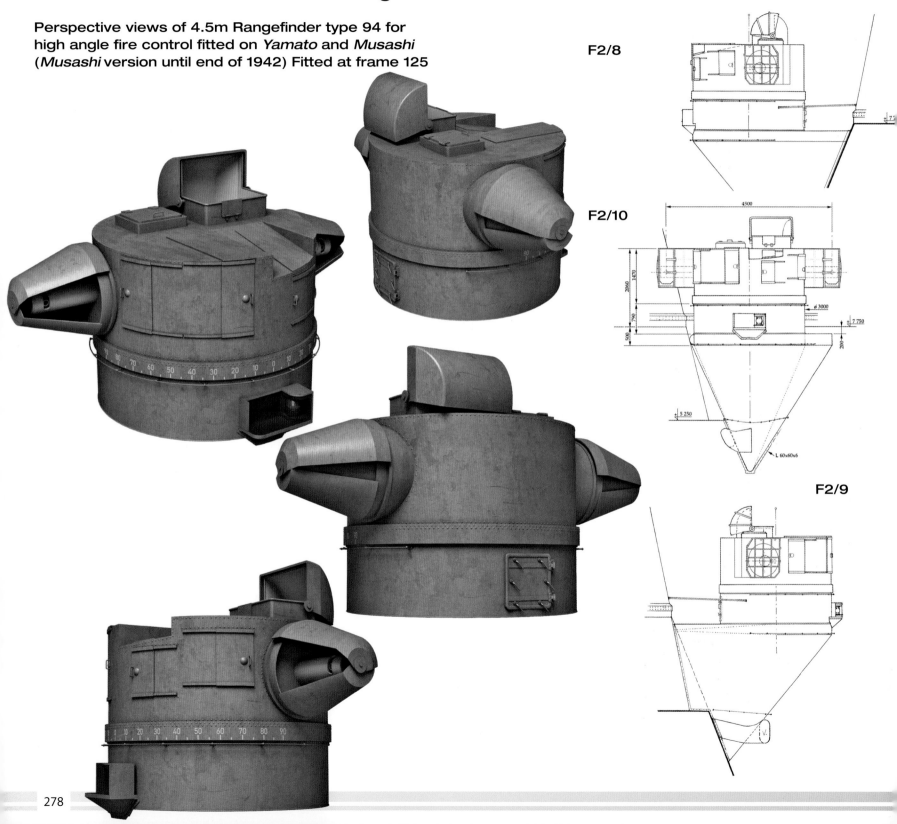

F2/8

F2/10

F2/9

4.5m Rangefinder type 94 on *Musashi* after modernisation in early 1943 (1/100 scale)

F2/8 Left profile

F2/9 Front elevation (port side)

F2/10 Right profile

F2/11 Plan

F2/12 Right profile with open windows

F2/13 Windows handle

F2/11

F2/12

F2/13

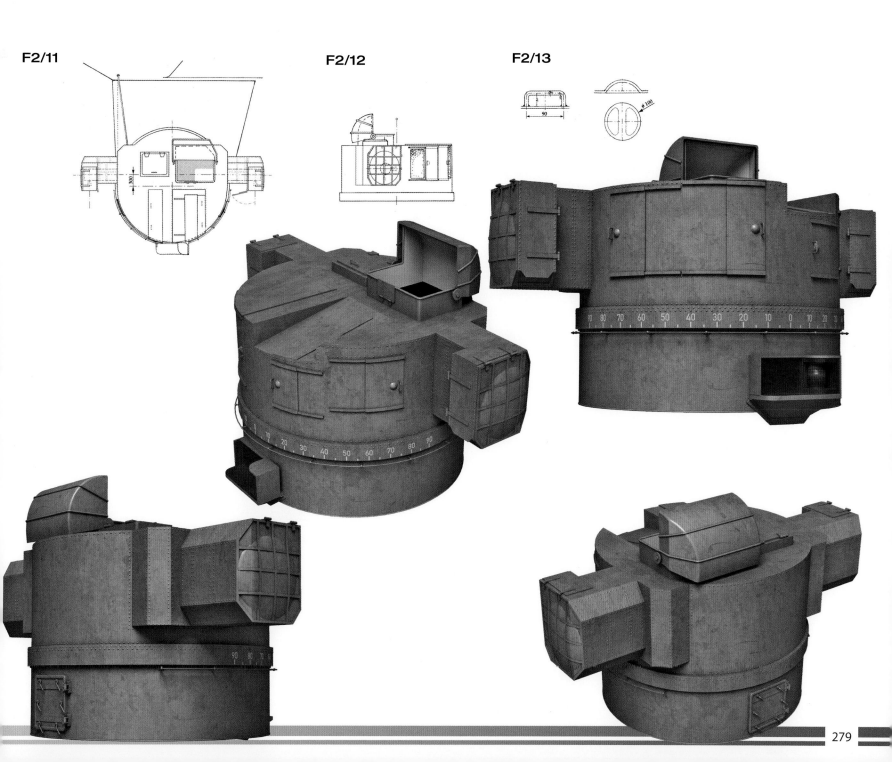

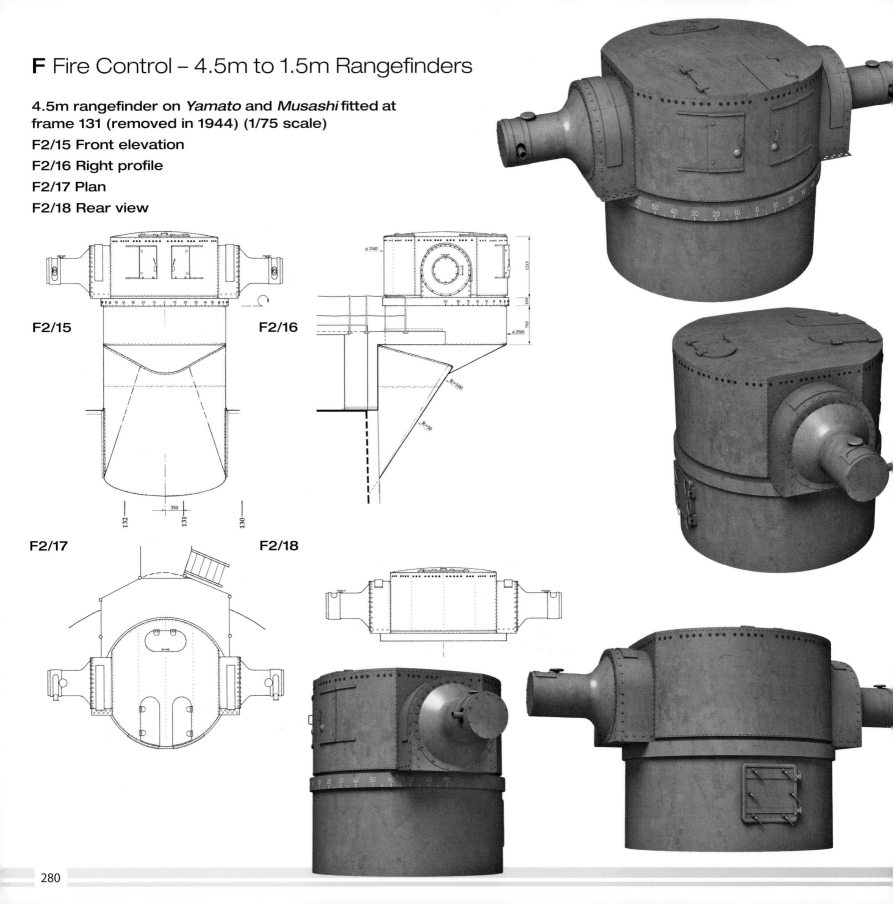

F Fire Control – 4.5m to 1.5m Rangefinders

4.5m rangefinder on *Yamato* and *Musashi* fitted at frame 131 (removed in 1944) (1/75 scale)

F2/15 Front elevation

F2/16 Right profile

F2/17 Plan

F2/18 Rear view

F2/15

F2/16

F2/17

F2/18

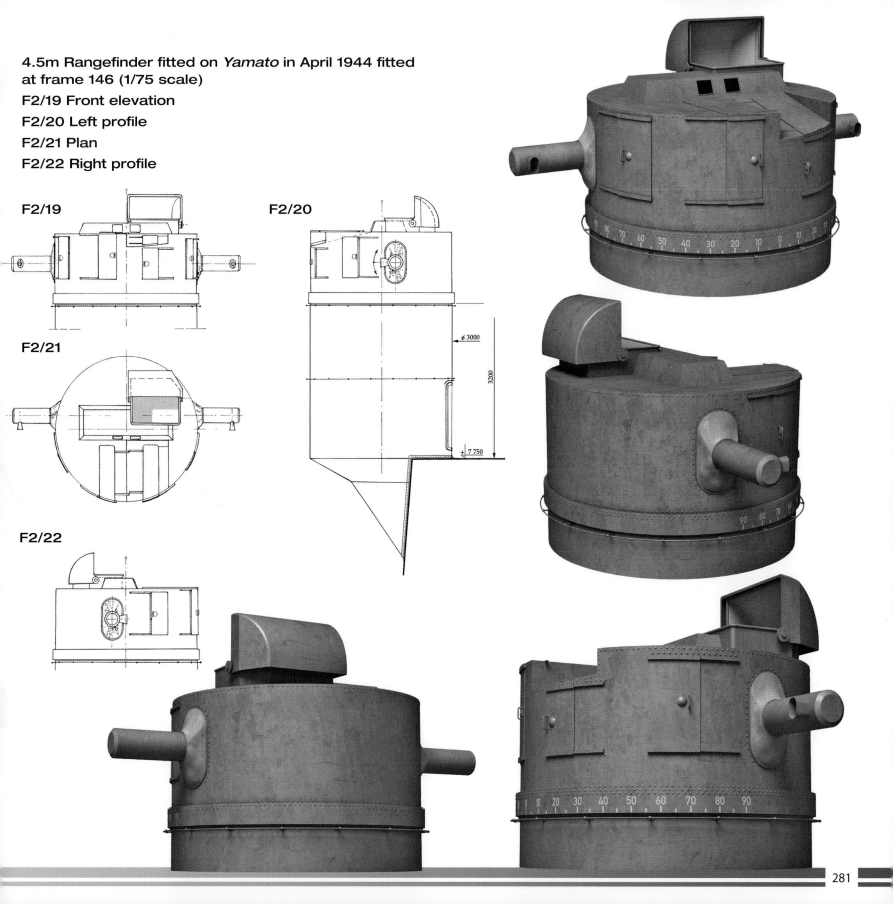

4.5m Rangefinder fitted on *Yamato* in April 1944 fitted at frame 146 (1/75 scale)

F2/19 Front elevation

F2/20 Left profile

F2/21 Plan

F2/22 Right profile

F2/19

F2/20

F2/21

F2/22

F Fire Control – 4.5m to 1.5m Rangefinders

**1.5m Type 14 navigation rangefinder from fore wall
of tower bridge (1/50 scale)**

F2/23 Profile view

F2/24 Front elevation

F2/25 Left profile

F2/26 Plan

F2/27 Sections of base column

F2/28 Roller bearing

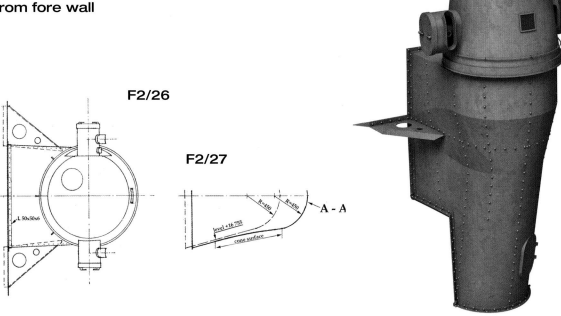

F2/26

F2/27

L 50x50x6

R=450 R=450 A - A

level +16 755 cone surface

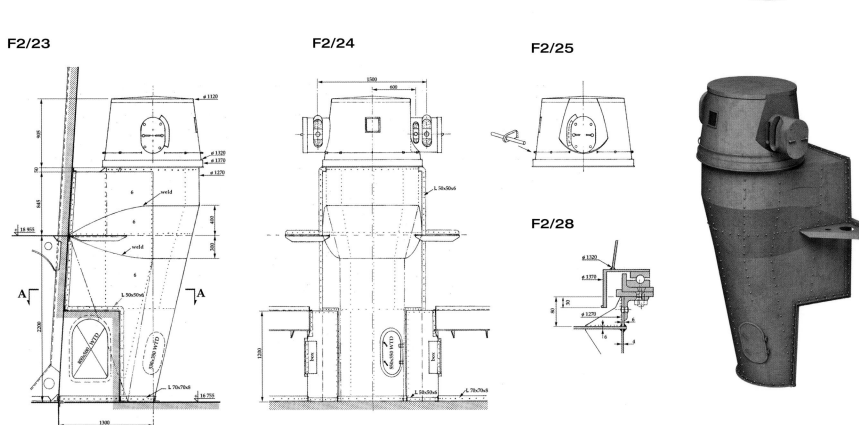

F2/23

ø 1120

905

50

845

18 955

6 weld

6

400

300

weld

6

A A

L 50x50x6

2200

800x500 WTD

550x350 WTD

L 70x70x8

16 755

1300

5900 from tower axis

ø 1320
ø 1370
ø 1270

F2/24

1500

600

L 50x50x6

1200

box

550x350 WTD

box

L 50x50x6 L 70x70x8

F2/25

F2/28

ø 1320

ø 1370

80

30

ø 1270

6

6

Type 85 machine gun fire control tower
F2/29 Plan of montage on compass bridge
F2/30 Right profile with base of compass bridge
F2/31 Front elevaton
F2/32 Plan
F2/33 Section A-A
F2/34 Author's study model

F2/29

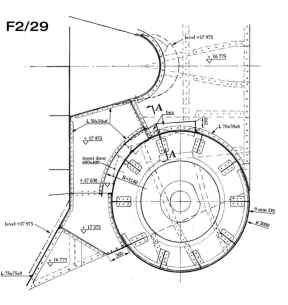

F2/30

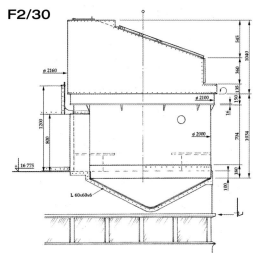

F2/33

A - A

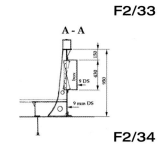

F2/34

F2/31

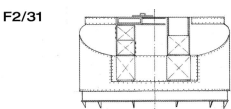

F2/32

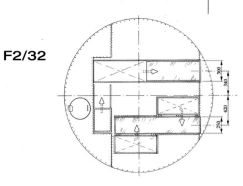

F Fire Control – 4.5m to 1.5m Rangefinders

Searchlight control tower (1/35 scale)
F2/35 Front view
F2/36 Profile
F2/37 Plan
F2/38 Rear view

Type 95 Kai 1 machine gun control tower (1/50 scale)
F2/39 Profile view with base at frame 154 (*Yamato* only)
F2/40 Rear view (*Yamato*)
F2/41 Plan (*Yamato*)
F2/42 Profile – other stands – *Yamato* and *Musashi*
F2/43 Roller bearing
F2/44 Section (scheme)

F2/35

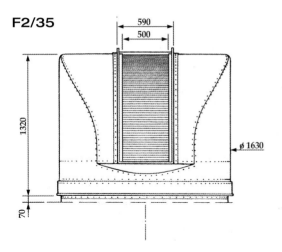

F2/36

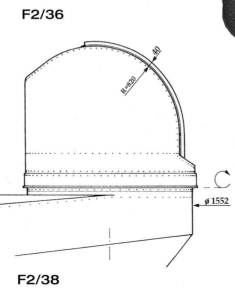

F2/37

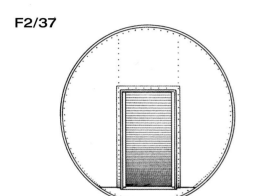

F2/38

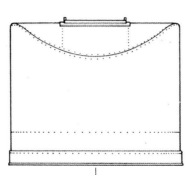

F2/39

F2/40

WTD 535x835

ø 2000

ø 800

F2/42

1780

760

1100

50

on frame ~ 216

F2/41

support fixed to superstructure

ladder

support fixed to rear tower bridge

F2/43

o 2200

150

o 2000

F2/44

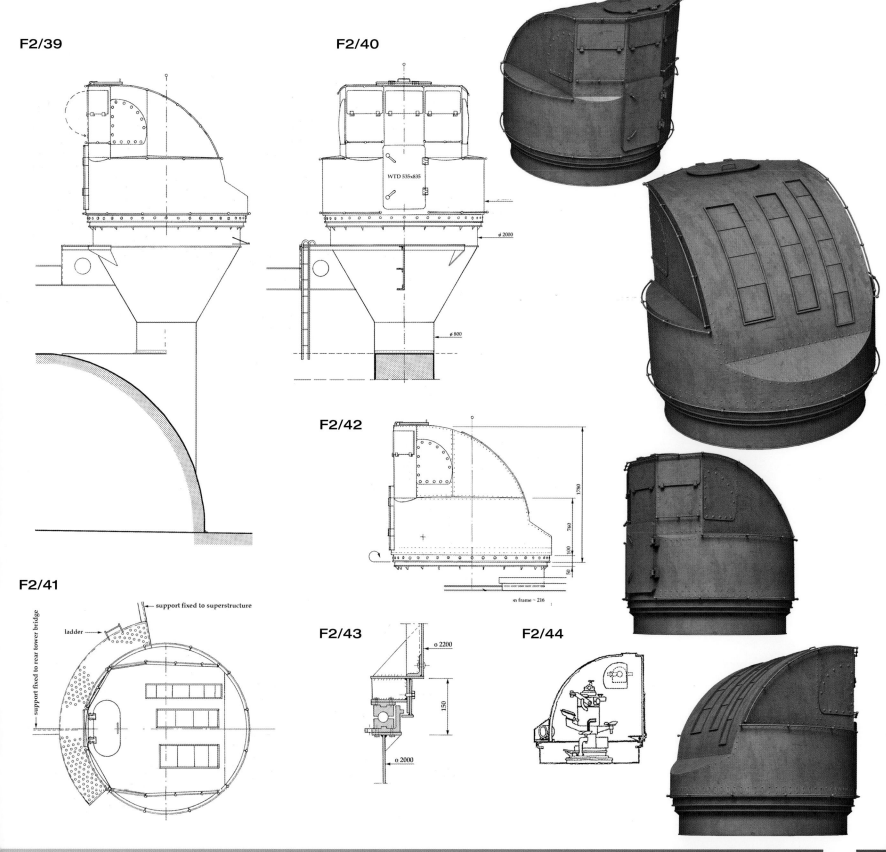

G Fittings – Searchlights

150cm searchlight (1/50 scale)

G1/1 Left profile

G1/2 Front view

G1/3 Right profile

G1/4 Rear view

G1/5 Plan

G1/6 Scheme

60cm signalling searchlight (1/50 scale)

G1/7 Left profile

G1/8 Front view

G1/9 Right profile

G1/10 Plan

G1/11 Rear cover

G1/12 60cm searchlight on sunken *Yamato*

G1/13 30cm Deck lamp (no scale)

G1/14 30cm Signalling lamp

G1/1

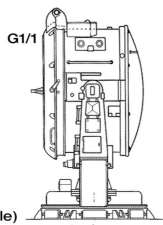

G1/2

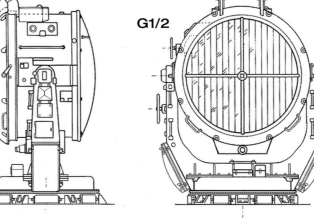

G1/3

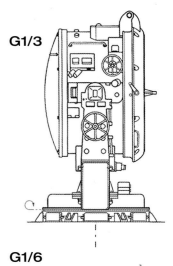

G1/4

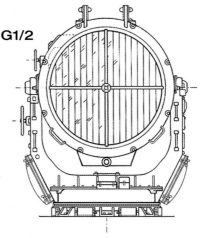

G1/5

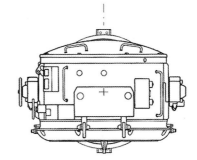

G1/6

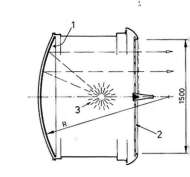

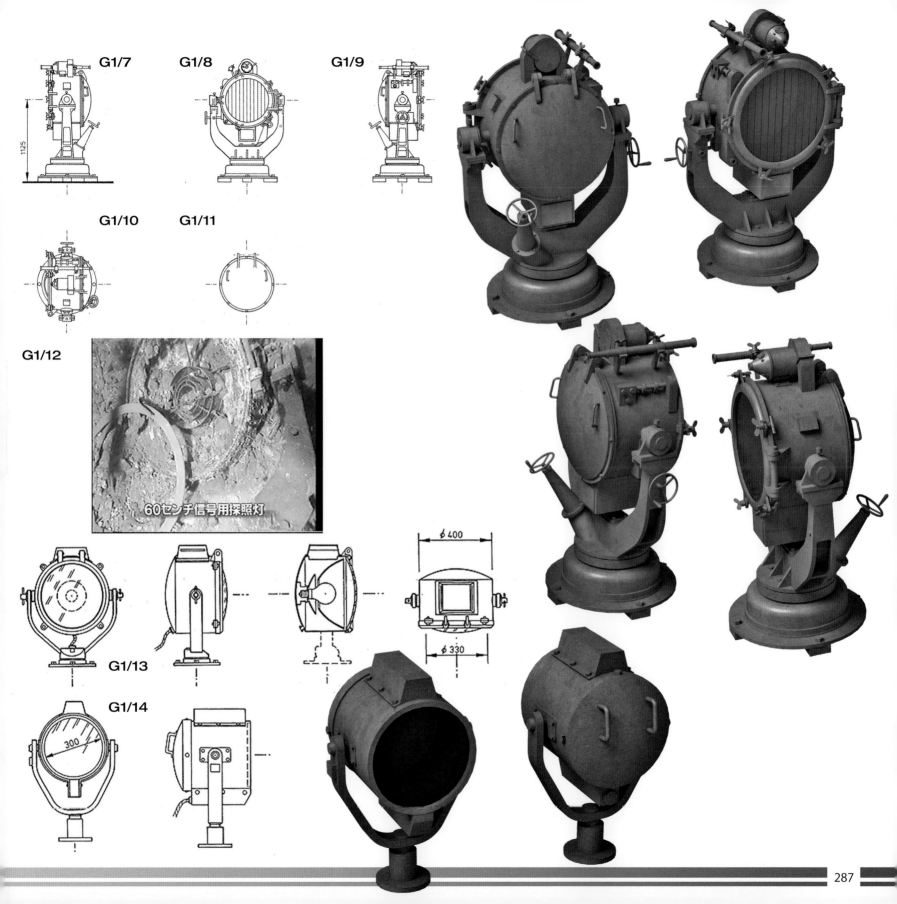

G1/7

G1/8

G1/9

1125

G1/10

G1/11

G1/12

60センチ信号用探照灯

G1/13

φ400

φ330

G1/14

300

G Fittings – Lanterns and Binoculars

G1/15 2kW daylight signal lantern (1/25 scale)

G1/16 Typical lantern

G1/17 8cm binoculars (1/25 scale)

G1/18 12cm binoculars

G1/19 6cm binoculars

G1/20 Typical mounting

G1/21 Binoculars with signalling lamp

G1/22 12cm Binoculars with infra-red message transmitter

G1/23 12cm binoculars (1/25 scale)

G1/24 12cm binoculars

G1/25 1.5 m rangefinder from air combat platform of tower bridge

G1/26 18cm binoculars

G1/27 18cm binoculars from closed compartments of tower bridge

G1/28 12cm binoculars mount from air combat platform on sunken *Yamato*

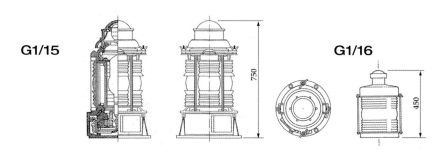

G1/15   G1/16

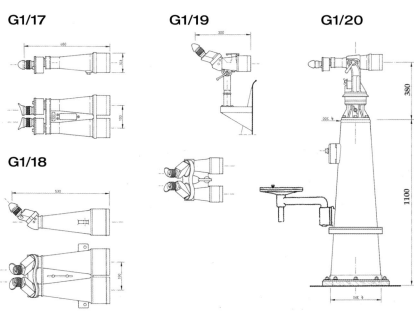

G1/17   G1/19   G1/20

G1/18

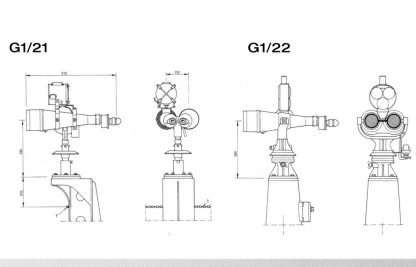

G1/21   G1/22

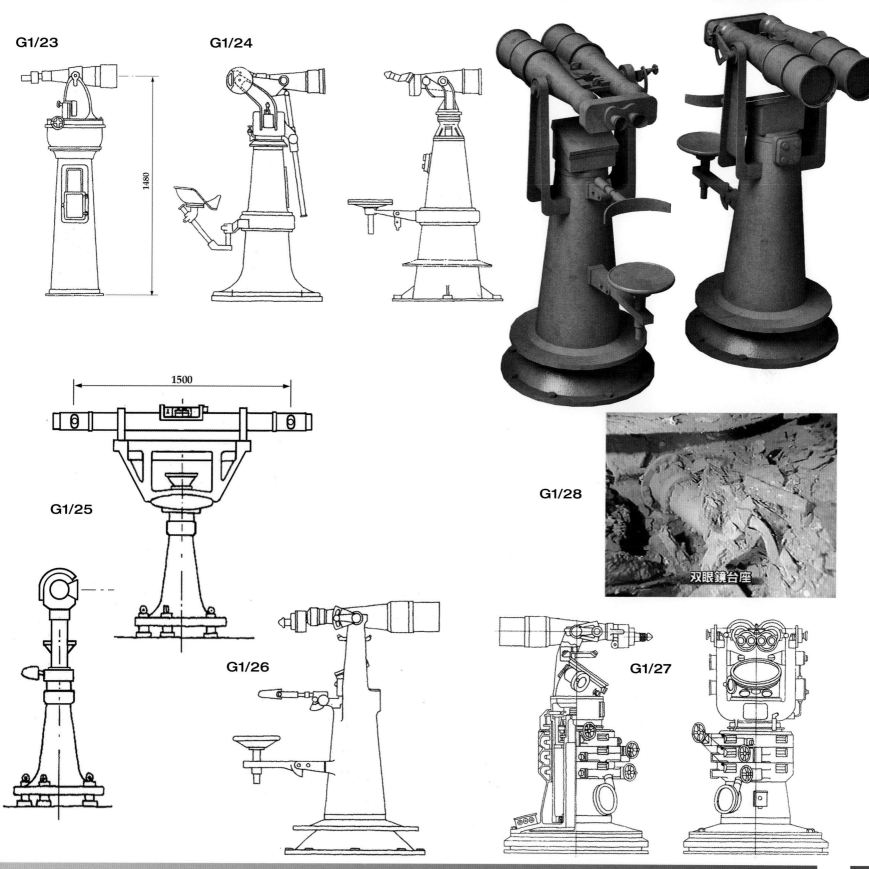

G1/23

G1/24

1480

1500

G1/25

G1/26

G1/27

G1/28

双眼鏡台座

G Fittings – Side Scuttles

Side Scuttle

G2/1 Inner view

G2/2 Section

G2/3 Front view of all types:

G2/3a side scuttle only *Musashi* at frames 101–104 and 116–126 (starboard side UD)

G2/3b side scuttle on UD and MD

G2/3c side scuttle of LD compartments and on super-structure walls

G2/3d side scuttle fitted on UD compartments at frames 156–162

G2/4 Hull scuttles blanked off by steel rings (diameter 50mm bigger than hole) after 1944 refit

Deck fittings

G2/5 Typical fairleads

G2/6 Bollards

G2/7 Davit

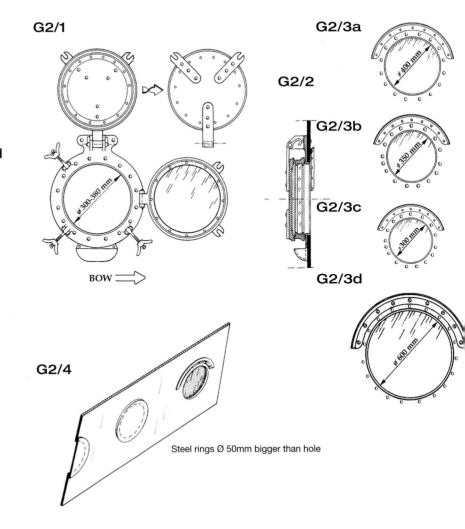

G2/1

G2/2

G2/3a

G2/3b

G2/3c

G2/3d

BOW

G2/4

Steel rings Ø 50mm bigger than hole

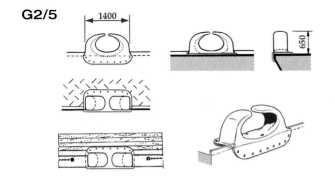

G2/5

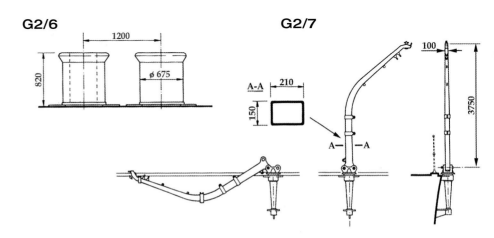

G2/6

G2/7

G2/8 Guardrails and edge of decks
G2/9 Profile view
G2/10 Section
G2/11 Guard rail stanchion
G2/12 Scupper
G2/13 View
G2/14 Plan

G2/8

G2/9

G2/10

G2/11

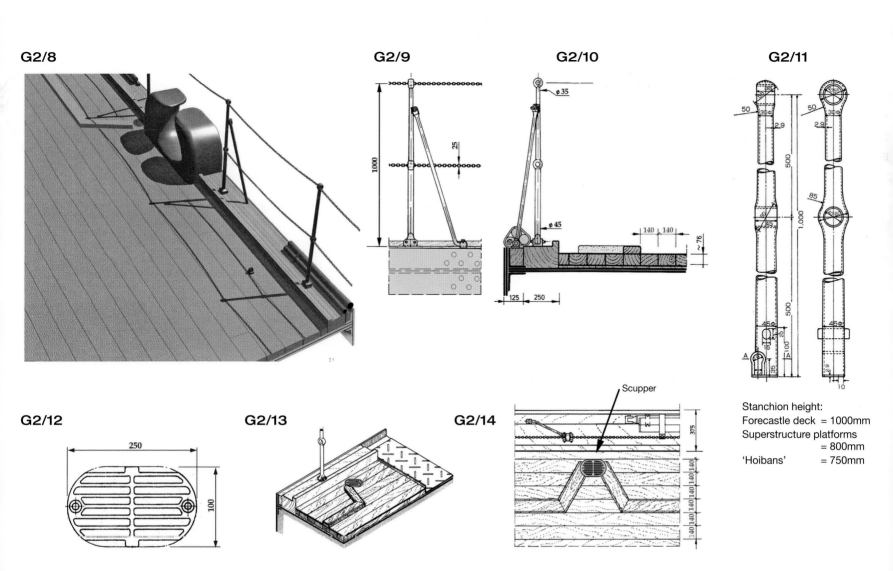

G2/12

G2/13

G2/14

Scupper

Stanchion height:
Forecastle deck = 1000mm
Superstructure platforms
                  = 800mm
'Hoibans'   = 750mm

G Fittings – Hatches and Ammunition Box

Deck hatch

G2/15 Plan

G2/16 Profile

G2/17 Rear view

G2/18 Profile of open hatch

25mm MG ammunition box for 240 rounds

G2/19 Profile

G2/20 Front view

G2/21 Plan

G2/19

G2/20

675

1065

466

24

G2/21

G2/15

1800

920

Manhole escape cover

G2/16

G2/17

G2/18

300

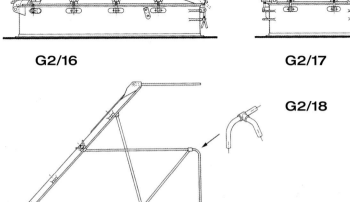

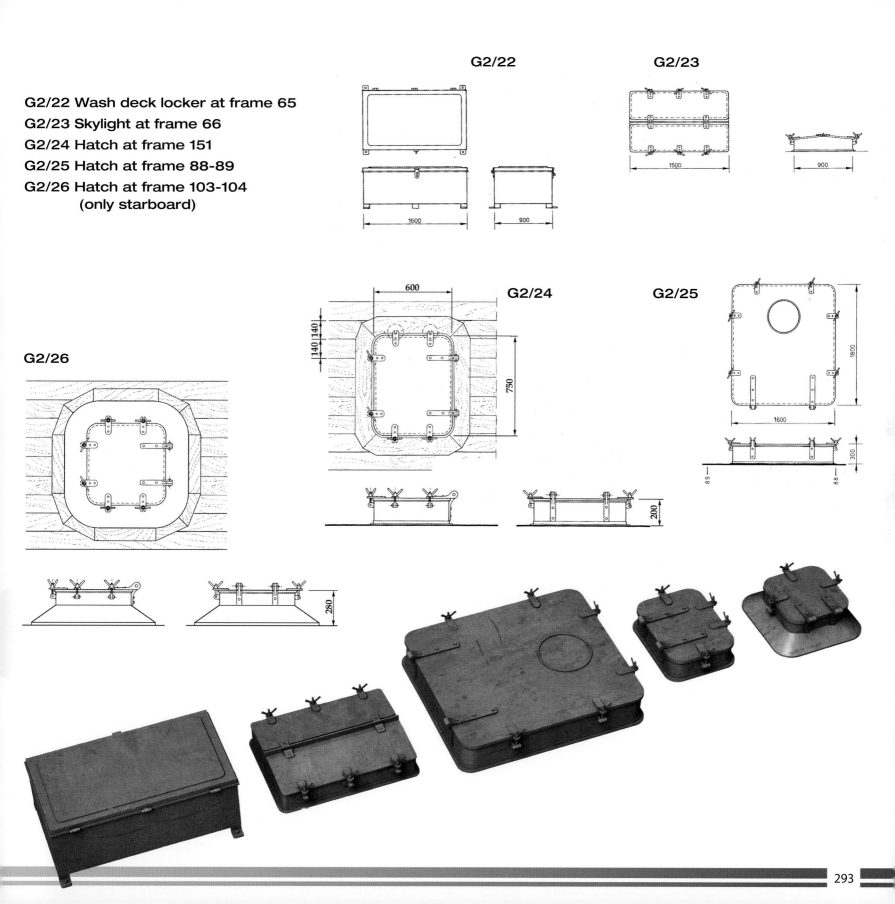

G2/22 Wash deck locker at frame 65

G2/23 Skylight at frame 66

G2/24 Hatch at frame 151

G2/25 Hatch at frame 88-89

G2/26 Hatch at frame 103-104
(only starboard)

G2/22

G2/23

G2/24

G2/25

G2/26

G Fittings – Water-tight Doors and Ladders

Water-tight doors

G2/27 Water-tight door of lower fore walls of superstructure

G2/28 Water-tight door from superstructure platforms

G2/29 Clip

G2/30 Water-tight door door from lower side walls of superstructure

G2/31 Clip

G2/27

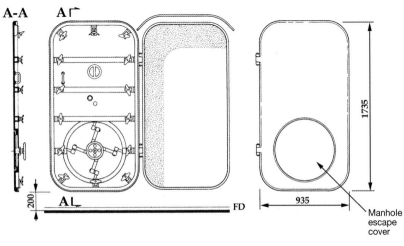

A-A   A

200

AL   FD

1735

935

Manhole escape cover

G2/29

G2/31

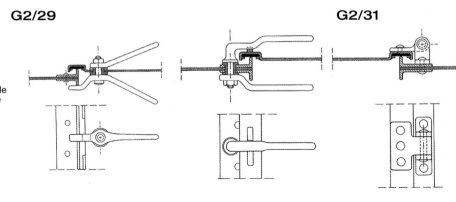

G2/28

a = white colour sign

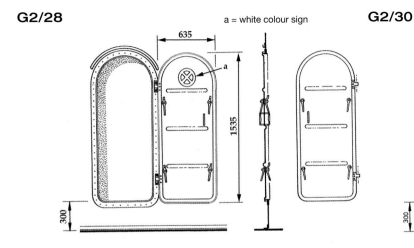

635

1535

300

G2/30

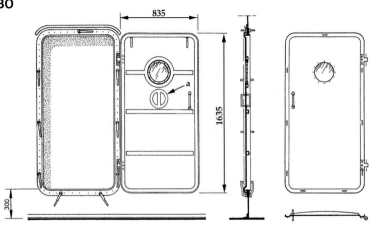

835

1635

300

a

Ladders

G2/32 Ladder from gunhouses, rangefinders

G2/33 From lower parts of superstructure

G2/34 From rear upper wall of tower bridge

G2/35 From signal platform

G2/33

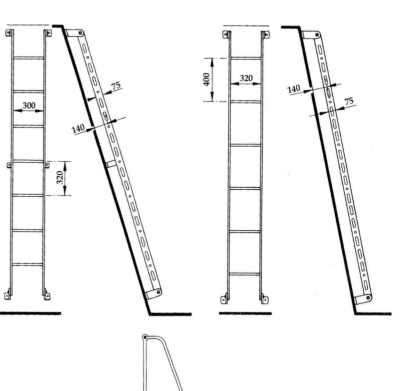

G2/32

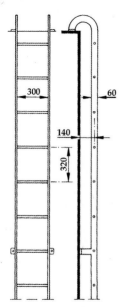

G2/34

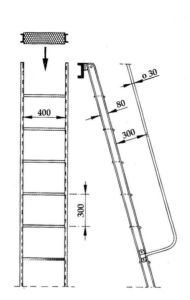

G2/35

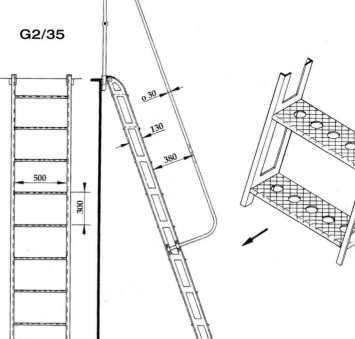

G Fittings – Reels And Parvane

Reels

G2/36 Type 'A' profile
G2/37 Type 'A' view
G2/38 Type 'B' profile
G2/39 Type 'B' view
G2/40 Type 'C'
G2/41 Type 'D'
G2/42 Type 'E'
G2/43 Type 'F'
G2/44 scheme of protection cover

Reels type A, B, C, D fitted at frame 60
Reels type D, E, F fitted at frames 65-66
Reels type B on frame 191, type C at frame 194

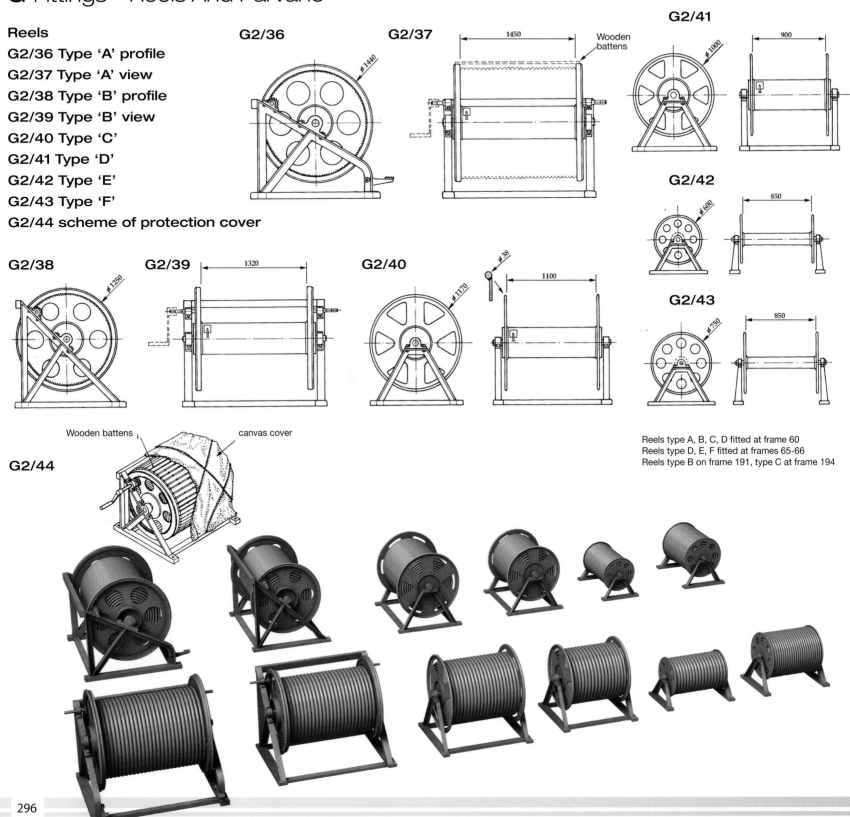

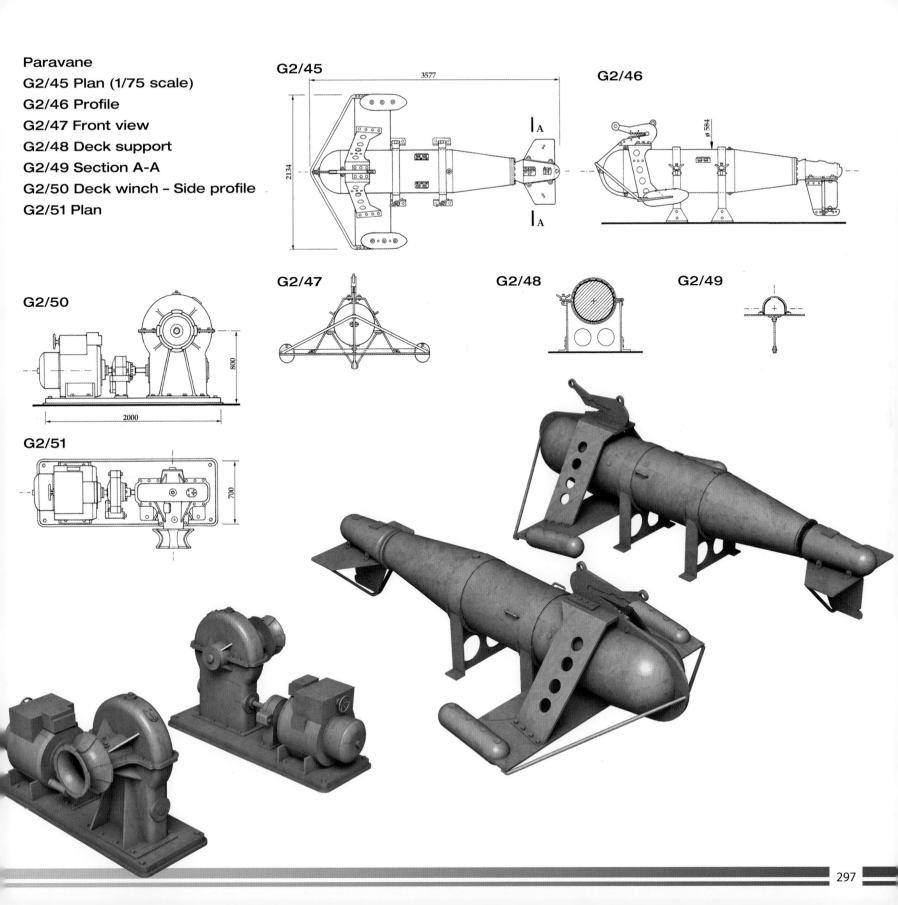

Paravane

G2/45 Plan (1/75 scale)

G2/46 Profile

G2/47 Front view

G2/48 Deck support

G2/49 Section A-A

G2/50 Deck winch – Side profile

G2/51 Plan

G2/45

G2/46

G2/47

G2/48

G2/49

G2/50

G2/51

G Fittings – Anchoring

Electric cable holder – port bower (1/75 scale)

G2/52 Profile view

G2/53 Plan

G2/54 Rear view

G2/55 Forecastle electric capstan – plan

G2/56 Profile

G2/57 Anchor cable

G2/58 Deck stopper (two per one anchor cable) profile
and view

Stern anchor (1/50 scale)

G2/59 Front view

G2/60 Profile

**15-ton main anchor (Imperial Japanese Navy design)
stockless type (1/50 scale)**

G2/61 View

G2/62 Profile

G2/63 Bottom view

G2/64 Sections

G2/52

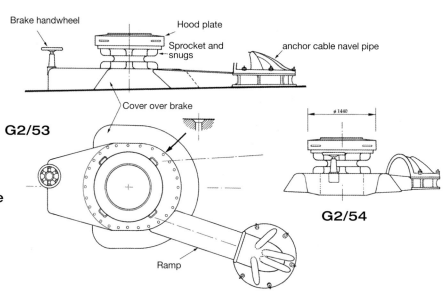

G2/53

G2/54

G2/55

G2/56

G2/57

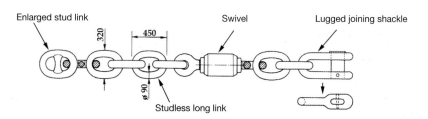

G2/58

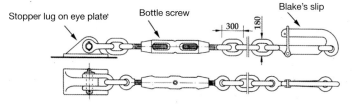

G2/59

G2/60

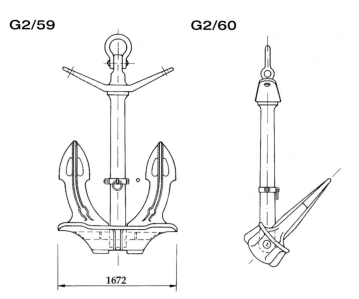

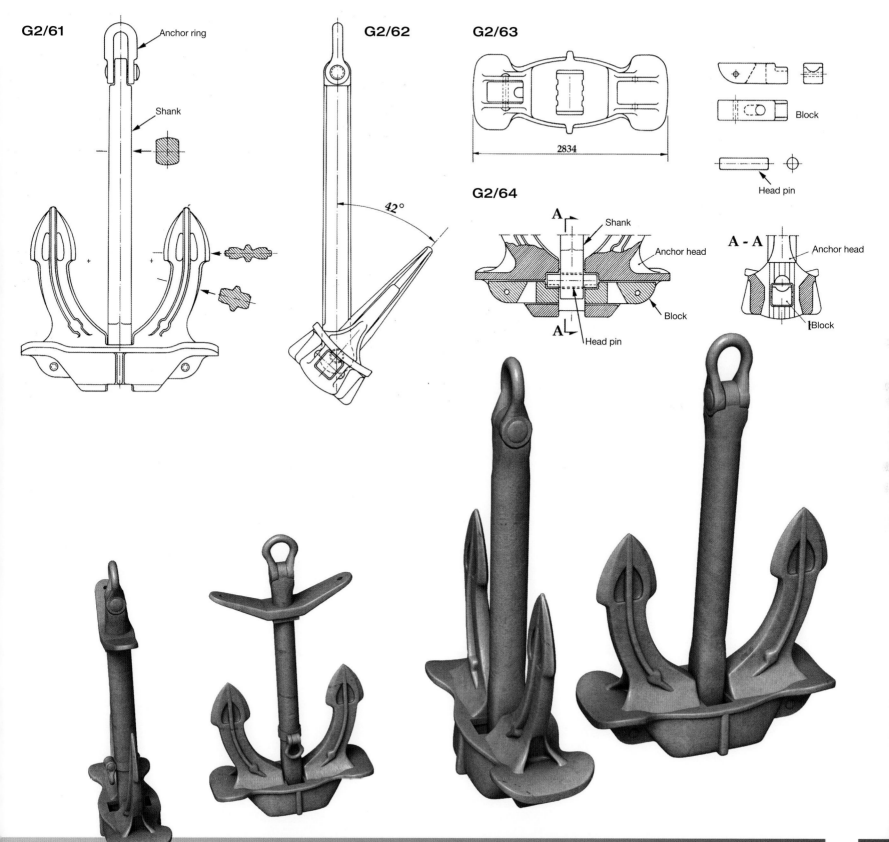

G2/61

Anchor ring

Shank

G2/62

42°

G2/63

2834

Block

Head pin

G2/64

A

Shank

Anchor head

Block

A

Head pin

A - A

Anchor head

Block

G Fittings

Lifebuoy frame (1/35 scale)
G2/65 Front view
G2/66 Profile
G2/67 Perspective

Wind intensity transmitter
G2/68 Front view
G2/69 Plan

Wind direction indicator
G2/70 Front view
G2/71 Plan

G2/72 Mounting for *Yamato* – port side profile
G2/73 Plan
G2/74 Mounting for *Musashi* – port side profile
G2/75 Plan

G2/66

G2/65

ø 800

G2/67

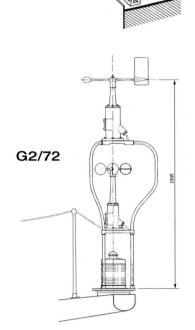

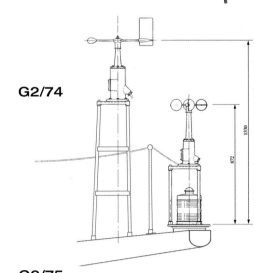

G2/68

180

430

G2/70

430

G2/72

1505

G2/74

1330

872

G2/69

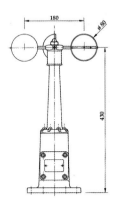

G2/71

260

223

G2/73

BOW

G2/75

BOW

G2/76

Yamato

Musashi

Tripod

Lantern

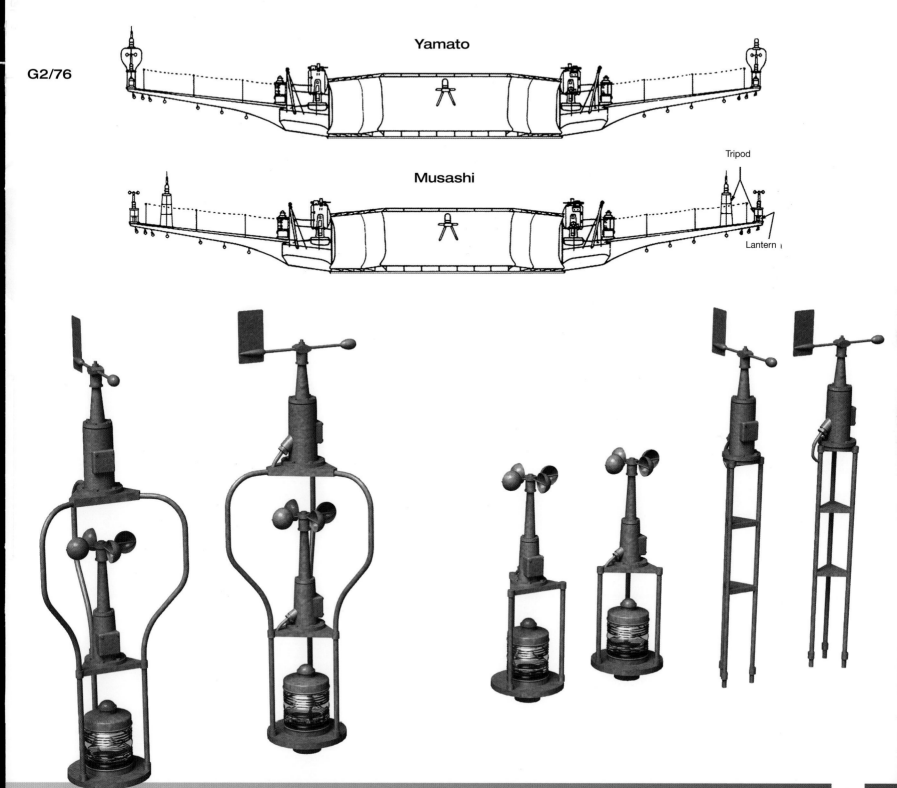

G Fittings

Antenna wires connecting tube

G-2/77 Plan

G-2/78 Front view

G-2/79 Profile

Ventilation intake fom superstructure walls

G2/80 Details of ventilator intake (1/15 scale)
  – Typical wire netting intake with railing for canvas shield
  – Ventilation intake shutter at back of conning tower

G2/81 Small ventilators from superstructure walls (1/15 scale)

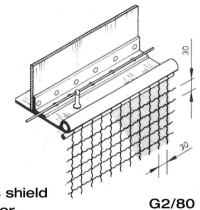
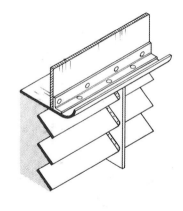

G2/80

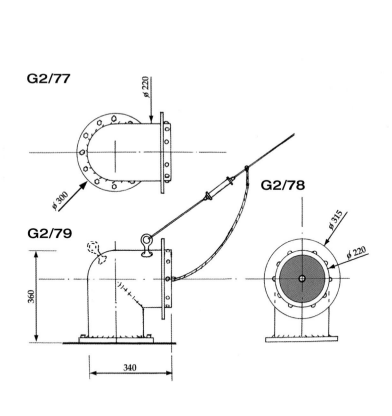

G2/77

G2/78

G2/79

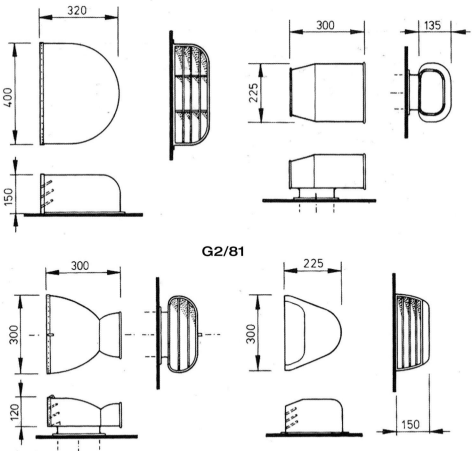

G2/81

G2/82 Detail of bulwarks

G2/83 Type 90 radio antenna from upper part of tower bridge
G2/84 Depth charge fitted on *Musashi* stern deck in 1944

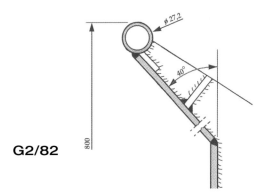

G2/82

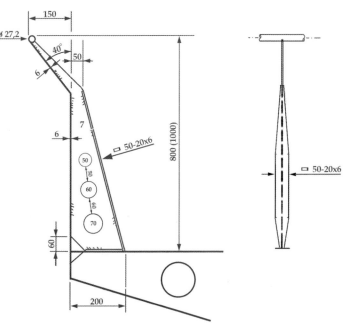

G2/83

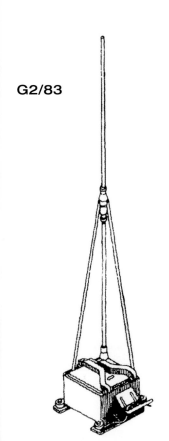

G2/84

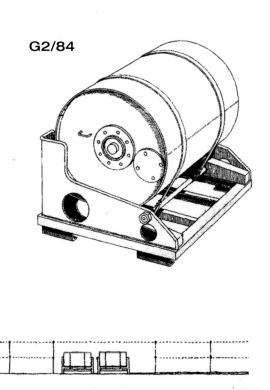

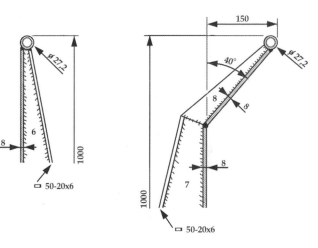

H Aircraft

H1/1 Catapult Kure Shiki 2 Gō 5 Gata –
     profile with aircraft trolley (1/150 scale)

H1/2 Front view

H1/3 Rear view

H1/4 Plan (with trolley)

H1/5 Perspective of fore part

H1/6 Details – wooden support for canvas cover

H1/7 Catapult cradle for single float plane

H1/8 Trolley for floatplane transport on deck rails

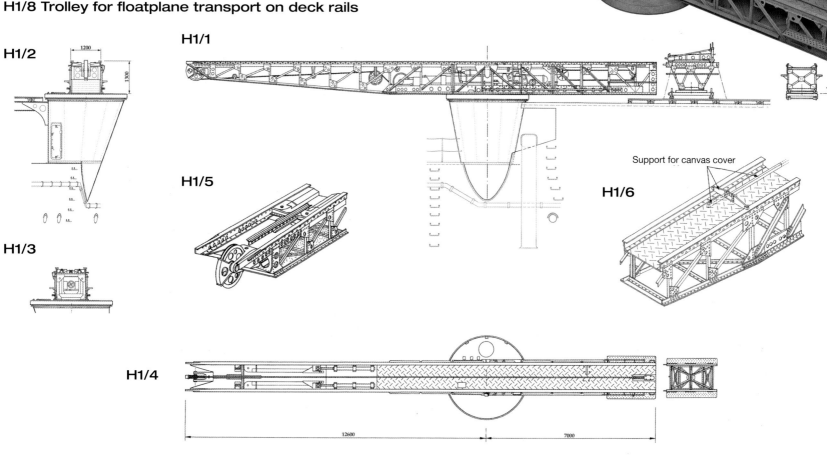

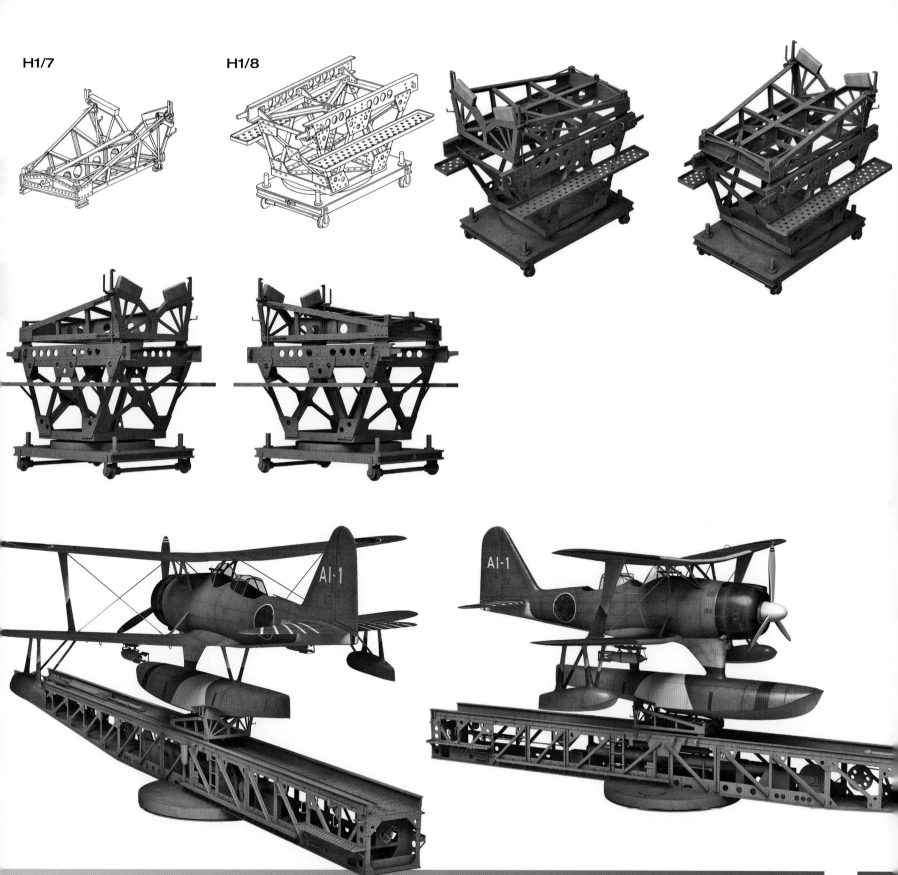

H1/7

H1/8

H Aircraft

H1/9 Turntable for aircraft deck rails plan and profile

H1/10 Deck rails section

H1/11 Profile view

H1/12 Aircraft hangar on middle deck for five F1M2 floatplanes

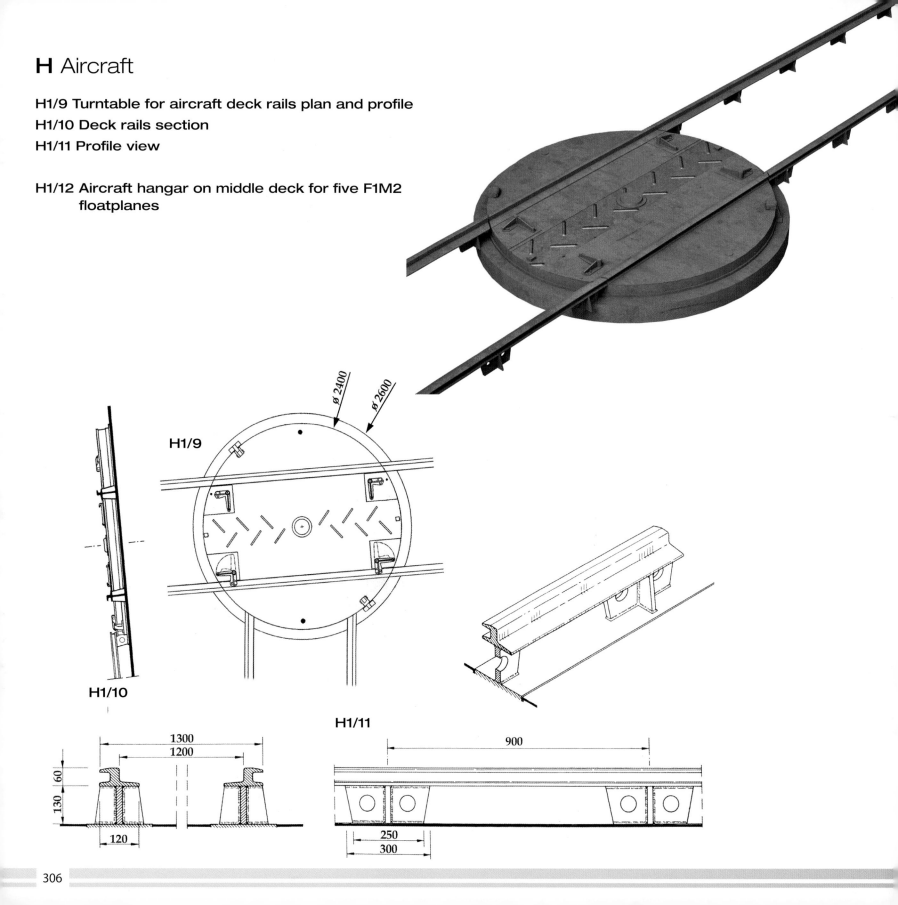

ø 2400
ø 2600

H1/9

H1/10

H1/11

1300
1200
60
130
120

900
250
300

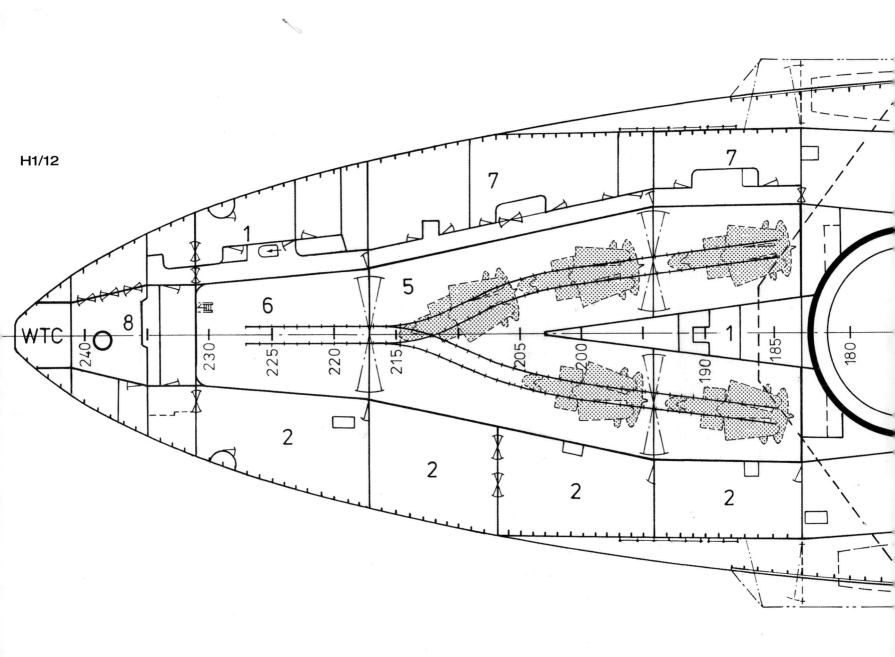

H1/12

WTC

240 · 230 · 225 · 220 · 215 · 205 · 200 · 190 · 185 · 180

8 · 1 · 6 · 5 · 7 · 7 · 1 · 2 · 2 · 2 · 2

H Aircraft

Mitsubishi F1M2 type '0' floatplane [only this type was used on *Yamato* and *Musashi*] (1/100 scale)

H1/12 Profile view

H1/13 Plan

H1/14 Front view

H1/15 Propeller

H1/16 60kg bomb

H1/17 Sections

H1/18 Tail markings

From left to right: Yamato 1941-43, Yamato 1944-45, Musashi 1944

H1/18

H1/13

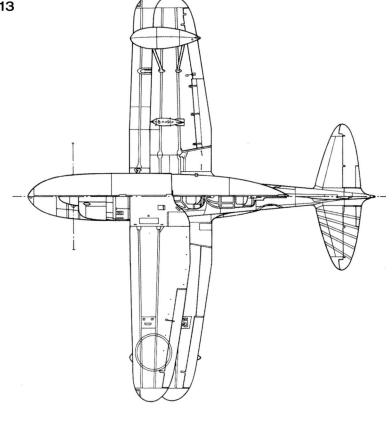

A   B   C   D

H1/12

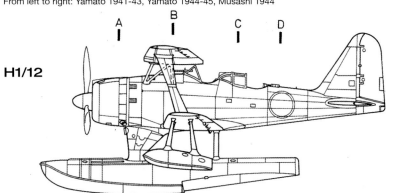

11 000

H1/14

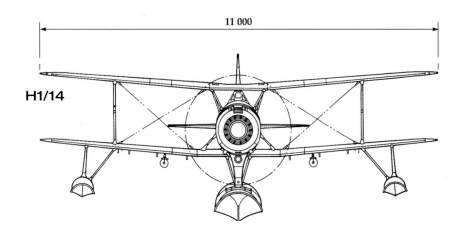

H1/15

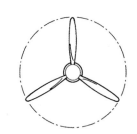

H1/16

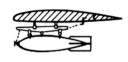

H1/17

A   B   C   D

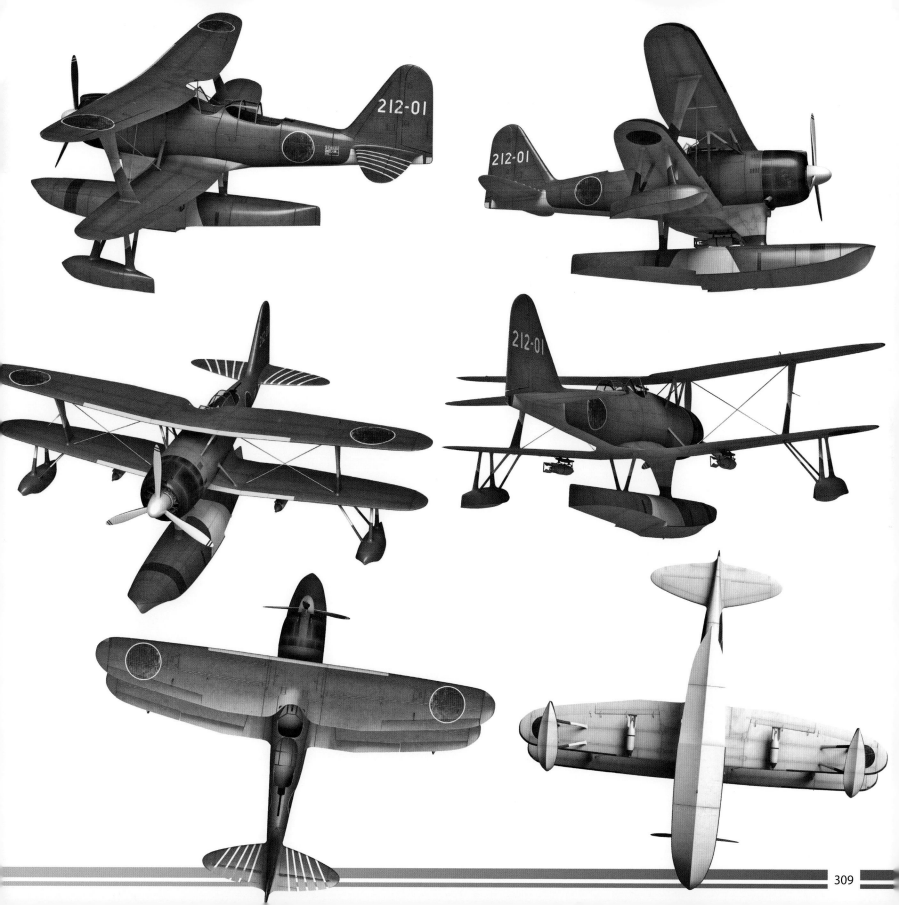

I Boats

17m Motor Pinnace – ceremonial barge (1/100 scale)

I1/1 Profile

I1/2 Plan

I1/3 Internal profile

I1/4 Internal plan

I1/5 Body plan

I1/6 Section – Frame 6
    with view to stern

I1/7 Rear view

I1/8 Detail of hull edge

I1/9 Navigation lights and lamp

I1/1

I1/2

I1/5

I1/6

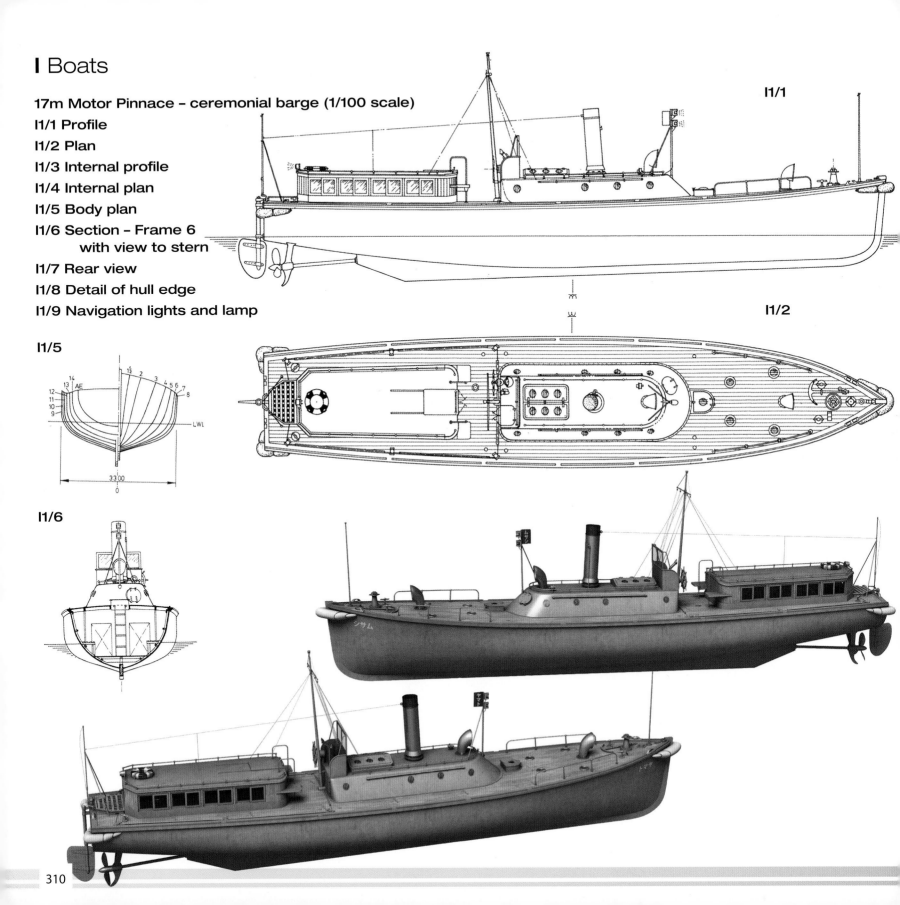

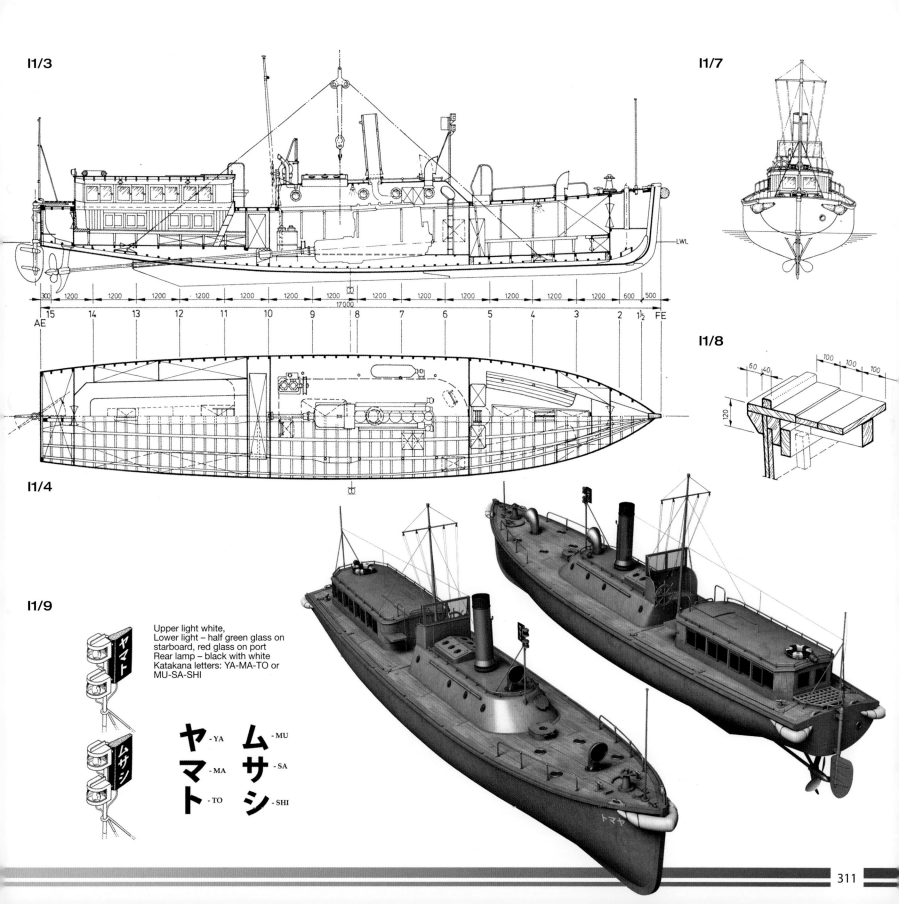

I1/3

I1/7

I1/8

I1/4

I1/9

Upper light white,
Lower light – half green glass on
starboard, red glass on port
Rear lamp – black with white
Katakana letters: YA-MA-TO or
MU-SA-SHI

ヤ -YA ム -MU
マ -MA サ -SA
ト -TO シ -SHI

I Boats

**15m / 150hp Motor Boat – ceremonial barge
(1/100 scale)**

I1/10 Profile

I1/11 Plan

I1/10

I1/11

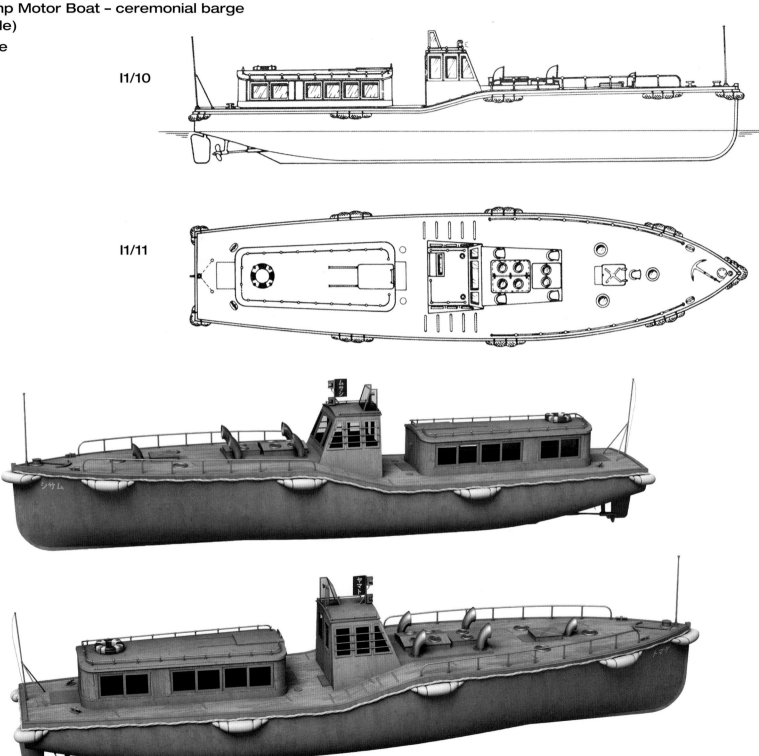

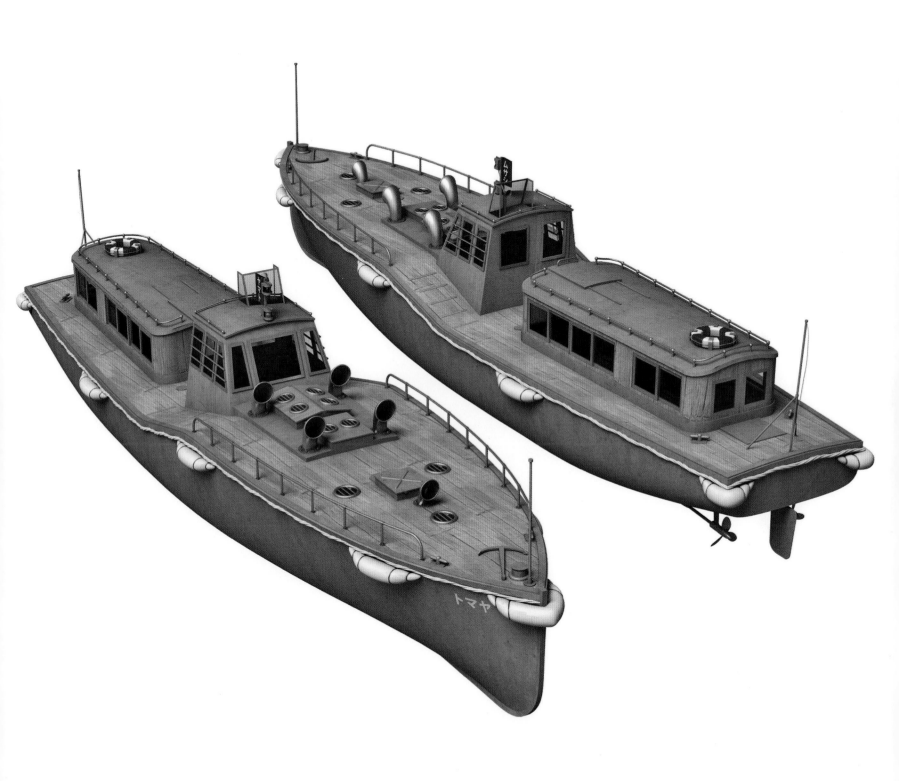

Boats

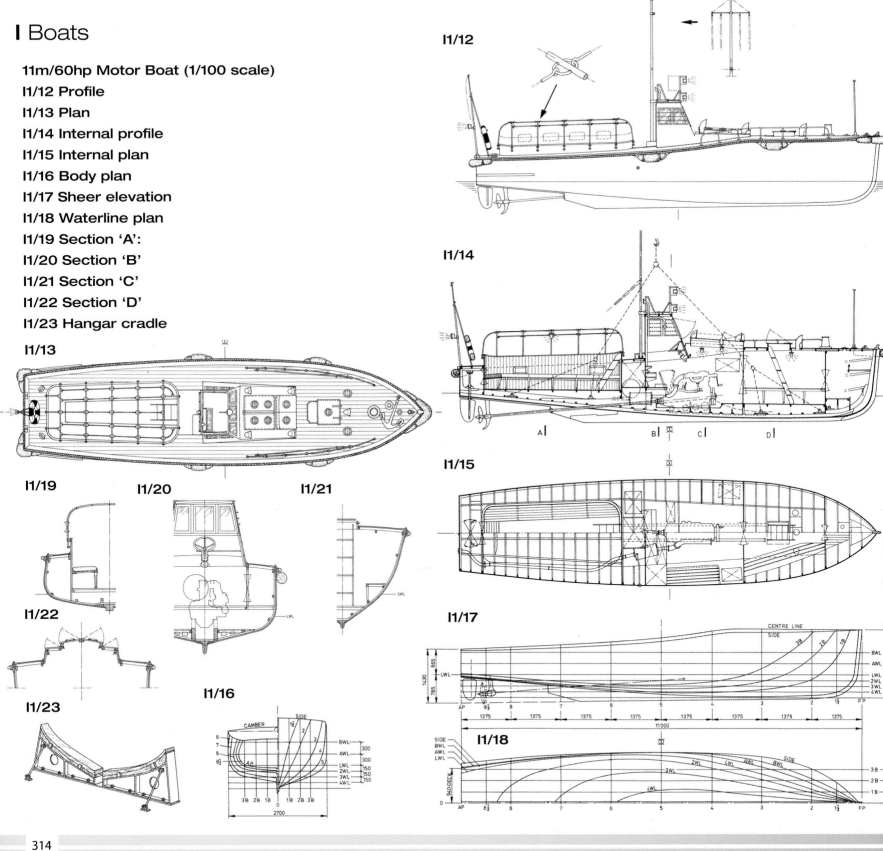

I1/12

I1/14

I1/15

I1/13

I1/19

I1/20

I1/21

I1/22

I1/23

I1/16

I1/17

I1/18

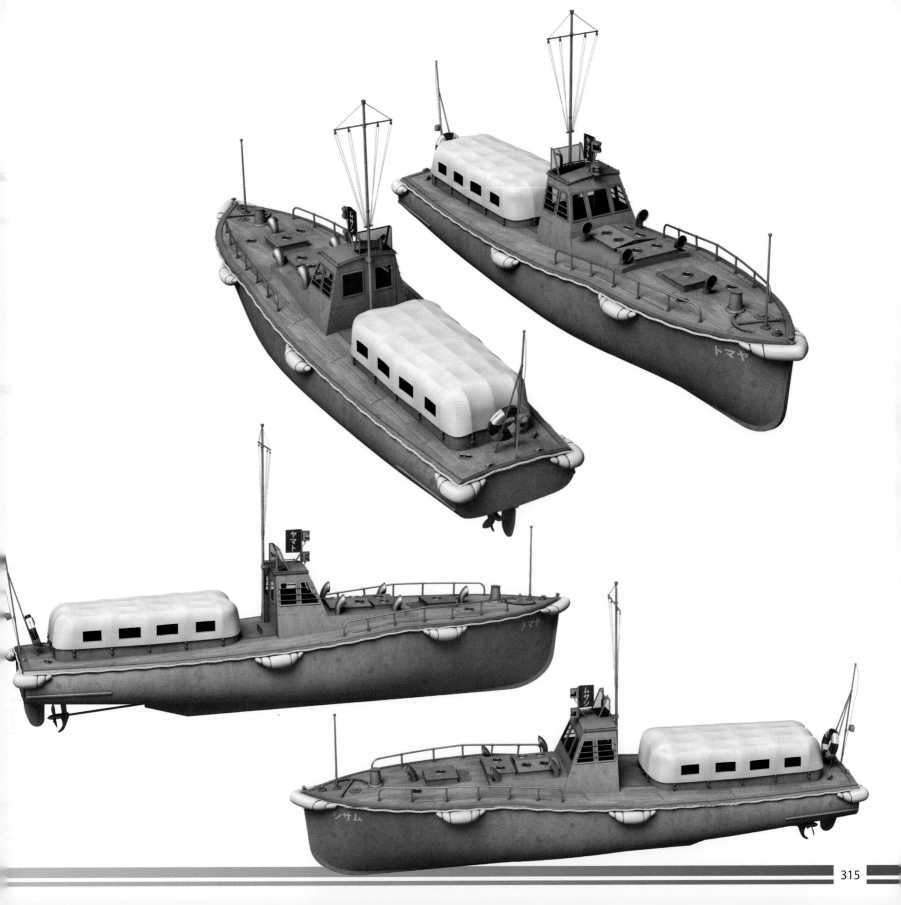

I Boats

12m /30hp Motor Launch (1/100 scale)

I1/24 Internal profile
    (canvas rack was used sporadically)

I1/25 Plan

I1/26 Body plan

I1/27 Sheer elevation

I1/28 Waterline plan

I1/29 Section 'A-A'

I1/30 Section 'A-A' enlarged x 2

I1/31 Section 'B-B'

I1/32 Cradle

I1/24

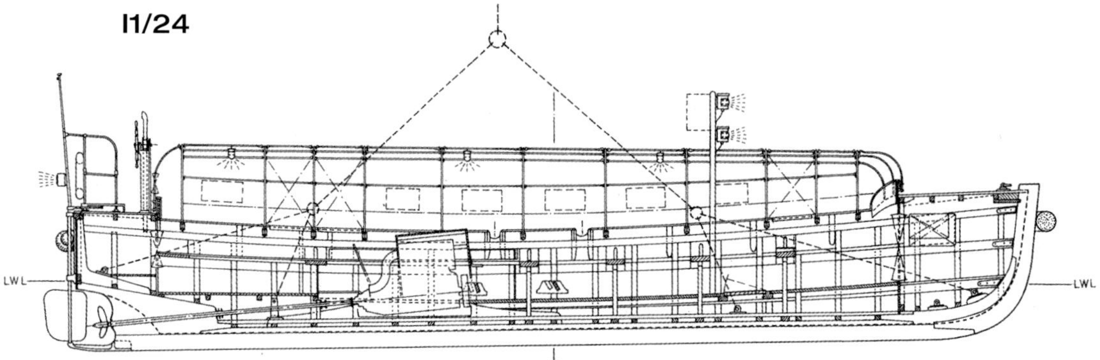

I1/25

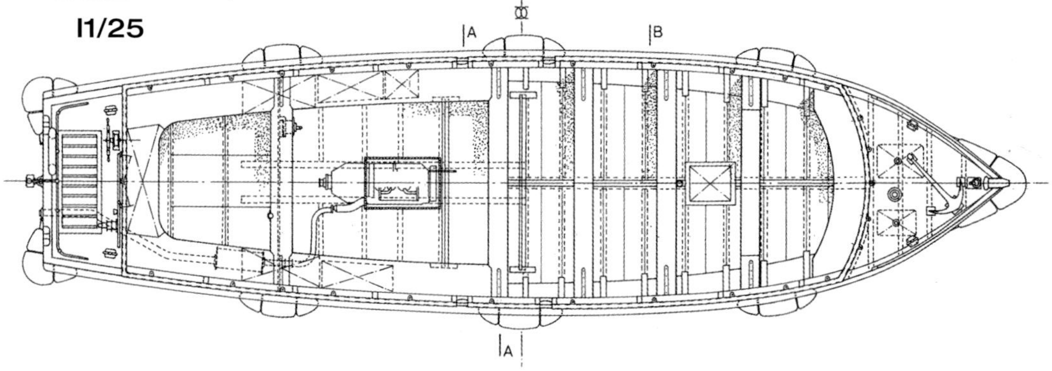

I1/29

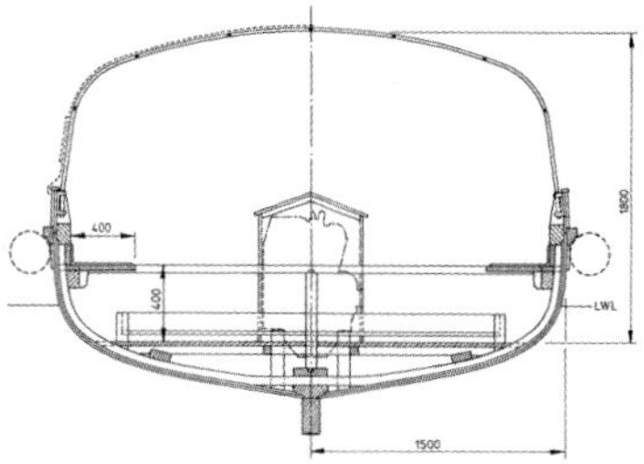

I1/30 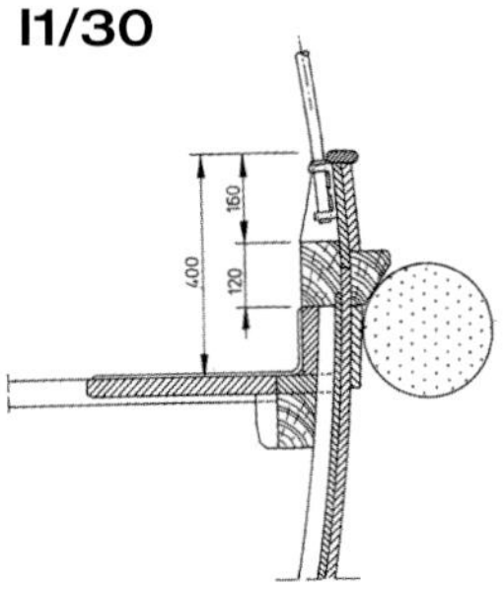   I1/31

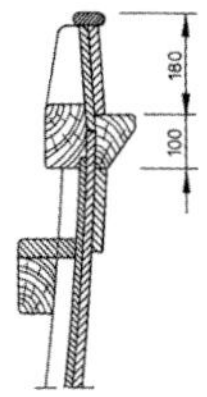

I1/26

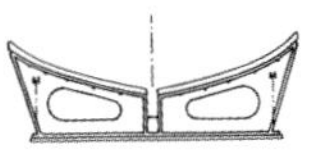

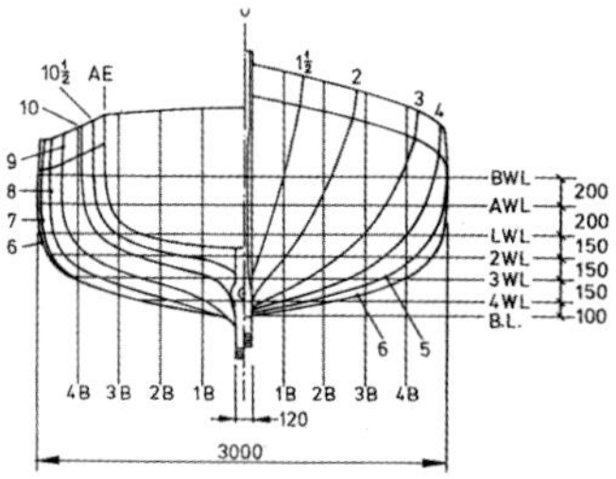

I1/27

I1/32

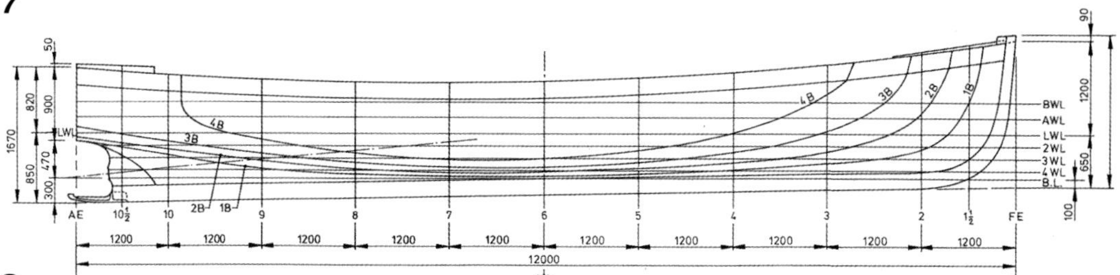

I1/28

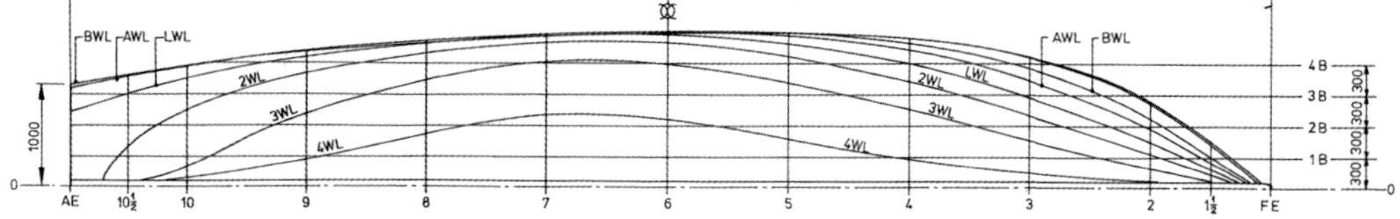

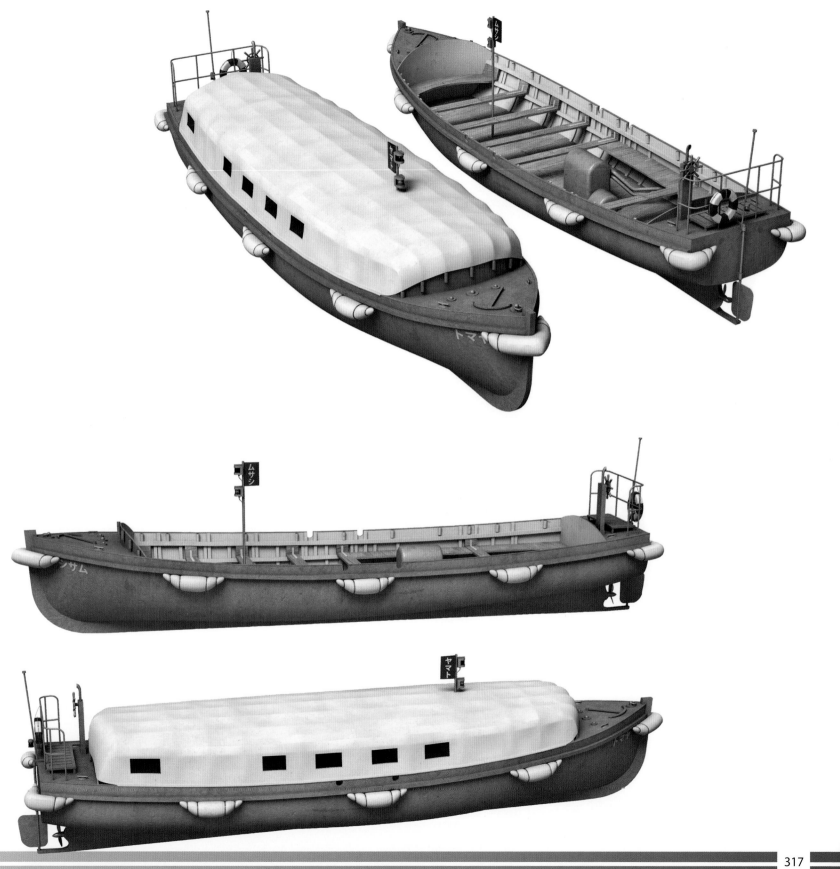

I Boats

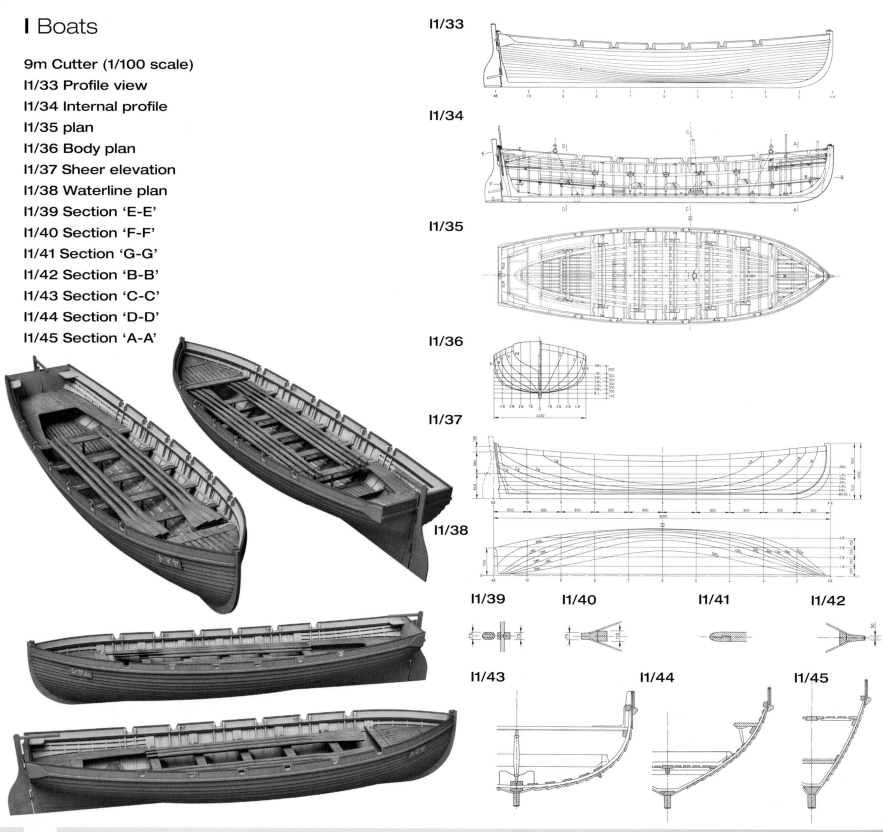

I1/33

I1/34

I1/35

I1/36

I1/37

I1/38

I1/39   I1/40   I1/41   I1/42

I1/43   I1/44   I1/45

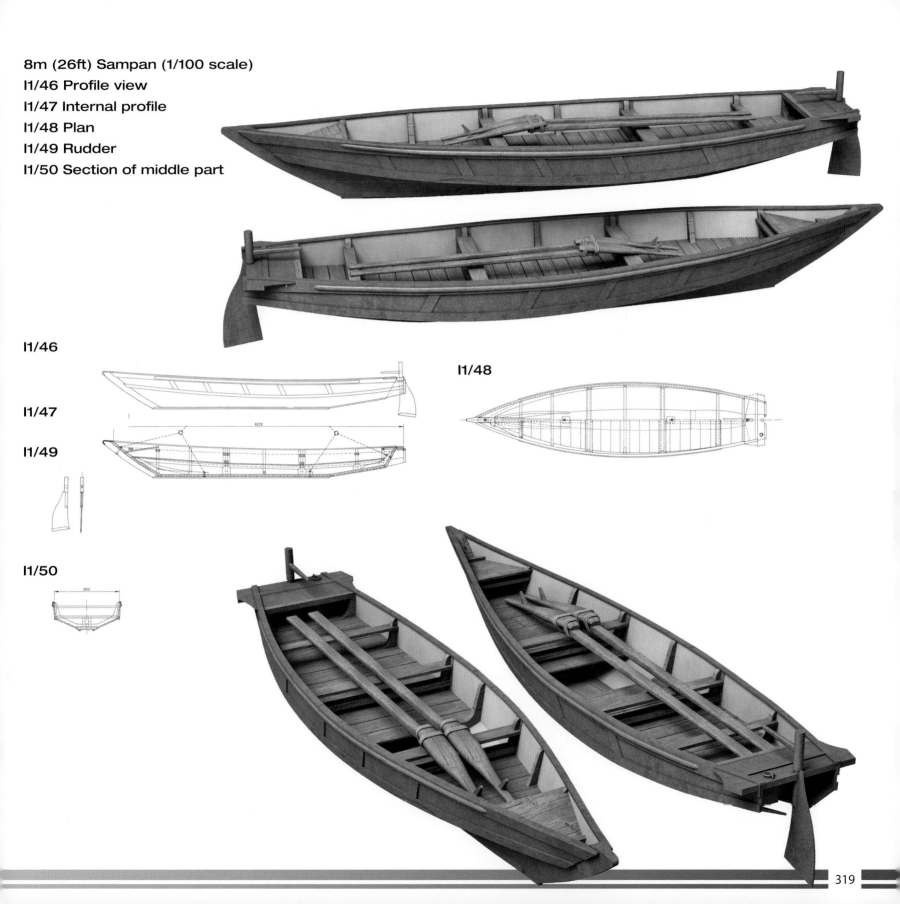

8m (26ft) Sampan (1/100 scale)

I1/46 Profile view

I1/47 Internal profile

I1/48 Plan

I1/49 Rudder

I1/50 Section of middle part

I1/46

I1/47

I1/49

I1/50

I1/48

I Boats

6m (20ft) Sampan (1/100 scale)

I1/51 Profile view

I1/52 Internal profile

I1/53 Plan

I1/54 Section of middle part

I1/55 Rudder

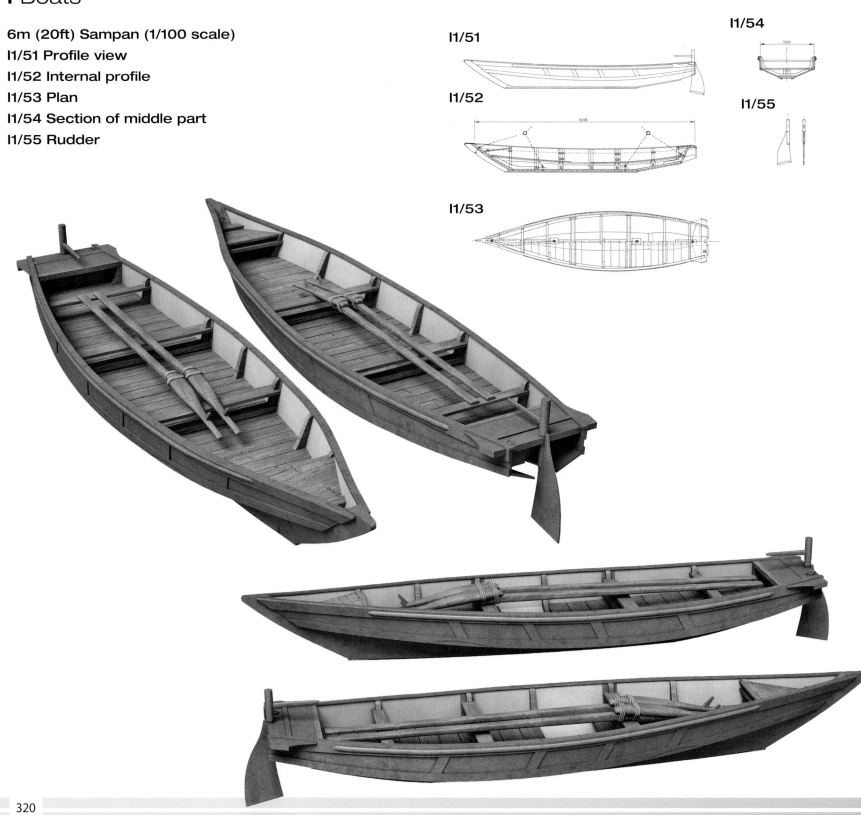

I1/51

I1/54

I1/52

I1/55

I1/53

I1/56 Katakana inscription on boat sides

I1/57 Boat stowage on upper deck (UD)
I1/58 Boat stowage on middle deck (MD)

I1/56

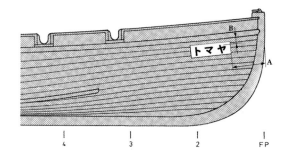

BOAT	A	B
12 m	650	150
9 m	500	130
8 m	450	55
6 m	450	40

トマヤ
TO MA YA

シサム
SHI SA MU

I1/57

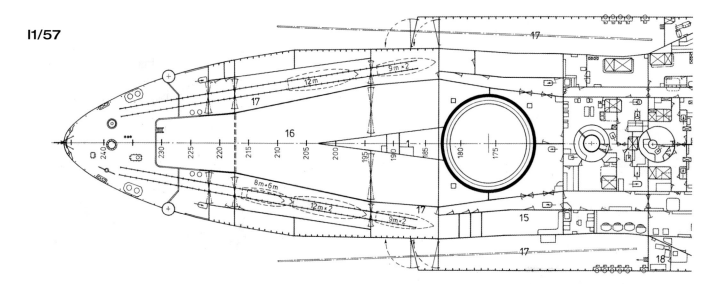

I1/58

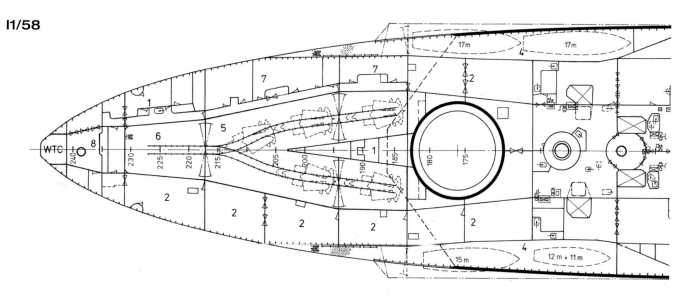

AUTHOR'S CONSTRUCTION MODEL

Study model at 1:50 scale of *Yamato*'s tower bridge and my assistant Pieszczotka the cat

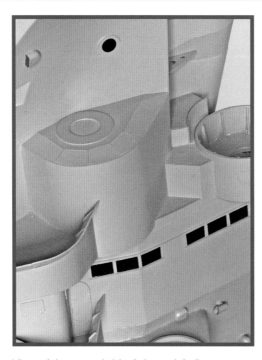

View of the tower bridge's lower LA director Type 98 'Hoiban' – level + 16,755

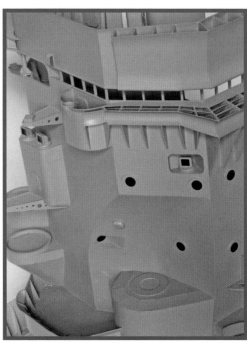

View of upper starboard part of the tower bridge

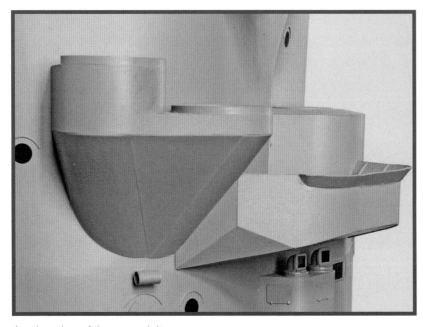

Another view of the rear pulpit

View of the 'pulpit' support of searchlight control towers on the ship level + 14,000

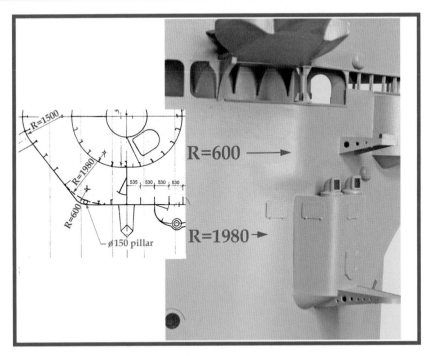

Details of the upper part of the tower bridge

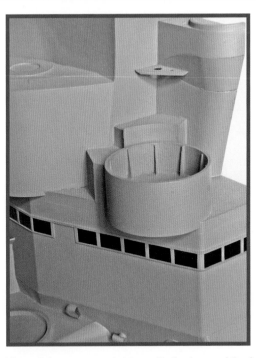

View of the compass bridge with the base of the MG control tower and the base of the 1.5m navigation rangefinder

The 'pulpit' of rear two searchlight control towers and platform on the ship's level + 16,755

Another view of the rear pulpit

YAMATO AND *MUSASHI* AT SEA

Yamato 1941

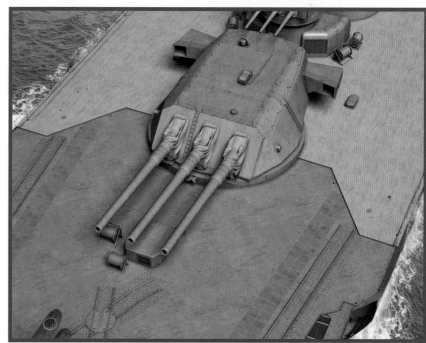

Yamato 1944

Yamato 1945

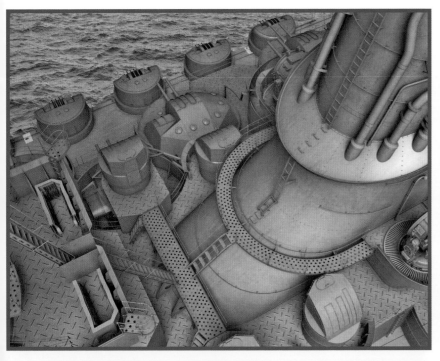

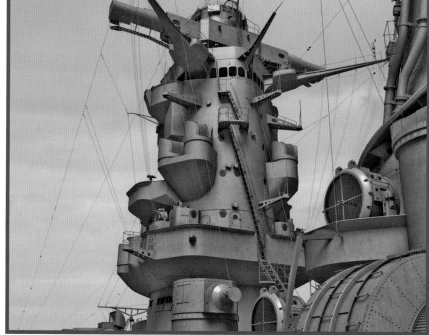

Musashi 1944

THE REMAINS OF *YAMATO* AND *MUSASHI*

EXPEDITIONS TO THE SUNKEN BATTLESHIPS

First expedition, 1985

On 1 August 1985, 40 years after the *Yamato* sank, a Japanese expedition, in the small research submarine *Research Submersible 2* (on loan from the UK), found the remains 345m below sea level and examined them carefully. They partly explained the secret of the *Yamato*'s last moments. Two huge and devastating explosions tore the ship apart leaving a large part of the hull (~170m long), the bow (~70m long) and some smaller fragments. Her remains have been slowly sinking into the sand ever since.

Second expedition, 1999

On 14 December 1999 the Japanese television station Asahi along with a French team and their research ship *Ocean Voyager* (that had, in 1998 investigated the wreck of *Titanic*) investigated the wreck once more. These expeditions discovered far more new information than the earlier ones. They concluded that after *Yamato* rolled over (listing 120°) there were two explosions – the first in the magazines of turrets No. 1 and No. 2 of 46cm guns with the magazines of the 15.5cm guns and probably AA gun ammunition, and the second explosion in the magazine of the rear 15.5cm guns. It caused a hole about 32m in diameter in the port side of the rear part of the hull. This is about 160m long and is now upside down. The fore part of the hull – from the bow to the 46cm gun tower barbette is about 90m long with a list to starboard of about 45°.

The top of the tower bridge stayed near the starboard side of the bow part of the hull and fragments of main mast stayed on the No.1 barbette. I think that these two parts of the hull must have locked together as the ship sunk, tearing off the mast and fragments of the tower bridge.

Third expedition

On 1 March 2015, after eight years of research, Paul G. Allen discovered the *Musashi* in the Sibuyan Sea. His M/Y *Octopus* found the remains of the *Musashi* in seas 1300m deep and with remains spread over a very wide field. Although *Musashi* sank as a complete ship with a list to starboard by the bow, moments after the sinking two huge underwater explosions were heard – caused, we can now say, by the fore and rear ammunition magazines. One or both of these blasts probably went on to completely flood the boiler and engine rooms and tore the midship area into smaller and larger pieces. As

on her sister ship *Yamato,* the largest fragments are the bow and rear part of the hull.

It is likely that the explosions on both battleships were ignited partly by 15.5cm, 12.7 and 25mm rounds, causing the explosion of the powder magazine and partly by the shells of the 46cm guns when the ships rolled over. With the explosion of *Yamato*'s aft magazines, it is possible that the fire that arose after the bomb struck the rear turret of the 15.5cm gun, was not extinguished.

Expedition to *Yamato*

The photos on the opposite page of the *Yamato* were taken during the First expedition by *Ocean Voyager* and Asahi TV in December 1999

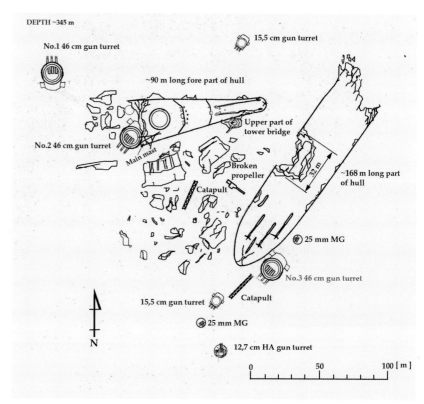

The condition of the sunken *Yamato* as examined on 14 December 1999

120cm diameter Chrysanthemum crest and the bow

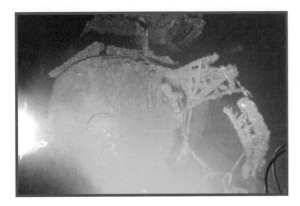

View of the 'Hoiban' roof without the lost periscope turret and broken small mast

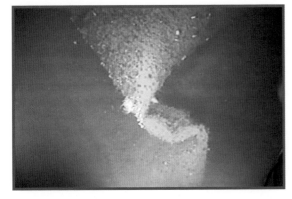

Sharp bend in the stern of *Yamato* probably caused by knocking the stern deck on the sea bottom (VHS)

The 'Hoiban' tower, main rangefinder compartment and fragment of the aft part of air defence platform of tower bridge

46cm AP shells in the broken lower part of gun turret

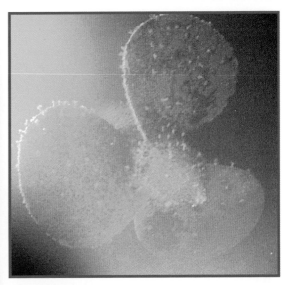

5m diameter propeller

5m diameter propeller

25mm MG turret on sea bottom

Expedition to *Musashi*

The photos on this page of the *Musashi* were taken by the Paul G. Allen expedition on 2 March 2015

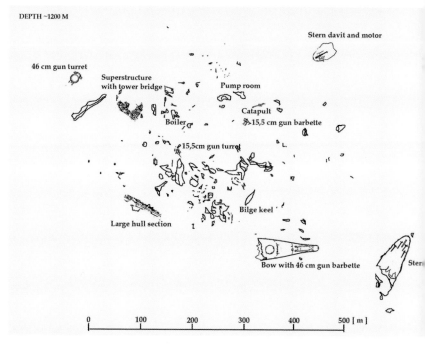

The condition of the sunken *Musashi* as discovered on 2 March 2015 and examined by the Paul G. Allen Expedition

The 'Hoiban' tower with the small rear mast and the aft wall of the 15.5m rangefinder with strengthening framework

Two starboard searchlight control towers from aft, middle part of tower bridge

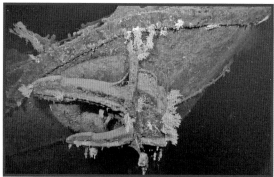

The bow of the *Musashi* at a depth of ~1300m with her lost chrysanthemum crest

Starboard 15-ton anchor, the port anchor was dropped into the sea about two hours before her sinking, to attempt to reduce the list.

Rear view of the catapult

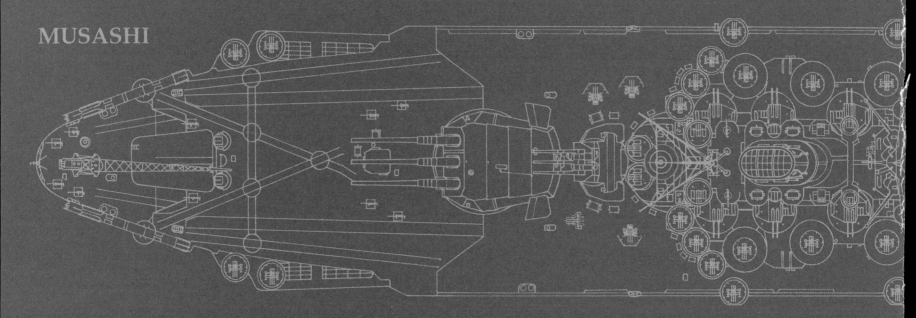

MUSASHI